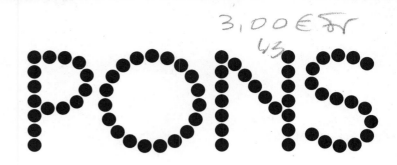

GRAMMATIK KOMPLETT
ENGLISCH

Das große Übungs- und Nachschlagebuch

D1438504

PONS GmbH
Stuttgart

PONS
GRAMMATIK KOMPLETT
ENGLISCH

Das große Übungs- und Nachschlagebuch

von
Darcy Bruce Berry und Dr. Alexander T.Bergs (Grammatik)
Samantha Scott (Verbtabellen)
Claudia Heidieker unter Mitarbeit von Esther Lorenz-Bottke (Übungsgrammatik)

PONS verpflichtet sich, die Download-Dateien zu diesem Buch mindestens bis Ende 2017 bereitzustellen.
Einen Anspruch der Nutzung darüber hinaus gibt es nicht.

Auflage A1 $^{4\ 3\ 2\ 1}$ / 2017 2016 2015 2014

© PONS GmbH Stuttgart, Rotebühlstraße 77, 70178 Stuttgart, 2014
PONS Produktinfos und Shop: www.pons.de
PONS Online-Wörterbuch: www.pons.eu
E-Mail: info@pons.de

Logoentwurf: Erwin Poell
Logoüberarbeitung: Sabine Redlin, Ludwigsburg
Einbandgestaltung: Anne Helbich, Stuttgart
Titelfoto: Thinkstock/Kollektion: iStockphoto
Layout: Andrea Grundmann Kommunikationsgestaltung, Karlsruhe; belugadesign, Stuttgart (Übungsgrammatik)
Satz: Satz und mehr, Besigheim
Illustrationen: Palmer-Lorenz Illustrationen, Steinbach
Anpassung der Illustrationen: Norberto Lombardi, Campana
Tonstudio: Ton in Ton Medienhaus, Stuttgart
Druck und Bindung: L.E.G.O. S.p.A., in Lavis (TN)

Printed in the EU
ISBN: 978-3-12-562677-5

Gesamtinhaltsverzeichnis

Willkommen in der Welt der englischen Sprache

PONS Grammatik Komplett Englisch ist ein umfassendes Nachschlage- und Übungswerk, das Sie in ihrer gesamten Sprachlernlaufbahn begleiten wird.

Es bietet Ihnen als Sprachanfänger oder fortgeschrittenem Lerner die Möglichkeit, die wichtigsten Bereiche und Aspekte der englischen Grammatik nachzuschlagen und zu üben:

- **Nachschlagegrammatik**

In diesem Kapitel finden Sie die wichtigsten Grammatikregeln an zahlreichen Beispielen sinnvoll veranschaulicht. Leicht verständliche Erklärungen und nützliche Tipps helfen Ihnen, typische Fehler zu vermeiden.

- **Verbtabellen**

Dieses Kapitel bietet Ihnen übersichtliche Konjugationstabellen der wichtigsten Verben. Zusätzlich finden Sie eine ausführliche Verbliste mit Verweisen auf das jeweilige Konjugationsmuster. Für einen besseren Überblick sind die Besonderheiten in den Konjugationen farbig hervorgehoben.

- **Übungsgrammatik**

In diesem Teil trainieren Sie mit einer kommunikativen Lernmethode intensiv die englische Grammatik und lernen, diese in lebensnahen Situationen anzuwenden. Die Lösungen und Tipps tragen dazu bei, dass Sie als Selbstlerner die englische Grammatik schnell beherrschen.

 Dieses Symbol zeigt Ihnen, dass Sie den Text der Übung auch anhören können, indem Sie die jeweilige Sounddatei unter www.pons.de/grammatik-komplett-englisch herunterladen.

Am Ende des Buches finden Sie zahlreiche Lerntipps, wie Sie schneller und besser die Sprache erlernen. Für alle Aspekte der Sprache und auch für jeden Lernertyp ist etwas dabei.

Viel Spaß und Erfolg beim Englischlernen!

1 | Nachschlagegrammatik

Inhalt

Einleitung

Sie wollen die Regeln der englischen Sprache auf einfache und verständliche Weise erlernen oder wiederholen, Sie möchten zu speziellen Fragen aber auch schnell und gezielt nachschlagen können.

Das Kapitel **Grammatik** bietet Ihnen eine **übersichtliche Darstellung** der aktuellen englischen Sprache in Nordamerika und Großbritannien. Die Regeln werden anhand **zahlreicher englischer Beispielsätze** mit deutschen Übersetzungen veranschaulicht.

Das Kapitel **Grammatik** warnt vor typischen Fehlern, die gerade deutschsprachigen Englischlernenden häufig passieren.

Bei der Arbeit mit diesem Kapitel helfen Ihnen die folgenden Hervorhebungen:

> Hier wird auf eine **Regel** oder eine **Besonderheit** hingewiesen, die man nicht übersehen sollte.

Kleine **Tipps** verraten Ihnen an dieser Stelle, wie Sie sich die Regeln besser merken können.

Hier werden Unterschiede zwischen dem Deutschen und dem Englischen aufgezeigt, die Sie besonders beachten sollten.

> Hier finden Sie **Varianten**, die im amerikanischen Englisch vorkommen.

▷ **Hier wird auf ein anderes Grammatikkapitel verwiesen, z.B.** ▷ **Kapitel Verbs – Verben.**

Wenn Sie etwas gezielt nachschlagen wollen, führt Sie das **ausführliche Stichwortregister** im Anhang schnell zur richtigen Stelle.

Viel Spaß und Erfolg!

Erklärung der Grammatikbegriffe

Englisch	Latein	Bedeutung
active	Aktiv	Tätigkeitsform
adjective	Adjektiv	Eigenschaftswort
adverb	Adverb	Umstandswort
article	Artikel	Begleiter
auxiliary	Hilfsverb	Hilfs-Tätigkeitswort
conjunction	Konjunktion	Bindewort
consonant	Konsonant	Mitlaut
continuous tense	Kontinuativ; Progressive Form	Verlaufsform
demonstrative pronoun	Demonstrativpronomen	hinweisendes Fürwort
future	Futur	Zukunft
gerund	Gerundium	ing-Form
imperative (form)	Imperativ	Befehlsform
imperfect (tense)	Imperfekt	einfache Vergangenheit
infinitive	Infinitiv	Grundform des Verbs
intransitive verb	intransitives Verb	Tätigkeitswort ohne direkte Ergänzung
noun	Nomen, Substantiv	Hauptwort
object	Objekt	Ergänzung
participle	Partizip	Mittelwort
passive	Passiv	Leideform
perfect (tense)	Perfekt	vollendete Gegenwart
personal pronoun	Personalpronomen	persönliches Fürwort
plural	Plural	Mehrzahl
possessive (pronoun)	Possessivpronomen	besitzanzeigendes Fürwort
preposition	Präposition	Verhältniswort
present (tense)	Präsens	Gegenwart
progressive (tense)	Progressive Form	Verlaufsform
pronoun	Pronomen	Fürwort
reflexive pronoun	Reflexivpronomen	rückbezügliches Fürwort
relative pronoun	Relativpronomen	bezügliches Fürwort
singular	Singular	Einzahl
subject	Subjekt	Satzgegenstand
transitive verb	transitives Verb	Tätigkeitswort mit direkter Ergänzung
verb	Verb	Tätigkeitswort
vowel	Vokal	Selbstlaut

1 Verbs | *Verben*

Vollverben

Verbarten

Es gibt zwei Arten von Verben: transitive und intransitive Verben.

- transitive Verben brauchen mindestens ein, manchmal zwei Objekte. Verben, die ein Objekt benötigen, heißen monotransitive Verben, solche mit zwei Objekten ditransitive Verben:

  Monotransitive Verben
Anne likes dogs.	*Anne mag Hunde.*
Peter kissed Mary.	*Peter küsste Mary.*

  Ditransitive Verben
Jeremy wrote me a letter.	*Jeremy schrieb mir einen Brief.*
Paul gave me a book.	*Paul gab mir ein Buch.*

- intransitive Verben brauchen dagegen kein Objekt:

Anne slept.	*Anne schlief.*
Usually Jeremy drives.	*Normalerweise fährt Jeremy.*

Manche Verben können sowohl transitiv als auch intransitiv sein:

John is reading a book.	*John liest gerade ein Buch.*
John is reading.	*John liest gerade.*

Regelmäßige und unregelmäßige Verben

Bei regelmäßigen Verben braucht man nur den Infinitiv (die erste Form, oder Grundform) um alle anderen Formen abzuleiten:

1. Form Infinitiv/Grundform	2. Form Simple Past	3. Form Past Participle
(to) **call**	called	called
(to) **kiss**	kissed	kissed

Bei unregelmäßigen Verben reicht der Infinitiv nicht, da sich das Simple Past bzw. Past Participle nicht ableiten lassen:

1. Form Infinitiv/Grundform	2. Form Simple Past	3. Form Past Participle
(to) **sing**	**sang**	**sung**
(to) **see**	**saw**	**seen**

Tenses | *Zeitformen*

Einfache Formen

Von den Zeiten werden nur die einfache Gegenwart und die einfache Vergangenheit ohne Hilfsverb gebildet:

Simple Present | *Einfache Gegenwartsform*

Das Simple Present ist bei fast allen Verben in allen Personen außer der dritten (**he/ she/it**) gleich dem Infinitiv (der Grundform). Vollverben in Sätzen mit Subjekten in der dritten Person haben in der Regel ein **-s** am Ende.

I like **hairy spiders.**	*Ich mag haarige Spinnen.*
You need **a haircut.**	*Du musst zum Friseur.*
He/she watches **TV every night.**	*Er sieht jeden Abend fern.*
Theresa prefers **white wine.**	*Theresa trinkt lieber Weißwein.*
Tom and Martha want **a new car.**	*Tom und Martha wollen ein neues Auto.*

Lediglich bei den Hilfsverben **be** und **have** und den Modalverben **may**, **can**, **will**, **should** usw. gibt es Abweichungen: (▷ Hilfsverben)

BE (*sein*)

I am **tired.**	*Ich bin müde.*
You are **tired.**	*Du bist müde.*
He/she/it is **boring.**	*Er/Sie/Es ist langweilig.*
Ballet is **boring.**	*Ballett ist langweilig.*
Peter, Paul, and Mary are **here.**	*Peter, Paul und Mary sind hier.*

HAVE (*haben*)

I have **a car.**	*Ich habe ein Auto.*
You have **a nice jacket.**	*Du hast eine hübsche Jacke.*
Mary-Jane has **a flat tire.**	*Mary-Jane hat einen Platten.*
They have **a swimming-pool.**	*Sie haben einen Swimming-Pool.*

Die Modalverben (▷ Modalverben) haben immer die gleiche Form:

I/you/he/she/it/they may **be here now.**	*Ich/Du/Er/Sie/Es könnte jetzt hier sein.*

Simple Past | *Einfache Vergangenheitsform*

Die regelmäßige Form des Simple Past fügt **-ed** ans Ende des Infinitivs. Dies gilt für jedes Subjekt, d.h. alle Personen.

I wanted **a new car.**	*Ich wollte ein neues Auto.*
My colleagues worked **yesterday.**	*Meine Kollegen arbeiteten gestern.*

Einige der wichtigsten unregelmäßigen Verben:

Infinitive	Simple Past	Past Participle	Übersetzung
be	was	been	*sein*
begin	began	begun	*beginnen*
bring	brought	brought	*bringen*
buy	bought	bought	*kaufen*
catch	caught	caught	*fangen, erwischen*
choose	chose	chosen	*auswählen*
come	came	come	*kommen*
cost	cost	cost	*kosten*
cut	cut	cut	*schneiden*
do	did	done	*tun, machen*
drink	drank	drunk	*trinken*
drive	drove	driven	*fahren*
eat	ate	eaten	*essen*
fall	fell	fallen	*(hin)fallen*
feel	felt	felt	*(sich) fühlen*
fly	flew	flown	*fliegen*
forget	forgot	forgotten (UK) forgot (US)	*vergessen*
get	got	got (UK), gotten (US)	*kriegen, werden*
give	gave	given	*geben, schenken*
go	went	gone	*(hin)gehen*
have	had	had	*haben*
hear	heard	heard	*hören*
keep	kept	kept	*behalten*
know	knew	known	*wissen, kennen*
leave	left	left	*weggehen, verlassen*
lend	lent	lent	*ausleihen*
lose	lost	lost	*verlieren*
make	made	made	*machen*
pay	paid	paid	*(be)zahlen*
put	put	put	*stellen, (hin)legen*
read	read	read	*lesen*

ride	rode	ridden	*reiten, (mit)fahren*
ring	rang	rung	*läuten, ringen*
run	ran	run	*laufen*
say	said	said	*sagen*
see	saw	seen	*sehen*
sell	sold	sold	*verkaufen*
sing	sang	sung	*singen*
sit	sat	sat	*sitzen*
sleep	slept	slept	*schlafen*
take	took	taken	*(mit)nehmen*
teach	taught	taught	*lehren, unterrichten*
tell	told	told	*erzählen, sagen*
think	thought	thought	*denken, glauben*
wake	woke	woken	*erwachen, aufwecken*
write	wrote	written	*schreiben*

Dazu gibt es Verben, die im Amerikanischen regelmäßig sind (also mit **–ed** gebildet werden), im britischen Englisch aber wie folgt:

Infinitive	Simple Past	Past Participle	Übersetzung
dream	dreamt (UK)	dreamt (UK)	*träumen*
	dreamed (US)	dreamed (US)	
lean	leant	leant	*(sich) anlehnen*
learn	learnt	learnt	*lernen*
spell	spelt	spelt	*buchstabieren*
spill	spilt	spilt	*verschütten*
spoil	spoilt	spoilt	*verderben, verwöhnen*

Das einzige Verb, wo dies umgekehrt passiert, ist **to dive** (*tauchen, hechten*):

Infinitive	Simple Past	Past Participle	Übersetzung
dive	dove (US)	dived (US)	*tauchen, hechten*
	dived (UK)	dived (UK)	

Zusammengesetzte Formen

Zusammengesetzte Formen bestehen aus mindestens einem Hilfsverb und der entsprechenden Form des Vollverbs.

Progressive | *Die Verlaufsform*

Um eine Progressive Form zu bilden, braucht man die richtige Form von **be** als Hilfsverb und die *ing*-Form des Vollverbs. Zur Bildung der *ing*-Form hängt man einfach **-ing** an den Infinitiv (die Grundform) des Vollverbs.

Present Progressive:	
The cat is sleeping.	*Die Katze schläft gerade.*
They are learning **English.**	*Sie lernen gerade Englisch.*

Past Progressive:	
George was wearing **a bow tie.**	*George trug eine Fliege.*
You were **all** driving **me crazy.**	*Ihr habt mich alle verrückt gemacht.*

Perfect Tenses | *Perfektformen*

Perfect Tenses bildet man immer mit dem Hilfsverb **have** und der dritten Form (dem Past Participle) des Vollverbs. Man unterscheidet zwischen dem gegenwarts-bezogenen Present Perfect und der Vorvergangenheit, dem Past Perfect.

Present Perfect:	
I have seen **her before.**	*Ich habe sie schon einmal gesehen.*
Carla has hidden **my shoes again.**	*Carla hat wieder meine Schuhe versteckt.*

Past Perfect – Vorvergangenheit:	
Deanna had chosen **a large SUV.**	*Deanna hatte sich einen großen Geländewagen ausgesucht.*
Wally had slipped **on a banana peel.**	*Wally war auf einer Bananenschale ausgerutscht.*

In der gesprochenen Sprache ist es üblich, die Gegenwarts- und Vergangenheitsformen von **have** zusammenzuziehen und an das Subjekt anzuhängen:

You have gone.	▷ **You've gone.**	*Du bist (fort)gegangen.*
She has gone.	▷ **She's gone.**	*Sie ist (fort)gegangen.*
We had gone.	▷ **We'd gone.**	*Wir waren (fort)gegangen.*

Future | *Zukunft:*

Englisch hat viele verschiedene Zukunftsformen, die sehr schwer zu unterscheiden sind (▷ Wie man über die Zukunft spricht). Sehr häufig aber bildet man die Zukunftsform einfach mit dem Hilfsverb **will** (das nie verändert wird) und dem Infinitiv (der Grundform) des Vollverbs:

They will move next year.	*Sie werden nächstes Jahr umziehen.*
She will never meet him again.	*Sie wird ihn nie wieder sehen.*

Passive Forms | *Passiv*

Das normale englische Passiv wird mit dem Hilfsverb **be** und dem Past Participle (der dritten Form) gebildet:

That song is sung at services.	*Dieses Lied wird beim Gottesdienst gesungen.*
The dishwasher was repaired today.	*Die Spülmaschine wurde heute repariert.*

Oft benutzt man auch eine Phrase, die zeigt, wer oder was etwas getan hat. Diese Phrase wird von **by** eingeleitet:

The dessert is brought by the butler.	*Der Nachtisch wird vom Butler gebracht.*
He was greeted by many people.	*Er wurde von vielen Leuten gegrüßt.*

Kombinationen von Hilfsverben

Es ist möglich, verschiedene Hilfsverben nach Bedarf aneinander zu reihen. Dabei bleibt die Reihenfolge gleich, man muss aber auf die richtigen Formen achten:

Modalverb – **have** *(perfect)* – **be** *(continuous)* – **be** *(passive)* – Vollverb

She had been **promoted.**	*Sie war befördert worden.*
They will have been being **taught French for a year now.**	*Sie werden jetzt wohl seit einem Jahr in Französisch unterrichtet.*
He can't be **eating again!**	*Er kann doch nicht schon wieder beim Essen sein!*

Used to | *früher*

Um vergangene Zustände und Gewohnheiten zu beschreiben, verwendet man häufig **used to**. Dies drückt dann ungefähr das gleiche aus wie das deutsche *früher*. Sehr oft beinhalten Formen mit **used to** den Hinweis, dass der Zustand bzw. die Gewohnheit nicht mehr gilt:

But you used to **like spinach.**	*Aber früher hast du Spinat doch gemocht.*
Mr. Jones used to **go for a walk every day.**	*Früher ist Herr Jones jeden Tag spazieren gegangen.*

Man setzt **used to** wie ein Hilfsverb zwischen das Subjekt und das Vollverb. **Used** ist dann das erste Verb des Satzes.

Zu beachten ist außerdem, dass **used to** im Kontext **be used to** + *ing*-Form *etwas gewöhnt sein* bedeutet (▶ **be used to, get used to**):

Carlos is used to washing **up the dishes.**	*Carlos ist es gewöhnt, das Geschirr abzuwaschen.*

Anwendung der verschiedenen Formen

1. Simple Present and Present Progressive

Simple Present wird hauptsächlich für Tatsachen und Gewohnheiten in der Gegenwart verwendet:

I like chocolate ice cream.	*Ich mag Schokoladeneis.*
The church bells ring every hour.	*Die Kirchenglocken läuten jede Stunde.*
The children watch TV every night.	*Die Kinder sehen jeden Abend fern.*

Present Progressive dagegen wird für momentan andauernde Zustände gebraucht. Solche Zustände können auch sich wiederholende Ereignisse sein:

I'm eating chocolate ice cream.	*Ich esse gerade Schokoladeneis.*
It's raining.	*Es regnet.*
What are you thinking about?	*Woran denkst Du gerade?*

2. Present Perfect

Present Perfect verwendet man für Zustände und Ereignisse, die in der Vergangenheit angefangen haben, in der Gegenwart als noch nicht abgeschlossen gelten, oder für diese immer noch größere Bedeutung haben:

The plumber has been here since 9 a.m.	*Der Klempner ist (schon) seit 9 Uhr morgens da.*
We've lived in London for five years.	*Wir leben seit fünf Jahren in London.*
Pete has called me twelve times last month.	*Pete hat mich zwölf Mal letzten Monat angerufen.*
I've worked all day, and now I want to relax.	*Ich habe den ganzen Tag gearbeitet, und jetzt will ich mich entspannen.*

Man verwendet das Present Perfect auch für Neuigkeiten:

Beatrice has written another novel.	*Beatrice hat noch einen Roman geschrieben.*
Playboy Clark has married for the seventh time.	*Der Playboy Clark hat (gerade) zum siebten Mal geheiratet.*

3. Present Perfect and Simple Past

Wie oben beschrieben kann man das Present Perfect nur dann verwenden, wenn ein Ereignis oder ein Zustand irgendwie aktuell ist. Wenn aber das Ereignis oder der Zustand abgeschlossen ist und eine Zeitangabe hierfür getroffen werden kann, muss man das Simple Past verwenden:

I have lived in London for five years.	*Ich lebe seit fünf Jahren in London. (Und tue dies immer noch!)*
I lived in London for five years.	*Ich habe fünf Jahre lang in London gelebt. (z.B. als ich ein Kind war!)*
We've met before.	*Wir sind uns schon mal begegnet. (irgend wann, ohne feste Zeitangabe)*
We met at a party last week.	*Wir haben uns letzte Woche auf einem Fest kennengelernt. (abgeschlossen, Zeitangabe)*

Im amerikanischen Englisch können einige Ausdrücke, die auf aktuelle Zustände hindeuten (z.B. **just, already**) auch mit dem Simple Past stehen:	
He has just left the hotel. (UK)	*Er hat gerade das Hotel verlassen.*
He just left the hotel. (US)	*Er hat gerade das Hotel verlassen.*

Wenn man einen Zeitausdruck benutzen will, der einen Zeitraum oder einen Zeitpunkt in der Vergangenheit bezeichnet, kann man das Present Perfect nicht verwenden:

I saw that play last year.	*Ich habe dieses Theaterstück letztes Jahr gesehen.*
I paid that bill on the first of the month.	*Ich habe diese Rechnung am Monatsersten bezahlt.*

4. Simple Past and Past Progressive

Einerseits verwendet man das Simple Past für Allgemeinheiten und Gewohnheiten in der Vergangenheit, ähnlich wie **used to**:

Leonard's cat liked spaghetti. **Leonard's cat used to like spaghetti.**	*Leonards Katze mochte Spaghetti.*
Professor Roberts always wrote on the blackboard. **Professor Roberts used to write on the blackboard.**	*Professor Roberts schrieb immer an die Tafel.*

Andererseits verwendet man das Simple Past auch für einzelne Ereignisse in der Vergangenheit:

Their daughter ran off with a hobo.	*Ihre Tochter ist mit einem Landstreicher durchgebrannt.*
Several plates fell off the shelves.	*Mehrere Teller fielen aus dem Regal.*

Dagegen verwendet man das Past Progressive für Ereignisse, die zu einem Zeitpunkt in der Vergangenheit gerade abliefen:

At that moment she was thinking about her problems at work.	*In dem Moment dachte sie gerade über ihre Probleme bei der Arbeit nach.*
When I saw him, he was dipping doughnuts in his coffee.	*Als ich ihn sah, war er dabei Doughnuts in seinen Kaffee zu tunken.*

Solche Zustände können auch sich wiederholende Ereignisse sein. Durch das Past Progressive deutet man an, dass der Zeitraum dieser Ereignisse nicht allzu lang dauerte:

At that time we were talking on the phone every day.	*Zu der Zeit telefonierten wir jeden Tag.*
In those days they were buying real estate like crazy.	*Damals haben sie Immobilien wie verrückt gekauft.*

5. Wie man über die Zukunft spricht

Wie unter den Verbformen schon erwähnt, bildet man in der Regel das Future Tense mit dem Hilfsverb **will**. Allerdings wird diese Zeitform nicht so häufig angewandt, wie man sich denken könnte. Die Zukunft mit **will** verwendet man hauptsächlich für Ereignisse, die nicht geplant werden, sondern einfach so passieren oder passieren könnten:

It will rain **soon.**	*Es wird bald regnen.*
If you aren't careful, you'll fall.	*Wenn du nicht aufpasst, fällst du hin.*
Business will improve **during the Christmas season.**	*Das Geschäft wird in der Vorweihnachtszeit besser laufen.*

Außerdem verwendet man diese Zukunftsform für Vorschläge und Ideen bei der Planung:

I'll buy the drinks for the party.	*Ich kann die Getränke für das Fest kaufen.*
Marty will drive Al home after the meeting.	*Marty fährt Al nach der Besprechung heim.*
Jon will take the car tomorrow, and we'll take the bus.	*Jon nimmt morgen das Auto mit, und wir fahren mit dem Bus.*

Wenn etwas aber schon geplant ist, so ist das Future Tense nicht üblich. Das gilt besonders für die gesprochene Sprache. Dann muss man auf andere Ausdrucksweisen ausweichen:

Be going to ist die allgemeine Zukunftsform der gesprochenen Sprache: man kann sie für geplante wie ungeplante Ereignisse (aber nicht für Vorschläge) verwenden:

I'm going to marry **in April.**	*Ich werde im April heiraten.*
It's going to rain.	*Es wird bald regnen.*

Present Progressive

Für fest geplante Ereignisse kann man auch das Present Progressive nehmen:

Mabel is flying **to Hawaii tomorrow.**	*Mabel fliegt morgen nach Hawaii.*
My parents are moving **next year.**	*Meine Eltern ziehen nächstes Jahr um.*

Future Progressive

Das Future Progressive ist eine Kombination aus **will** und Progressive (**be** + *ing*-Form). Diese Bildung verwendet man, wenn das Ereignis sowieso passieren wird, also nicht extra geplant werden muss:

I can ask Randy. I'll be seeing **him tonight.**	*Ich kann Randy fragen. Ich sehe ihn heute abend sowieso.*

Simple Present

Man kann das Simple Present für Ereignisse in der Zukunft verwenden, wenn es um einen fest geplanten Zeitpunkt geht:

My cousin arrives **on Monday.**	*Meine Kusine kommt am Montag an.*
Dr. Curtis and her husband travel **to Moscow on the 27th.**	*Dr. Curtis und ihr Mann reisen am 27. nach Moskau.*

6. Zukunft in der Vergangenheit

Manchmal ist es notwendig, aus der Perspektive der Vergangenheit von etwas zu berichten, das damals noch in der Zukunft lag.

Yesterday morning **Sue** was going to be **late.**	*Gestern früh war Sue drauf und dran zu spät zu kommen.*

Hierzu kann man natürlich die oben erwähnten Zukunfsformen in entsprechende Vergangenheitsformen umwandeln. Allerdings geht dies nicht immer. Man kann z.B. **would** als die Vergangenheit von **will** normalerweise nur in der indirekten Rede benutzen:

Harold said that Sue would be **late.**	*Harold sagte, dass Sue später kommen würde.*

Ansonsten hat **will** überhaupt keine Vergangenheitsform. Deshalb muss man auf einen Ersatz, eine Umschreibung zurückgreifen, nämlich **going to**:

Last week they were going to drive **me crazy.**	*Letzte Woche waren sie auf dem Weg mich in den Wahnsinn zu treiben.*

Wenn man das Simple Present in das Simple Past verwandelt, hat der Satz nur eine normale Vergangenheitsbedeutung:

My cousin arrived **on Monday.**	*Meine Kusine kam am Montag an.*

Hier ist es also besser entweder **going to** oder das Past Progressive zu verwenden:

My cousin was going to arrive **on Monday.**	*Meine Kusine wollte/sollte am Montag ankommen.*
My cousin was arriving **on Monday.**	*Meine Kusine wollte/sollte am Montag ankommen.*

Auxiliaries | *Hilfsverben*

Hilfsverben im Englischen stehen zwischen dem Subjekt und dem Vollverb:

The dog has **eaten my homework.**	*Der Hund hat meine Hausaufgaben gefressen.*
They are **looking for Easter eggs.**	*Sie suchen gerade Ostereier.*

Unentbehrliche Hilfsverben

Bestimmte grammatische Strukturen können ohne Hilfsverb nicht gebildet werden. Wenn kein Hilfsverb vorhanden ist (nämlich bei einfacher Gegenwart oder Vergangenheit), muss man das Spezialhilfsverb **do** nehmen. Dieses merkwürdige Hilfsverb hat keine Bedeutung! Es erfüllt nur diese Erfordernis der Grammatik.

Yes-No Questions | *Ja-Nein-Fragen*

Fragen, auf die man mit ja oder nein antwortet, werden mit einem Hilfsverb eingeleitet. Wenn das Hilfsverb im entsprechenden Aussagesatz schon vorhanden ist, setzt man es einfach an den Satzanfang. Wenn aber der Aussagesatz nur ein Vollverb enthält, muss das Spezialhilfsverb **do** einspringen:

Have you seen the new film?	*Hast du den neuen Film gesehen?*
Do you want to marry me?	*Willst Du mich heiraten?*
Does he like chocolate?	*Mag er Schokolade?*

Die entsprechenden Aussagesätze sind:

You have seen the new film.	*Du hast den neuen Film gesehen.*
You want to marry me.	*Du willst mich heiraten.*
He likes chocolate.	*Er mag Schokolade.*

Der erste Aussagesatz enthält das Hilfsverb **have**, das dann an erster Stelle in der Frage steht. Der zweite und der dritte Aussagesatz enthalten kein Hilfsverb. Da man die Frage ohne Hilfsverb gar nicht anfangen kann, setzt man die passende Form von **do** an den Satzbeginn. Bei zwei oder mehr Hilfsverben in der Aussage wird nur die erste vorangezogen.

Aussage:

The letters have been sent. *Die Briefe sind abgeschickt worden.*

Frage:

Have the letters been sent? *Sind die Briefe abgeschickt worden?*

Eine kleine Besonderheit findet sich bei Ja-Nein Fragen mit **have** bzw. **have got** (*haben, besitzen*). Im britischen English werden entsprechende Aussagesätze häufig mit **have got** gebildet. Dann ist das erste Hilfsverb für die Frage **have**. Im amerikanischen Englisch werden die entsprechenden Aussagesätze eher mit dem einfachen **have** gebildet. Dies gilt dann natürlich als Vollverb und braucht zur Fragebildung noch das Hilfsverb **do**:

Aussage:

She has got a red car. (UK) *Sie hat ein rotes Auto.*
She has a red car. (US) *Sie hat ein rotes Auto.*

Frage:

Has she got a red car? (UK) *Hat sie ein rotes Auto?*
Does she have a red car? (US) *Hat sie ein rotes Auto?*

Negation | *Verneinung*

Die normale Satzverneinung mit **not** verlangt ein Hilfsverb. Dabei steht **not** zwischen dem Hilfsverb und dem Vollverb:

The guests had not arrived yet. *Die Gäste waren noch nicht angekommen.*
We did not like the beer. *Wir mochten das Bier nicht.*

Ohne **do** (in diesem Fall die Vergangenheitsform **did**) hätte der zweite Satz kein Hilfsverb. Der entsprechende nicht verneinte Satz lautet nämlich:
We liked the beer. *Wir mochten Bier.*

Diesen Satz kann man nicht verneinen, indem man nur **not** in den Satz einschiebt!

In der gesprochenen Sprache verwendet man das volle Wort **not** nur zur ausdrücklichen, betonten Verneinung und sonst eher selten. Stattdessen verwendet man die reduzierte Form **-n't**, die an das Hilfsverb angehängt wird:

The guests hadn't **arrived yet.**	*Die Gäste waren noch nicht angekommen.*
We didn't **like the beer.**	*Wir mochten das Bier nicht.*

Wenn man nun eine **Yes-No Question** mit einem verneinten Satz bilden will, muss man das Hilfsverb voranziehen. Dabei geht **-n't** mit.

Didn't **you like the beer?**	*Habt ihr das Bier denn nicht gemocht?*

Kurzantworten

Wenn man eine Frage gestellt bekommt, ist es meist nicht notwendig mit einem vollständigen Satz zu antworten. Bei einer **Yes-No Question** kann man natürlich einfach nur **yes** oder **no** sagen. Dies wird aber oft als abgehackt und unhöflich empfunden. Daher hat man die Möglichkeit, einen abgekürzten Satz hinzuzufügen.

Bei der Antwort **yes** besteht der abgekürzte Satz nur aus Subjekt und Hilfsverb:

Did **you see the film on Monday?**	*Hast du am Montag den Film gesehen?*
Yes, I did**.**	*Ja, habe ich.*
Can **you pass me the salt?**	*Kannst Du mir das Salz geben?*
Yes, I can**.**	*Ja, kann ich.*

Bei der Antwort **no** besteht der abgekürzte Satz aus Subjekt und Hilfsverb mit angehängter Verneinung (**-n't**):

Did **you see the film on Monday?**	*Hast du am Montag den Film gesehen?*
No, I didn't.	*Nein, habe ich nicht.*
Can **you pass me the salt?**	*Kannst Du mir das Salz geben?*
No, I can't.	*Nein, kann ich nicht.*

Sehr wichtig bei Kurzantworten ist, dass das Hilfsverb immer dasselbe ist wie in der vorangegangenen Frage.

Es gibt auch noch spezielle Kurzantworten auf Subjektsfragen, d. h. Fragen, bei denen das Fragewort das Subjekt ist. Hier besteht die Kurzantwort aus dem Subjekt und dem entsprechenden Hilfsverb.

Who's [= has] been to Paris?	*Wer war schon mal in Paris?*
Terry and Larry have.	*Terry und Larry waren schon mal dort.*
Who bought the present for Susan?	*Wer hat das Geschenk für Susan gekauft?*
Harry did.	*Harry hat das gemacht.*

Tag Questions | *Frageanhängsel*

Eine sehr übliche Bildung im Englischen ist der Aussagesatz mit **Tag Question**. Das **Tag** (Anhängsel) hat die Form von einer Kurzfrage: Hilfsverb + Subjekt.

Laura hasn't taken my sweater, has she**?**	*Laura hat meinen Pullover nicht mitgenommen, oder?*

Das Subjekt der **Tag Question** ist immer das Pronomen, das dem Subjekt der vorangegangenen Aussage entspricht:

The children have returned, haven't they**?**	*Die Kinder sind zurück, oder?*

Wenn das einzige oder erste Verb in der Aussage kein Hilfsverb, sondern ein Vollverb ist, verwendet man **do** im **Tag** (Anhängsel).

You know my friend Sebastian, don't you**?**	*Du kennst meinen Freund Sebastian schon, nicht wahr?*

Wichtig ist, dass hinter einer bejahenden Aussage das verneinende **Tag** (Anhängsel) steht, und hinter einer verneinenden Aussage das bejahende **Tag** (Anhängsel).

Billie had left, hadn't she**?**	*Billie war schon gegangen, nicht wahr?*
Billie hadn't left, had she**?**	*Billie war noch nicht gegangen, nicht wahr?*

Formal betrachtet ist das Frageanhängsel eine Bitte um Bestätigung.

Modalverben

Formen

Modalverben sind eine Untergruppe der Hilfsverben und verhalten sich meist auch wie diese. Die wichtigsten Modalverben des Englischen sind **can, could, will, would, shall, should, may, might** und **must**. Es wird oft gesagt, dass die meisten dieser Hilfsverben sich in Gegenwarts-Vergangenheits-Paare einordnen lassen:

Gegenwartsform	Vergangenheitsform	Übersetzung
can	could	*können*
will	would	*werden, wollen*
shall	should	*werden, sollen*
may	might	*dürfen, können*

Diese Behauptung stimmt bezüglich der indirekten Rede. Ansonsten stimmt die Aussage in der Regel nicht. Nur **could** wird tatsächlich manchmal als Vergangenheitsform von **can** verwendet:

Gegenwart:

You can open the door.	*Du kannst die Tür aufmachen.*

Vergangenheit:

You could open the door, after all.	*Du konntest die Tür doch aufmachen.*

Es ist viel einfacher, die Bedeutungen der einzelnen Formen auswendig zu lernen.

can	*kann*	could	*konnte, könnte*
will	*wird*	would	*würde*
shall	*wird, soll*	should	*sollte, soll, dürfte*
may	*darf, kann*	might	*könnte*
must	*muss*		

Das englische **will** ist im modernen Sprachgebrauch nicht gleich dem deutschen *will* (*wollen*). Das deutsche Verb *wollen* wird mit dem Vollverb **want** übersetzt.

They will have dinner soon.	*Sie werden bald zu Abend essen.*
They want to have dinner soon.	*Sie wollen bald zu Abend essen.*

Parallel dazu heißt **would** *würde* (und nicht *wollte*).

Ms. Fielding would **do it.**	*Frau Fielding würde es tun.*
Ms. Fielding wanted **to do it.**	*Frau Fielding wollte es tun.*

Wenn man über eine Zeit in der Vergangenheit spricht, so kann man **would** auch einsetzen, um Gewohnheiten auszudrücken:

He would go in and order five hamburgers.	*Er ging einfach rein und bestellte fünf Hamburger.*

Gerade in der gesprochenen Sprache wird **will** oft zu **'ll** bzw. **would** zu **'d** verkürzt und an das Ende des Subjekts angehängt:

I'll bring my special tuna and ketchup salad.	*Ich bringe meinen Tunfisch-und-Ketschup-Spezialsalat mit.*
They'd buy a yacht if they had the money.	*Sie würden sich eine Jacht kaufen, wenn sie das Geld hätten.*

Fehlende Formen und Alternativen

Bei den Modalverben gibt es ein besonderes Problem: sie besitzen nicht alle nötigen Formen. Ein Modalverb kann immer nur das erste Verb im Satz (Haupt- oder Nebensatz) sein und es kann nicht hinter **to** stehen:

We can bake the cookies.	*Wir können die Kekse backen.*

Aus diesem Grund ist der Gebrauch von Modalverben natürlich ziemlich eingeschränkt. Trotzdem kommt es vor, dass man die Bedeutung eines Modalverbs an einer problematischen Stelle ausdrücken möchte. Dafür gibt es verschiedene Alternativen, mit denen man Modalverben ersetzen kann:

Modalverb	Alternative	Übersetzung
can, could	be able to	*können*
will, shall	be going to	*werden*
may	be allowed to	*dürfen*
must	have to	*müssen*
should	be supposed to	*sollen*

| We have been able to to bake the cookies. | *Wir konnten die Kekse backen.* |
| They hoped to be able to bake the cookies. | *Sie hofften, die Kekse backen zu können.* |

Verneinte Formen

Formen mit der verkürzten Version von **not** gibt es auch bei den Modalverben. Im Allgemeinen hängt man **n't** wie bei **have** und **do** an das Ende des Modalverbs an. Aber in ein paar Fällen muss man eine besondere Form verwenden:

can	+	n't		=	can't
will	+	n't		=	won't
shall	+	n't		=	shan't

Man beachte, dass **won't** manchmal die Bedeutung *will nicht* (im Sinne einer Verweigerung) haben kann:

| **The gardener won't rake the leaves.** | *Der Gärtner will das Laub nicht zusammenrechen.* |
| **The car won't start.** | *Das Auto will nicht anspringen.* |

Parallel dazu bedeutet **wouldn't** manchmal *wollte nicht*:

| **The gardener wouldn't rake the leaves.** | *Der Gärtner wollte das Laub nicht zusammenrechen.* |
| **The car wouldn't start.** | *Das Auto wollte nicht anspringen.* |

Gebrauch im Satz

Die Modalverben unterscheiden sich von den anderen Verben darin, dass ihre Form sich bei einem **he/she/it**-Subjekt nicht verändert:

| **I can go.** | *Ich kann hingehen.* |
| **She can go.** | *Sie kann hingehen.* |

Modalverben kommen an denselben Stellen im Satz vor wie andere Hilfsverben. Das Modalverb verlangt, dass das nächste Verb in der einfachen Grundform steht:

James can meet you at the airport.	*James kann dich vom Flughafen abholen.*
James can't meet you at the airport.	*James kann dich nicht vom Flughafen abholen.*
Should Cathy take her car?	*Soll Cathy mit ihrem Auto kommen?*
No, she shouldn't.	*Nein, das soll sie nicht.*
They'll just do it again, won't they?	*Sie werden es einfach wieder tun, oder?*

Das modalverbähnliche **ought (to)** bedeutet ungefähr das gleiche wie **should**. Im Gegensatz zu den Modalverben folgt aber immer ein Infinitiv mit **to**:

You ought to bathe sometimes.	*Du solltest dich ab und zu baden.*

Sonderfunktionen der Modalverben

Oft setzt man Modalverben ein, um klarzustellen, dass es sich bei einer Äußerung um eine Vermutung handelt. Die Wahl des Modalverbs zeigt die Wahrscheinlichkeit der Aussage an.

May und **might** können beide eine Möglichkeit ausdrücken. Dabei ist **may** ein bisschen sicherer oder wahrscheinlicher als **might.**

Ms. Young may know.	*Frau Young weiß es vielleicht.*
Ms. Young might know.	*Frau Young weiß es vielleicht.*

In **should** steckt die Annahme, dass ein Zustand existieren müsste oder sollte:

Ms. Young should know.	*Frau Young sollte es wissen.*
Walter should be feeding the cat now.	*Walter müsste jetzt die Katze füttern.*

Must ist stärker als **should** und bedeutet entweder eine starke Verpflichtung, oder dass der Sprecher annimmt, dass etwas der Fall sein muss (z.B. aufgrund von sichtbaren Beweisen):

Ms. Young must know.	*Frau Young muss es erfahren!*
The thief must have forgotten the money. There's still some of it lying on the floor.	*Der Dieb muss das Geld vergessen haben. Da liegt immer noch etwas auf dem Fussboden.*

Bei Verbketten, die aus einem Modalverb gefolgt von einer Perfektform bestehen, gibt es zwei Bedeutungsklassen. Die Bedeutung hängt immer vom Modalverb ab.

Vermutung:

They will have **paid the conman.**	*Sie werden den Schwindler bezahlt haben.*
They may have **paid the conman.**	*Sie könnten den Schwindler bezahlt haben.*
They might have **paid the conman.**	*Sie können den Schwindler vielleicht bezahlt haben.*
They must have **paid the conman.**	*Sie müssen den Schwindler bezahlt haben.*
They can't have **paid the conman.**	*Sie können den Schwindler nicht bezahlt haben.*

Unwirkliches in der Vergangenheit:

They would have **paid the conman.**	*Sie hätten den Schwindler bezahlt.*
They could have **paid the conman.**	*Sie hätten den Schwindler bezahlen können.*
They should have **paid the conman.**	*Sie hätten den Schwindler bezahlen sollen.*
They might have **paid the conman.**	*Sie hätten den Schwindler doch bezahlen können.*

Dabei sieht man, dass nur **might** in beide Klassen fällt.

Höflichkeitsformen

Would und **could** gelten in bittenden Fragen als besonders höflich:

Would you please close the door?	*Würden Sie bitte die Türe schließen?*
Could you bring me one too?	*Könntest du mir auch eins bringen?*

Spezielle Verben

Be | *Formen*

Simple Present		Simple Past	
I am	*ich bin*	**I was**	*ich war*
you are	*du bist*	**you were**	*du warst*
he/she/it is	*er/sie/es ist*	**he/she/it was**	*er/sie/es war*
we are	*wir sind*	**we were**	*wir waren*
you are	*ihr seid*	**you were**	*ihr wart*
they are	*sie sind*	**they were**	*sie waren*

In der gesprochenen Sprache verwendet man gern Kurzformen in der Gegenwart:

I am	▷	**I'm**
she is	▷	**she's**
you are	▷	**you're**
They are	▷	**they're**

I'm here – under the table!	*Ich bin hier – unter dem Tisch!*
She's nice.	*Sie ist nett.*
You're not alone.	*Du bist nicht allein.*

Anwendung

Be kann auch als Vollverb eingesetzt werden. Dann verbindet es das Subjekt mit einer anderen Phrase:

John is **in the kitchen.**	*John ist in der Küche.*
Such problems are **normal.**	*Solche Probleme sind normal.*
Susan is **an excellent ice hockey player.**	*Susan ist eine ausgezeichnete Eishockeyspielerin.*

Im Normalfall muss ein Vollverb in gewissen Situationen wie z.B. Verneinung oder **Yes-No-Questions** von einem Hilfsverb begleitet werden (▶ Hilfsverben). Bei **be** ist es anders – auch als Vollverb verhält sich **be** wie ein Hilfsverb: **be** steht vor **not**, leitet Fragen ein und taucht in Kurzantworten und Frageanhängseln auf:

Verneinung:

John isn't **in the kitchen.**	*John ist nicht in der Küche.*

Ja-Nein-Frage:

Is **John in the kitchen?**	*Ist John in der Küche?*

Kurzantworten:

Yes, he is**.**	*Ja, ist er.*
No, he isn't**.**	*Nein, ist er nicht.*

Frageanhängsel:

John is **in the kitchen,** isn't **he?**	*John ist in der Küche, oder?*

Be wird als Hilfsverb im Passiv und in den Progressive Formen benutzt, aber nicht im Present Perfect:

Food is prepared **here.**	*Hier wird Essen zubereitet.*
Frank was reading**.**	*Frank las gerade.*

There is/There are

There is (Singular) und **there are** (Plural) drücken meist Existenz, Anwesenheit oder Erscheinen aus:

There is **a squirrel in the garden.**	*Ein Eichhörnchen ist im Garten.*
There are **squirrels in the garden.**	*Ein paar Eichhörnchen sind im Garten.*
There are **twelve months in a year.**	*Das Jahr hat zwölf Monate.*

Bei dieser Verwendung handelt es sich um unbestimmte Dinge. Das bedeutet, dass man in der Regel keine bestimmten Artikel, Demonstrative oder Eigennamen nach **there is/ there are** benutzen darf:

There was **a stranger at the party.**	*Da war ein Fremder auf dem Fest.*

There is/there are kann auch bei Aufzählungen verwendet werden:

Frage:	
What chores do you still have to do?	*Was musst du noch an Hausarbeit machen?*
Antwort:	
Well, there's the washing and the ironing. Then there are the dishes.	*Also, da wäre das Waschen und Bügeln. Dann muss ich auch noch abspülen.*

Have und have got | *Gegenwartsformen von have*

I have	*Ich habe*
you have	*Du hast*
he, she, it has	*Er, sie, es hat*
we have	*Wir haben*
you have	*Du hast*
they have	*Sie haben*

Anwendung

Have kann ebenfalls als Vollverb gebraucht werden. Am häufigsten bedeutet **have** *haben* im Sinne von *besitzen, bei sich haben*, usw.:

The Smiths have a yellow car. | *Die Smiths haben ein gelbes Auto.*

Eine Alternative zu diesem **have** ist **have got**:
The Smiths have got a yellow car. | *Die Smiths haben ein gelbes Auto.*

Im Amerikanischen gilt **have got** als umgangssprachlich und wird in formellen Situationen nicht verwendet.

Have mit und ohne Hilfsverb

Das tückische bei **have** sind die Situationen, in denen man ein Hilfsverb braucht und keines vorhanden ist. (Die englischen Muttersprachler sind sich nämlich nicht einig, wie man die Sätze bilden soll!)

Strategie 1: **have** wird wie ein Hilfsverb gebraucht:

They haven't a bicycle. *Sie haben kein Fahrrad.*
Have you a car? *Hast du ein Auto?*

Obwohl diese Strategie wohl am einfachsten ist, bringt sie gewisse Probleme mit sich: Erstens wird sie im Amerikanischen nur noch in ein paar alten Ausdrücken überhaupt verwendet und kommt den Leuten fremd vor. Zweitens kommt sie in Großbritannien auch aus der Mode; dort wird sie hauptsächlich von älteren Leuten benutzt.

Strategie 2: **have** wird wie ein Vollverb gebraucht:

Dies ist die gängige Strategie des Amerikanischen. Sie hat zur Folge, dass man **do** einsetzt, wenn ein Hilfsverb gebraucht wird:

They don't have a bicycle. *Sie haben kein Fahrrad.*
Do you have a car? *Hast du ein Auto?*

Strategie 3: **have** wird durch **have got** ersetzt:

They haven't got **a bicycle.**	*Sie haben kein Fahrrad.*
Have you got **a car?**	*Hast du ein Auto?*

Diese Strategie stellt die moderne Lösung in Großbritannien dar. Sie hat den Vorteil, dass man sie in der Umgangssprache überall anwenden kann. Im Amerikanischen gehört sie zum lockeren Sprachgebrauch; in der Standardsprache muss man Strategie 2 nehmen.

Weitere Bedeutungen von have

Have wird auch in anderen Zusammenhängen und festen Verbindungen verwendet, die man am besten auswendig lernt:

We have breakfast at 8:00.	*Wir frühstücken um 8.00.*
I had a cup of coffee.	*Ich habe eine Tasse Kaffee getrunken.*
Lisa is having a baby.	*Lisa bekommt ein Kind.*
Keith had a smoke.	*Keith rauchte eine.*

Bei den obigen Beispielen muss man Strategie 2 anwenden:

Did they have breakfast with you?	*Haben sie mit euch gefrühstückt?*
I didn't have a cup of coffee.	*Ich habe keine Tasse Kaffee getrunken.*
Keith didn't have a smoke.	*Keith hat nicht geraucht.*

Do | *Gegenwartsformen*

I do	*Ich mache*
you do	*Du machst*
he/she/it does	*Er/sie/es macht*
we do	*wir machen*
you do	*Ihr macht*
they do	*Sie machen*

Anwendung

Do ist nicht nur das Spezialhilfsverb, das bei den Vollverben aushilft, sondern wird auch selbst als Vollverb eingesetzt:

The children did **their homework.**	*Die Kinder machten ihre Hausaufgaben.*
What are **you** doing?	*Was machst du?*

Wenn nun ein Hilfsverb unentbehrlich ist und nur das Vollverb **do** zur Verfügung steht, muss man auch das Hilfsverb **do** einsetzen. Dann enthält der Satz zweimal **do:**

The children didn't do **their homework.**	*Die Kinder haben ihre Hausaufgaben nicht gemacht.*
What did **you** do?	*Was hast du gemacht?*

Get

Get ist ein meist umgangssprachliches Verb mit der Grundbedeutung *kriegen* bzw. *bekommen*:

I got **a watch for my birthday.**	*Ich habe eine Uhr zum Geburtstag bekommen.*
We finally got **the door open.**	*Endlich haben wir die Tür aufgekriegt.*
I couldn't get **the cat down from the tree.**	*Ich habe die Katze nicht vom Baum runterkriegen können.*

Get kann aber auch *werden* bedeuten:

We were getting **tired.**	*Wir wurden allmählich müde.*
It gets **hot here in summer.**	*Es wird hier im Sommer heiß.*
Tony got **hit by car.**	*Tony wurde von einem Auto angefahren.*

Be used to und get used to

Die Phrase **be used to** bedeutet *etwas gewöhnt sein*. Sie wird mit **be** verwendet um einen Zustand des Gewöhntseins auszudrücken:

She's used to **the noise.**	*Sie ist den Lärm gewöhnt.*
Ms. Thompson is used to **teaching large classes.**	*Frau Thompson ist es gewöhnt große Klassen zu unterrichten.*

Get used to hingegen bedeutet *sich an (etwas) gewöhnen*.

She got used to **the noise quickly.**	*She gewöhnte sich schnell an den Lärm.*
I can't get used to **English pronunciation.**	*Ich kann mich an die englische Aussprache nicht gewöhnen.*
Ms. Thompson is getting used **to teaching large classes.**	*Frau Thompson gewöhnt sich daran große Klassen zu unterrichten.*

2 Prepositions | *Verhältniswörter*

Zeitangaben

- Die Uhrzeiten werden mit **at** angegeben:

I'll be home at seven.	*Ich bin um sieben Uhr wieder zu Hause.*
We had lunch at noon.	*Wir aßen um zwölf zu Mittag.*

- **Morning, afternoon** und **evening** verlangen die Präposition **in** und den bestimmten Artikel **the**:

Stretch before you get up in the morning.	*Strecken Sie sich, bevor Sie morgens aufstehen.*
The children always play in the afternoon.	*Nachmittags spielen die Kinder immer.*
In the evening **we went out.**	*Am Abend gingen wir aus.*

- **Night** verlangt meist die Präposition **at** und tritt dann ohne Artikel auf:

Owls hunt at night.	*Eulen gehen nachts auf die Jagd.*
My friend Steve, a catburglar, works at night.	*Mein Freund Steve, ein Fassadenkletterer, arbeitet nachts.*

Vorsicht, denn der Abend wird auch sehr häufig als **night** bezeichnet:

What did you do last night?	*Was habt ihr gestern Abend gemacht?*
When I get home at night, I make dinner.	*Wenn ich abends nach Hause komme, mache ich das Abendessen.*

- Wochentage werden häufig mit **on** angegeben:

I have an appointment on Wednesday.	*Ich habe am Mittwoch einen Termin.*
Most museums are closed on Mondays.	*Die meisten Museen sind montags geschlossen.*

Jedoch kann man **on** in der gesprochenen Sprache auch weglassen:

I have an appointment Wednesday.	*Ich habe am Mittwoch einen Termin.*
Most museums are closed Mondays.	*Die meisten Museen haben montags zu.*

In Großbritannien sagt man **at the weekend**, in Nordamerika stattdessen **on the weekend**.

- Einzelne Feiertage brauchen normalerweise **on**:

We get half the day off on Christmas Eve.	*Heiligen Abend bekommen wir den halben Tag frei.*
Many people go to church at sunrise on Easter.	*An Ostern gehen viele Leute bei Sonnenaufgang in die Kirche.*

At oder **over** weisen nicht nur auf den Feiertag hin, sondern auch auf die Zeit um den Feiertag herum:

I saw my aunt and uncle at Christmas.	*Ich habe meine Tante und meinen Onkel zu Weihnachten gesehen.*
I'm flying home over Easter.	*Ich fliege zu Ostern nach Hause.*

- Monate und Jahreszeiten werden mit **in** angegeben:

It happened in July.	*Es ist im Juli passiert.*
The neighbors barbecued every day in August.	*Im August grillten die Nachbarn jeden Tag.*
In winter **we need to heat the house.**	*Im Winter müssen wir das Haus heizen.*

- Man braucht **in** auch immer bei Jahreszahlen:

In 1492 **Columbus discovered America.**	*1492 entdeckte Columbus Amerika.*
Sales figures fell in 1996.	*Die Verkaufszahlen sind 1996 gefallen.*

Während

In der Regel wird *während* mit **during** ausgedrückt:

I fell asleep during the opera.	*Ich bin während der Oper eingeschlafen.*
She arrived during the winter.	*Sie kam im Laufe des Winters an.*

Als Übersetzung für *während des/der ganzen* ... nimmt man meist **throughout:**

The postal service is very busy throughout the Christmas season.	*Die Post hat während der ganzen Weihnachtszeit sehr viel zu tun.*
Evergreens stay green throughout the year.	*Immergrüne Pflanzen bleiben das ganze Jahr über grün.*

Bei **day, night, month, year** geht es ohne Präposition – man setzt einfach all davor:

The cats sang outside my window all night.	*Die Katzen haben die ganze Nacht vor meinem Fenster miaut.*
Evergreens stay green all year.	*Immergrüne Pflanzen bleiben das ganze Jahr über grün.*

For gibt an, wie lange ein Ereignis dauert:

Nigel and Joo didn't talk to each other for a year.	*Nigel und Joo sprachen ein Jahr lang nicht miteinander.*
They worked for five more hours.	*Sie arbeiteten fünf weitere Stunden.*

Das deutsche Wort *vor* hat zwei verschiedene Übersetzungen. Wenn sich *vor* auf einen Zeitpunkt bezieht, übersetzt man es mit **before**:

Before the flood **we lived in the valley.**	*Vor der Überflutung lebten wir im Tal.*
We had to get up before daybreak.	*Wir mussten vor Tagesanbruch aufstehen.*

Wenn man stattdessen eine Zeitspanne nennt, verwendet man im Englischen keine Präposition, sondern setzt **ago** nach dem Zeitraum:

We met six years ago.	*Wir haben uns vor sechs Jahren kennen gelernt.*
Three days ago **my car broke down.**	*Vor drei Tagen ist mein Auto kaputtgegangen.*

Ortsangaben

Die wichtigsten Präpositionen für die Ortsangabe sind **in** und **on**:

We stayed in New York.	*Wir wohnten in New York.*
There's a frog on my desk.	*Auf meinem Schreibtisch ist ein Frosch.*

Man muss **on** (*auf*) und **at** (*an*) unterscheiden:

We all sat down on the table.	*Wir setzten uns alle auf den Tisch.*
We all sat down at the table.	*Wir setzten uns alle an den Tisch.*

An den obigen Beispielsätzen sieht man, dass Phrasen wie **sit down, lie down, set down, lay down** nicht immer zu den jeweiligen Präpositionen passen. Man lernt daher diese Phrasen in ihren einzelnen Zusammensetzungen am besten auswendig.

At verwendet man auch für Anwesenheit in Läden und auf Veranstaltungen:

I ran into Ralph at the pharmacy.	*Ich traf Ralph in der Apotheke.*
The adults are at the circus,	*Die Erwachsenen sind im Zirkus,*
but the children are at the museum.	*aber die Kinder sind im Museum.*
Who was at the party?	*Wer war alles auf der Party?*

Problemfälle

Der Ausdruck **at home** heißt immer *zu Hause*:

I often stay at home.	*Ich bleibe oft zu Hause.*

Bei einer Ortsangabe bedeutet **by** *ganz in der Nähe von*, nicht *bei*:

Vera lives by Jonathan.	*Vera wohnt ganz in der Nähe von Jonathan.*
Vera lives at Jonathan's.	*Vera wohnt bei John.*

In der Nähe von heißt auf Englisch oft einfach **near**:

Newark is near New York City.	*Newark liegt in der Nähe von New York.*
There's a telephone booth near the church.	*In der Nähe der Kirche ist eine Telefonzelle.*

Richtung

Into (*in/hinein*) und **onto** (*auf*) zeigen die räumliche oder zeitliche Richtung oder Orientierung eines Geschehens. Im Gegensatz zu **on** oder **in** steht hier das jeweilige Verb bzw. Geschehen im Mittelpunkt.

The rabbit jumped into a hole.	*Das Kaninchen ist in ein Loch gesprungen.*
Jeff got into trouble.	*Jeff geriet in Schwierigkeiten.*
Bonzo fell onto my foot.	*Bonzo fiel mir auf den Fuss.*

Manchmal kann man aber auch **into** und **onto** mit **in** und **on** ersetzen:

We got into/in the car.	*Wir sind ins Auto gestiegen.*
She put chocolate in/into the cake.	*Sie hat Schokolade in den Kuchen getan.*
The ball rolled onto/on the street.	*Der Ball rollte auf die Strasse.*

To deutet an, dass sich etwas nicht nur in eine Richtung bewegt, sondern auch ankommt:

We went to the supermarket.	*Wir sind zum Supermarkt gegangen.*
Let's go to Switzerland!	*Fahren wir in die Schweiz!*

To wird auch häufig anstatt des Wemfalles (Dativ) verwendet:

The librarian showed the visitor the books.	*Die Bibliothekarin zeigte dem Besucher die Bücher.*
▶ **The librarian showed the books** to the visitor.	*Die Bibliothekarin zeigte dem Besucher die Bücher.*
She explained the problem to me.	*Sie erklärte mir das Problem.*
They recommended a cheap restaurant to me.	*Sie haben mir ein billiges Restaurant empfohlen.*

Die Phrase **go to (someone)** bedeutet, dass man zu der Person als solche gegangen ist, nicht zu deren Wohnung o.ä.:

I went to Mary **and told her the story.**	*Ich ging zu Mary und erzählte ihr die Geschichte.*

From sagt uns, woher jemand oder etwas kommt:

Kyle is from Athens, Georgia. **We drove** from the bank **to the restaurant next door.**	*Kyle stammt aus Athens in Georgia. Wir sind mit dem Auto von der Bank zum Restaurant nebenan gefahren.*

From verwendet man auch bei Entfernungen:

Oakville is five miles from here. **It's four inches** from the doorframe **to the wall.**	*Oakville liegt fünf Meilen von hier entfernt. Vom Türrahmen zur Wand sind es etwa zehn Zentimeter.*

Of ist ein vielseitiges Wort. Besonders schriftsprachlich muss man meist **of** anstelle des Besitzfalles (Possessive) bei Besitzern und Verursachern verwenden, wenn etwas nach dem Kernwort der Noun Phrase steht:

Possessive:	
The funny young man's favorite aunt	*Die Lieblingstante des komischen jungen Mannes*
Tom's advice	*Toms Rat*
Of-Phrase:	
The favorite aunt of the man wearing a silk suit	*Die Lieblingstante des Mannes im Seidenanzug*
The advice of a stranger	*Der Rat eines Fremden*

Eine sehr wichtige Anwendung von **of** drückt Zugehörigkeit oder Zuordnung aus:

An association of scientists **was having a meeting.**	*Eine Gruppe Wissenschaftler tagte gerade.*
The man was standing naked on the roof of the house.	*Der Mann stand nackt auf dem Dach des Hauses.*

Man verwendet **of** zusammen mit Mengen- und Inhaltsangaben:

a pinch of salt	*eine Prise Salz*
a box of matches	*eine Schachtel Streichhölzer*
a glass of water	*ein Glas Wasser*
I ate a bowl of soup, a slice of bread, and a can of beans, and drank two big glasses of grape juice.	*Ich aß einen Teller Suppe, eine Scheibe Brot und eine Dose Bohnen und trank zwei große Gläser Traubensaft.*

Das Wort **pair** (**of**) bezieht sich immer auf zwei Gegenstände oder Leute:

Rene bought a pair of socks.	*Rene kaufte ein Paar Socken.*
They made a pretty pair.	*Sie waren ein hübsches Pärchen.*

Häufig markiert **of** die entsprechende Phrase nach dem verwandten Nomen (*Noun*):

The delay of the flight **worried the passengers.**	*Die Verspätung des Fluges beunruhigte die Passagiere.*
The classification of bats **is a difficult business.**	*Die Klassifizierung von Fledermäusen ist ein schwieriges Unterfangen.*
The baking of cookies **leads to overeating.**	*Das Plätzchenbacken führt dazu, dass man zu viel isst.*

Of gibt auch die Todesursache an:

My grandmother died of old age.	*Meine Großmutter ist an Altersschwäche gestorben.*
Timothy Toast almost died of overeating.	*Timothy Toast starb fast an zuviel Essen.*

By drückt aus von wem oder was etwas gemacht worden ist:

I'm reading an exciting book by Sara Paretsky.	*Ich lese gerade ein spannendes Buch von Sara Paretsky.*
Who**'s the article** by**?**	*Von wem ist der Artikel?*

Komplexe Präpositionen

Einige wenige Präpositionen bestehen aus zwei oder mehr Wörtern:

because of	*aufgrund, wegen*
in spite of	*trotz*
instead of	*(an)statt*
out of	*aus*
from under	*von unter*

The game was cancelled because of **the snowstorm.**	*Das Spiel wurde wegen des Schneesturms abgesagt.*
In spite **of their promise, they behaved badly.**	*Trotz ihres Versprechens haben sie sich schlecht benommen.*
Clint came out of **the bathroom half dressed.**	*Clint kam halb angezogen aus dem Bad.*
Betsy crawled out from under **the bed.**	*Betsy kam unter dem Bett hervorgekrochen.*

3 Phrasal Verbs | *Partikelverben*

Allgemeines

Phrasal Verb wird oft als ein Überbegriff für mehrere Bildungstypen aus einem Verb und mindestens einem zusätzlichen Element verwendet. Dabei muss man zwischen zwei Arten von ähnlichen zusätzlichen Elementen unterscheiden: Präpositionen und Partikel. Präpositionen verlangen immer eine *Noun Phrase*, mit anderen Worten ihr eigenes Objekt. Dieses Objekt muss – außer in Fragewort-Fragen, Relativsätzen u.ä. – nach der Präposition stehen. Partikel treten zwar häufig zusammen mit Noun Phrases auf, aber die Noun Phrase ist nicht das Objekt der Partikel und muss daher nicht dahinter stehen. Das Schwierige bei der Sache ist natürlich, dass Präpositionen und Partikel oft gleich aussehen! Ein relativ einfacher Test ist die Verschiebbarkeit des Elements. Kann es hinter der Noun Phrase oder dem Fürwort (Pronoun) stehen, so ist es ein Partikel. Muss es immer vor der Noun Phrase oder dem Pronoun stehen, ist es eine Präposition.

Präposition:	
The woman pushed the stroller up the street.	*Die Frau schob den Sportwagen die Straße hoch.*
Partikel:	
The woman looked up the telephone number. **The woman looked the telephone number up.**	*Die Frau schlug die Telefonnummer nach.*

Es gibt auch verschiedene Kombinationsmöglichkeiten:

Verb	+	Partikel					
Verb	+	Partikel	+	Noun Phrase			
Verb	+	Präposition	+	Noun Phrase			
Verb	+	Partikel	+	Präposition	+	Noun Phrase

Beispiele für Verb + Partikel

come along	*mitkommen*	**grow up**	*aufwachsen, erwachsen*
get in	*einsteigen (ins Auto)*		*werden*
get on	*einsteigen (in den Bus,*	**make up**	*sich versöhnen*
	Zug, Flugzeug)	**run away**	*weglaufen*
get up	*aufstehen*	**sit down**	*sich hinsetzen*
go along	*mitgehen*	**take off**	*abheben, abfliegen,*
go away	*weggehen*		*sich davonmachen*
go back	*zurückgehen*	**wake up**	*aufwachen*

Die Partikel steht unmittelbar nach dem Verb:

I have to get up **so early every morning!**	*Ich muss jeden Morgen so früh aufstehen!*
The others wanted to go to the party without me, but I went along **anyway.**	*Die anderen wollten ohne mich auf die Party, aber ich bin trotzdem mitgegangen.*
The unhappy teenager ran away **from home.**	*Der unglückliche Teenager ist von zu Hause weggelaufen.*

Beispiele für Verb + Partikel + *Noun Phrase*

bring along	*mitbringen*	**put on**	*anziehen*
bring back	*zurückbringen*	**ring up**	*anrufen (UK)*
call off	*absagen*	**run over**	*überfahren*
call up	*anrufen (US)*	**stand up**	*versetzen, sitzen lassen*
let in	*hereinlassen*	**take along**	*mitnehmen*
look up	*nachschlagen*	**take off**	*ausziehen*
make up	*schminken; (Geschichte)*	**turn down**	*kleiner oder leiser stellen*
	erfinden	**turn off**	*ausschalten*
pick up	*abholen*	**turn on**	*einschalten*

In der Wortfolge stehen Partikel und Noun Phrase nach dem Verb und vor anderen Elementen wie z. B. Adverbien. Bei voller Noun Phrase ist es grammatisch gesehen egal, ob die Partikel vor der Noun Phrase steht oder umgekehrt – obwohl manchmal die eine oder andere Wortfolge üblicher wird. Wenn aber die Noun Phrase ein Pronomen (Fürwort) ist, muss sie vor der Partikel stehen.

Judith stood up **Mel.**	*Judith hat Mel sitzen lassen.*
Judith stood **Mel** up.	*Judith hat Mel sitzen lassen.*
Judith stood **him** up.	*Judith hat ihn sitzen lassen.*

Casey called **us** up **last night.**	*Casey hat uns gestern Abend angerufen.*
Lenny made **that story** up.	*Lenny hat diese Geschichte erfunden.*
When they called off **the wedding, the make-up artist was already** making up **the bride.**	*Als sie die Hochzeit absagten, war die Visagistin schon dabei, die Braut zu schminken.*

Beispiele für Verb + Präposition + *Noun Phrase*

call for	*rufen nach; fordern; abholen*	**look at**	*anschauen*
		look for	*suchen*
care for	*pflegen*	**run after**	*hinterherlaufen*
do without	*auskommen ohne*	**run across**	*stoßen auf*
listen to	*zuhören; hören auf*	**run into**	*zufällig treffen; rennen/ fahren gegen*
look after	*hüten; sich kümmern um*		

Man verwendet die Präposition genauso wie sonst, d.h. sie stehen immer vor ihrer Noun Phrase oder dem Pronoun:

You never listen to **me!**	*Du hörst mir nie zu!*
I can't possibly do without **my waffle iron.**	*Ich kann unmöglich ohne mein Waffeleisen auskommen.*
I was looking for **a job and** ran across **an unusual advertisement.**	*Ich habe nach einer Stelle gesucht und bin dabei auf eine ungewöhnliche Anzeige gestoßen.*

Die Präposition und ihr Objekt stehen meist vor anderen Phrasen, die hinten im Satz stehen können.

The babysitter looks after the children **on weekdays.**	*Die Babysitterin passt an Wochentagen auf die Kinder auf.*
A nurse cares for their sick child **at their home.**	*Eine Krankenschwester pflegt ihr krankes Kind bei ihnen zu Hause.*

Beispiele für Verb + Partikel + Präposition + *Noun Phrase*

catch up with	*einholen*	**look forward to**	*sich freuen auf*
do away with	*abschaffen; umbringen*	**look out for**	*achten auf; Ausschau*
fall back on	*zurückgreifen auf*		*halten nach*
	herumkommen um;	**put up with**	*sich gefallen lassen*
get out of	*herauskommen aus*	**rub off on**	*abfärben auf*
keep up with	*Schritt halten mit;*	**run out of**	*kein ... mehr haben*
	mithalten mit	**watch out for**	*achten auf*
look down on	*herabsehen auf*		

Man muss die Wortfolge beachten: Nach dem Verb kommt zunächst die Partikel, dann die Präposition und erst dann die Noun Phrase.

Watch out for **pickpockets at the fair!**	*Achtet auf Taschendiebe auf dem Jahrmarkt!*
His bad mood rubbed off on **the others.**	*Seine schlechte Laune färbte sich auf die anderen ab.*
We ran out of **milk yesterday.**	*Uns ist gestern die Milch ausgegangen.*
My boyfriend is running out of **excuses.**	*Meinem Freund gehen langsam die Ausreden aus.*
I promised to go, and now I can't get out of **it.**	*Ich habe versprochen hinzugehen, und jetzt komme ich nicht mehr drum herum.*
Audrey is always on the run; no one can keep up with **her.**	*Audrey ist ständig auf Achse, keiner kann mit ihr mithalten.*

4 Nouns | *Hauptwörter*

Groß- und Kleinschreibung

Im Englischen werden die meisten Hauptwörter (Nouns) kleingeschrieben:

The boy bought a hamburger and a salad.	*Der Junge hat einen Hamburger und einen Salat gekauft.*

Eigennamen aber werden großgeschrieben:

In London, George and Marilyn went to see the Tate Gallery.	*In London haben George und Marilyn die Tate Gallery besucht.*

Die Namen der Wochentage, Monate sowie auch Nationalitäten, Sprachen und Religionen bzw. Religionszugehörigkeiten gelten als Eigennamen:

Mr. Firth normally comes on Mondays, but this Monday he wasn't there.	*Herr Firth kommt normalerweise montags, aber diesen Montag ist er nicht gekommen.*
It's nearly always cold in February.	*Im Februar ist es fast immer kalt.*
The Americans took pictures, while the New Zealanders talked.	*Die Amerikaner machten Fotos, während die Neuseeländer redeten.*
I speak English, German and Chinese.	*Ich spreche Englisch, Deutsch und Chinesisch*
In this part of town, Jews, Christians and Muslims live together peacefully.	*In diesem Stadtviertel leben Juden, Christen, und Muslime friedlich miteinander.*

The Plural | *die Mehrzahl*

Den regelmäßigen Plural bildet man mit **-s**:

The gardeners asked for pails, shovels, and rakes.	*Die Gärtner baten um Eimer, Schaufeln und Rechen.*

Wenn nun das Wort mit einem Zischlaut endet, kann man das **-s** (auch ein Zischlaut) nicht direkt an den ersten Zischlaut hängen, sondern man braucht einen kleinen Vokal dazwischen.

- Wenn der Singular mit einem ungesprochenen **e** endet, hängt man im Plural das **-s** einfach daran und spricht das **es** dann als eigene Silbe aus:

prince (einsilbig):	**princes** (zweisilbig)	*Prinze(n)*
garage (zweisilbig):	**garages** (dreisilbig)	*Garagen*

- Wenn der Singular nicht mit einem ungesprochenen Buchstaben endet, hängt man gleich **-es** daran und spricht dies genauso als eigene Silbe aus:

church (einsilbig):	**churches** (zweisilbig)	*Kirche(n)*
bush (einsilbig):	**bushes** (zweisilbig)	*Büsche*

- Wenn die Singularform einen Konsonanten und dann **-y** am Ende hat, wird das **-y** im Plural meist zu **ie** vor dem **-s**:

ferry	**ferries**	*Fähren*
copy	**copies**	*Kopien, Ausgaben (Bücher)*

Es gibt zwölf Nouns, die in **-f** oder **-fe** enden, und dieses gegen **-ves** tauschen, wenn sie in den Plural gesetzt werden:

wife	**wives**	*Ehefrauen*
wolf	**wolves**	*Wölfe*
thief	**thieves**	*Diebe*

(ebenso: **calf, half, knife, leaf, life, loaf, self, sheaf, shelf**). **Hoof, carf, wharf** können beide Formen **–s** oder **–ves** annehmen.

Das Englische hat darüber hinaus genau wie das Deutsche natürlich noch eine Reihe von unregelmässigen Pluralformen, die auswendig gelernt müssen:

man	men	*Männer*
woman	women	*Frauen*
foot	feet	*Füße*
mouse	mice	*Mäuse*
tooth	teeth	*Zähne*
child	children	*Kinder*
phenomenon	phenomena	*Phänomene*

Possessive | *besitzanzeigende Form*

Die besitzanzeigende Form wird normalerweise mit **'s** gebildet:

Cathy's mouse escaped.	*Cathys Maus ist entkommen.*
Bill's best friend's tennis racket broke.	*Der Tennisschläger von Bills bestem Freund ist kaputtgegangen.*

Wenn das Noun im Plural steht und deswegen ein **-s** am Ende hat, lässt man das **'s** der besitzanzeigenden Form weg. Dann hängt man nur **'** (einen Apostroph) ans Ende des Noun. Natürlich hört man danach keinen Unterschied zur normalen Pluralform, aber man sieht sie in schriftlichen Texten:

The boys' tennis rackets broke.	*Die Tennisschläger der Jungen sind kaputtgegangen.*
The boy's tennis racket broke.	*Der Tennisschläger des Jungen ist kaputtgegangen.*

Wenn der Plural nicht mit **-s** gebildet wird, benutzt man die besitzanzeigende Form des Plurals mit **'s**:

The children's toys are in the way.	*Das Spielzeug der Kinder steht im Weg.*
Those deer's antlers grow quickly.	*Das Geweih dieser Rehe wächst schnell.*

Bei manchen Eigennamen (vor allem bei berühmten Persönlichkeiten), die mit **-s** enden, lässt man das **s** der besitzanzeigenden Form wie bei dem **s**-Plural weg:

The Beatles' words always impressed their followers.	*Die Worte der Beatles beeindruckten ihre Anhänger immer.*

Dieselben Ausspracheregeln wie beim Plural gelten auch beim Possessive **'s**.
Wenn das Kernwort der Noun Phrase einen Artikel hat, lässt man ihn weg:

The daughter of a queen is a princess.	*Die Tochter einer Königin ist eine Prinzessin.*
▶ **A queen's daughter is a princess.**	*Die Tochter einer Königin ist eine Prinzessin.*

Problemfälle

Folgende Bildung ist für die meisten Leute etwas unerwartet, kommt im Englischen aber häufig vor:

A friend of my mother's tapdanced at the wedding.	*Eine Freundin meiner Mutter steppte bei der Hochzeit.*
Two books of Helen's got lost.	*Zwei von Helens Bücher sind verloren gegangen.*

Man kann die Possessiv-Form alleine verwenden um die Wohnung der genannten Person zu bezeichnen.

There was a wild party at Leo's **last night.**	*Bei Leo gab es gestern Abend eine wilde Party.*
We're going to the Millers' **for a meeting.**	*Wir gehen zu einer Besprechung zu den Millers.*
I'll be at my mother's.	*Ich werde bei meiner Mutter sein.*

Viele Geschäfte werden nach demselben Prinzip benannt: sie bekommen den Namen des Inhabers in der besitzanzeigenden Form:

I bought all my dishes at Jenner's.	*Ich habe mein ganzes Geschirr bei Jenner gekauft.*
After breakfast at Tiffany's, **we went to** Sotheby's.	*Nach dem Frühstück bei Tiffany sind wir zu Sotheby gegangen.*

Man kann auch auf Geschäfte, Praxen usw. nach der Berufsbezeichnung des Inhabers hinweisen.

I spent the morning at the doctor's.	*Ich habe den Vormittag beim Arzt verbracht.*
I got this exotic orchid at the florist's.	*Ich habe diese exotische Orchidee vom Floristen.*

Man verwendet Possessive **'s** zusammen mit bestimmten Zeitangaben:

It was in Tuesday's **paper.** **The older generation is agreed that** today's **youth is lazy –** **and their parents said the same thing 30 years ago.**	*Es war in der Zeitung vom Dienstag.* *Die ältere Generation ist sich darüber einig, dass die Jugend von heute faul sei – und ihre Eltern sagten vor 30 Jahren das gleiche.*

Zählbare und nicht zählbare Nouns

Im Allgemeinen kann man Nouns in zwei Klassen einteilen: zählbare und nicht zählbare. Die zählbaren Nouns bezeichnen einzelne Dinge, die man zählen kann:

I want a pineapple.	*Ich möchte eine Ananas.*
I want three pineapples.	*Ich möchte drei Ananas.*

Die nicht zählbaren Nouns bezeichnen Sachen, die als Mengen oder Massen betrachtet werden. Man verwendet dabei immer den Singular:

The milk **always goes off.**	*Die Milch wird immer schlecht.*
The wheat **is being harvested.**	*Der Weizen wird gerade geerntet.*
I'd like some jam.	*Ich hätte gern Marmelade.*

Es ist möglich, manche von diesen Wörtern im Plural zu verwenden, wobei sie meistens als Portionen oder Sorten zu verstehen sind:

Two coffees **and** eight beers**, please.**	*Zwei Kaffee und acht Bier, bitte.*
They grow three different wheats **here.**	*Hier bauen sie drei verschiedene*
I've tried all the jams.	*Weizensorten an.*
	Ich habe alle Marmeladensorten schon
	probiert.

Trotzdem gibt es nicht zählbare Nouns, die so nicht verwendet werden können:

His information **was always unreliable.**	*Die Informationen von ihm waren immer unzuverlässig.*
She has had a lot of experience.	*Sie hat schon eine Menge Erfahrung gesammelt.*
The room was full of furniture.	*Der Raum war voller Möbel.*

Das Wort **news** (ebenso wie **mumps**) sieht aus wie Plural, ist aber Singular:

All the news **in the paper** was **good that day.**	*An diesem Tag waren alle Nachrichten in der Zeitung gut.*
The good news is **that we have a** spare tire; the bad news is **that we don't have the necessary tools to mount it.**	*Die gute Nachricht ist, dass wir einen Ersatzreifen haben, die schlechte Nachricht ist, dass wir das notwendige Werkzeug nicht haben, um ihn zu montieren.*

Es gibt unterschiedliche Verwendungsweisen für Bezeichnungen von Institutionen und Personengruppen (collective nouns) wie etwa **police, government, team, family,** je nachdem, ob man diese als Einheit oder eine Anzahl Individuen sieht:

Our family is **the best.** **Our family** are **wearing their motto shirts now.**	*Unsere Familie ist die beste.* *Unsere Familienmitglieder tragen jetzt ihre Mottohemden.*

Pair Nouns

Es gibt Nouns, die einen Gegenstand bezeichnen, aber trotzdem als Paare aufgefasst werden (**pair** = Paar). Normalerweise handelt es sich um Gegenstände, die aus zwei Teilen bestehen:

This pair of scissors is blunt. **Bring me** a pair of pliers**!** **I need** a new pair of glasses**.**	*Diese Schere ist stumpf.* *Bring mir eine Zange!* *Ich brauche eine neue Brille.*

Oft verwendet man sie ohne **pair of** im Plural:

These scissors **are blunt.**	*Diese Schere ist stumpf.*
Bring me the pliers!	*Bring mir die Zange!*
I need new glasses.	*Ich brauche eine neue Brille.*
I'm looking for a pair of paisley trousers.	*Ich suche eine Hose mit Paisleymuster.*
My pants **have shrunk.**	*Meine Hose (US)/Unterhose (UK) ist eingelaufen.*
These jeans **don't fit.**	*Diese Jeans passt nicht.*

Solche Wörter lassen sich nur paarweise zählen:

I'd like two pairs of green jeans. | *Ich hätte gern zwei grüne Jeans.*

Proper Names: Titles

Abkürzungen von Titeln werden im britischen Englisch ohne Punkt und im Amerikanischen mit Punkt geschrieben.

Der allgemeine Titel für Männer ist **Mr.**:

Mr. Johnson | *Herr Johnson*

Bei den Frauen ist die Lage komplizierter: Es gibt zwei herkömmliche Titel – **Miss** für unverheiratete Frauen (z. B. **Miss Johnson** = *Fräulein Johnson*) und **Mrs.** für verheiratete (z. B. **Mrs. Johnson** = *Frau Johnson*, also die Ehefrau von einem **Mr. Johnson**). Inzwischen aber gibt es auch einen dritten, allgemeinen Titel für alle Frauen, ganz gleich, ob sie verheiratet sind oder nicht: **Ms.** (z. B. **Ms. Johnson** = *Frau Johnson*). **Ms.** ist auch der einzige korrekte Titel für Frauen, die in der Ehe ihren eigenen Nachnamen beibehalten haben.

Dr. und Prof.

In der englischsprachigen Welt werden Titel nicht vor dem Namen angesammelt: Man spricht eine Person mit nur einem Titel an. Mit anderen Worten gibt es keine Bildungen wie im Deutschen: *Herr Dr. Mayer* und *Frau Prof. Dr. Reis*.

Wer den Doktor- oder Professorengrad schon erreicht hat, verdient auch den dazugehörigen Titel. Also ist es höflicher, diesen Titel statt eines allgemeinen, geschlechtbezogenen Titels zu gebrauchen:

Dr. Beale and Prof. Sinclair arrived at the conference on Friday.	*Herr Dr. Beale und Frau Prof. Sinclair kamen am Freitag auf die Konferenz.*
Drs. Corcoran and Lowe, a husband-and-wife research team, have been invited to speak.	*Man hat Dr. Corcoran und Dr. Lowe, ein Forscherpaar, eingeladen einen Vortrag zu halten.*

5 Pronouns | *Fürwörter*

Pronouns ersetzen nicht, wie viele glauben, einzelne Nouns, sondern Phrases, die ein Noun als Kern haben. So eine Phrase nennt man eine Noun Phrase. Eine Noun Phrase kann schon aus einem einzigen Noun bestehen, aber dies ist nur Zufall: sie kann auch aus zehn oder mehr Wörtern bestehen:

William **fell into a hole.**	*William ist in ein Loch gefallen.*
▶ He **fell into a hole.**	*Er ist in ein Loch gefallen.*
The tall blond man wearing a yellow overcoat **fell into a hole.**	*Der große blonde Mann, der einen gelben Mantel trug, ist in ein Loch gefallen.*
▶ He **fell into a hole.**	*Er ist in ein Loch gefallen.*

Im ersten Satz ist **William** das Noun. Im zweiten ist **man** das Noun, während die volle Phrase aus **the tall blond man wearing a yellow overcoat** besteht. An diesem Beispiel kann man deutlich sehen, dass das Fürwort die ganze Phrase (und nicht nur das Noun) ersetzt.

Personal Pronouns | *persönliche Fürwörter*

Die Personal Pronouns sind die normalen Fürwörter, also diejenigen, mit denen man von *ich* oder *du* redet oder auch von bekannten Dritten.

Subject Pronouns

Singular		Plural	
I	*ich*	we	*wir*
you	*du, Sie*	you	*ihr, Sie*
he	*er*		
she	*sie*	they	*sie*
it	*es*		

Bei den persönlichen Fürwörtern sollte man sich gleich zwei Unterschiede zum Deutschen merken: Erstens gibt es nur eine Form für *du, ihr* und *Sie*: nämlich **you**. Das Fürwort **you** kann – der Situation entsprechend – Singular oder Plural ausdrücken. Im Englischen gibt es kein formelles Fürwort wie im Deutschen *Sie*:

You're **mean!**	*Du bist gemein!*
You two should do your **homework.**	*Ihr zwei solltet eure Hausaufgaben machen.*
Would you **like coffee, tea, or juice?**	*Möchten Sie Kaffee, Tee oder Saft?*

Zweitens sind **he, she** und **it** anders zu unterscheiden als im Deutschen. Während im Deutschen die Hauptwörter alle ihr eigenes Geschlecht haben, ist das im Englischen nicht so. Das Geschlecht, das zu einem Noun passt, entspricht einfach dem Geschlecht des bezeichneten Menschen oder Gegenstands in der Wirklichkeit.

The girl tried to laugh at his jokes.	*Das Mädchen versuchte, über seine Witze zu lachen.*
▷ **She tried to laugh at his jokes.**	*Sie versuchte, über seine Witze zu lachen.*

Nur Menschen und Tiere können in der Regel als **he** oder **she** bezeichnet werden (obwohl manche Leute andere Dinge wie z. B. ihr Auto als „Haustiere" betrachten und entsprechend bezeichnen). Alles andere bekommt das Fürwort *it*.

The table collapsed.	*Der Tisch brach zusammen.*
▷ **It collapsed.**	*Er brach zusammen.*

Im Gegensatz zu den Nouns haben die Personal Pronouns andere Formen für Objekte als für Subjekte.

Object Pronouns

Singular		Plural	
me	*mich; mir*	**us**	*uns*
you	*dich; dir; Sie;*	**you**	*euch; Sie; Ihnen*
him	*Ihnen*		
her	*ihn; ihm*	**them**	*sie; ihnen*
it	*sie; ihr*		
	es; ihm		

Die Objektsformen verwendet man u. a. für Objekte (Noun Phrases direkt nach dem Verb) und nach Präpositionen:

Archibald took them.	*Archibald hat sie genommen.*
Thelma gave her **a good scolding.**	*Thelma hat sie tüchtig ausgeschimpft.*
I threw the stick, and Rover ran after it.	*Ich habe den Stock geworfen, und Rover ist ihm nachgelaufen.*
Paul fixed our car for us.	*Paul hat uns unser Auto repariert.*

Wenn man ein Fürwort allein verwenden will, gebraucht man die Objektform:

Who's there? – Me.	*Wer ist da? – Ich.*
It's me.	*Ich bin's.*
It's them.	*Sie sind's.*
Was it you?	*Warst du es?*

Possessive Forms | *besitzanzeigende Formen*

Jedes Personal Pronoun hat nicht nur eine, sondern zwei besitzanzeigende Formen!
* Eine Form benutzt man vor einem Noun in einer Noun Phrase.

Possessive Forms before Nouns

Singular		Plural	
My	*mein*	**our**	*unser*
your	*dein; Ihr*	**your**	*euer; Ihr*
his	*sein*		
her	*ihr*	**their**	*ihr*
its	*sein*		

My friend Barbara is getting divorced.	*Meine Freundin Barbara lässt sich scheiden.*
They wouldn't take our brilliant advice.	*Sie weigerten sich, unseren genialen Rat zu befolgen.*

Bei Körperteilen, Kleidung u. ä. von Individuen muss man besitzanzeigende Formen verwenden:

I broke my arm.	*Ich habe mir den Arm gebrochen.*
They took off their clothes but not their hats.	*Sie zogen sich die Kleidung aus, aber setzten ihre Hüte nicht ab.*
He touched her shoulder.	*Er berührte ihre Schulter.*
Our stomachs hurt.	*Wir hatten Bauchschmerzen.*

aber:

She kicked him in the stomach.	*Sie hat ihn in den Bauch getreten.*

* Die andere Form ist nicht vom *Noun* abhängig.

Independent Possessive Forms

Singular		Plural	
mine	*meins, das meine*	**ours**	*unseres, das*
yours	*deins, das deine,*	**yours**	*unsere*
	Ihres, das Ihre		*eures, das eure,*
his	*seines, das seine*		*Ihres, das Ihre*
hers	*ihres, das ihre*	**theirs**	
(its)	*seines, das seine*		*ihres, das ihre*

Its wird sehr selten benutzt. Es darf nicht verwechselt werden mit **it's** (**it** + Apostroph) als Kurzform für **it has** oder **it is.**

Diese Form gilt als unabhängig, weil sie allein stehen kann:

My **shirt's clean, but** hers **is dirty.**	*Mein Hemd ist sauber, aber ihres ist schmutzig.*
Ellen has her **own locker, but she likes to put** her **things in** his.	*Ellen hat ihr eigenes Schließfach, aber sie stellt ihre Sachen gern in seines.*

Wie sagt man *ein Freund/eine Freundin von mir*? Eigentlich genau wie im Deutschen – aber mit der unabhängigen Form:

A friend of mine **is coming to visit.**	*Ein Freund/eine Freundin von mir kommt zu Besuch.*
A notebook of mine **is missing.**	*Ein Notizbuch von mir ist weg.*

Wenn es mal unpersönlich wird

Was macht man, wenn man *man* meint? Da gibt es zwei Lösungen.
In der gesprochenen Sprache sagt man meist **you**:

You **have to be really stupid to do a thing like that.**	*Man muss wirklich dumm sein, um so was Blödes zu machen.*
You **can get good shoes and bags there.**	*Man bekommt dort gute Schuhe und Taschen.*

Aber die „offizielle" Übersetzung von *man* ist **one.** Allerdings wirkt **one** ziemlich formell. Die besitzanzeigende Form von **one** ist einfach **one's.**

One **should always wash** one's **hands before meals.**	*Man sollte sich vor jeder Mahlzeit die Hände waschen.*
One **needs to update** one's **wardrobe once in a while.**	*Man muss seine Garderobe ab und zu der aktuellen Mode anpassen.*

Es ist ein Problem, wenn man von einer Person redet, die entweder männlich oder weiblich sein könnte. Früher wurde gelehrt, dass man in solchen Situationen das männliche Fürwort (personal pronoun) **he** verwenden soll, aber heutzutage wird dies als sexistisch und altmodisch betrachtet. Es ist viel besser, **he or she** zu sagen:

If the customer is not satisfied, he or she **may return the item for a full refund.**	*Wenn der Kunde/die Kundin nicht zufrieden ist, kann er oder sie die Ware gegen eine volle Rückerstattung des Kaufpreises zurückbringen.*
A typical fan wants to wear his or her **favorite player's number.**	*Der typische Fan will die Nummer seines Lieblingsspielers tragen.*

In der gesprochenen Sprache hat sich eine schlichtere Lösung entwickelt: man verwendet die Pluralform:

Apparently someone **called up Harlan last night, and** they **started threatening him.**	*Anscheinend hat gestern abend jemand Harlan angerufen, und der jenige hat angefangen, ihn zu bedrohen.*
If the person **is hungry,** they **can get something at the fast-food place across the street.**	*Wenn die Person Hunger hat, kann sie etwas beim Schnellimbiss gegenüber bekommen.*

Reflexive Pronouns | *rückbezügliche Fürwörter*

Das deutsche Wort *sich* ist etwas merkwürdig: eigentlich hat es eine ganze Reihe von Formen, aber außer *sich* sind alle gleich mit dem Wen- oder Wemfall (z. B. *mich*, *mir*). Deshalb: wenn man nicht sicher ist, ob man es in einem deutschen Satz mit einem *sich*-Wort zu tun hat, sollte man den Satz mit einem er/sie/es-Subjekt probieren. Wenn das Fürwort dann zu *sich* wird, ist es ein *sich*-Wort!

Sich hat mehrere Anwendungen. Wenn man mit dem Englischen zurechtkommen will, muss man diese auseinander halten.

Wenn ein *sich*-Wort ungefähr *dieselbe Person* bedeutet, wird es normalerweise mit speziellen Fürwörtern, den Reflexive Pronouns, übersetzt:

Reflexive Pronouns

Singular		Plural	
Myself	*mich; mir*	**ourselves**	*uns*
yourself	*dich; dir; sich*	**yourselves**	*euch; sich*
himself	*sich*		
herself	*sich*	**themselves**	*sich*
itself	*sich*		
oneself	*sich*		

Wie man an der Tabelle sehen kann, ist es sehr problematisch, wenn man immer versucht, alles direkt zu übersetzen. Am besten überlegt man, ob das Subjekt seine Handlung, sein Gefühl usw. auf sich selber richtet.

The man admired himself **in the mirror.**	*Der Mann bewunderte sich im Spiegel.*
I told myself **I should be careful.**	*Ich sagte mir, ich sollte aufpassen.*

Wenn man *sich selbst/selber* meint, kann man ein Reflexive Pronoun benutzen.

We're always laughing at ourselves.	*Wir lachen dauernd über uns selbst.*
Frieda was angry with herself.	*Frieda ärgerte sich über sich selbst.*

Manchmal sagt man *selbst* oder *selber* ohne *sich* um das Subjekt zu betonen. Im Englischen verwendet man auch hier die Reflexive Pronouns.

You know that yourself.	*Das weißt du doch selbst.*
Dean said so himself.	*Dean sagte es selbst.*

Wenn das *sich*-Wort *einander* oder *jeder den/dem anderen* bedeutet, verwendet man im Englischen meist **each other**. Dieser Ausdruck ist unveränderlich:

The two dogs chased each other.	*Die zwei Hunde jagten einander.*
Mark and Carla gave each other **socks for Christmas.**	*Mark und Carla schenkten sich Socken zu Weihnachten.*
We haven't seen each other **for a long time.**	*Wir haben uns schon lange nicht mehr gesehen.*

Es gibt auch etliche Verben im Deutschen, die ganz einfach ein *sich*-Wort verlangen. Manchmal übersetzt man das *sich*-Wort ins Englische, aber oft auch nicht. Folgende Ausdrücke haben kein Reflexive Pronoun im Englischen:

get dressed	*sich anziehen*	**comb one's hair**	*sich kämmen*
get/be angry	*sich ärgern*	**open**	*sich öffnen*
move; (Fitness)	*sich bewegen*	**close**	*sich schließen*
exercise		**argue**	*sich streiten*
concentrate	*sich konzentrieren*	**meet**	*sich treffen*
turn	*sich drehen*	**change [one's**	*sich umziehen*
remember	*sich erinnern an*	**clothes]**	
be interested	*sich interessieren*		

Suddenly I remembered **the cake in the oven.**	*Plötzlich erinnerte ich mich an den Kuchen im Backofen.*
Aaron concentrated **real hard.**	*Aaron konzentrierte sich sehr.*
The wheel was turning.	*Das Rad drehte sich.*

Das Verb **meet** kann in Bezug auf Menschen folgende Bedeutungen haben:
- *zum ersten Mal kennen lernen*
- *sich zum ersten Mal kennen lernen*
- *treffen*
- *sich treffen*

I met my wife at a party.	*Ich habe meine Frau auf einer Party kennen gelernt.*
Don and Kelly originally met in Las Vegas.	*Don und Kelly haben sich in Las Vegas kennen gelernt.*
Guess who I met in town!	*Rate mal, wen ich in der Stadt getroffen habe!*
Let's meet at the pub.	*Treffen wir uns in der Kneipe.*

Verschiedene Wörter, die sonst als Adjektive, Adverbien usw., verwendet werden, finden auch Einsatz als Fürwörter.

Demonstrative Pronouns | *hinweisende Fürwörter*

Die Demonstrative Pronouns **this** (Plural **these**) und **that** (Plural **those**) können wie Artikel vor einem Noun stehen oder auch allein als Fürwörter:

These are the best plums I've ever eaten.	*Diese sind die besten Pflaumen, die ich je gegessen habe.*
I saw that.	*Das habe ich gesehen.*

All | *alles, alle*

Meist braucht **all** eine ergänzende Phrase hinter sich. Diese kann eine Noun Phrase sein:

The cats ate all the fish.	*Die Katzen fraßen den ganzen Fisch.*
All the visitors **were cranky.**	*Alle Besucher waren schlecht gelaunt.*

Bei persönlichen Fürwörtern stellt man **all** hinter das Pronoun!	
I beat them all.	*Ich schlug sie alle.*
We all **ordered cheesecake.**	*Wir bestellten alle Käsekuchen.*

Man kann die Phrase auch mit **of** einleiten:

The cats ate all of the fish.	*Die Katzen fraßen den ganzen Fisch.*
All of the visitors **were cranky.**	*Alle Besucher waren schlecht gelaunt.*

Bei Subjekten besteht eine dritte Möglichkeit: Man setzt die Noun Phrase allein in die Subjektsposition und **all** danach – entweder gleich nach dem Subjekt oder nach dem (ersten) Hilfsverb:

The painters all **went home early.**	*Die Maler sind alle früh heimgegangen.*
The books **have** all **fallen off the shelf.**	*Die Bücher sind alle aus dem Regal gefallen.*
The parents all **have written to the governor.**	*Die Eltern haben alle dem Gouverneur geschrieben.*

Das Vollverb **be** verhält sich wie ein Hilfsverb, d. h. **all** darf dahinterstehen:

You were all **there too.**	*Ihr wart auch alle da.*
The employees were all **happy.**	*Die Arbeitnehmer waren alle zufrieden.*

Obwohl man **all** in ganz wenigen Fällen allein und ohne Bezug zu einer anderen Phrase verwenden kann, muss man im Normalfall jedoch auf die viel üblicheren Wörter **everything** (*alles*) und **everyone** bzw. **everybody** (*alle*) zurückgreifen:

Rex worries about everything.	*Rex macht sich über alles Sorgen.*
Everything **was fine.**	*Alles war in Ordnung.*
Everyone **came.**	*Alle sind gekommen.*
I gave one to everyone.	*Ich habe jedem eins gegeben.*
Everybody **was talking about**	*Alle haben von Roseannes neuer Nase*
Roseanne's new nose.	*geredet.*
Aunt Becky kissed everybody **good-bye.**	*Tante Becky küsste alle zum Abschied.*

Both | *alle beide*

Both betont, dass nicht nur eins von zwei, sondern alle beide gemeint sind.
Man kann **both** wie **all** vor einer Noun Phrase, vor einer **of**-Phrase oder wieder aufgreifend nach dem Subjekt einsetzen.

We met both her sons.	*Wir lernten ihre beiden Söhne kennen.*
Both our cars **are old.**	*Unsere beiden Autos sind alt.*
Both of the bottles **exploded.**	*Alle beide Flaschen explodierten.*
I gave both of the letters **to Jess.**	*Ich gab Jess beide Briefe.*
The eggs for the cake both **broke.**	*Die Eier für den Kuchen zerbrachen beide.*
Mac and Toni were both **screaming.**	*Mac und Toni haben beide geschrien.*
Now the teacher and the substitute	*Jetzt waren die Lehrerin und ihre*
were both **sick.**	*Vertretung beide krank.*

Im Gegensatz zu **all** kann **both** auch völlig allein stehen:

I was worried about the packages, but both **arrived safely.**	*Ich machte mir Sorgen um die Pakete, aber alle beide sind heil angekommen.*
Which flavor is better: chocolate or vanilla? – Both **are good.**	*Welcher Geschmack ist besser: Schokolade oder Vanille? – Alle beide sind gut.*

Each | *jedes, jeder, je*

Each kann vor einer **of**-Phrase oder auch nach dem Subjekt stehen. Es kann dagegen nicht vor einer Noun Phrase stehen:

Each of the pipes **had to be repaired.**	*Jede Leitung musste repariert werden.*
The boss spoke to each of the employees **individually.**	*Die Chefin sprach mit jedem der Mitarbeiter einzeln.*
Five robbers each **decided to break into the same bank the same night.**	*Fünf Räuber beschlossen in derselben Nacht jeweils in dieselbe Bank einzubrechen.*
Mandy, Phil, Candice, and Henry have each **given us a toaster as a wedding gift.**	*Mandy, Phil, Candice und Henry haben uns je einen Toaster zur Hochzeit geschenkt.*

> **Each** betont, dass jeder als einzelnes Individuum bzw. jedes als einzelner Gegenstand gemeint ist.

Häufig bezieht sich **each** auf das erste von zwei Objekten. Dann steht **each** meist nach dem ersten Objekt:

The nurse gave the children each **a toy.**	*Die Krankenschwester gab jedem der Kinder ein Spielzeug.*

Aber wenn man die Zahl des zweiten Objekts hervorheben will, setzt man **each** (oder auch **apiece**) erst danach:

Uncle Willy gave the boys five dollars each**.**	*Onkel Willy gab jedem der Jungen fünf Dollar.*
We ate four muffins apiece**.**	*Jeder von uns hat vier Muffins gegessen.*

Bei Stückpreisen ist es üblich, **each** oder **apiece** (*pro Stück*) nach dem Preis zu sagen:

These pens are 95 cents each.	*Diese Kugelschreiber kosten 95 Cent pro Stück.*
The bouquets cost ten pounds apiece.	*Die Blumensträuße kosten zehn Pfund pro Stück.*

One | *eines*

One ist ein unbestimmtes Fürwort für zählbare Dinge im Singular. Es kann unabhängig oder mit einer **of**-Phrase auftreten:

Have one!	*Nimm eins!*
I had never seen an armadillo until we encountered one **at the zoo.**	*Ich hatte noch nie ein Gürteltier gesehen, bis wir eins im Zoo entdeckt haben.*
One **of the books was about horse races.**	*Eins der Bücher handelte von Pferderennen.*

Man kann **one** auch als eine Art Kleinfürwort für das Hauptwort nach einem Artikel verwenden. **One** ist hier oft völlig unentbehrlich:

Which one **do you want?**	*Welches willst du?*
I'll take the blue one.	*Ich nehme das blaue.*
Grace hoped for some chocolates when she got home, but Julie had eaten every one.	*Als Grace heim kam, hoffte sie noch ein paar Pralinen zu erwischen, aber Julie hatte alle aufgegessen.*

Either und neither

Either bedeutet soviel wie *entweder das eine oder das andere*:

Should we take the stew or the roast? – Either **would be fine.**	*Sollen wir den Eintopf oder den Braten nehmen? – Beides wäre gut.*
Either **of the boys will be glad to help you – if you pay him.**	*Jeder der beiden Jungen hilft dir gern – wenn du ihn bezahlst.*

Neither bedeutet *weder das eine noch das andere*:

Neither really appeals to me.	*Keiner der beiden sagt mir wirklich zu.*
Neither of them did a good job.	*Keiner der beiden hat seine Arbeit gut gemacht.*

Wenn **either** irgendwo hinter einem verneinenden Wort steht, ergibt sich die Bedeutung *keiner der beiden*:

The parrots wouldn't describe either of the robbers.	*Die Papageien wollten keinen der Räuber beschreiben.*
I never saw either of them again.	*Ich habe keinen der beiden jemals wieder gesehen.*

Some | *manche, einige, welche*

Das unbestimmte Fürwort **some** kann sich auf den Singular oder auf eine unzählbare Menge beziehen:

I'd like some, please.	*Ich hätte gern welche.*
Roger didn't really want licorice, but he bought some anyway.	*Roger wollte eigentlich keine Lakritze, aber er kaufte trotzdem welche.*
Some of the waiters were more elegant than the patrons.	*Einige Kellner waren eleganter als die Kunden.*

None | *keins, keiner*

Außer im formellen Sprachgebrauch sollte man **none** immer mit einer *of-Phrase* verwenden. Solche *none-Phrases* eignen sich hauptsächlich als Subjekte; sonst verwendet man lieber **not ... any**:

None of the mice likes cheese.	*Keine der Mäuse mag Käse.*
None of her furniture was comfortable.	*Keine ihrer Möbel waren bequem.*

Trotz seiner Verwandtschaft zu **one** kann man ein Verb im Plural nach einer *none-Phrase* bringen, vorausgesetzt, es handelt sich um ein zählbares Noun:

None of your greedy clients were there.	*Keiner deiner gierigen Klienten war da.*

Wenn man *keiner* im Sinne von *kein Mensch* sagen will, verwendet man **no one** oder **nobody**:

No one **was home.**	*Keiner war zu Hause.*
Nobody **said you had to believe it.**	*Niemand hat gesagt, dass du es glauben musst.*

Any

Nach dem Verb in negativen Sätzen muss man **any** anstelle von **some** verwenden. Im Deutschen sagt man in solchen Fällen *keine*:

I asked for secondhand computers, but they didn't **have** any.	*Ich verlangte gebrauchte Computer, aber sie hatten keine.*
I haven't **heard from** any **of them.**	*Ich habe bislang von keinem von ihnen gehört.*
My shoes weren't **in** any **of the closets or under** any **of the beds in the house.**	*Meine Schuhe waren in keinem der Schränke und auch unter keinem der Betten im Haus.*

6 Articles and Related Words |
Artikel und verwandte Wörter

Artikel (articles) stehen am Anfang einer Noun Phrase. Die Wortfolge vor dem Noun innerhalb einer Noun Phrase ist

Article–Number–Adjective(s)–**Noun**

D. h. ein Artikel kann vor einer Zahl, einem Adjektiv oder dem Substanitv selber stehen, je nachdem, ob sich etwas zwischen dem Artikel und dem Substantiv befindet:

The **marmot**	*Das Murmeltier*
The **sleepy marmot**	*Das schläfrige Murmeltier*
The **five marmots**	*Die fünf Murmeltiere*
The **five sleepy marmots**	*Die fünf schläfrigen Murmeltiere*

Nicht nur der unbestimmte und der bestimmte Artikel, sondern auch noch verschiedene andere Wörter, z.B. Demonstrativpronomen wie **this, that, these** und **those** oder besitzanzeigende Formen wie **my, her, their** und **John's** können an dieser Stelle stehen.

This **marmot**	*Dieses Murmeltier*
My **sleepy marmot**	*Mein schläfriges Murmeltier*
Their **five marmots**	*Ihre fünf Murmeltiere*
John's **five sleepy marmots**	*Johns fünf schläfrige Murmeltiere*

Der unbestimmte Artikel

Der unbestimmte Artikel für zählbare Nouns im Singular ist **a**:

A **passing car skidded to** a **stop.**	*Ein vorbeifahrendes Auto rutschte und kam zum Halten.*
A **monkey wrench is** a **useful thing to have.**	*Es ist nützlich, einen Engländer* zu haben.* *(*verstellbarer Schraubenschlüssel)*

Wenn man den unbestimmten Artikel vor einem Vokallaut gebraucht, hat er die Form **an**:

An anteater and an elephant went for a stroll.	*Ein Ameisenbär und ein Elefant gingen zusammen spazieren.*
Please buy me an orange and an apple.	*Kauf mir bitte eine Orange und einen Apfel.*
He was wearing an old shirt.	*Er trug ein altes Hemd.*

Das entscheidende Kriterium der Wahl zwischen **a** und **an** ist nicht der nächste Buchstabe, sondern der nächste Laut:

She intended to join a **union.**	*Sie hatte vor, in eine Gewerkschaft einzutreten.*
This graph shows an x-**axis and** a y-**axis.**	*Dieses Diagramm zeigt eine x-Achse und eine y-Achse.*

Anwendungstipps

Man verwendet den unbestimmten Artikel **a**, wenn man den Beruf einer einzelnen Person angibt:

Stephanie is a welder.	*Stephanie ist Schweißerin.*
Julian is a singer.	*Julian ist Sänger.*

Im Plural fällt dieser natürlich weg:

Liza and Victor are nurses.	*Liza und Victor sind Krankenpfleger.*

Man kann – besonders in informellen Situationen – **one** am Anfang von größeren Zahlen durch **a** ersetzen:

Simon just won a **hundred thousand dollars.**	*Simon hat gerade hunderttausend Dollar gewonnen.*
We expected a **hundred people at the opening.**	*Wir erwarteten hundert Leute bei der Eröffnung.*

In der Regel gebraucht man den unbestimmten Artikel nach **with** und **without**, wenn das Noun zählbar ist und im Singular steht:

The boss was wearing a blouse with a bow.	*Die Chefin trug eine Bluse mit Schleife.*
Al left the house without a jacket.	*Al ging ohne Jacke aus dem Haus.*
You can have the chicken with or without a salad.	*Sie können das Hähnchen mit oder ohne Salat haben.*

Nach **as** gebraucht man auch den unbestimmten Artikel bei einem zählbaren Noun, das im Singular steht:

As a politician, **Lisle was success-ful;** as a human being, **he was not.**	*Als Politiker war Lisle erfolgreich, als Mensch war er es nicht.*
Lillian came dressed as a witch, **but no one realized that she was in costume.**	*Lillian kam als Hexe verkleidet, aber keiner merkte, dass sie kostümiert war.*
We can use the bed as a couch.	*Wir können das Bett als Couch benutzen.*

Der bestimmte Artikel

Der bestimmte Artikel ist **the**. Im Gegensatz zum deutschen *der/die/das* wird er nie verändert:

This is the **only bridge over** the **river.** The **cats are sitting on top of** the **bookcase.**	*Das ist die einzige Brücke über den Fluss. Die Katzen sitzen oben auf dem Bücherregal.*

Anwendungstipps

- Gattungen oder Gruppen bezeichnet man eher ohne **the**:

Crows are intelligent, amusing animals.	*Krähen sind intelligente, witzige Tiere.*
Canadians speak a North American dialect of English.	*Die Kanadier sprechen eine nordamerikanische Variante des Englischen.*
Archaeologists like the outdoors.	*Archäologen sind gerne draußen.*

- Wochentage, Monate und die meisten Feiertage haben keinen bestimmten Artikel:

We could meet on Monday.	*Wir könnten uns am Montag treffen.*
January is a dreary month.	*Der Januar ist ein öder Monat.*
Easter would be a good day for a party.	*Der Ostersonntag wäre ein guter Tag für ein Fest.*

- Mahlzeiten bezeichnet man ohne bestimmten Artikel, außer wenn es sich um eine ganz bestimmte Mahlzeit als Ereignis oder um das servierte Essen handelt:

We had lunch at a restaurant.	*Wir haben in einem Restaurant zu Mittag gegessen.*
Joan invited me over for tea.	*Joan hat mich zu sich zum Tee eingeladen.*
The four of them met for dinner at Sophy's.	*Die vier trafen sich bei Sophy zum Abendessen.*
The charity dinner was a success.	*Das Abendessen für wohltätige Zwecke war ein Erfolg.*
I didn't like the lunch.	*Ich mochte das Mittagessen nicht.*

- Folgende Bezeichnungen für Einrichtungen verwendet man meist ohne **the: school** (*Schule,* auch *Hochschule, Berufsschule*), **college** (*Hochschule, Universität* bis zum ersten Abschluss), **jail/gaol** (*Gefängnis, Untersuchungsgefängnis*), **prison** (*Gefängnis*), **church** (*Kirche*). Im britischen Englisch erscheint auch kein Artikel vor **university** (*Universität*) und **hospital** (*Krankenhaus*):

My daughter has to go to school in the morning, unless she can think of a good excuse.	*Meine Tochter muss morgens in die Schule gehen, es sei denn, sie lässt sich eine gute Ausrede einfallen.*
The murderer escaped from prison.	*Der Mörder ist aus dem Gefängnis ausgebrochen.*
We go to church every Sunday.	*Wir gehen jeden Sonntag in die Kirche.*

Für alle Wörter gilt allerdings: wenn man ein bestimmtes Gebäude oder Gelände meint, gebraucht man den Artikel:

The school is fairly large.	*Die Schule ist ziemlich groß.*
The prison was always cold.	*Das Gefängnis war immer kalt.*
We went into the church.	*Wir sind in die Kirche hineingegangen.*

Demonstrativpronomen

Die Demonstrativpronomen **this** (Plural **these)** und **that** (Plural **those**) gebraucht man wie Artikel am Anfang der Noun Phrase:

With this drink you'll add ten years to your life.	*Mit diesem Getränk verlängern Sie Ihr Leben um zehn Jahre.*
These boots are killing me!	*Diese Stiefel bringen mich um!*
What does that man want?	*Was will dieser Mann da?*
Those two jokers had better watch out!	*Die beiden Spaßvögel dort sollten sich in Acht nehmen!*

Man wählt **this** bzw. **these,** um auszudrücken, dass das Bezeichnete in der direkten Nähe ist, z.B. dass man es bei sich hat. Umgekehrt wählt man **that** bzw. **those,** um auszudrücken, dass das Bezeichnete etwas weiter weg ist, z.B. weil es jemand anderes hat, oder es gerade nicht verfügbar ist. Distanz und Nähe kann man also auch im weiteren Sinn verstehen, z. B. zeitlich oder emotional.

This house is bigger than that house.	*Dieses Haus hier ist größer als das Haus da.*
Those applicants weren't as good as the current ones.	*Jene Berwerber waren nicht so gut wie die jetzigen.*

Beim Erzählen kann man **this** gebrauchen, um subtil anzudeuten, dass es sich um eine ungewöhnliche bzw. komische Sache handelt. Dies hilft oft, die Geschichte lebendiger zu machen:

Alison came in wearing this weird hat.	*Alison ist hereingekommen mit diesem merkwürdigen Hut auf dem Kopf.*
And then she ate this huge chocolate cake right after lunch.	*Und dann aß sie diesen riesigen Schokokuchen direkt nach dem Mittagessen.*

Andere artikelähnliche Wörter

Andere artikelähnliche Wörter stellt man auch an den Anfang einer Noun Phrase.

Some (*etwas, einiges, manches*) kann sich auf den Plural oder auf eine unzählbare Menge beziehen. Beim Singular eines zählbaren Hauptwortes gebraucht man **a** oder **one:**

Could I have some hot tea, please?	*Könnte ich bitte etwas heißen Tee haben?*
Some drunks were singing outside my window.	*Einige Betrunkene sangen vor meinem Fenster.*

In seiner Artikelfunktion deutet **all** auf die gesamte Menge von etwas hin. Daher sind Sätze mit **all** in der Regel allgemeine Aussagen:

All **passengers must pay attention during the safety briefing.** **The course covers** all **basic problems.**	*Alle Passagiere müssen während der Sicherheitsunterweisung aufpassen.* *Der Kurs behandelt alle elementaren Probleme.*

Every bedeutet jedes Mitglied einer Gruppe. Es steht immer im Singular.

In the US every **town has at least one motel.** Every **person in the room stood up.** **I think Ken knows** every **single rock on the shore.**	*In den USA hat jede Stadt mindestens ein Motel.* *Alle Leute im Raum standen auf.* *Ich glaube, Ken kennt jeden einzelnen Stein am Ufer.*

Each bezeichnet jedes Mitglied einer Gruppe und betont, dass die Mitglieder als Einzelne zu betrachten sind:

Each **toy is inspected individually.** **We admired** each **item in the window.**	*Jedes Spielzeug wird einzeln untersucht.* *Wir bewunderten jedes Stück im Schaufenster.*

Both bedeutet *alle beide*, d. h. es betont, dass jeder von zweien gemeint ist:

Both **companies sell green sunscreen.** **Each crook tried to blame the other, but in the end** both **men were convicted.**	*Alle beide Firmen verkaufen grünes Sonnenschutzmittel.* *Jeder der beiden Gauner versuchte, dem anderen die Schuld zu geben, aber schließlich wurden alle beide Männer verurteilt.*

Wenn man dies nicht betonen will, nimmt man stattdessen **the two**:

The two **friends talked on the phone every day.** **The** two **companies work together.**	*Die beiden Freunde telefonierten jeden Tag miteinander.* *Die beiden Firmen arbeiten zusammen.*

Either bezieht sich meistens auf *entweder der/das eine oder der/das andere*; d. h. es bezeichnet genau zwei Leute, Gegenstände usw., separat betrachtet:

Either dog would be good.	*Jeder der beiden Hunde wäre gut.*
You can have either one but not both.	*Du kannst das eine oder das andere haben, aber nicht beide.*
I don't care; you can give me either kind.	*Mir ist es egal, du kannst mir entweder das eine oder das andere geben.*

Manchmal aber bedeutet **either** *jeder von beiden*:

The actress came down the corridor with a bodyguard on either side.	*Die Schauspielerin kam mit einem Leibwächter auf beiden Seiten den Gang entlang.*

Neither bedeutet *keine/keiner/keins der beiden*:

Neither girl was interested in dolls.	*Keins der beiden Mädchen interessierte sich für Puppen.*
Neither textbook contains any useful information.	*Keins der beiden Lehrbücher enthält irgendwelche nützliche Informationen.*

No gebraucht man als negativen Artikel, aber im Gegensatz zu vielen artikelähnlichen Wörtern kann es nicht als Pronoun (Pronomen) allein stehen. Das entsprechende Pronoun ist **none**:

No news is good news.	*Keine Nachrichten sind gute Nachrichten.*
We waited for celebrities, but none showed up.	*Wir haben auf Berühmtheiten gewartet, aber Keiner tauchte auf.*

No findet hauptsächlich bei Noun Phrases Gebrauch, die Subjekte sind. Sonst gebraucht man normalerweise **not ... any**:

Having worked in a chocolate factory, I didn't like any cookies.	*Da ich in einer Schokoladenfabrik gearbeitet hatte, mochte ich keine Kekse.*

7 Quantities and Measurements
Mengen- und Maßangaben

Entscheidend für Mengen- und Maßangaben im Englischen ist der Unterschied zwischen zählbaren und nicht zählbaren Dingen. Wenn man z. B. fragt: *Wie viel Milch habt ihr gekauft?*, dann kann eine grammatisch korrekte Antwort nicht *zwei* lauten, weil man Milch nicht zählen kann. Dagegen ist *zwei* eine durchaus befriedigende Antwort auf die Frage: *Wie viele Hemden hast du gekauft?*

Fragen

Im Englischen fängt der Unterschied schon mit den Fragen nach Maß und Menge an. Man verwendet also **How many ...?,** wenn das Noun als einzelnes ohne weitere Mengenangabe wie Liter, Kilogramm, usw. zählbar ist. Wenn man eine maßangebende Antwort wie z.B. *drei Liter* hören möchte, benötigt man die Frage **How much ...? How much ...?** ist also für nicht zählbare *Nouns*:

How many calves **are there?**	*Wie viele Kälber sind es?*
How much milk **have we got?**	*Wie viel Milch haben wir noch?*

Oft kann man etwas Unzählbares sozusagen zählbar machen, indem man entsprechende Gefäße nennt, die einzeln zählbar sind.

How much wine **should I buy?**	*Wie viel Wein soll ich kaufen?*
How many bottles of wine **should I buy?**	*Wie viele Flaschen Wein soll ich kaufen?*

Wenn die Maßeinheit schon in der Frage genannt wird, und die Antwort somit auch zählbare Einheiten ergibt, ist auch **how many...?** zu verwenden:

How many liters of wine **should I buy?** | *Wieviel Liter Wein sollte ich kaufen?*

Money (*Geld*) ist im üblichen Sinn nicht zählbar:	
How much money **do you have on you?**	*Wie viel Geld hast du dabei?*
How much money **has that rich man got?**	*Wie viel Geld hat der reiche Mann?*

Gleichzeitig aber werden Antworten auf Fragen nach Geldmengen oft in zählbaren Währungseinheiten angegeben:

How much money **do you have on you?**	
I have five dollars and twenty-five cents.	*Ich habe fünf Dollar und fünfundzwanzig Cent.*
He has three million pounds.	*Er hat drei Millionen Pfund.*

Bei zählbaren Nouns verwendet man **many** für *viele*, **few** für *nur wenige* und **a few** für *einige wenige, ein paar*:

That library has many **good books.**	*Diese Bibliothek hat viele gute Bücher.*
Many **people disagree.**	*Viele Leute sind anderer Meinung.*
Eleanor took few **blouses along on her trip.**	*Eleanor nahm nur wenige Blusen auf die Reise mit.*
Few **people like to swim in cold water.**	*Nur wenige Leute schwimmen gern in kaltem Wasser.*
A few **coins fell on the floor.**	*Einige Münzen fielen auf den Boden.*
There were a few **candles in the drawer.**	*Da waren ein paar Kerzen in der Schublade.*

Der Ausdruck **quite a few** bedeutet *relativ viele, nicht wenige*:

Ralph read quite a few **books while he was recovering.**	*Ralph hat nicht wenige Bücher gelesen, während er sich erholt hat.*
Quite a few **people have read Shakespeare.**	*Ziemlich viele Leute haben Shakespeare gelesen.*

Bei nicht zählbaren Nouns verwendet man **much** für *viel*, little für *nur wenig* und **a little** für *ein wenig, ein bisschen*:

There isn't much **to eat in the house.**	*Es gibt im Haus nicht viel zu essen.*
Don't make so much **noise!**	*Mach nicht so viel Lärm!*
The employees had little **to do.**	*Die Mitarbeiter hatten nur wenig zu tun.*
Olga ate little **soup but** much **cake.**	*Olga hat wenig Suppe, aber viel Kuchen gegessen.*
A little **rest would do you good.**	*Ein bisschen Ausruhen würde dir gut tun.*
Would you like a little **milk with your coffee?**	*Möchten Sie ein bisschen Milch in Ihren Kafee?*

A lot (of) ist ein umgangsprachlicher Ausdruck mit der Bedeutung *viel*, der sowohl für zählbare als auch für nicht zählbare Nouns geeignet ist. Besonders in positiven Sätzen hört er sich viel natürlicher an als **much**. Andererseits kann man **a lot** nicht mit **too** (*zu* im Sinne von *übermäßig*, z.B. *zu schnell*) verwenden:

We ate a lot of **lasagna.**	*Wir haben viel Lasagne gegessen.*
We talked to a lot of **people that we knew.**	*Wir haben mit vielen Leuten gesprochen, die wir kannten.*

aber:

We ate too much **lasagna.**	*Wir haben zu viel Lasagne gegessen.*
We talked to too many **people.**	*Wir haben mit zu vielen Leuten gesprochen.*

8 Adjectives | *Eigenschaftswörter*

Allgemeine Bemerkungen

Im Gegensatz zu deutschen Adjektiven haben englische *Adjectives* keine Endungen, die zwischen verschiedenen Fällen oder auch zwischen Singular und Plural unterscheiden. *Adjectives* im Englischen bleiben also in ihrer Grundform (▶ Kapitel Verben) immer gleich:

The hungry **dog stole the sausage.**	*Der hungrige Hund hat die Wurst gestohlen.*
I fed a hungry **dog.**	*Ich habe einen hungrigen Hund gefüttert.*
The two hungry **dogs were fighting over some meat.**	*Die beiden hungrigen Hunde haben um ein Stück Fleisch gekämpft.*

Adjectives werden oft aus Participles (Partizipien), wie etwa dem Past Participle gebildet. Das Past Participle, das man ja in der Passivbildung verwendet, hat als Adjective meist eine Passivbedeutung:

The lost **keys turned up in the pocket of a thief.**	*Die verlorenen Schlüssel tauchten in der Tasche eines Diebes auf.*
The needed **funds were provided by a local millionaire.**	*Die benötigten Gelder wurden von einem hiesigen Millionär bereitgestellt.*

Daher können solche Sätze mit Kombinationen aus Adjective (Past Participle) und Noun auch ganz einfach als Passivsätze ausgedrückt werden:

The keys that were lost **turned up in the pocket of a thief.**	*Die Schlüssel, die verloren worden waren, tauchten in der Tasche eines Diebes auf.*
The funds that were needed **were provided by a local millionaire.**	*Die Gelder, die benötigten wurden, wurden von einem hiesigen Millionär bereitgestellt.*

Die **ing**-Form eines Verbs ist auch ein Partizip. Wie in den Progressive Tenses (▷ Hilfsverben) deutet sie häufig aber nicht immer an, dass ein Ereignis im Gange ist. Sie hat
immer eine Aktivbedeutung. Diese Form gleicht dem deutschen *-end*:

The falling tree hit Cassie's house.	*Der herunterfallende Baum traf Cassies Haus.*
Let sleeping dogs lie.	*Schlafende Hunde soll man nicht wecken.*

Manchmal ist aber die deutsche Übersetzung mit *–end* sehr eigenartig. In solchen Fällen übersetzt man besser z.B. mit einem Relativsatz:

The losing team must pay for the beer.	*Die Mannschaft, die verliert, muss das Bier bezahlen.*

Nationalitätsbezeichnende Adjectives werden wie die entsprechenden Nouns großgeschrieben (▷ Groß- und Kleinschreibung).

Let's order an English breakfast.	*Bestellen wir uns ein englisches Frühstück.*
Bobby finally woke up from the American dream.	*Bobby wachte schließlich aus dem amerikanischen Traum auf.*

Steigerungsformen

Viele Adjectives haben Steigerungsformen:

tall	*groß*	**taller**	*größer*	**tallest**	*am größten*
late	*spät*	**later**	*später*	**latest**	*am spätesten*

Neben der Grundform gibt es eine *mehr*-Form (comparative) und eine *meist*-Form (superlative). Das Comparative bildet man oft dadurch, dass man **-er** an das Ende der Grundform anhängt. Für das Superlative hängt man **-est** an die Grundform:

Vincent is tall, but Nick is taller.	*Vincent ist groß, aber Nick ist größer.*
That elephant is the biggest.	*Der Elefant da ist der größte.*
Harold's newest **tie has red lobsters on a white background.**	*Harolds neueste Krawatte hat rote Hummer auf einem weißen Hintergrund.*

Bei Adjectives, die mit Konsonant **+ y** enden, wird das **y** zu **ie**, wenn **-er** oder **-est** angehängt wird:

funny ▶ **funnier** ▶ **funniest**	*witzig, merkwürdig*
No one is funnier than Jerry Lewis.	*Keiner ist lustiger als Jerry Lewis.*

Es gibt aber auch einige unregelmäßig gebildete Steigerungsformen. Diese muss man auswendig lernen:

Grundform	*Comparative*	*Superlative*	Übersetzung
bad	**worse**	**worst**	*schlecht, schlimm*
good	**better**	**best**	*gut*
well	**better**	**best**	*gesund*
far	**farther, further**	**farthest, furthest**	*weit*
little	**less**	**least**	*wenig*
much	**more**	**most**	*viel*
many	**more**	**most**	*viele*

The patient looked better **after a while.**	*Nach einer Weile sah der Patient besser aus.*
That was the worst **day of my life!**	*Das war der schlimmste Tag in meinem Leben!*

Adjectives ohne Steigerungsformen

Die meisten Adjectives mit mehr als zwei Silben besitzen keine eigene Steigerungsformen. Trotzdem können solche Wörter gesteigert werden – durch die Umschreibung mit **more** und **most**:

It was the most interesting **thing in the world!**	*Es war das interessanteste Ding der Welt!*
The painting became more beautiful **every day.**	*Das Gemälde wurde jeden Tag schöner.*
This room is most comfortable**.**	*Dieser Raum ist am bequemsten.*

Bei zweisilbigen Adjektiven entscheidet oft eher das Sprachgefühl als die Regel:

I have never seen a plan that was simpler**!**	*Ich habe noch nie einen einfacheren Plan gesehen!*
I have never seen a plan that was more simple**!**	

Auch kürzere, aus dem Lateinischen oder Griechischen stammende *Adjectives* haben meist keine eigenen Steigerungsformen und benötigen **more** und **most**:

Her style has become more modern**.**	*Ihr Stil ist moderner geworden.*
Al isn't the most patient **person.**	*Al ist nicht der geduldigste Mensch.*

Adjectives, die von den Partizipformen der Verben abgeleitet sind, besitzen normalerweise ebenfalls keine Steigerungsformen:

The new clerk made the most glaring **errors.**	*Der neue Sachbearbeiter machte die schlimmsten Fehler.*
Ron thought geometry was more boring **than biology, but Delia thought it was the** most fascinating **subject.**	*Ron meinte, Geometrie sei langweiliger als Biologie, aber Delia meinte, es sei das faszinierendste Fach.*

Adjectives, die Zugehörigkeit zu Gruppen (Nationen, Religionen, Städte etc.) ausdrücken, brauchen auch **more** oder **most**:

The immigrants were more French **than the French themselves.**	*Die Einwanderer waren mehr französisch als die Franzosen selbst.*

Adjectives in the Noun Phrase

Meistens stehen Adjectives direkt vor dem Noun in der Noun Phrase:

The furious **passenger wanted his money back.** **The** small **TV is more expensive.**	*Der wütende Passagier wollte sein Geld zurück.* *Der kleine Fernseher ist teurer.*

Einige Adjektive verlangen eine von einer Präposition eingeleitete Phrase. Dies ist dann aber vor dem Noun zu viel, und das ganze Gebilde muss hinter das Noun gesetzt werden:

Parents proud of their children **like to tell others about them.** Anybody as furious about a delayed flight **would want their money back, too.**	*Eltern, die stolz auf ihre Kinder sind, erzählen gern anderen Leuten von ihnen.* *Jeder, der so wütend über einen verspäteten Flug ist, würde auch sein Geld zurückhaben wollen.*

Wenn das Noun überflüssig ist

Wenn es schon klar ist, um welches Noun es sich handelt, kann man im Deutschen das Substantiv einfach weglassen und nur das Adjektiv verwenden: z. B. *Ich nehme den Gelben*. Im Englischen kann man das meist nicht machen; man braucht eben immer ein Noun oder ein entsprechendes Fürwort. Es reicht zum Teil schon das Fürwort **one**:

I'll take the yellow one. **Do you mean** the fat one **or** the skinny one?	*Ich nehme den Gelben.* *Meinst du den Dicken oder den Dürren?*

Adjectives nach Verben

Man kann Adjectives auch nach gewissen Verben wie **be** (*sein*), **seem** und **appear** (*scheinen, vorkommen*), **get** und **become** (*werden*) oder **stay** und **remain** (*bleiben*) verwenden. Dabei passen **seem, get** und **stay** besser zur gesprochenen Sprache als **appear, become** und **remain:**

You're crazy!	*Du bist verrückt!*
The book on basket weaving seemed interesting.	*Das Buch über Korbflechten schien interessant zu sein.*
You won't get rich **that way.**	*So wirst du nicht reich.*
The class remained quiet.	*Die Klasse blieb ruhig.*

Besonders bei Farben verwendet man **turn** für *werden*:

Julia turned red **with embarrassment.**	*Julia wurde rot vor Verlegenheit.*
When I washed my new jeans, the water turned blue **– and so did all the other clothes.**	*Als ich meine neue Jeans gewaschen habe, ist das Wasser blau geworden – und die andere Kleidung auch.*

Andererseits kann man sie gut mit bestimmten Verben wie **look** (*aussehen*), **sound** (*klingen, sich anhören*), **taste** (*schmecken*), **smell** (*riechen*) und **feel** (*sich anfühlen*) verwenden:

Everyone looked great.	*Alle haben toll ausgesehen.*
This old Easter egg smells rotten.	*Dieses alte Osterei stinkt.*
It felt right.	*Es fühlte sich richtig an.*

Good/well

Als Eigenschaftswörter bedeuten **good** *gut, brav* und **well** *gesund*. **Good** ist ein sehr allgemeines Wort mit vielen Anwendungen, während das Adjective **well** sich nur auf die Gesundheit bezieht:

They enjoyed the good **meal.**	*Sie haben das gute Essen genossen.*
The children were being good**.**	*Die Kinder waren im Moment brav.*
I don't feel well**.**	*Ich fühle mich krank.*
His old mother isn't looking well**.**	*Seine alte Mutter sieht zur Zeit recht krank aus.*

Own

Das Adjective **own** kann nur nach einem besitzanzeigenden Fürwort (Pronoun) stehen:

She makes all her own **hats herself.**	*Sie macht ihre Hüte alle selbst.*
I feel like a stranger in my own **house.**	*Ich fühle mich wie ein Fremder im eigenen Haus.*

Vergleichende Anwendungen

Man verwendet das Comparative (**-er, more**), wenn man zwei Dinge vergleicht, während man das Superlative (**-est, most**) verwendet, wenn man mehr als zwei Dinge vergleicht:

Geraldine is the older of the two sisters**.**	*Geraldine ist die ältere der zwei Schwestern.*
Geraldine is the oldest of the three sisters**.**	*Geraldine ist die älteste der drei Schwestern.*

Vergleiche mit than

Wenn man einen direkten Vergleich zwischen zwei Dingen herstellt und meint, dass eins mehr von einer Eigenschaft hat als das andere, verwendet man **than**:

Kate is happier than **Stephanie.**	*Kate ist glücklicher als Stephanie.*
My computer is more powerful than **your computer.**	*Mein Computer ist leistungsfähiger als dein Computer.*

Dies gilt auch, wenn das erste weniger von der Eigenschaft hat:

The stepsisters were less beautiful than **Cinderella.**	*Die Stiefschwestern waren nicht so schön wie Aschenputtel.*

Bei dieser Verwendung, wo **than** keinen Nebensatz einleitet, nehmen die Personal Pronouns zumindest in der gesprochenen Sprache die Objektform an:

His brother is much taller than **him.**	*Sein Bruder ist viel größer als er.*

Than

Sehr üblich sind Äußerungen, in denen man das Subjekt und das entsprechende Hilfsverb nach **than** setzt:

Sarah looks older than Jessica does.	*Sarah sieht älterer aus als Jessica.*
Stephen was less experienced in catching potato bugs than Meredith was.	*Stephen hatte weniger Erfahrung im Fangen von Kartoffelkäfern als Meredith.*

Man kann statt des Hilfsverbs auch ein Vollverb verwenden:

Law is more interesting than it looks.	*Jura ist interessanter als man denkt.*

Vergleiche mit as ... as

Wenn man sagen will, dass zwei Dinge gleich viel von einer Eigenschaft haben, verwendet man **as ... as,** wobei man die Grundform zwischen die beiden **as** schiebt:

My pregnant cousin is as big as **a house.**	*Meine schwangere Kusine ist so rund wie eine Tonne.*
Gary looks as healthy as **his father.**	*Gary sieht so gesund aus wie sein Vater.*

Ebenso wie **than** kann das zweite **as** einen Nebensatz einleiten:

The soup tastes just as sweet as the cake does.	*Die Suppe schmeckt genauso süß wie der Kuchen.*
Their children are as fat as they are.	*Ihre Kinder sind genauso dick wie sie.*
Paddy was as pleasant as I had expected him to be.	*Paddy war so liebenswürdig wie ich ihn mir vorgestellt hatte.*

Am meisten

Nach einem Verb kann man das Superlative eines Adjektivs mit oder ohne **the** verwenden:

The old lady was (the) friendliest.	*Die alte Dame war am freundlichsten.*
That building is the most modern.	*Das Gebäude da ist am modernsten.*

Wenn man die Gruppe nennen will, aus der man das Extrembeispiel nimmt, leitet man diese mit **of** ein. In diesem Fall braucht man **the:**

Brady was the stupidest of our students.	*Brady war der dümmste unserer Studenten.*
That story was the funniest of all.	*Diese Geschichte war die witzigste von allen.*

Allgemeine Fragen

Die allgemeinste Frage nach den Eigenschaften einer Sache ist: **What is it like?** (*Wie ist es?*). Natürlich kann man diese Frage je nach Zeit, Modalverb usw. entsprechend umgestalten:

What's the weather been like?	*Wie war das Wetter in letzter Zeit?*
What should the drawing be like?	*Wie soll die Zeichnung aussehen?*

Eine verwandte Frage lautet: **How is it?** (*Wie ist es?*). Damit fragt man mehr nach dem Empfinden des Gesprächspartners. Man erwartet dann eine Beurteilung:

How's the pumpkin salad?	*Wie ist der Kürbissalat?*

Vergleichen Sie folgende Dialoge:

Sprecher A:	
What was the music like?	*Wie war die Musik?*
Sprecher B:	
It was a mixture of jazz and blues.	*Es war eine Mischung aus Jazz und Blues.*

Sprecher A:	
How was the music?	*Wie war die Musik?*
Sprecher B:	
It was too loud, the pianist wasn't very good, but otherwise it was all right.	*Sie war zu laut, der Klavierspieler war nicht sehr gut, aber sonst war sie in Ordnung.*

Wenn man die Frage **How is/are...?** auf Personen bezieht, wird sie zu einer Frage nach deren Gesundheit bzw. deren Wohlbefinden:

How are your parents?	*Wie geht's deinen Eltern?*
Hi! How've you been?	*Hallo! Was treibst du so?*

Wenn man nach der Farbe von etwas fragt, verwendet man **What color** und die richtige Form von **be**:

Sprecher A:	
What color is it?	*Welche Farbe hat es?*
Sprecher B:	
It's blue and green.	*Es ist blau und grün.*

Fragen mit wahrnehmungsbezogenen Verben

Das allgemeine Schema für Fragen mit den in diesem Kapitel aufgeführten wahrnehmungsbezogenen Verben ist: **What ... like?**

What does it look like?	*Wie sieht es aus?*
What did the perfume smell like?	*Wie hat das Parfüm gerochen?*

9 Adverbs | *Umstandswörter*

Der Unterschied zwischen Adjective und Adverb

Im Deutschen sehen Adjectives (Eigenschaftswörter) und Adverbs (Umstandswörter) genau gleich aus. Daher kann es am Anfang schwer sein, sie voneinander zu unterscheiden.

Adjectives beschreiben immer ein Noun oder eine Noun Phrase.

The little mouse was nervous.	*Die kleine Maus war nervös.*

Ein Adverb beschreibt dagegen etwas anderes: ein Verb, ein Adjective, ein anderes Adverb oder den Satz selbst.

Es beschreibt ein *Verb*:	
The jogger ran into the house fast and immediately disappeared into the bathroom.	*Der Jogger lief schnell ins Haus und verschwand sofort ins Bad.*
Es beschreibt ein *Adjective*:	
The rather relieved parents welcomed their extremely tardy son home.	*Die Eltern waren ganz erleichtert und hießen ihren Sohn, der sehr spät nach Hause kam, willkommen.*
Es beschreibt ein *Adverb*:	
You've weeded the garden very thoroughly.	*Du hast den Garten aber sehr gründlich gejätet.*

Die Bildung von Adverbs

Viele (aber nicht alle!) Adverbs werden auf der Grundlage von Adjectives gebildet, in dem man man **-ly** ans Adjective hängt.

Adjective		Adverb	Übersetzung
probable	▷	**probably**	*wahrscheinlich*
quick	▷	**quickly**	*schnell*
horrible	▷	**horribly**	*schrecklich*

In der Umgangssprache lässt man aber manchmal das **-ly** einfach weg.

He drank real quick. | *Er trank echt schnell.*

Wichtige Ausnahmen

Manche Adverbs haben die gleiche Form wie die entsprechenden Adjectives:

back	*zurück*	**high**	*hoch*
close	*nahe*	**late**	*spät*
deep	*tief*	**left/right**	*links/rechts*
early	*früh*	**long**	*lang*
enough	*genug*	**near**	*nah*
far	*weit*	**right/wrong**	*richtig/falsch*
fast	*schnell*	**straight**	*gerade, direkt*
hard	*kräftig, hart*		

Bei diesen Adjectives und Adverbs muss man natürlich besonders darauf achten, um was es sich handelt:

Adjectives:	
Their service **is** fast.	*Ihr Service ist schnell.*
But that hotel **is too** far **from the train station.**	*Aber das Hotel ist zu weit vom Bahnhof entfernt.*
Who knows the right answer**?**	*Wer weiß die richtige Antwort?*

Adverbs:	
Our secretary types fast.	*Unsere Sekretärin kann schnell tippen.*
On a clear day you can see far.	*Bei klarem Wetter kann man weit sehen.*
Can't you do anything right**?**	*Kannst du denn nichts richtig machen?*

Manche dieser Adjectives haben zu dem auch noch eine **-ly** Form, die dann aber eine etwas andere Bedeutung oder Verwendung hat:

hardly	*kaum*	**nearly**	*beinahe, fast*
deeply	*tief*	**closely**	*nah*
lately	*kürzlich, vor kurzem*		

I hardly know him!	*Ich kenne ihn kaum.*
They nearly missed the train.	*Sie hätten fast den Zug verpasst.*
She's done a lot of charity lately.	*Sie hat vor kürzlich bei vielen Wohl-tätigkeitsaktionen gemacht.*

Well

Well als Adverb bedeutet *gut*. Als Adjective dagegen bedeutet es etwa *gesund*.
Adjective:

He was well when I last was there.	*Das letzte Mal als ich dort war, war er gesund.*

Adverb:

They did their work well.	*Sie machten ihre Arbeit gut.*

Well kann in der gesprochenen Sprache aber auch ganz anders, in der Art von *nun*
oder *ääh* verwendet werden:

Well, sometimes it's hard to see.	*Nun, manchmal ist es schwer zu erkennen.*
Well... can I ask you something?	*Ääh... kann ich Dich was fragen?*

Adjectives mit der Endung -ly

Es gibt auch Adjectives, die mit **-ly** enden: **elderly** (*betagt*), **sickly** (*kränklich*), **kindly**
(*liebenswürdig*), **likely** (*wahrscheinlich*) und **friendly** (*freundlich*) können sogar **nur** als
Adjectives gebraucht werden:

A nurse takes care of their sickly child.	*Eine Krankenschwester pflegt ihr kränkliches Kind.*
A kindly woman helped us.	*Eine liebenswürdige Frau hat uns geholfen.*
It was likely that they would start fighting again.	*Sehr wahrscheinlich würden sie wieder anfangen miteinander zu streiten.*
There comes that friendly man with his dachshund.	*Da kommt dieser freundliche Herr mit seinem Dackel.*

Wenn man ein Adverb mit der Bedeutung *wahrscheinlich* verwenden möchte, greift man am besten auf **probably** zurück. Man kann aber auch **more likely** und **most likely** als gesteigerte Adverbs gebrauchen!

They probably **went home already.**	*Wahrscheinlich sind sie schon nach Hause gegangen.*
Eric most likely **was after the ice cream.**	*Sehr wahrscheinlich hatte es Eric auf das Eis abgesehen.*

Friendly

Friendly hat kein Adverb. Um eine adverbiale Bedeutung zu erzielen, muss man es deshalb umschreiben: Man setzt **friendly** in eine Phrase wie **in a friendly way**, oder formeller, **in a friendly manner**. Beide bedeuten *freundlich*.

Whitney looked up in a friendly manner.	*Whitney schaute freundlich auf.*
The business partners shook hands in a friendly way.	*Die Geschäftspartner gaben sich freundlich die Hand.*

Home

Alleine verwendet bedeutet das Wort **home** fast immer *nach Hause*:

Ray got fed up and went home.	*Ray hatte die Nase voll und ging nach Hause.*
Everybody was driving home **from vacation on the same day.**	*Alle fuhren am selben Tag aus dem Urlaub nach Hause.*

Wenn man **home** nach **be, stay, remain** gebraucht, heißt es *zu Hause*. Wenn man sonst *zu Hause* sagen will, muss man **at home** benutzen:

They were home **but refused to open the door.**	*Sie waren zu Hause, aber wollten nicht aufmachen.*
Many college students live at home **with their parents.**	*Viele Studenten wohnen zu Hause bei ihren Eltern.*

Die Steigerung

Genau wie bei den Adjectives (▶ Adjektive) haben kurze, höchstens zweisilbige Adverbs oft regelmäßig gesteigerte Formen im Comparative und Superlative:

Grundform	*Comparative*	*Superlative*	Übersetzung
close	closer	closest	*nahe*
early	earlier	earliest	*früh*
fast	faster	fastest	*schnell*
hard	harder	hardest	*hart, kräftig*
wide	wider	widest	*weit, breit*

Lange Adverbs mit mehr als drei Silben werden in der Regel mit **more** und **most** gesteigert:

Grundform	*Comparative*	*Superlative*	Übersetzung
beautifully	more beautifully	most beautifully	*schön*
effectively	more effectively	most effectively	*effektiv, wirkungsvoll*

He sang the most beautifully. | *Er sang am schönsten.*

Natürlich gibt es auch unregelmäßige Steigerungsformen, die man auswendig lernen muss:

Grundform	*Comparative*	*Superlative*	Übersetzung
badly	worse	worst	*schlecht*
far	farther, further	farthest, furthest	*weit*
little	less	least	*wenig*
much	more	most	*viel*
well	better	best	*gut*

The sound of jets overhead bothers us less than our neighbors' music.	*Der Lärm von Düsenflugzeugen stört uns weniger als die Musik von unseren Nachbarn.*
Who can get there the fastest?	*Wer kann am schnellsten dort sein?*

Verb- und satzbeschreibende Adverbs

Während Adverbs, die Adjectives und Adverbs beschreiben, ganz einfach vor diesem Wort stehen, ist die Platzierung im Satz der verb- und satzbeschreibenden Adverbs viel lockerer geregelt.

Adverbs der Art und Weise stehen manchmal vor dem *Verb*:

Dustin had carefully brushed his coat.	*Dustin hatte seinen Mantel sorgfältig gebürstet.*
Ruby cheerfully hummed a song.	*Ruby summte fröhlich ein Lied.*

Sie können auch nach dem Objekt des Verb stehen. Hat das Verb kein Objekt, dann setzt man das Adverb direkt nach dem Verb:

Dustin had brushed his coat carefully.	*Dustin hatte seinen Mantel sorgfältig gebürstet.*
Ruby hummed a song cheerfully.	*Ruby summte fröhlich ein Lied.*
The police appeared quickly.	*Die Polizei erschien schnell.*

Das Adverb kann aber niemals zwischen Verb und Objekt stehen.

Adverbs der Häufigkeit stehen meistens unmittelbar vor oder nach dem (ersten) Hilfsverb. Wenn kein Hilfsverb da ist, kommt das Adverb zwischen Subjekt und Vollverb:

Jo would **never do such a thing.**	*Jo würde so was nie machen.*
I sometimes have **seen him there.**	*Ich habe ihn manchmal dort gesehen.*
The train usually arrives **on time.**	*Der Zug kommt meistens pünktlich an.*

Die Adverbs **always, usually, often, frequently, sometimes, occasionally** können zur Betonung auch am Satzanfang stehen.

Usually the train arrives on time, but where is it today?	*Meistens kommt der Zug pünktlich an, aber wo bleibt er denn heute?*
Occasionally they visit Mr. McMurtry, but more often they stay home and gossip about him.	*Gelegentlich besuchen sie Mr. McMurtry, aber öfter bleiben sie daheim und tratschen über ihn.*
Evidently they've gone to look for a bar.	*Sie sind offenbar eine Bar suchen gegangen.*
Possibly Ross has frightened off all the clients.	*Ross hat vielleicht alle Klienten abgeschreckt.*

Man kann auch Adverbs mit negativer Bedeutung, wie z.B. **never** (*niemals*), an den Satzanfang stellen (▷ Kapitel Verneinung). Dann vertauschen aber Subjekt und erstes Verb ihre Position, d.h. es kommt zur sogenannten *Inversion*:

Never had I felt so embarrassed!	*Nie habe ich mich so geschämt!*

Das gleiche geschieht oft auch mit Adverbs, die Zeit, Ort oder Richtung eines Ereignisses betonen (z.B. **here, now, down, up, there** usw.):

Here comes the bus.	*Da kommt der Bus.*
Now is the time to say goodbye.	*Jetzt ist es an der Zeit, sich zu verabschieden.*
Down came the rain.	*Da fiel der Regen literweise!*
There stood a confused student.	*Da stand ein verwirrter Schüler.*

10 Coordinating Conjunctions |
Bindewörter

Einzelwörter

Die Bindewörter **and** (*und*), **but** (*aber*) und **or** (*oder*) können sowohl zwischen Hauptsätzen als auch zwischen anderen Satzteilen stehen.

Zwischen Hauptsätzen

Carol chose a book on difficult parents, and her mother chose one on difficult children.	*Carol suchte sich ein Buch über schwierige Eltern aus, und ihre Mutter suchte sich eins überschwierige Kinder aus.*
The boy wanted an ice cream cone, but his parents wouldn't buy him one before dinner.	*Der Junge wollte ein Eis, aber seine Eltern weigerten sich, ihm eins vor dem Abendessen zu kaufen.*
Perhaps Jerry was looking for a raccoon, or perhaps he was going to dig holes in the flower garden.	*Vielleicht hat Jerry nach einem Waschbär gesucht, oder vielleicht ist er auch Löcher im Blumengarten graben gegangen.*

Zwischen anderen Satzteilen

We looked for Perry in his room but not under the bed. **My cat loves strawberries and cream – or at least the cream.**	*Wir haben Perry in seinem Zimmer gesucht, aber nicht unterm Bett.* *Meine Katze liebt Erdbeeren mit Sahne – oder zumindest die Sahne.*

Mehrwortbildungen

Es gibt auch noch die komplexeren Bildungen **both ... and, either ... or** und dessen
verneinendes Gegenstück **neither ... nor**:

Both our dog and our cat love to go for walks.	*Sowohl unser Hund als auch unsere Katze gehen gern spazieren.*
Either Harvey is lying, or there's an elephant hiding in the backyard.	*Entweder Harvey lügt, oder ein Elefant hat sich im Hinterhof versteckt.*
The travellers found neither an oasis nor the promised camels.	*Die Reisenden fanden weder eine Oase noch die versprochenen Kamele vor.*

Wenn man **neither ... nor** in zwei Sätzen benutzen möchte, muss man etwas aufpassen:
Im ersten Satz steht **neither** nach dem Subjekt, und im zweiten muss ein Hilfsverb vor
dem Subjekt stehen:

Sylvia neither intended to get married, nor did she approve of living together.	*Sylvia hatte weder vor zu heiraten, noch hielt sie viel vom Zusammenleben.*

11 Sentence Construction | *Satzbau*

Der Aussagesatz

Im Deutschen beginnt ein Hauptsatz meistens mit einer einzigen Phrase, die vor dem (ersten) Verb steht. Diese Phrase kann das Subjekt sein – oder auch nicht. Wenn sie nicht das Subjekt ist, dann steht das Subjekt hinter dem Verb.

Im Englischen ist dies anders. Egal was am Satzanfang steht: man muss das Subjekt vor dem (ersten) Verb platzieren:

After the conference some of us **went out for a drink.**	*Nach der Konferenz sind einige von uns etwas trinken gegangen.*
The chewing gum, she **liked;** **the cream pie,** she **didn't like.**	*Den Kaugummi mochte sie, die Cremetorte mochte sie nicht.*

Auch wenn der Satz mit einem Nebensatz anfängt, steht das Subjekt des Hauptsatzes vor dem Verb:

Although it was late, we **didn't go home.**	*Obwohl es spät war, sind wir nicht nach Hause gegangen.*

Was nach dem Verb kommt

Eine ganze Reihe von Phrasen kann nach dem Vollverb eines Satzes stehen. Wenn es ein Objekt gibt (eine Noun Phrase), kommt dieses unmittelbar nach dem Verb. Danach stehen Phrasen, die eine enge Verbindung zum Verb haben. Diese haben eine vom Verb verlangte Präposition, wie z.B. die *woher*- und *wohin*-Phrasen. Dahinter setzt man Phrasen, die das bezeichnen, womit die Handlung ausgeführt wird. Erst danach kommen *wo*-Phrasen und als Schlusslicht *wann*-Phrasen. Natürlich enthält nicht jeder Satz alle diese Phrasenarten gleichzeitig, aber in dieser Reihenfolge werden sie geordnet:

Rick ate at the restaurant on Tuesday.	*Rick hat am Dienstag in dem Restaurant gegessen.*
The guru explained yoga to his pupils.	*Der Guru erklärte seinen Schülern Yoga.*
The cook chased the intruders out of the kitchen with a rolling pin that day.	*An jenem Tag jagte die Köchin die Eindringlinge mit einem Nudelholz aus der Küche.*

Ein störender Faktor bei dieser Regel ist die Länge der Phrasen: Lange Phrasen stehen gern hinten. Nebensätze tauchen oft am Satzende auf und nicht da, wo man sie sonst erwarten würde:

I finally found the missing papers yesterday where no one would ever think to look.	*Schließlich habe ich die Papiere dort gefunden, wo es niemandem in den Sinn käme zu schauen.*

Nebensatz-Fragen

Nebensatz-Fragen sind keine direkten Fragen, so wie sie einem immer gestellt werden, sondern Fragen, von denen berichtet wird. Typischerweise werden sie von Hauptsatz-Verben wie **ask, wonder** (*sich etwas fragen*), **learn** (*erfahren*), know, hear usw. eingeleitet. Nebensatz-Fragen lassen sich in zwei Klassen einteilen: ob-Fragen und Fragewort-Fragen:

Ob-Fragen

She asked whether **I ski.**	*Sie fragte, ob ich Ski fahre.*
He asked **his friend** whether **she had seen that film.**	*Er fragte seine Freundin, ob sie den Film schon gesehen hätte.*

Im Englischen gibt es zwei Wörter für *ob* – **if** und **whether:**

They hadn't heard whether **Karen was working in town.**	*Sie hatten nicht gehört, ob Karen in der Stadt arbeitete.*
I'm not sure if **we need cheese for the pizza.**	*Ich bin mir nicht sicher, ob wir Käse für die Pizza brauchen.*

Beide Wörter sind grundsätzlich gleich, auch wenn **whether** etwas formeller klingt.

Indirect Speech | *Indirekte Rede*

Zeitanpassung

Es gibt zwei Möglichkeiten davon zu berichten, was jemand gesagt hat: Man kann die Person wörtlich zitieren, oder man kann einfach von dem Inhalt erzählen. Die erste Methode heißt direct speech (direkte Rede) und die zweite indirect speech (indirekte Rede).

Direct Speech:	**She said, "Rover bit the policeman."**
Indirect Speech:	**She said that Rover had bitten the policeman.**

Bei der direct speech hat man am Gesagten natürlich nichts zu ändern.

Bei der indirect speech hingegen passt sich die Zeit des Nebensatzes an die des Hauptsatzes an. Wenn der Hauptsatz in der Gegenwart oder Zukunft steht, kann man die Zeit des Nebensatzes so lassen, wie sie ist. Wenn der Hauptsatz aber in der Vergangenheit steht, so müssen gewöhnlich alle Zeiten in der berichteten Aussage eine Stufe zurückgesetzt werden. Aus der einfachen Gegenwart wird dann die einfache Vergangenheit, aus der einfachen Vergangenheit wird das Past Perfect (die Vorvergangenheit), bei der Zukunft gelten die Regeln für Modalverben:

Hauptsatz in der Gegenwart oder Zukunft	
He says **that the painting** is finished. **She** will want **to know what you**'ve done.	*Er sagt, dass das Gemälde fertig ist. Sie wird wissen wollen, was ihr getan habt.*
They have often told **me that** they plan **to import coconuts.**	*Sie haben mir oft gesagt, dass sie vorhaben, Kokosnüsse zu importieren.*

Hauptsatz in der Vergangenheit

• Aus der Gegenwart wird Vergangenheit:

The painting is **finished.** **He** said **that the painting** was **finished.**	*Das Gemälde ist fertig.* *Er sagte, dass das Gemälde fertig sei.*

• Aus der Vergangenheit wird Plusquamperfekt (Vorvergangenheit):

France won **the game.** **She** said **that France** had won **the game.**	*Frankreich gewann das Spiel.* *Sie sagte, dass Frankreich das Spiel gewonnen hatte.*

Modalverben in der indirekten Rede

Bei der Vergangenheit der indirekten Rede verwendet man die Vergangenheitsformen der Modalverben:

Elliot claimed that he could read **minds.**	*Elliot behauptete, dass er Gedanken lesen könne.*
We wondered what they would **do next.**	*Wir haben uns gefragt, was sie wohl als Nächstes tun würden.*

Pronouns | *Fürwörter*

Man muss bei der indirekten Rede darauf achten, dass die Pronouns stimmen. D. h. ein *ich* im direkten Zitat ist nicht immer gleich mit dem *ich*, das jetzt von der Äußerung berichtet: Wenn es in der **direct speech** heisst **I see him** (*Ich sehe ihn*), wie soll man von dieser Aussage berichten? Wenn man es selbst gesagt hat, sagt man natürlich: **I said that I saw him.** Wenn es eine Äußerung des jetzigen Gesprächspartners war, so sagt man: **You said that you saw him.** Oder wenn es jemand anderes, z.B. Anne gesagt hat, sagt man: **She/Anne said that she saw him.**

Adverbiale Nebensätze

Adverbiale Nebensätze sind Sätze, die ungefähr die gleiche Funktion haben wie Adverbien. Solche Nebensätze haben meist die gleiche Wortfolge wie Aussagesätze:

Adverbien

Therefore **the glass was empty.**	*Deshalb war das Glas leer.*
Something will happen soon.	*Bald wird etwas passieren.*

Adverbiale Nebensätze

Because my friend had passed by and seen the wine, **the glass was empty.**	*Weil mein Freund vorbeigekommen war und den Wein gesehen hatte, war das Glas leer.*
Something will happen when the monkeys are let out of the cage.	*Wenn die Affen aus dem Käfig gelassen werden, wird etwas passieren.*

Man sollte sich einprägen, dass zukünftige Ereignisse in Nebensätzen selten mit **will** oder **shall** ausgedrückt werden. Vielmehr verwendet man Gegenwartsbildungen:

As soon as you get home, **turn on the heater.**	*Sobald du heimkommst, dreh die Heizung auf.*
Before the players take the field, **the coach will remind them of the strategy.**	*Bevor die Spieler auf das Feld kommen, erinnert sie der Trainer an ihre Strategie.*

Wenn-Sätze

If (*falls*) und **when** (*wenn*) werden leicht verwechselt, weil sie beide oft als *wenn* übersetzt werden. **If** bedeutet *wenn* im Sinne von *falls* oder *wenn es stimmt, dass*; es drückt Möglichkeit aus:

We can go to the zoo if you want.	*Wir können in den Zoo gehen, wenn du willst.*
If it rains today, **I'll stay home.**	*Wenn es heute regnet, bleibe ich daheim.*

Dagegen ist **when** immer zeitlich zu verstehen:

When you see Gina tonight, **give her this book for me.**	*Wenn du heute abend Gina siehst, gib ihr dieses Buch von mir.*
I always stay home when it rains.	*Ich bleibe immer zu Hause, wenn es regnet.*

When wird auch mit *als* übersetzt, wenn es Vergangenheitssätze einleitet:

We were glad when they left.	*Wir waren froh, als sie gingen.*
When he started to sing, **everyone left the room.**	*Als er anfing zu singen, verließen alle den Raum.*

Man sieht deutlich den Unterschied in diesen beiden Sätzen:

When you get up tomorrow, **call me up.**	*Sobald du morgen aufstehst, ruf mich an.*
If you get up tomorrow, **call me up.**	*Falls du morgen aufstehst, ruf mich an.*

Verbformen mit if-Sätzen

Im Allgemeinen kann man Gegenwart und Vergangenheit in if-Sätzen wie im Hauptsatz ausdrücken:

If **she's tired, let her go to bed.**	*Wenn sie müde ist, lass sie ins Bett gehen.*
If **they've been doing their homework, why are they covered with dirt?**	*Wenn sie gerade ihre Hausaufgaben gemacht haben, warum sind sie dann mit Dreck verschmiert?*
If **she was tired, she didn't say so.**	*Wenn sie müde war, so hat sie es nicht gesagt.*
If **they were sleeping at the time, the telephone surely woke them up.**	*Wenn sie um diese Zeit geschlafen haben, so hat sie das Telefon ganz sicher geweckt.*

Wenn es im if-Satz um ein Ereignis in der Zukunft geht, hat der if-Satz meist eine Gegenwartszeit:

If **that dog bites me, I'll sue you.**	*Falls mich dieser Hund beißt, werde ich Sie verklagen.*
If **you go to Russia next year, I will go to the States.**	*Wenn Du nächstes Jahr nach Russland fährst, fahre ich in die Staaten.*

Um auszudrücken, dass das Ereignis geplant oder vorhergesagt ist, verwendet man **be going to** (▷ Wie man über die Zukunft spricht):

If **they** are going to **tear down that hotel, it must not be doing well.**	*Wenn sie vorhaben, das Hotel abzureißen, dann läuft das Geschäft dort wahrscheinlich nicht gut.*
If **prices** are going to **rise, we should stock up on chocolate bars.**	*Wenn es stimmt, dass die Preise steigen werden, sollten wir uns einen Vorrat an Schokoladenriegeln zulegen.*

Wenn man **will** im if-Satz verwendet, deutet es darauf hin, dass die Subjektsperson ein-
willigt die Handlung auszuführen – mehr oder weniger, dass sie so nett ist, es zu tun:

If you will just close the window, **we can get started.**	*Wenn Sie das Fenster zumachen wollen, können wir anfangen.*
If Jasper will do the washing, **the others can concentrate on the repairs.**	*Wenn Jasper bereit ist die Wäsche zu waschen, können sich die anderen auf die Reparaturen konzentrieren.*

Oft will man mit einem if-Satz eine Situation beschreiben, die eigentlich nicht real ist,
die aber – zumindest in der Fantasie – stattfinden könnte. Dafür braucht man das
Past Subjunctive.

If **I** were **an ostrich, I would run 50 km every day.**	*Wenn ich ein Strauß wäre, würde ich jeden Tag 50 km laufen.*
If **Jackie** had **more Money, we would buy a yacht.**	*Falls Jackie mehr Geld hätte, würden wir eine Jacht kaufen.*

Wenn das Nichtexistierende in der Vergangenheit war, so nimmt man das Past Perfect:

If **I** had been **an ostrich at the time, I would have run 50 km every day.**	*Wenn ich damals ein Strauß gewesen wäre, wäre ich jeden Tag 50 km gelaufen.*
If **Anne** hadn't brought **the drinks, we couldn't have held the party.**	*Wenn Anne die Getränke nicht gebracht hätte, hätten wir das Fest nicht feiern können.*

Andere adverbiale Nebensätze

- Adverbiale Nebensätze können zeitliche Verhältnisse beschreiben:

After Colin had his coffee, **he read the newspaper.**	*Nachdem Colin seinen Kaffee getrunken hatte, las er die Zeitung.*
Before Alberta went to work, **she called five clients.**	*Bevor Alberta zur Arbeit ging, hat sie noch fünf Kunden angerufen.*
As soon as the results are made public, **the company will act.**	*Sobald die Ergebnisse bekannt gegeben worden sind, wird die Firma handeln.*
Since he's been here, **there's been nothing but trouble.**	*Seitdem er hier ist, hat's nichts als Ärger gegeben.*
As long as Perry thinks you're here, **he won't get suspicious.**	*Solange Perry glaubt, dass du hier bist, wird er nicht stutzig werden.*

Es gibt ein allgemeines Wort für *während*, nämlich **while**.

Im britischen Englisch kann man im sehr gehobenen Sprachgebrauch auch **whilst** sagen.

While Naomi was singing in the bathtub, **the man left with the contents of her wallet.**	*Während Naomi noch in der Badewanne sang, ist der Mann mit dem Inhalt ihrer Brieftasche verschwunden.*
Whilst Moira played the piano, **Francis worked in the garden.**	*Während Moira Klavier spielte, arbeitete Francis im Garten.*

- Adverbiale Nebensätze die sonstige Umstände (z.B. Gründe, Bedingungen) beschreiben:

Because there was a lot of snow last night, **we have to stay indoors today.**	*Weil es letzte Nacht viel geschneit hat, müssen wir heute drinnen bleiben.*
Since you think you're so smart, **you can finish the work yourself.**	*Da du dich für so gescheit hältst, kannst du die Arbeit selber zu Ende machen.*
Although Tim wanted a car, **he only bought himself a bike.**	*Obwohl Tim ein Auto wollte, kaufte er sich nur ein Fahrrad.*
Unless the weather improves, **we'll have to stay indoors.**	*Falls das Wetter nicht besser wird, werden wir drinnen bleiben müssen.*
As long as you're here, **you can help me with the chores.**	*Wenn du sowieso da bist, kannst du mir im Haushalt helfen.*
So long as Patsy and Mark don't try to climb the trees, **they can come too.**	*Solange Patsy and Mark nicht ver-suchen auf die Bäume zu klettern, dürfen sie auch mitkommen.*

Infinitivsätze

Wo immer man einen **to-**Infinitiv findet, handelt es sich um einen Nebensatz. Aus diesem Grund kann nach **to** entweder ein Vollverb alleine oder ein Hilfsverb(en) + Vollverb stehen.

Unter anderem können bestimmte Verbs (Verben), Adjectives (Eigenschaftswörter) und Nouns (Hauptwörter) einen Infinitivsatz verlangen. Der Infinitivsatz beginnt jeweils mit **to**.

We meant to send you a card.	*Wir hatten vor, euch eine Karte zu schicken.*
My parents would be sorry to have to see you again.	*Meine Eltern würden es bedauern, dich wieder sehen zu müssen.*
Greta Garbo's desire to be alone disappointed her fans.	*Greta Garbos Wunsch alleine zu sein, enttäuschte ihre Fans.*
To have danced badly would have been embarrassing.	*Schlecht getanzt zu haben wäre peinlich gewesen.*

Bei gewissen Verben kann ein Objekt zwischen dem Verb und dem Infinitivsatz stehen:

I asked the committee **to pay for it.**	*Ich habe das Komitee darum gebeten, es zu bezahlen.*
The owner told the rowdy customers **to get out of the bar.**	*Der Besitzer forderte die randalierenden Gäste auf, seine Bar zu verlassen.*

Ein paar Verben erlauben, dass der Infinitivsatz sein eigenes Subjekt hat. Bei **want** und **need** gibt es übrigens keine andere Möglichkeit, dieses Subjekt auszudrücken: sie vertragen keinen **that**-Satz!

The athletes wanted the spectators **to cheer them up.**	*Die Athleten wollten vom Publikum aufgemuntert werden.*
They expect it **to stop raining tomorrow.**	*Sie nehmen an, dass es morgen aufhört zu regnen.*
I need him **to move furniture for me.**	*Ich hätte gern, dass er für mich Möbel umstellt.*

Wenn das Subjekt des Infinitivsatzes allerdings mit dem Subjekt des Hauptsatzes identisch ist, so erscheint das Subjekt nur im Hauptsatz:

We **wanted to see New York in spring.**	*Wir wollten New York im Frühjahr sehen.*
They **expect to find some buried treasures soon.**	*Sie erwarten, bald vergrabene Schätze zu finden.*
I **need to call the movers.**	*Ich muss die Spedition anrufen.*

Adverbiale Anwendung

Mit einem Infinitivsatz kann man den Sinn und Zweck einer Handlung ausdrücken: Entweder man setzt **to** an den Anfang des Infinitivsatzes, oder man leitet den Satz mit **in order to** ein:

Mrs. Green went to the party to **keep an eye on her daughters.**	*Mrs. Green ist zu der Party gegangen, um ihre Töchter im Auge zu behalten.*
You need to turn on the light in order to see **properly.**	*Du musst das Licht anmachen, um besser sehen zu können.*

ing-Sätze

Man kann die *ing*-Form als Verb eines Nebensatzes verwenden. Dies ist aber sprachlich etwas formell:

Desperately needing **money, they started a small business.**	*Da sie dringend Geld benötigten, gründeten sie ein kleines Geschäft.*
Having **lost his car keys, he continued his journey on foot.**	*Da er seine Autoschlüssel verloren hatte, setzte er seine Reise zu Fuß fort.*

Man kann einen *ing*-Satz am Ende des Hauptsatzes anhängen um zu zeigen, was das Subjekt gleichzeitig tut, d.h. welche Handlungen gerade ablaufen:

Maurice was at home eating steaks for breakfast.	*Maurice war zu Hause und aß zum Frühstück Steaks.*
Sabrina crawled around on the floor picking up the fallen coins.	*Sabrina kroch auf dem Boden herum und hob alle Münzen auf, die heruntergefallen waren.*

Before, after, without, while können auch mit einer *ing*-Form als Nebensatz verwendet werden. Dies geht aber nur, wenn sich der Inhalt des Nebensatzes auf das Subjekt des längeren Satzes (d. h. des Hauptsatzes) bezieht:

Clean up after finishing your work.	*Räumt auf, wenn ihr mit eurer Arbeit fertig seid.*
Before bathing, **he looked at the clock.**	*Bevor er badete, schaute er auf die Uhr.*
He put up his feet without removing his shoes.	*Er legte seine Füße hoch, ohne seine Schuhe auszuziehen.*
The chef prepared the salad while flipping pancakes.	*Der Koch bereitete den Salat zu, während er Pfannkuchen in der Luft herumwirbelte.*

Instead of und **by** müssen mit einer *ing*-Form verwendet werden:

Instead of buying **groceries, he spent the money on pinball.**	*Anstatt Lebensmittel zu kaufen, gab er das Geld für Flipperspiele aus.*
You could try to fix it by pressing **that button.**	*Du könntest versuchen es zu reparieren, in dem du diesen Knopf drückst.*

Ein *ing*-Satz kann auch als Subjekt eines längeren Satzes dienen:

Climbing mountains **can be great fun.**	*Auf Berge steigen kann viel Spaß machen.*
Seeing their incompetence **drives me crazy.**	*Es macht mich wahnsinnig, wenn ich mir ansehen muss, wie unfähig sie sind.*

Verben, nach denen eine ing-Form steht

Nach bestimmten Verben kann oder muss man eine *ing*-Form verwenden:

enjoy	*sehr gern tun, genießen*	**mind**	*etwas ausmachen*
finish	*beenden, aufhören, etwas*	**miss**	*vermissen*
	zu Ende machen	**practice**	*üben*
go	*gehen*	**remember**	*sich an etwas erinnern*
imagine	*sich etwas vorstellen*	**stop**	*aufhören*
keep	*weitermachen*	**try**	*versuchen*
like	*gern tun*	**start**	*anfangen*

They finally stopped banging **the pans together.**	*Endlich hörten sie damit auf, Pfannen zusammenzuknallen.*
I enjoy swimming **in warm water.**	*Ich schwimme sehr gern in warmem Wasser.*
We didn't mind walking **the ten miles.**	*Es machte uns nichts aus, die zehn Meilen zu Fuß zu gehen.*
Let's go swimming **tomorrow!**	*Gehen wir morgen schwimmen!*
Pauline kept bothering **me.**	*Pauline hat mich ständig gestört.*

Vorsicht! Bei **stop** gibt es sowohl eine Ergänzung mit *ing*-Form als auch mit **to**-Infinitiv. Beide haben völlig unterschiedliche Bedeutungen: **stop doing something** heißt *aufhören, etwas zu tun,* **stop to do something** heißt aufhören, *um etwas zu tun:*

They finally stopped shouting **at me.**	*Sie hörten endlich auf, mich anzuschreien.*
They finally stopped to shout **at me.**	*Sie hörten endlich auf, um mich anzuschreien.*

Nach einer Präposition braucht man fast immer einen *ing*-Satz:

be afraid of	*davor Angst haben*	**believe in**	*daran glauben*
be for/against	*dafür/dagegen sein*	**feel like**	*dazu Lust haben*
be good/bad at	*darin gut/schlecht sein*	**insist on**	*darauf bestehen*
be interested in	*daran interessiert sein*	**look forward to**	*sich darauf freuen*
be tired of	*es satt haben*	**think about**	*daran denken, sich*
be used to	*es gewohnt sein*		*überlegen*

I look forward to hearing **from you.**	*Ich freue mich darauf, von Ihnen zu*
I feel like having **a swim.**	*hören.*
I didn't feel like working.	*Ich habe Lust zu schwimmen.*
My grandmother believes in eating	*Ich hatte keine Lust zu arbeiten.*
porridge for breakfast every day.	*Meine Großmutter ist davon überzeugt,*
	dass man jeden Tag Haferbrei zum
	Frühstück essen sollte.

Vorsicht: Wenn die scheinbare Präposition **to** ist, gebraucht man oft die Grundform, da es sich eigentlich um das **to** des *to*-Infinitivs handelt:	
I was prepared to do **anything.**	*Ich war bereit, alles zu tun.*
The group went on to discuss	*Die Gruppe unterhielt sich anschließend*
the weather.	*über das Wetter.*
He used to call **me up in the**	*Früher hat er mich mitten in der*
middle of the night.	*Nacht angerufen.*

Einige Ergänzungen haben aber tatsächlich die Präposition **to**, die einen *–ing*-Satz fordert:

I have no objection to waiting.	*Ich habe nichts dagegen, zu warten.*
Next to sleeping, **my favorite**	*Neben Schlafen ist Fernsehen meine*
activity is watching TV.	*Lieblingsbeschäftigung.*
I'm used to hearing **his complaints.**	*Ich bin es gewohnt, seine Klagen zu hören.*

Bei bestimmten Verben und Präpositionen kann man ein Element vor der *ing*-Form ein-schieben. Dieses Element kann entweder in der Objektform oder in der Possessivform stehen:

appreciate	*zu schätzen wissen*	**remember**	*sich daran erinnern*
excuse	*entschuldigen*	**resent**	*übel nehmen*
mind	*etwas dagegen haben*	**understand**	*verstehen*
miss	*vermissen*		

I remember him/his burning the photo.	*Ich erinnere mich daran, wie er das Foto verbrannte.*
I can understand them/their wanting to be alone.	*Ich kann es verstehen, dass sie alleine sein wollen.*

be afraid of	*davor Angst haben*	**hear about**	*davon hören*
be fed up with	*die Nase voll von …*	**look forward**	*sich darauf freuen*
	haben	**to**	*etwas dagegen haben*
be used to	*es gewöhnt sein*	**object to**	

I'm fed up with you/your running around with other women.	*Ich habe die Nase voll davon, dass du mit anderen Frauen herumläufst.*
They objected to people('s) sunbathing naked.	*Sie hatten etwas dagegen, dass Leute nackt sonnenbaden.*

Lassen

Das deutsche Verb *lassen* bringt oft eine Art „kleinen Satz" mit sich. Wie ein normaler Satz hat auch dieser kleine Satz sein eigenes Verb. Es gibt zwei verschiedene Arten den kleinen Satz zu bilden. Da kommt es darauf an, ob das Verb des kleinen Satzes eine normale Aktivbedeutung oder eher eine Passivbedeutung hat.

Normale Sätze	Kleine Sätze
Die Angestellten gehen.	*Die Chefin lässt die Angestellten früh gehen.*
Der Hund hat die Möbel zerstört.	*Frieda hat den Hund die Möbel zerstören lassen.*
Mein Rock ist gereinigt worden.	*Ich habe meinen Rock reinigen lassen.*

Dieses *lassen* hat zweierlei Bedeutungen: *erlauben, zulassen* und *veranlassen*. Wenn es *erlauben* heißt, übersetzt man es oft mit **let**. Wenn es *veranlassen* heißt, übersetzt man es meist mit **have** oder **make**. Dabei drückt **have** aus, dass man jemanden beauftragt hat, während **make** (bei absichtlichen Handlungen) andeutet, dass man diesen jemanden dazu gezwungen hat – oder zumindest seine Autorität über den anderen ausgeübt hat.

Let | *erlauben, zulassen*

In der Aktivbedeutung bildet man nach **let** einen kleinen Satz. Dieser besteht aus mindestens einem Subjekt und einem Verb im Infinitiv (der Grundform) ohne **to**. Andere Elemente (z. B. Objekt, Adverb) können folgen, je nachdem, was das Verb verlangt und was man sagen will:

Despite the complaints, the police let **them** sing.	*Trotz der Beschwerden hat die Polizei sie singen lassen.*
He let **the sand** run **through his fingers.**	*Er hat den Sand durch seine Finger rieseln lassen.*

Man kann nach **let** auch ein Passiv mit dem Passivhilfsverb **be** bilden:

The guards let **the money** be **stolen.**	*Die Wächter haben es zugelassen, dass das Geld gestohlen wurde.*
The injured athlete let **himself** be carried **off the field.**	*Der verletzte Spieler ließ sich vom Feld tragen.*

Have | *veranlassen, in Auftrag geben*

In der Aktivbedeutung verwendet man **have** wie **let**: Man bildet einen kleinen Satz, dessen Verb im Infinitiv (der Grundform) ohne **to** steht:

The Ellisons are having **the carpenter** make **them a kitchen cabinet.**	*Die Ellisons lassen sich vom Schreiner einen Küchenschrank machen.*
Merle had **her daughter** do **the dishes.**	*Merle hat ihre Tochter abspülen lassen.*

In der Passivbedeutung verwendet man keine Infinitivform (Grundform), sondern ein Past Participle (die dritte Form):

The priest has **the church bells** rung **before weddings.**	*Der Priester lässt die Kirchenglocken vor Hochzeiten läuten.*
I had **my suit** cleaned **only last week.**	*Ich habe meinen Anzug erst letzte Woche reinigen lassen.*

Make | *veranlassen, zwingen*

Make kann man nur in der Aktivbedeutung verwenden. Wie oben schon erwähnt, enthält es bei absichtlichen Handlungen die Andeutung, dass jemand gezwungen wurde.

Mrs. Grundy made **her children** give **their teacher a present.**	*Mrs. Grundy zwang ihre Kinder, ihrer Lehrerin einen Geschenk zu machen.*
Sherrie always makes **her little brother** take **out the garbage.**	*Sherrie läßt immer ihren kleinen Bruder den Müll nach draußen bringen.*

Make wählt man auch, um auszudrücken, dass ein Gegenstand, Ereignis usw. etwas unabsichtlich verursacht:

Howard's thoughtless remark made **his listeners** see **red.**	*Howards gedankenlose Bemerkung ließ seine Zuhörer rotsehen.*
The loud bang made **the passers-by** run **away in fright.**	*Der laute Knall ließ die Passanten vor Schreck weglaufen.*

12 Questions Words | *Fragewort-Fragen*

Die englischen Fragewörter:

what	*was*	**when**	*wann*
which	*welches*	**where**	*wo*
who	*wer, wen, wem*	**why**	*warum*
whose	*wessen*	**how**	*wie*
whom	*wen, wem*		

Anwendung

Genau wie im Deutschen verwendet man Fragewörter, um Phrasen zu bilden, mit denen man nach fehlenden Informationen fragen kann. Fragewort-Phrasen stehen meist am Satzanfang:

What do you want?	*Was willst du?*
How much does that gold ring cost?	*Wie viel kostet dieser Goldring?*

Um großes Erstaunen auszudrücken, kann man aber auch die Wortfolge eines Aussagesatzes kopieren und die entsprechende Stelle (meist eine Noun Phrase), die zur Überraschung geführt hat, durch das jeweilige Fragewort ersetzen. Auf gleiche Art kann man auch – relativ unhöflich und umgangssprachlich – nachfragen, wenn man einen einzelnen Satzteil nicht verstanden hat:

Sprecher A:	
Leah's been eating peach sandwiches.	*Leah hat in letzter Zeit Pfirsichbrote gegessen.*
Sprecher B:	
Leah's been eating WHAT?	*Leah hat WAS in letzter Zeit gegessen?*

Man kann sogar das Verb durch die entsprechende Form von **do** und die Noun Phrase durch ein Fragewort ersetzen:

Sprecher A:	
Gonzuela gave Peter the car.	*Gonzuela hat Peter das Auto gegeben.*
Sprecher B:	
Gonzuela did WHAT?	*Gonzuela hat WAS getan?*

Das Fragewort **whom** (*wen, wem*) existiert kaum noch in der gesprochenen Sprache.

Vor allem in den USA ist **whom** fast völlig verschwunden. An seiner Stelle verwendet man *who*:

Who **did she see?**	*Wen hat sie gesehen?*
Who **were you talking to just now?**	*Mit wem hast du gerade gesprochen?*

Whom findet man jedoch noch in der formellen Schriftsprache:

Whom **did she see?**	*Wen hat sie gesehen?*
To whom **must one speak about such matters?**	*Mit wem muss man über solche Angelegenheiten sprechen?*

Wenn man eine Präposition (**on, by, in, to** usw.) in der Fragekonstruktion braucht, gibt es zwei Möglichkeiten, um diese zu positionieren.

1. In sehr formellen, hauptsächlich schriftlichen Situationen stellt man die Präposition an den Anfang der Fragewort-Phrase:

On which **corner was the musician standing?**	*An welcher Ecke stand der Musikant?*
To which **thief did the docent show the collection?**	*Welchem Dieb zeigte die Museums-pädagogin die Sammlung?*

Dies ist auch der einzige Fall, wo man gelegentlich noch **whom** hört oder liest:

To whom did you turn then? | *An wen haben Sie sich dann gewandt?*

2. Im normalen Sprachgebrauch aber steht die Präposition am Ende oder in der Mitte des Satzes:

Which **corner was the musician standing** on?	*An welcher Ecke ist der Musikant gestanden?*
Which **thief did the docent show the collection** to?	*Welchem Dieb hat die Museumspädagogin die Sammlung gezeigt?*
Who **did you turn** to **then?**	*An wen haben Sie sich dann gewandt?*

Fragewort-Fragen im Nebensatz

Fragewort-Fragen im Nebensatz haben normalerweise eine andere Wortfolge als im Hauptsatz. Im Nebensatz nämlich schiebt man kein Hilfsverb zwischen Fragewort-Phrase und Subjekt. Wenn ein Hilfsverb vorhanden ist, steht es nach dem Subjekt, wie in einem Aussagesatz. Wenn von der Bedeutung her kein Hilfsverb notwendig ist, setzt man auch keines hinein.

Fragewort-Fragen im Hauptsatz:	
What did you say?	*Was hast du gesagt?*
How many would you like?	*Wie viele möchten Sie?*
What do we want?	*Was wollen wir?*
Fragewort-Fragen im Nebensatz:	
She asked him what he'd said.	*Sie fragte ihn, was er gesagt hatte.*
The salesclerk asked how many they would like.	*Die Verkäuferin fragte, wie viele sie möchten.*
Simon and Bonnie don't know what they want.	*Simon und Bonnie wissen nicht, was sie wollen.*

13 Relative Clauses | *Relativsätze*

Relativsätze sind Nebensätze, die in der Regel ein Noun (Hauptwort) oder eine Noun Phrase beschreiben:

The girl who swims fastest **wins a prize.**	*Das Mädchen, das am schnellsten schwimmt, gewinnt einen Preis.*
The fish which jumped out of the water **was a salmon.**	*Der Fisch, der aus dem Wasser sprang, war ein Lachs.*

Die Beispielsätze zeigen, dass hier der Relativsatz ein notwendiger Teil des Satzes ist, da er definiert, wer genau gemeint ist. Wenn man den Relativsatz weglassen würde, wüsste man nicht, welche Person einen Preis gewinnt oder welcher Fisch ein Lachs war. Zum Vergleich: in den beiden folgenden Beispielsätzen wäre trotzdem klar, wer oder was gemeint ist: **The fastest one** bzw. **Peter** sagt schon alles, so dass der Relativsatz zwar eine zusätzliche Information bringt, jedoch nicht notwendig zur Identifikation beiträgt.

The fastest one, who of course wins, **receives a prize.**	*Die Schnellste, die natürlich gewinnt, bekommt einen Preis.*
Peter, who was a bit shy, **kept quiet.**	*Peter, der ein bisschen schüchtern war, blieb still.*

Kommaregel für Relativsätze

In der geschriebenen Sprache unterscheidet man zwischen den beiden genannten Relativsatztypen durch die Interpunktion. Wo nämlich der Relativsatz zur Identifikation des gemeinten notwendig ist, benutzt man weder davor noch danach ein Komma. Wo der Relativsatz lediglich zusätzliche Informationen gibt, also nur beschreibt und nicht notwenig ist (und deshalb weggelassen werden kann), benutzt man jeweils vor und nach dem Relativsatz ein Komma:

Those books which everyone has read **are boring.**	*Die Bücher, die jeder gelesen hat, sind langweilig.*
His new book, which everyone has read, **is boring.**	*Sein neues Buch, das jeder gelesen hat, ist langweilig.*

Wenn die Zeichensetzung im Englischen sonst auch relativ unwichtig ist, so ist die Unterscheidung zwischen den beiden Typen sehr wichtig, da sie zu großen Missverständnissen führen kann:

Mary knows few boys who are knitting. *Mary kennt nur wenige Jungs, die häkeln.*

Mary knows few boys, who are knitting. *Mary kennt nur wenige Jungs, und die Jungs häkeln alle.*

In der gesprochenen Sprache muss man sich auf sein Ohr verlassen. Das Komma der geschriebenen Sprache entspricht hier in etwa einer kleinen Pause.

Relative Pronouns | *Relativpronomen*

Die Relativpronomen im Englischen lauten: **who, whom, whose, which, when, where** und **why**.

- **Who**, **whose** und **whom** werden für Menschen und manchmal auch für Haustiere verwendet:

I met a man who **can walk on his hands.**	*Ich habe einen Mann getroffen, der auf seinen Händen laufen kann.*
A woman who **was sweeping the sidewalk gave us directions.**	*Eine Frau, die gerade den Gehweg kehrte, erklärte uns den Weg.*
That dog, who **did tricks, followed me home.**	*Dieser Hund, der Kunststücke machen konnte, folgte mir nach Hause.*

Wie bei den Fragewörtern (▷ Kapitel Fragewort-Fragen) findet **whom** selten Gebrauch in der gesprochenen Sprache. Dafür verwendet man **who**:

The police officer whom **you saw.**	*Der Polizist, den/Die Polizistin, die du gesehen hast.*
▷ The police officer who **you saw.**	

Im Gegensatz zu **who** und **whom** kann man **whose** auch bei Gegenständen benutzen:

A chest, whose **hinges were broken, stood in the corner.**	*Eine Kiste, deren Scharniere kaputt waren, stand in der Ecke.*

Die gleichwertige Alternative für Gegenstände ist **of which,** dieses benötigt jedoch manchmal schwierige Satzstellungen:

A chest, **the hinges** of which **were broken, stood in the corner.**	*Eine Kiste, deren Scharniere kaputt waren, stand in der Ecke.*

* **Which** verwendet man ausschliesslich für Gegenstände und Lebewesen, zu denen man wenig Bezug hat.

The cookies which **I dropped made Fido happy.**	*Die Kekse, die mir aus der Hand gefallen sind, machten Fido glücklich.*

In der gesprochenen Sprache lässt man eine Präposition wie bei Fragen am Ende des Relativsatzes:

The businesswoman who **Graham was talking** to **was his aunt.** The vegetables which **the chef had asked** for **were delivered.**	*Die Geschäftsfrau, mit der Graham gesprochen hat, war seine Tante. Das Gemüse, um das der Koch gebeten hatte, wurde geliefert.*

Im sehr formellen Sprachgebrauch jedoch kommt die Präposition vor dem Relative Pronoun, das bei Personen dann *whom* lautet:

The businesswoman to whom **Graham was talking was his aunt.**	*Die Geschäftsfrau, mit der Graham gesprochen hat, war seine Tante.*

- **When, where** und **why**
  When kann man nach verschiedenen Zeitangaben verwenden:

Do you remember the time when **Walt scared the neighbors with his trumpet?**	*Erinnerst du dich daran, als Walt mit seiner Trompete die Nachbarn erschreckte?*
That was the night when **the electricity went out.**	*Das war der Abend, an dem der Strom ausgefallen ist.*

Where kann sowohl für Ortsangaben als auch für andere Dinge verwendet werden:

The city where **I left my heart was San Francisco.**	*Die Stadt, wo ich mein Herz verlor, war San Francisco.*
I know a restaurant where **you get all you can eat for ten dollars.**	*Ich kenne ein Restaurant, wo man für zehn Dollar so viel bekommt, wie man essen kann.*
It was a situation where **nobody could win.**	*Es war so eine Situation, wo keiner gewinnen konnte.*
I was having a day where **everything went wrong.**	*Ich hatte gerade so einen Tag, wo alles schief geht.*

Why verwendet man nur als Relativpronomen, um einen gemeinten Grund zu verdeutlichen:

I never understood the reason why **he left her.**	*Ich habe nie verstanden, warum er sie verlassen hat.*

That

Sehr häufig verzichtet man ganz auf Relativpronomen und verwendet stattdessen das unveränderliche Wort **that.** In der gesprochenen Sprache hört sich **that** viel natürlicher an als das Relativpronomen für Gegenstände, **which:**

The lamp that **we bought was very expensive.**	*Die Lampe, die wir gekauft haben, war sehr teuer.*
The mouse that **lives in my kitchen is quite clever.**	*Die Maus, die in meiner Küche lebt, ist ganz schön schlau.*

Präpositionen bleiben bei **that** grundsätzlich am Ende des Relativsatzes:

The chair that **Andrew was sitting** on **collapsed.**	*Der Stuhl, auf dem Andrew saß, ist zusammengebrochen.*
The young woman that **he was talking** about **doesn't like us.**	*Die junge Frau, von der er geredet hat, mag uns nicht.*

That eignet sich nur für Relativsätze, die unbedingt nötig sind, weil sie etwas näher definieren. Wenn man einen Relativsatz bilden will, der nur zusätzliche Informationen bietet, aber nicht unbedingt nötig ist, muss man ein Relativpronomen verwenden. **That** kann das besitzanzeigende Relativpronomen **whose** nicht ersetzen.

Manchmal braucht man weder ein Relativpronomen noch **that.** Diese Form von Relativsatz ist besonders in der gesprochenen Sprache sehr üblich:

The hotel ____ **they took Debbie** to **had a swimming pool.**	*Das Hotel, in das sie Debbie einluden, hatte einen Swimmingpool.*

Es gibt zwei wichtige Regeln, die man beachten muss, wenn man das Relativpronomen bzw. **that** ganz weglassen möchte:

1. Man kann diese Wörter nur bei Relativsätzen weglassen, die unbedingt nötig sind. Ist ein Relativsatz nicht nötig, d.h. er steht zwischen zwei Kommas, dann muss das entsprechende Relativpronomen benutzt werden.
2. Das Relativpronomen bzw. **that** darf nicht als das Subjekt des Relativsatzes fungieren, wenn es ersetzt werden soll.

the man who/that saw the movie star	*der Mann, der den Filmstar sah*
the man (who/that) the movie star saw	*der Mann, den der Filmstar sah*
the man (who/that) I saw the movie star with	*der Mann, mit dem ich den Filmstar sah*
Peter, who saw the movie star, kissed the girl.	*Peter, der den Filmstar sah, küsste das Mädchen.*

Im ersten Beispielsatz kann man das Relativpronomen bzw. **that** nicht weglassen, weil **who/that** das Subjekt innerhalb des Relativsatzes ist. Im zweiten und dritten Beispiel dagegen kann man das Relativpronomen bzw. **that** weglassen. Im vierten Beispielsatz kann **who** nicht weggelassen werden, da der Relativsatz nur Zusatzinformationen gibt, aber nicht zur Identifikation von Peter notwendig ist.

Free Relatives | *freie Relativsätze*

Ein Free Relative ist eine Art Relativsatz, der eine Noun Phrase nicht ergänzen, sondern alleine eine bilden kann. Mit anderen Worten: diese Relativsätze können selbst als Subjekte, Objekte usw. fungieren.

Subjekt:	
What irritated me so much was their attitude.	*Was mich so ärgerte, war ihre Einstellung.*
Objekt:	
He likes what he cooks.	*Er mag, was er kocht.*

In Free Relatives kann man **what, where, when** und manchmal **who** verwenden:

What you need **is exercise.**	*Was du brauchst, ist Bewegung.*
I have what you want**.**	*Ich habe, was du willst.*
It wasn't where it was supposed to be**.**	*Es war nicht dort, wo es hätte sein sollen.*
They came and went when they pleased**.**	*Sie kamen und gingen, wann es ihnen passte.*
I'm going to thrash who did it**.**	*Ich werde den verprügeln, der es gemacht hat.*

Ausserdem kann man diese Fürwörter mit **–ever** ergänzen. Sie bedeuten dann soviel wie *was auch immer (***whatever***), wo auch immer (***wherever***), wann auch immer (***whenever***)* und *wer auch immer (***whoever***)*.

Whoever **told you that was lying.**	*Wer immer dir das auch gesagt hat, hat gelogen.*
I'll bring whatever **you need.**	*Ich bringe dir, was immer du brauchst.*
They simply went wherever **the bus took them.**	*Sie sind einfach dorthin gefahren, wo der Bus gerade hinfuhr.*
We can leave whenever **you're ready.**	*Wir können gehen, wann immer du fertig bist.*

14 Negation | *Verneinung*

Negative Ausdrücke

Ein paar grammatische Abweichungen kommen hauptsächlich in verneinten Sätzen vor. Dabei zählen nicht nur die offensichtlich verneinenden Ausdrücke (wie z. B. **not, never, no**) als negativ, sondern auch die untenstehenden:

few	*nur wenige*
rarely, seldom	*selten*
hardly, scarcely, barely	*kaum*

Any-Wörter

Das Wort **any** und seine Zusammensetzungen, wie **anyone, anywhere** verwendet man in verneinten Sätzen, wo man in nicht verneinten Sätzen **some** und verwandte Wörter, wie **someone, somewhere** gebraucht. Das entsprechende Wort für die Zeitangabe enthält aber kein **any,** es heißt **ever.**

1. Wenn das Subjekt negativ ist, verwendet man **any**-Wörter hinten im Satz:

No one **ever said** anything.	*Keiner hat jemals etwas gesagt.*
Few sloths **went** anywhere.	*Nur wenige Faultiere sind irgendwohin gegangen.*

2. Wenn man vor dem Verb ein negatives Adverb benutzt, braucht man nach dem Verb anstatt **some**-Wörter **any**-Wörter:

Kerry seldom **talked to** anybody.	*Kerry hat selten mit irgend jemand gesprochen.*
Duncan almost never **does** anything.	*Duncan tut fast nie etwas.*

3. Im Deutschen verwendet man gern negative Objekte, Zeitangaben, usw. Wenn diese im englischen Satz nach dem Verb stehen würden, ist es viel üblicher, **not** plus **any-**Wort zu verwenden:

There weren't **any more.**	*Es gab keine mehr.*
I couldn't **find my gloves anywhere.**	*Ich konnte meine Handschuhe nirgendwo finden.*

In Ja-Nein-Fragen sind any-Wörter auch sehr üblich

Has anybody seen my raincoat?	*Hat jemand meinen Regenmantel gesehen?*
Has Toby blabbed the secret to anyone yet?	*Hat Toby das Geheimnis schon irgend jemandem ausgeplaudert?*

15 Glossary | *Glossar*

Active

dt.: Aktiv. Eine Satzform, in der das vom Verb verlangte Subjekt auch tatsächlich als Subjekt dient. Vgl. Passive.

Adjective

dt.: Eigenschaftswort, Adjektiv. Ein Adjective beschreibt ein Noun oder eine Noun Phrase.

Adverb

dt.: Umstandswort, Adverb. Ein Adverb ist ein *Wort*, das ein Verb, ein Adjective, ein anderes Adverb oder einen Satz beschreibt.

Article

dt.: Artikel. Ein Article steht am Anfang einer Noun Phrase und zeigt an, ob diese bestimmt oder unbestimmt ist.

Auxiliary

▶ Hilfsverb.

Full verb

▶ Vollverb.

Hauptsatz

Ein Hauptsatz ist ein Satz, der das Hauptereignis bzw. der Hauptzustand eines Satzes ausdrückt. In **They said that the tree was old** ist **They said** der Hauptsatz, weil der Satz primär ausdrückt, dass jemand etwas gesagt hat.

Hilfsverb

Ein Hilfsverb ist eine Art Verb, welches das Vollverb unterstützt – in der Zeitbildung, der Vervollständigung der Bedeutung (bei manchen Modalverben), oder der Erfüllung grammatischer Bedingungen. Im Englischen stehen die Hilfsverben immer vor dem Vollverb.

Infinitive

dt.: Infinitiv, Grundform des Verbs. Der Infinitive ist die erste Form des Verbs und diejenige, die am wenigsten zeitliche Information enthält.

Modalverb

Die primären englischen Modalverben sind **can, could, will, would, shall, should, may, might** und **must. Need, dare** und **ought to** verhalten sich ähnlich wie Modalverben. Das englische Modalverb besitzt weder Infinitiv noch Partizipformen und ändert seine Form nicht, um mit dem Subjekt übereinzustimmen.

Nebensatz

Ein Nebensatz ist ein Teilsatz, der einem Hauptsatz beigefügt ist.

Noun

dt.: Hauptwort, Substantiv, Nomen. Ein Noun ist ein Wort, das in der Regel einen Gegenstand, ein Lebewesen oder einen abstrakten Begriff bezeichnet.

Noun Phrase

dt.: Nominalphrase. Eine Noun Phrase ist eine Phrase mit einem Noun als Kern, oder auch ein Pronoun. Sie kann z.B. als Subjekt oder Objekt im Satz fungieren. Vgl. Phrase

Objekt

Ein Objekt ist eine Noun Phrase, die nach dem Verb kommt. Manche Verben lassen zwei Objekte zu: Das erste heißt dann das indirekte Objekt und das zweite das direkte Objekt.

Participle

dt.: Partizip. Ein Participle ist eine Form des Verbs, die zum einen als Verb, zum anderen als Adjective auftreten kann. In ihrer Funktion als Verb können Partizipien im englischen Hauptsatz nur hinter einem Hilfsverb stehen; im Nebensatz können sie allein auftreten. Vgl. Past Participle

Passive

dt.: Passiv. Eine Satzform, bei der das normale Subjekt des Vollverbs seinen Status als Subjekt verliert und entweder nach einer Präposition erscheint (im Englischen **by**) oder sogar verschwindet. Im Deutschen bildet man den Passiv mit dem Hilfsverb *werden*, im Englischen mit **be** oder manchmal mit **get.**

Past Participle

dt.: Partizip Perfekt, dritte Form. Das Past Participle wird bei der Bildung der Perfect Tenses (Hilfsverb: **have**) und des Passivs (Hilfsverb: **be**) verwendet.

Perfect Tenses

dt.: Perfekttempora, „vollendete" Zeiten. Die Perfect Tenses werden mit **have** + Past Participle gebildet. Sie beschreiben, dass ein Ereignis oder Zustand vor einem gegebenen Zeitpunkt geschehen ist bzw. gegolten hat.

Phrase

dt.: Phrase. Eine Phrase ist eine Reihe von Wörtern, die eine bestimmte „Stelle" oder Funktion in der Wortfolge einnehmen können: z. B. die Subjektsfunktion. Eine Phrase kann aus einem Wort bestehen: insbesondere sind alle Fürwörter gleichzeitig auch Phrases. Vgl. Noun Phrase

Possessive

dt.: possessiv, besitzanzeigend. Possessive Formen erklären, wem etwas gehört, zuzuorden ist, usw.

Preposition

dt.: Präposition, Verhältniswort. Eine Preposition gibt in erster Linie an, wo jemand oder eine Sache sich befindet oder in welche Richtung sich etwas oder jemand bewegt bzw. bewegt wird.

Progressive Tenses

dt.: Verlaufsformen. Die Progressive Tenses sind Zeiten, die darauf hinweisen, dass ein Geschehen zu einem bestimmten Zeitpunkt im Gange ist.

Pronoun

dt.: Fürwort. Pronouns sind einzelne Wörter, deren Funktion es ist, ein Noun oder ganze Phrasen zu ersetzen. Vgl. Phrase

Reflexive Pronoun

dt.: Reflexivpronomen, rückbezügliches Fürwort. Ein Reflexive Pronoun ist ein Pronoun, das sich auf dieselbe Person oder dasselbe Ding wie das Subjekt bezieht.

Relative Pronoun

dt.: Relativpronomen. Ein Relative Pronoun steht am Anfang eines Relativsatzes, um diesen mit dem davorstehenden Noun bzw. der Noun Phrase zu verbinden.

Relative Clause

dt.: Relativsatz. Ein Relativsatz ist ein Nebensatz, der ein Noun oder eine Noun Phrase beschreibt. Vgl. Noun, Noun Phrase

Subject

dt.: Subjekt. Das Subjekt ist das Element, um das es im Satz oder Teilsatz geht. Im Deutschen steht das Subjekt fast immer im Nominativ (Werfall) und oft am Satzanfang. Im Englischen steht das Subjekt in der Regel vor dem ersten Verb im Satz, nicht unbedingt direkt am Anfang.

Tense

dt.: Tempus, Zeit. Eine Tense ist eine grammatische Zeit.

Verb

Im Deutschen auch „Tunwort" genannt. Das Verb beschreibt ein Ereignis bzw. einen Zustand oder hilft einem anderen Verb. Vgl. Vollverb, Hilfsverb

Vollverb

Das Vollverb ist das Verb, das die meiste Bedeutung in den Satz bringt. Im Englischen muss jeder vollständige Haupt- bzw. Nebensatz ein Vollverb enthalten, wobei es immer als letztes der Verben auftritt. Vgl. Verb, Hilfsverb

Stichwortregister

2 | Verbtabellen

Grammatikbegriffe in der Übersicht

Englisch	Lateinischer Ursprung	Deutsch
active	Aktiv	Tätigkeitsform
auxiliary	Hilfsverb	Hilfszeitwort
conditional present	Konditional I	Bedingungsform I
conditional past	Konditional II	Bedingungsform II
conjugation	Konjugation	Beugung des Zeitworts
continuous form	progressive Form	Verlaufsform
consonant	Konsonant	Mitlaut
future	Futur I	unvollendete Zukunft
future 2 (future perfect)	Futur II	vollendete Zukunft
gerund	Gerundium	Gerundium
imperative	Imperativ	Befehlsform
infinitive	Infinitiv	Grundform des Zeitworts
irregular verb	unregelmäßiges Verb	unregelmäßiges Zeitwort
modal verb	Modalverb	Modalverb
participle	Partizip	Mittelwort
passive	Passiv	Leideform
past	Präteritum	Vergangenheit
past participle	Partizip Perfekt	Mittelwort der Vergangenheit
past perfect	Plusquamperfekt	Vorvergangenheit
plural	Plural	Mehrzahl
present	Präsens	Gegenwart
present perfect	Perfekt	vollendete Gegenwart
pronoun	Pronomen	Fürwort
reflexive verb	reflexives Verb	rückbezügliches Zeitwort
regular verb	regelmäßiges Verb	regelmäßiges Zeitwort
simple form	—	einfache Form
singular	Singular	Einzahl
subject	Subjekt	Satzgegenstand
verb	Verb	Zeitwort
vowel	Vokal	Selbstlaut

AE = amerikanisches Englisch
BE = britisches Englisch

Inhalt

Einleitung

Sie wollen sich die Formen eines bestimmten Verbs einprägen und dabei auf Besonderheiten und Unregelmäßigkeiten aufmerksam gemacht werden, Sie möchten aber auch eine seltene Verbform rasch und gezielt nachschlagen können.

Aufbau der Konjugationstabellen

Das Kapitel Verbtabellen bietet Ihnen übersichtliche Konjugationstabellen in alphabetischer Reihenfolge zu 84 regelmäßigen und unregelmäßigen Musterverben.

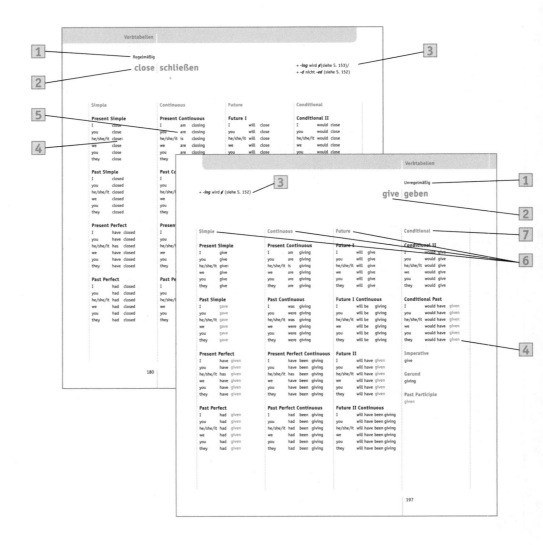

Diese Konjugationsmuster zeigen Ihnen alle Formen auf einen Blick; auf Besonderheiten wird durch farbige Hervorhebung und praktische Faustregeln hingewiesen.

1 Konjugationstyp: Mit diesem Hinweis lassen sich die englischen Verben der regelmäßigen bzw. der unregelmäßigen Konjugation zuordnen.

2 Verb mit Übersetzung: Sie finden in den Konjugationstabellen eine Auswahl englischer Verben, die im täglichen Sprachgebrauch häufige Verwendung finden. Die gängigste deutsche Übersetzung für diese Verben wurde ausgewählt.

3 Kurzcharakteristik: Merksatz zu den Besonderheiten/Unregelmäßigkeiten des Konjugationsmusters.

4 Farbige Hervorhebung: Formen, die vom regelmäßigen Konjugationsschema abweichen
bzw. Besonderheiten der englischen Sprache (z. B. 3. Person Singular -s), sind orange hervorgehoben.

5 Vollformen: In den Konjugationstabellen wurde grundsätzlich das Hilfsverb in der ausgeschriebenen Form angegeben. Die Verwendung der Kurzform können Sie auf Seite 155 ersehen.

6 Gliederung der Tabelle: In der ersten Spalte finden Sie die einfachen Formen des Verbs, in der zweiten Spalte die Verlaufsformen und in der dritten Spalte alle Zukunftsformen.

7 Conditional: Da Conditional I und Futur I gleich gebildet werden, wurde bewusst auf die Aufführung von Conditional I verzichtet.

In der Liste der unregelmäßigen Verben am Ende des Kapitels Verbtabellen finden Sie 100 der gebräuchlichsten unregelmäßigen Verben. Im Anschluss daran können Sie in einer alphabetischen deutsch-englischen Verbliste alle in diesem Band konjugierten Verben nachschlagen und erhalten zugleich einen entsprechenden Seitenverweis. Übrigens: Im Vorspann zu den Konjugationstabellen erhalten Sie wertvolle Informationen. Sie finden auf Seite 152 und 154 einen systematischen Überblick über wichtige orthographische Besonderheiten sowie Angaben zur Aussprache. Auf Seite 155 können Sie die Reflexivpronomen nachschlagen. Kurze, präzise Angaben zum Gebrauch der Zeiten werden ab Seite 156 gemacht.

Viel Erfolg!

Orthographische Besonderheiten

Verben können die folgenden Endungen haben:
1. **Verb + -s/-es**
2. **Verb + -ed/-d/-ied**
3. **Verb + -ing**

Dabei erfahren manche Verben orthographische Änderungen.

1. Verb + -s/-es

für die 3. Person Singular im *Simple Present* – in der einfachen Gegenwart

Verben, die auf *-ch, -sh, -ss, -o, -x* enden	Anhängen von *-es*	watch	watches
		push	pushes
		go	goes
Verben, die auf einen Konsonanten + *-y* enden	Anhängen von *-ies* Wegfall von *-y*	study	studies
		try	tries
		carry	carries
Aber: Verben, die auf einen Vokal + *-y* enden	Anhängen von *-s*	play	plays
		buy	buys
		enjoy	enjoys

2. Verb + -ed/-d/-ied

Die Endung *-ed* wird für regelmäßige Verben im *Simple Past* – in der einfachen Vergangenheit und für das *Past Participle* von regelmäßigen Verben benutzt.

Verben, die auf *-e* enden	Anhängen von *-d*	arrive	arrived
		change	changed
Verben, die auf einen Konsonanten + *-y* enden	*-y* wird zu *-ied*	carry	carried
		try	tried
		study	studied
Verben, die auf einen Vokal + Konsonant enden	Konsonant wird verdoppelt	stop	stopped
		plan	planned
Verben mit zwei Silben, die auf einen Konsonant enden	Konsonant wird nur verdoppelt, wenn die letzte Silbe betont wird	prefer	preferred
		aber	
		visit	visited
		offer	offered

AUSNAHME – Im BE wird ein *-l* am Ende auch bei unbetonter Silbe verdoppelt.
Im AE trifft dies nicht zu. Beispielsweise:

	travel	travelled (BE)
	travel	traveled (AE)

3. Verb + *-ing*

Die Endung *-ing* wird im Partizip Präsens und Gerundium benutzt.

Verben, die auf *-e* enden	Wegfall von *-e* Anhängen von *-ing*	have dance	hav**ing** danc**ing**
Verben, die auf *-ee* enden	Anhängen von *-ing*	see	see**ing**
Verben, deren Endkonsonant betont ist und einem Vokal folgt	Konsonant wird verdoppelt	stop plan get begin	stop**ping** plan**ning** get**ting** begin**ning**

AUSNAHME – Im BE wird ein *-l* am Ende, das einem Vokal folgt, auch bei unbetonter Silbe verdoppelt. Beispielsweise:

	cancel	cancelling (BE)
	cancel	canceling (AE)

Aussprache

Aussprache des -ed im Past Simple und Past Participle

Die Endung -ed wird gesprochen:

nach stimmlosen Konsonanten (nach -p, -f, -ss usw.)	stimmlos (-t)	asked looked stopped	wie t in „Takt" z. B. [ɑːskt]
nach stimmhaften Konsonanten und Vokalen (nach -b, -v, -g usw.)	stimmhaft (-d)	allowed listened opened	wie d in „Ende" z. B. [ˈəʊpənd]
nach -d und -t	silbisch (-id)	needed waited wanted	wie id in „Widder" z. B. [ˈniːdɪd]

Aussprache des -s, in der 3. Person Singular Present Simple

Die Endung -s wird gesprochen:

nach stimmlosen Konsonanten	stimmlos* (-s)	waits gets cuts	wie ss in „nass" z. B. [gets]
nach stimmhaften Konsonanten und Vokalen	stimmhaft* (-z)	runs opens allows	wie s in „Sahne" z. B. [rʌnz]
nach einem Zischlaut, bei Bildung der 3. Person Sing. Present Simple auf -es	silbisch (-iz)	changes watches washes	wie das erste -s in „business" z. B. [ˈwɒʃɪz]

* Es gibt zwei Arten von Konsonanten (Mitlauten) im Englischen:
stimmhafte Konsonanten – Sie fühlen eine Vibration am Kehlkopf.
stimmlose Konsonanten – Sie fühlen keine Vibration am Kehlkopf.

Kurzformen

Kurzformen werden im Allgemeinen in der gesprochenen Sprache benutzt. In der geschriebenen Sprache werden die Vollformen benutzt.

BE			HAVE		
I am	→	I'm	I have	→	I've
you are	→	you're	you have	→	you've
he/she/it is	→	he's/she's/it's	he/she/it has	→	he's/she's/it's
we are	→	we're	we have	→	we've
you are	→	you're	you have	→	you've
they are	→	they're	they have	→	they've
HAD			**WILL**		
I had	→	I'd	I will	→	I'll
you had	→	you'd	you will	→	you'll
he/she/it had	→	he'd/she'd/it'd	he/she/it will	→	he'll/she'll/it'll
we had	→	we'd	we will	→	we'll
you had	→	you'd	you will	→	you'll
they had	→	they'd	they will	→	they'll
WOULD					
I would	→	I'd			
you would	→	you'd			
he/she/it would	→	he'd/she'd/it'd			
we would	→	we'd			
you would	→	you'd			
they would	→	they'd			

Reflexivpronomen
Rückbezügliche Fürwörter

werden benutzt, wenn man die Handlung auf den Handelnden rückbeziehen kann. Die Reflexivpronomen *myself, yourself, himself* usw. entsprechen dem deutschen mich, dich, sich usw. Vorsicht! Es gibt nicht zu jedem deutschen Reflexivverb ein entsprechendes englisches und umgekehrt – z. B. sich erinnern – *remember*.

I	enjoy	**myself**	we	enjoy	**ourselves**
you	enjoy	**yourself**	you	enjoy	**yourselves**
he	enjoys	**himself**	they	enjoy	**themselves**
she	enjoys	**herself**			
it	enjoys	**itself**			

Zeitformen

Im Englischen gibt es 14 Zeiten. Man unterscheidet zwischen *Simple Form* (einfache Form) und *Continuous Form* (Verlaufsform).

Die **Simple Form** wird verwendet für
- regelmäßige, wiederkehrende Handlungen oder Zustände
- Tatsachen
- Zustände unbegrenzter Dauer.

Die **Continuous Form** wird verwendet für
- eine Handlung, die im Augenblick abläuft
- gerade verlaufende Handlungen, in die eine zweite Handlung eintritt
- zwei parallell verlaufende Handlungen.

Es gibt auch eine Reihe von Verben, die nicht in der Verlaufsform verwendet werden können. Beispielsweise: *like, hope, know, love.*

Present Simple

Das *Present Simple* wird mit der Grundform des Verbs gebildet.
Nur die 3. Person Singular (*he/she/it*) wird verändert, indem ein *-s* angehängt wird.

Aussage		Verneinung			Frage		
I/we/you/they	live.	I/we/you/they	do not (don't)	live.	Do	I/we/you/they	live?
he/she/it	lives.	he/she/it	does not (doesn't)	live.	Does	he/she/it	live?
		Verneinte Sätze werden durch Hinzufügen von don't/doesn't gebildet.			Fragen werden gebildet, indem do/does am Satz anfang hinzugefügt wird. Hier bleibt die Grundform des Verbs erhalten.		

Present Simple Continuous

Das *Present Simple Continuous* wird mit der passenden Form von to be (*is/am/are*) + Anhängen von *-ing* an die Grundform des Verbs gebildet.

Aussage			Verneinung			Frage		
I	am	living.	I	am not ('m not)	living.	Am	I	living?
he/she/it	is	living.	he/she/it	is not ('s not)	living.	Is	he/she/it	living?
we/you/they	are	living.	we/you/they	are not ('re not)	living.	Are	we/you/they	living?
			Verneinte Sätze werden durch Hinzufügen von *not* nach dem Pronomen gebildet.			Bei der Frageform steht *am/is/are* am Anfang des Satzes.		

Past Simple

Das *Past Simple* wird gebildet, indem man *-ed* an die Grundform des Verbs anhängt. Eine Liste mit unregelmäßigen Verben befindet sich auf den Seiten 246 bis 250.

Aussage		Verneinung			Frage		
I	lived.	I	did not (didn't)	live.	Did	I	live?
he/she/it		he/she/it				he/she/it	
we/you/they		we/you/they				we/you/they	
		Die Verneinung wird mit *did not* (*didn't*) und der Grundform gebildet.			Fragen werden mit dem Hilfsverb *do* gebildet. *Did* ist die Vergangenheitsform von *do/does* und steht am Anfang des Satzes. Das Verb steht in der Grundform.		

Achtung! Eine der gebräuchlichsten Vergangenheitsformen ist das *Past Simple*. Mit dem *Past Simple* berichtet man über Vorgänge in der Vergangenheit, die keinen direkten Bezug zur Gegenwart haben.

Past Continuous

Das *Past Continuous* wird mit *was/were* + *-ing* Form des Verbs gebildet.

Aussage			Verneinung			Frage		
I/he/she/it	was	living.	I/he/she/it	was not	living.	Was	I/he/she/it	living?
we/you/they	were	living.	we/you/they	were not	living.	Were	we/you/they	living?
			Verneinte Sätze werden durch Hinzufügen von *not* nach *was* bzw. *were* gebildet.			Bei der Frageform steht *was/were* am Anfang des Satzes.		

Present Perfect

Das *Present Perfect* wird mit *have/has* + Partizip Perfekt (dritte Form des Verbs) gebildet. Regelmäßige Formen werden durch Anhängen von *-ed* gebildet. Die unregelmäßigen Formen befinden sich auf den Seiten 246 bis 250.

Aussage			Verneinung			Frage		
I/we/you/they	have	lived.	I/we/you/they	have not (haven't)	lived.	Have	I/we/you/they	lived?
he/she/it	has	lived.	he/she/it	has not (hasn't)	lived.	Has	he/she/it	lived?
			Verneinte Sätze werden durch Hinzufügen von *not* vor dem Partizip Perfekt gebildet.			Bei der Frageform steht *have/has* am Anfang des Satzes.		

Achtung! Das *Present Perfect* ist streng von der *Past Simple* Form zu unterscheiden, da es entgegen der einfachen Vergangenheit einen Bezug zur Gegenwart hat. Das *Present Perfect* bildet eine Brücke zwischen Vergangenheit und Gegenwart.

Present Perfect Continuous

Das *Present Perfect Continuous* wird mit *have/has been* + *-ing* Form des Verbs gebildet.

Aussage			Verneinung			Frage		
I/we/you/they	have	been living.	I/we/you/they	have not (haven't)	been living.	Have	I/we/you/they	been living?
he/she/it	has	been living.	he/she/it	has not (hasn't)	been living.	Has	he/she/it	been living?
			Verneinte Sätze werden durch Hinzufügen von *not* vor dem Verb gebildet.			Bei der Frageform steht *have/has* am Anfang des Satzes.		

Past Perfect

Das *Past Perfect* wird mit *had* + Partizip Perfekt (dritte Form des Verbs) gebildet. Regelmäßige Formen werden durch Anhängen von -ed gebildet. Die unregelmäßigen Formen befinden sich auf den Seiten 246 bis 250.

Aussage			Verneinung			Frage		
I	had	lived.	I	had not (hadn't)	lived.	Had	I	lived?
he/she/it			he/she/it				he/she/it	
we/you/they			we/you/they				we/you/they	
			Verneinte Sätze werden durch Hinzufügen von *not* nach *had* gebildet.			Bei der Frageform steht *had* am Anfang des Satzes.		

Past Perfect Continuous

Das *Past Perfect Continuous* wird mit *had been* + *-ing* Form des Verbs gebildet.

Aussage			Verneinung			Frage		
I	had	been living.	I	had not (hadn't)	been living.	Had	I	been living?
he/she/it			he/she/it				he/she/it	
we/you/they			we/you/they				we/you/they	
			Verneinte Sätze werden durch Hinzufügen von *not* zwischen *had* und *been* gebildet.			Bei der Frageform steht *had* am Anfang des Satzes.		

Future I

Das *Future I* wird mit *will* und der Grundform des Verbs gebildet.

Aussage			Verneinung			Frage		
I	will	live.	I	will not (won't)	live.	Will	I	live?
he/she/it			he/she/it				he/she/it	
we/you/they			we/you/they				we/you/they	
			Verneinte Sätze werden durch Hinzufügen von *not* nach *will* gebildet. Achtung! Kurzform → *won't*			Bei der Frageform steht *will* am Anfang des Satzes.		

Future I Continuous

Das *Future I Continuous* wird mit *will be* + *-ing* Form des Verbs gebildet.

Aussage			Verneinung			Frage		
I	will be	living.	I	will not be (won't)	living.	Will	I	be living?
he/she/it			he/she/it				he/she/it	
we/you/they			we/you/they				we/you/they	
			Verneinte Sätze werden durch Hinzufügen von *not* zwischen *will* und *be* gebildet.			Bei der Frageform steht *will* am Anfang des Satzes.		

Future II

Das *Future II* wird mit *will have* + Partizip Perfekt (dritte Form des Verbs) gebildet.

Aussage			Verneinung			Frage		
I	will have	lived.	I	will not have (won't)	lived.	Will	I	have lived?
he/she/it			he/she/it				he/she/it	
we/you/they			we/you/they				we/you/they	
			Verneinte Sätze werden durch Hinzufügen von *not* zwischen *will* und *have* gebildet.			Bei der Frageform steht *will* am Anfang des Satzes.		

Future II Continuous

Das *Future II Continuous* wird mit *will have been* + *-ing* Form des Verbs gebildet.

Aussage			Verneinung			Frage		
I	will	living.	I	will not have	living.	Will	I	have
he/she/it	have		he/she/it	been			he/she/it	been
we/you/they	been		we/you/they	(won't)			we/you/they	living?
			Verneinte Sätze werden durch Hinzufügen von *not* nach *will* gebildet.			Bei der Frageform steht *will* am Anfang des Satzes.		

Conditional II

Das *Conditional II* wird mit *would* + Grundform des Verbs gebildet.

Aussage			Verneinung			Frage		
I	would	live.	I	would not	live.	Would	I	live?
he/she/it			he/she/it	(wouldn't)			he/she/it	
we/you/they			we/you/they				we/you/they	
			Verneinte Sätze werden durch Hinzufügen von *not* nach *would* gebildet.			Bei der Frageform steht *would* am Anfang des Satzes.		

Conditional Past

Das *Conditional Past* wird mit *would have* + Partizip Perfekt gebildet.

Aussage			Verneinung			Frage		
I	would	lived.	I	would not have	lived.	Would	I	have
he/she/it	have		he/she/it	(wouldn't)			he/she/it	lived?
we/you/they			we/you/they				we/you/they	
			Verneinte Sätze werden durch Hinzufügen von *not* nach *would* gebildet.			Bei der Frageform steht *would* am Anfang des Satzes.		

Das Passiv wird mit dem Hilfsverb *to be* (*is/was/has been* usw.) und dem Partizip Perfekt (*cleaned/ done/sold* usw.) gebildet.

Passiv | Leideform

Simple

Present Simple

I	am	taught
you	are	taught
he/she/it	is	taught
we	are	taught
you	are	taught
they	are	taught

Past Simple

I	was	taught
you	were	taught
he/she/it	was	taught
we	were	taught
you	were	taught
they	were	taught

Present Perfect

I	have	been taught
you	have	been taught
he/she/it	has	been taught
we	have	been taught
you	have	been taught
they	have	been taught

Past Perfect

I	had	been taught
you	had	been taught
he/she/it	had	been taught
we	had	been taught
you	had	been taught
they	had	been taught

Continuous

Present Continuous

I	am	being taught
you	are	being taught
he/she/it	is	being taught
we	are	being taught
you	are	being taught
they	are	being taught

Past Continuous

I	was	being taught
you	were	being taught
he/she/it	was	being taught
we	were	being taught
you	were	being taught
they	were	being taught

Present Perfect Continuous

I	have been being taught
you	have been being taught
he/she/it	has been being taught
we	have been being taught
you	have been being taught
they	have been being taught

Past Perfect Continuous

I	had	been being taught
you	had	been being taught
he/she/it	had	been being taught
we	had	been being taught
you	had	been being taught
they	had	been being taught

Future

Future I

I	will	be taught
you	will	be taught
he/she/it	will	be taught
we	will	be taught
you	will	be taught
they	will	be taught

Future I Continuous

I	will be	being taught
you	will be	being taught
he/she/it	will be	being taught
we	will be	being taught
you	will be	being taught
they	will be	being taught

Future II

I	will have been taught
you	will have been taught
he/she/it	will have been taught
we	will have been taught
you	will have been taught
they	will have been taught

Future II Continuous

I	will have been being taught
you	will have been being taught
he/she/it	will have been being taught
we	will have been being taught
you	will have been being taught
they	will have been being taught

Conditional

Conditional II

I	would be taught
you	would be taught
he/she/it	would be taught
we	would be taught
you	would be taught
they	would be taught

Conditional Past

I	would have been taught
you	would have been taught
he/she/it	would have been taught
we	would have been taught
you	would have been taught
they	would have been taught

Imperative

be + Past Participle*

Gerund

being taught

Regelmäßig

allow | erlauben

Simple

Present Simple

I	allow
you	allow
he/she/it	allows
we	allow
you	allow
they	allow

Past Simple

I	allowed
you	allowed
he/she/it	allowed
we	allowed
you	allowed
they	allowed

Present Perfect

I	have	allowed
you	have	allowed
he/she/it	has	allowed
we	have	allowed
you	have	allowed
they	have	allowed

Past Perfect

I	had	allowed
you	had	allowed
he/she/it	had	allowed
we	had	allowed
you	had	allowed
they	had	allowed

Continuous

Present Continuous

I	am	allowing
you	are	allowing
he/she/it	is	allowing
we	are	allowing
you	are	allowing
they	are	allowing

Past Continuous

I	was	allowing
you	were	allowing
he/she/it	was	allowing
we	were	allowing
you	were	allowing
they	were	allowing

Present Perfect Continuous

I	have	been	allowing
you	have	been	allowing
he/she/it	has	been	allowing
we	have	been	allowing
you	have	been	allowing
they	have	been	allowing

Past Perfect Continuous

I	had	been	allowing
you	had	been	allowing
he/she/it	had	been	allowing
we	had	been	allowing
you	had	been	allowing
they	had	been	allowing

Future

Future I

I	will	allow
you	will	allow
he/she/it	will	allow
we	will	allow
you	will	allow
they	will	allow

Future I Continuous

I	will be allowing
you	will be allowing
he/she/it	will be allowing
we	will be allowing
you	will be allowing
they	will be allowing

Future II

I	will have allowed
you	will have allowed
he/she/it	will have allowed
we	will have allowed
you	will have allowed
they	will have allowed

Future II Continuous

I	will have been allowing
you	will have been allowing
he/she/it	will have been allowing
we	will have been allowing
you	will have been allowing
they	will have been allowing

Conditional

Conditional II

I	would allow
you	would allow
he/she/it	would allow
we	would allow
you	would allow
they	would allow

Conditional Past

I	would have allowed
you	would have allowed
he/she/it	would have allowed
we	would have allowed
you	would have allowed
they	would have allowed

Imperative

allow

Gerund

allowing

Past Participle

allowed

Regelmäßig

answer | antworten

Simple

Present Simple

I	answer
you	answer
he/she/it	answers
we	answer
you	answer
they	answer

Past Simple

I	answered
you	answered
he/she/it	answered
we	answered
you	answered
they	answered

Present Perfect

I	have	answered
you	have	answered
he/she/it	has	answered
we	have	answered
you	have	answered
they	have	answered

Past Perfect

I	had	answered
you	had	answered
he/she/it	had	answered
we	had	answered
you	had	answered
they	had	answered

Continuous

Present Continuous

I	am	answering
you	are	answering
he/she/it	is	answering
we	are	answering
you	are	answering
they	are	answering

Past Continuous

I	was	answering
you	were	answering
he/she/it	was	answering
we	were	answering
you	were	answering
they	were	answering

Present Perfect Continuous

I	have been answering
you	have been answering
he/she/it	has been answering
we	have been answering
you	have been answering
they	have been answering

Past Perfect Continuous

I	had been answering
you	had been answering
he/she/it	had been answering
we	had been answering
you	had been answering
they	had been answering

Future

Future I

I	will	answer
you	will	answer
he/she/it	will	answer
we	will	answer
you	will	answer
they	will	answer

Future I Continuous

I	will be	answering
you	will be	answering
he/she/it	will be	answering
we	will be	answering
you	will be	answering
they	will be	answering

Future II

I	will have	answered
you	will have	answered
he/she/it	will have	answered
we	will have	answered
you	will have	answered
they	will have	answered

Future II Continuous

I	will have been answering
you	will have been answering
he/she/it	will have been answering
we	will have been answering
you	will have been answering
they	will have been answering

Conditional

Conditional II

I	would answer
you	would answer
he/she/it	would answer
we	would answer
you	would answer
they	would answer

Conditional Past

I	would have answered
you	would have answered
he/she/it	would have answered
we	would have answered
you	would have answered
they	would have answered

Imperative

answer

Gerund

answering

Past Participle

answered

Regelmäßig

arrive | ankommen

+ *-ing* wird ø (siehe S. 153)/
+ *-d* nicht *-ed* (siehe S. 152)

Simple

Present Simple

I	arrive
you	arrive
he/she/it	arrives
we	arrive
you	arrive
they	arrive

Past Simple

I	arrived
you	arrived
he/she/it	arrived
we	arrived
you	arrived
they	arrived

Present Perfect

I	have	arrived
you	have	arrived
he/she/it	has	arrived
we	have	arrived
you	have	arrived
they	have	arrived

Past Perfect

I	had	arrived
you	had	arrived
he/she/it	had	arrived
we	had	arrived
you	had	arrived
they	had	arrived

Continuous

Present Continuous

I	am	arriving
you	are	arriving
he/she/it	is	arriving
we	are	arriving
you	are	arriving
they	are	arriving

Past Continuous

I	was	arriving
you	were	arriving
he/she/it	was	arriving
we	were	arriving
you	were	arriving
they	were	arriving

Present Perfect Continuous

I	have	been	arriving
you	have	been	arriving
he/she/it	has	been	arriving
we	have	been	arriving
you	have	been	arriving
they	have	been	arriving

Past Perfect Continuous

I	had	been	arriving
you	had	been	arriving
he/she/it	had	been	arriving
we	had	been	arriving
you	had	been	arriving
they	had	been	arriving

Future

Future I

I	will	arrive
you	will	arrive
he/she/it	will	arrive
we	will	arrive
you	will	arrive
they	will	arrive

Future I Continuous

I	will be	arriving
you	will be	arriving
he/she/it	will be	arriving
we	will be	arriving
you	will be	arriving
they	will be	arriving

Future II

I	will have arrived
you	will have arrived
he/she/it	will have arrived
we	will have arrived
you	will have arrived
they	will have arrived

Future II Continuous

I	will have been arriving
you	will have been arriving
he/she/it	will have been arriving
we	will have been arriving
you	will have been arriving
they	will have been arriving

Conditional

Conditional II

I	would	arrive
you	would	arrive
he/she/it	would	arrive
we	would	arrive
you	would	arrive
they	would	arrive

Conditional Past

I	would have arrived
you	would have arrived
he/she/it	would have arrived
we	would have arrived
you	would have arrived
they	would have arrived

Imperative

arrive

Gerund

arriving

Past Participle

arrived

Regelmäßig

ask | fragen

Simple

Present Simple
I	ask
you	ask
he/she/it	asks
we	ask
you	ask
they	ask

Past Simple
I	asked
you	asked
he/she/it	asked
we	asked
you	asked
they	asked

Present Perfect
I	have	asked
you	have	asked
he/she/it	has	asked
we	have	asked
you	have	asked
they	have	asked

Past Perfect
I	had	asked
you	had	asked
he/she/it	had	asked
we	had	asked
you	had	asked
they	had	asked

Continuous

Present Continuous
I	am	asking
you	are	asking
he/she/it	is	asking
we	are	asking
you	are	asking
they	are	asking

Past Continuous
I	was	asking
you	were	asking
he/she/it	was	asking
we	were	asking
you	were	asking
they	were	asking

Present Perfect Continuous
I	have	been	asking
you	have	been	asking
he/she/it	has	been	asking
we	have	been	asking
you	have	been	asking
they	have	been	asking

Past Perfect Continuous
I	had	been	asking
you	had	been	asking
he/she/it	had	been	asking
we	had	been	asking
you	had	been	asking
they	had	been	asking

Future

Future I
I	will	ask
you	will	ask
he/she/it	will	ask
we	will	ask
you	will	ask
they	will	ask

Future I Continuous
I	will be	asking
you	will be	asking
he/she/it	will be	asking
we	will be	asking
you	will be	asking
they	will be	asking

Future II
I	will have	asked
you	will have	asked
he/she/it	will have	asked
we	will have	asked
you	will have	asked
they	will have	asked

Future II Continuous
I	will have been asking
you	will have been asking
he/she/it	will have been asking
we	will have been asking
you	will have been asking
they	will have been asking

Conditional

Conditional II
I	would ask
you	would ask
he/she/it	would ask
we	would ask
you	would ask
they	would ask

Conditional Past
I	would have	asked
you	would have	asked
he/she/it	would have	asked
we	would have	asked
you	would have	asked
they	would have	asked

Imperative
ask

Gerund
asking

Past Participle
asked

Unregelmäßig
Voll- und Hilfsverb

be | sein

Die Verlaufsformen von *be*
werden für die Bildung des
Passivs verwendet.

Simple

Present Simple
I	am
you	are
he/she/it	is
we	are
you	are
they	are

Past Simple
I	was
you	were
he/she/it	was
we	were
you	were
they	were

Present Perfect
I	have	been
you	have	been
he/she/it	has	been
we	have	been
you	have	been
they	have	been

Past Perfect
I	had	been
you	had	been
he/she/it	had	been
we	had	been
you	had	been
they	had	been

Continuous

Present Continuous
I	am	being
you	are	being
he/she/it	is	being
we	are	being
you	are	being
they	are	being

Past Continuous
I	was	being
you	were	being
he/she/it	was	being
we	were	being
you	were	being
they	were	being

Present Perfect Contlimous
I	have	been	being
you	have	been	being
he/she/it	has	been	being
we	have	been	being
you	have	been	being
they	have	been	being

Past Perfect Continuous
I	had	been	being
you	had	been	being
he/she/it	had	been	being
we	had	been	being
you	had	been	being
they	had	been	being

Future

Future I
I	will	be
you	will	be
he/she/it	will	be
we	will	be
you	will	be
they	will	be

Future I Continuous
I	will be	being
you	will be	being
he/she/it	will be	being
we	will be	being
you	will be	being
they	will be	being

Future II
I	will have	been
you	will have	been
he/she/it	will have	been
we	will have	been
you	will have	been
they	will have	been

Future II Continuous
I	will have been being
you	will have been being
he/she/it	will have been being
we	will have been being
you	will have been being
they	will have been being

Conditional

Conditional II
I	would be
you	would be
he/she/it	would be
we	would be
you	would be
they	would be

Conditional Past
I	would have	been
you	would have	been
he/she/it	would have	been
we	would have	been
you	would have	been
they	would have	been

Imperative
be

Gerund
being

Past Participle
been

Unregelmäßig

+ -ing wird ø (siehe S. 153)

become | werden

Simple

Present Simple

I	become
you	become
he/she/it	becomes
we	become
you	become
they	become

Past Simple

I	became
you	became
he/she/it	became
we	became
you	became
they	became

Present Perfect

I	have	become
you	have	become
he/she/it	has	become
we	have	become
you	have	become
they	have	become

Past Perfect

I	had	become
you	had	become
he/she/it	had	become
we	had	become
you	had	become
they	had	become

Continuous

Present Continuous

I	am	becoming
you	are	becoming
he/she/it	is	becoming
we	are	becoming
you	are	becoming
they	are	becoming

Past Continuous

I	was	becoming
you	were	becoming
he/she/it	was	becoming
we	were	becoming
you	were	becoming
they	were	becoming

Present Perfect Continuous

I	have	been	becoming
you	have	been	becoming
he/she/it	has	been	becoming
we	have	been	becoming
you	have	been	becoming
they	have	been	becoming

Past Perfect Continuous

I	had	been	becoming
you	had	been	becoming
he/she/it	had	been	becoming
we	had	been	becoming
you	had	been	becoming
they	had	been	becoming

Future

Future I

I	will	become
you	will	become
he/she/it	will	become
we	will	become
you	will	become
they	will	become

Future I Continuous

I	will be	becoming
you	will be	becoming
he/she/it	will be	becoming
we	will be	becoming
you	will be	becoming
they	will be	becoming

Future II

I	will have	become
you	will have	become
he/she/it	will have	become
we	will have	become
you	will have	become
they	will have	become

Future II Continuous

I	will have been becoming
you	will have been becoming
he/she/it	will have been becoming
we	will have been becoming
you	will have been becoming
they	will have been becoming

Conditional

Conditional II

I	would	become
you	would	become
he/she/it	would	become
we	would	become
you	would	become
they	would	become

Conditional Past

I	would have	become
you	would have	become
he/she/it	would have	become
we	would have	become
you	would have	become
they	would have	become

Imperative

become

Gerund

becoming

Past Participle

become

Unregelmäßig

begin | beginnen/anfangen

Konsonantenverdopplung
(siehe S. 152)

Simple	Continuous	Future	Conditional

Present Simple
I	begin
you	begin
he/she/it	begins
we	begin
you	begin
they	begin

Present Continuous
I	am	beginning
you	are	beginning
he/she/it	is	beginning
we	are	beginning
you	are	beginning
they	are	beginning

Future I
I	will	begin
you	will	begin
he/she/it	will	begin
we	will	begin
you	will	begin
they	will	begin

Conditional II
I	would	begin
you	would	begin
he/she/it	would	begin
we	would	begin
you	would	begin
they	would	begin

Past Simple
I	began
you	began
he/she/it	began
we	began
you	began
they	began

Past Continuous
I	was	beginning
you	were	beginning
he/she/it	was	beginning
we	were	beginning
you	were	beginning
they	were	beginning

Future I Continuous
I	will be	beginning
you	will be	beginning
he/she/it	will be	beginning
we	will be	beginning
you	will be	beginning
they	will be	beginning

Conditional Past
I	would have	begun
you	would have	begun
he/she/it	would have	begun
we	would have	begun
you	would have	begun
they	would have	begun

Present Perfect
I	have	begun
you	have	begun
he/she/it	has	begun
we	have	begun
you	have	begun
they	have	begun

Present Perfect Continuous
I	have	been	beginning
you	have	been	beginning
he/she/it	has	been	beginning
we	have	been	beginning
you	have	been	beginning
they	have	been	beginning

Future II
I	will have	begun
you	will have	begun
he/she/it	will have	begun
we	will have	begun
you	will have	begun
they	will have	begun

Imperative
begin

Gerund
beginning

Past Participle
begun

Past Perfect
I	had	begun
you	had	begun
he/she/it	had	begun
we	had	begun
you	had	begun
they	had	begun

Past Perfect Continuous
I	had	been	beginning
you	had	been	beginning
he/she/it	had	been	beginning
we	had	been	beginning
you	had	been	beginning
they	had	been	beginning

Future II Continuous
I	will have been beginning
you	will have been beginning
he/she/it	will have been beginning
we	will have been beginning
you	will have been beginning
they	will have been beginning

Regelmäßig

book | buchen

Simple

Present Simple

I	book
you	book
he/she/it	books
we	book
you	book
they	book

Past Simple

I	booked
you	booked
he/she/it	booked
we	booked
you	booked
they	booked

Present Perfect

I	have	booked
you	have	booked
he/she/it	has	booked
we	have	booked
you	have	booked
they	have	booked

Past Perfect

I	had	booked
you	had	booked
he/she/it	had	booked
we	had	booked
you	had	booked
they	had	booked

Continuous

Present Continuous

I	am	booking
you	are	booking
he/she/it	is	booking
we	are	booking
you	are	booking
they	are	booking

Past Continuous

I	was	booking
you	were	booking
he/she/it	was	booking
we	were	booking
you	were	booking
they	were	booking

Present Perfect Continuous

I	have	been	booking
you	have	been	booking
he/she/it	has	been	booking
we	have	been	booking
you	have	been	booking
they	have	been	booking

Past Perfect Continuous

I	had	been	booking
you	had	been	booking
he/she/it	had	been	booking
we	had	been	booking
you	had	been	booking
they	had	been	booking

Future

Future I

I	will	book
you	will	book
he/she/it	will	book
we	will	book
you	will	book
they	will	book

Future I Continuous

I	will be		booking
you	will be		booking
he/she/it	will be		booking
we	will be		booking
you	will be		booking
they	will be		booking

Future II

I	will have	booked
you	will have	booked
he/she/it	will have	booked
we	will have	booked
you	will have	booked
they	will have	booked

Future II Contlimous

I	will have been booking
you	will have been booking
he/she/it	will have been booking
we	will have been booking
you	will have been booking
they	will have been booking

Conditional

Conditional II

I	would book
you	would book
he/she/it	would book
we	would book
you	would book
they	would book

Conditional Past

I	would have booked
you	would have booked
he/she/it	would have booked
we	would have booked
you	would have booked
they	would have booked

Imperative
book

Gerund
booking

Past Participle
booked

Unregelmäßig

break | (zer)brechen

Simple

Present Simple
I	break
you	break
he/she/it	breaks
we	break
you	break
they	break

Past Simple
I	broke
you	broke
he/she/it	broke
we	broke
you	broke
they	broke

Present Perfect
I	have	broken
you	have	broken
he/she/it	has	broken
we	have	broken
you	have	broken
they	have	broken

Past Perfect
I	had	broken
you	had	broken
he/she/it	had	broken
we	had	broken
you	had	broken
they	had	broken

Continuous

Present Continuous
I	am	breaking
you	are	breaking
he/she/it	is	breaking
we	are	breaking
you	are	breaking
they	are	breaking

Past Continuous
I	was	breaking
you	were	breaking
he/she/it	was	breaking
we	were	breaking
you	were	breaking
they	were	breaking

Present Perfect Continuous
I	have	been	breaking
you	have	been	breaking
he/she/it	has	been	breaking
we	have	been	breaking
you	have	been	breaking
they	have	been	breaking

Past Perfect Continuous
I	had	been	breaking
you	had	been	breaking
he/she/it	had	been	breaking
we	had	been	breaking
you	had	been	breaking
they	had	been	breaking

Future

Future I
I	will	break
you	will	break
he/she/it	will	break
we	will	break
you	will	break
they	will	break

Future I Continuous
I	will be	breaking
you	will be	breaking
he/she/it	will be	breaking
we	will be	breaking
you	will be	breaking
they	will be	breaking

Future II
I	will have	broken
you	will have	broken
he/she/it	will have	broken
we	will have	broken
you	will have	broken
they	will have	broken

Future II Continuous
I	will have been breaking
you	will have been breaking
he/she/it	will have been breaking
we	will have been breaking
you	will have been breaking
they	will have been breaking

Conditional

Conditional II
I	would	break
you	would	break
he/she/it	would	break
we	would	break
you	would	break
they	would	break

Conditional Past
I	would have	broken
you	would have	broken
he/she/it	would have	broken
we	would have	broken
you	would have	broken
they	would have	broken

Imperative
break

Gerund
breaking

Past Participle
broken

bring | (mit)bringen

Simple

Present Simple
I	bring
you	bring
he/she/it	brings
we	bring
you	bring
they	bring

Past Simple
I	brought
you	brought
he/she/it	brought
we	brought
you	brought
they	brought

Present Perfect
I	have	brought
you	have	brought
he/she/it	has	brought
we	have	brought
you	have	brought
they	have	brought

Past Perfect
I	had	brought
you	had	brought
he/she/it	had	brought
we	had	brought
you	had	brought
they	had	brought

Continuous

Present Continuous
I	am	bringing
you	are	bringing
he/she/it	is	bringing
we	are	bringing
you	are	bringing
they	are	bringing

Past Continuous
I	was	bringing
you	were	bringing
he/she/it	was	bringing
we	were	bringing
you	were	bringing
they	were	bringing

Present Perfect Continuous
I	have	been	bringing
you	have	been	bringing
he/she/it	has	been	bringing
we	have	been	bringing
you	have	been	bringing
they	have	been	bringing

Past Perfect Continuous
I	had	been	bringing
you	had	been	bringing
he/she/it	had	been	bringing
we	had	been	bringing
you	had	been	bringing
they	had	been	bringing

Future

Future I
I	will	bring
you	will	bring
he/she/it	will	bring
we	will	bring
you	will	bring
they	will	bring

Future I Continuous
I	will be	bringing
you	will be	bringing
he/she/it	will be	bringing
we	will be	bringing
you	will be	bringing
they	will be	bringing

Future II
I	will have	brought
you	will have	brought
he/she/it	will have	brought
we	will have	brought
you	will have	brought
they	will have	brought

Future II Continuous
I	will have been	bringing
you	will have been	bringing
he/she/it	will have been	bringing
we	will have been	bringing
you	will have been	bringing
they	will have been	bringing

Conditional

Conditional II
I	would bring
you	would bring
he/she/it	would bring
we	would bring
you	would bring
they	would bring

Conditional Past
I	would have	brought
you	would have	brought
he/she/it	would have	brought
we	would have	brought
you	would have	brought
they	would have	brought

Imperative
bring

Gerund
bringing

Past Participle
brought

Unregelmäßig

buy | kaufen

Simple

Present Simple
I	buy
you	buy
he/she/it	buys
we	buy
you	buy
they	buy

Past Simple
I	bought
you	bought
he/she/it	bought
we	bought
you	bought
they	bought

Present Perfect
I	have	bought
you	have	bought
he/she/it	has	bought
we	have	bought
you	have	bought
they	have	bought

Past Perfect
I	had	bought
you	had	bought
he/she/it	had	bought
we	had	bought
you	had	bought
they	had	bought

Continuous

Present Continuous
I	am	buying
you	are	buying
he/she/it	is	buying
we	are	buying
you	are	buying
they	are	buying

Past Continuous
I	was	buying
you	were	buying
he/she/it	was	buying
we	were	buying
you	were	buying
they	were	buying

Present Perfect Continuous
I	have been	buying
you	have been	buying
he/she/it	has been	buying
we	have been	buying
you	have been	buying
they	have been	buying

Past Perfect Continuous
I	had been	buying
you	had been	buying
he/she/it	had been	buying
we	had been	buying
you	had been	buying
they	had been	buying

Future

Future I
I	will	buy
you	will	buy
he/she/it	will	buy
we	will	buy
you	will	buy
they	will	buy

Future I Continuous
I	will be	buying
you	will be	buying
he/she/it	will be	buying
we	will be	buying
you	will be	buying
they	will be	buying

Future II
I	will have	bought
you	will have	bought
he/she/it	will have	bought
we	will have	bought
you	will have	bought
they	will have	bought

Future II Continuous
I	will have been buying
you	will have been buying
he/she/it	will have been buying
we	will have been buying
you	will have been buying
they	will have been buying

Conditional

Conditional II
I	would buy
you	would buy
he/she/it	would buy
we	would buy
you	would buy
they	would buy

Conditional Past
I	would have	bought
you	would have	bought
he/she/it	would have	bought
we	would have	bought
you	would have	bought
they	would have	bought

Imperative
buy

Gerund
buying

Past Participle
bought

Regelmäßig

call | (an)rufen

Simple

Present Simple
I	call
you	call
he/she/it	calls
we	call
you	call
they	call

Past Simple
I	called
you	called
he/she/it	called
we	called
you	called
they	called

Present Perfect
I	have	called
you	have	called
he/she/it	has	called
we	have	called
you	have	called
they	have	called

Past Perfect
I	had	called
you	had	called
he/she/it	had	called
we	had	called
you	had	called
they	had	called

Continuous

Present Continuous
I	am	calling
you	are	calling
he/she/it	is	calling
we	are	calling
you	are	calling
they	are	calling

Past Continuous
I	was	calling
you	were	calling
he/she/it	was	calling
we	were	calling
you	were	calling
they	were	calling

Present Perfect Continuous
I	have	been	calling
you	have	been	calling
he/she/it	has	been	calling
we	have	been	calling
you	have	been	calling
they	have	been	calling

Past Perfect Continuous
I	had	been	calling
you	had	been	calling
he/she/it	had	been	calling
we	had	been	calling
you	had	been	calling
they	had	been	calling

Future

Future I
I	will	call
you	will	call
he/she/it	will	call
we	will	call
you	will	call
they	will	call

Future I Continuous
I	will be	calling
you	will be	calling
he/she/it	will be	calling
we	will be	calling
you	will be	calling
they	will be	calling

Future II
I	will have	called
you	will have	called
he/she/it	will have	called
we	will have	called
you	will have	called
they	will have	called

Future II Continuous
I	will have been	calling
you	will have been	calling
he/she/it	will have been	calling
we	will have been	calling
you	will have been	calling
they	will have been	calling

Conditional

Conditional II
I	would	call
you	would	call
he/she/it	would	call
we	would	call
you	would	call
they	would	call

Conditional Past
I	would have	called
you	would have	called
he/she/it	would have	called
we	would have	called
you	would have	called
they	would have	called

Imperative
call

Gerund
calling

Past Participle
called

Unregelmäßig
Modalverb

can/be able to | können

Unvollständiges Modalverb –
Can bzw. *could* werden nur im
Present Simple und *Past Simple*
verwendet.
Can/could/be able to haben keine
Verlaufsform.

Simple

Present Simple
I	can/am	able to
you	can/are	able to
he/she/it	can/is	able to
we	can/are	able to
you	can/are	able to
they	can/are	able to

Past Simple
I	could/was	able to
you	could/were	able to
he/she/it	could/was	able to
we	could/were	able to
you	could/were	able to
they	could/were	able to

Present Perfect
I	have been	able to
you	have been	able to
he/she/it	has been	able to
we	have been	able to
you	have been	able to
they	have been	able to

Past Perfect
I	had been	able to
you	had been	able to
he/she/it	had been	able to
we	had been	able to
you	had been	able to
they	had been	able to

Continuous

Present Continuous
—

Past Continuous
—

Present Perfect Continuous
—

Past Perfect Continuous
—

Future

Future I
I	will	be able to
you	will	be able to
he/she/it	will	be able to
we	will	be able to
you	will	be able to
they	will	be able to

Future I Continuous
—

Future II
I	will have been	able to
you	will have been	able to
he/she/it	will have been	able to
we	will have been	able to
you	will have been	able to
they	will have been	able to

Future II Continuous
—

Conditional

Conditional II
I	would	be able to
you	would	be able to
he/she/it	would	be able to
we	would	be able to
you	would	be able to
they	would	be able to

Conditional Past
I	would have been able to
you	would have been able to
he/she/it	would have been able to
we	would have been able to
you	would have been able to
they	would have been able to

Imperative
be able to

Gerund
being able to

Past Participle
been able to

Im AE wird das **-l** nicht verdoppelt.

cancel | absagen/stornieren

Simple

Present Simple

I	cancel
you	cancel
he/she/it	cancels
we	cancel
you	cancel
they	cancel

Past Simple

I	cancelled
you	cancelled
he/she/it	cancelled
we	cancelled
you	cancelled
they	cancelled

Present Perfect

I	have cancelled
you	have cancelled
he/she/it	has cancelled
we	have cancelled
you	have cancelled
they	have cancelled

Past Perfect

I	had cancelled
you	had cancelled
he/she/it	had cancelled
we	had cancelled
you	had cancelled
they	had cancelled

Continuous

Present Continuous

I	am	cancelling
you	are	cancelling
he/she/it	is	cancelling
we	are	cancelling
you	are	cancelling
they	are	cancelling

Past Continuous

I	was	cancelling
you	were	cancelling
he/she/it	was	cancelling
we	were	cancelling
you	were	cancelling
they	were	cancelling

Present Perfect Continuous

I	have been	cancelling
you	have been	cancelling
he/she/it	has been	cancelling
we	have been	cancelling
you	have been	cancelling
they	have been	cancelling

Past Perfect Continuous

I	had been	cancelling
you	had been	cancelling
he/she/it	had been	cancelling
we	had been	cancelling
you	had been	cancelling
they	had been	cancelling

Future

Future I

I	will	cancel
you	will	cancel
he/she/it	will	cancel
we	will	cancel
you	will	cancel
they	will	cancel

Future I Continuous

I	will be cancelling
you	will be cancelling
he/she/it	will be cancelling
we	will be cancelling
you	will be cancelling
they	will be cancelling

Future II

I	will have	cancelled
you	will have	cancelled
he/she/it	will have	cancelled
we	will have	cancelled
you	will have	cancelled
they	will have	cancelled

Future II Continuous

I	will have been cancelling
you	will have been cancelling
he/she/it	will have been cancelling
we	will have been cancelling
you	will have been cancelling
they	will have been cancelling

Conditional

Conditional II

I	would cancel
you	would cancel
he/she/it	would cancel
we	would cancel
you	would cancel
they	would cancel

Conditional Past

I	would have cancelled
you	would have cancelled
he/she/it	would have cancelled
we	would have cancelled
you	would have cancelled
they	would have cancelled

Imperative

cancel

Gerund

cancelling

Past Participle

cancelled

Regelmäßig

carry | tragen

-y wird *-ie* vor *-s/-y* wird *-i* vor *-ed* (siehe S. 152)

Simple

Present Simple

I	carry
you	carry
he/she/it	carries
we	carry
you	carry
they	carry

Past Simple

I	carried
you	carried
he/she/it	carried
we	carried
you	carried
they	carried

Present Perfect

I	have	carried
you	have	carried
he/she/it	has	carried
we	have	carried
you	have	carried
they	have	carried

Past Perfect

I	had	carried
you	had	carried
he/she/it	had	carried
we	had	carried
you	had	carried
they	had	carried

Continuous

Present Continuous

I	am	carrying
you	are	carrying
he/she/it	is	carrying
we	are	carrying
you	are	carrying
they	are	carrying

Past Continuous

I	was	carrying
you	were	carrying
he/she/it	was	carrying
we	were	carrying
you	were	carrying
they	were	carrying

Present Perfect Continuous

I	have	been	carrying
you	have	been	carrying
he/she/it	has	been	carrying
we	have	been	carrying
you	have	been	carrying
they	have	been	carrying

Past Perfect Continuous

I	had	been	carrying
you	had	been	carrying
he/she/it	had	been	carrying
we	had	been	carrying
you	had	been	carrying
they	had	been	carrying

Future

Future I

I	will	carry
you	will	carry
he/she/it	will	carry
we	will	carry
you	will	carry
they	will	carry

Future I Continuous

I	will be carrying
you	will be carrying
he/she/it	will be carrying
we	will be carrying
you	will be carrying
they	will be carrying

Future II

I	will have carried
you	will have carried
he/she/it	will have carried
we	will have carried
you	will have carried
they	will have carried

Future II Continuous

I	will have been carrying
you	will have been carrying
he/she/it	will have been carrying
we	will have been carrying
you	will have been carrying
they	will have been carrying

Conditional

Conditional II

I	would	carry
you	would	carry
he/she/it	would	carry
we	would	carry
you	would	carry
they	would	carry

Conditional Past

I	would have carried
you	would have carried
he/she/it	would have carried
we	would have carried
you	would have carried
they	would have carried

Imperative

carry

Gerund

carrying

Past Participle

carried

Unregelmäßig

+ *-es* in 3. Person Singular
(siehe S. 152)

catch | fangen

Simple

Present Simple

I	catch
you	catch
he/she/it	catches
we	catch
you	catch
they	catch

Past Simple

I	caught
you	caught
he/she/it	caught
we	caught
you	caught
they	caught

Present Perfect

I	have	caught
you	have	caught
he/she/it	has	caught
we	have	caught
you	have	caught
they	have	caught

Past Perfect

I	had	caught
you	had	caught
he/she/it	had	caught
we	had	caught
you	had	caught
they	had	caught

Continuous

Present Continuous

I	am	catching
you	are	catching
he/she/it	is	catching
we	are	catching
you	are	catching
they	are	catching

Past Continuous

I	was	catching
you	were	catching
he/she/it	was	catching
we	were	catching
you	were	catching
they	were	catching

Present Perfect Continuous

I	have	been	catching
you	have	been	catching
he/she/it	has	been	catching
we	have	been	catching
you	have	been	catching
they	have	been	catching

Past Perfect Continuous

I	had	been	catching
you	had	been	catching
he/she/it	had	been	catching
we	had	been	catching
you	had	been	catching
they	had	been	catching

Future

Future I

I	will	catch
you	will	catch
he/she/it	will	catch
we	will	catch
you	will	catch
they	will	catch

Future I Continuous

I	will be catching
you	will be catching
he/she/it	will be catching
we	will be catching
you	will be catching
they	will be catching

Future II

I	will have	caught
you	will have	caught
he/she/it	will have	caught
we	will have	caught
you	will have	caught
they	will have	caught

Future II Continuous

I	will have been catching
you	will have been catching
he/she/it	will have been catching
we	will have been catching
you	will have been catching
they	will have been catching

Conditional

Conditional II

I	would	catch
you	would	catch
he/she/it	would	catch
we	would	catch
you	would	catch
they	would	catch

Conditional Past

I	would have	caught
you	would have	caught
he/she/it	would have	caught
we	would have	caught
you	would have	caught
they	would have	caught

Imperative

catch

Gerund

catching

Past Participle

caught

Regelmäßig

change | ändern/wechseln

+ *-ing* wird ∅ (siehe S. 153)/
+ *-d* nicht *-ed* (siehe S. 152)

Simple	Continuous	Future	Conditional

Present Simple
I	change
you	change
he/she/it	changes
we	change
you	change
they	change

Past Simple
I	changed
you	changed
he/she/it	changed
we	changed
you	changed
they	changed

Present Perfect
I	have	changed
you	have	changed
he/she/it	has	changed
we	have	changed
you	have	changed
they	have	changed

Past Perfect
I	had	changed
you	had	changed
he/she/it	had	changed
we	had	changed
you	had	changed
they	had	changed

Present Continuous
I	am	changing
you	are	changing
he/she/it	is	changing
we	are	changing
you	are	changing
they	are	changing

Past Continuous
I	was	changing
you	were	changing
he/she/it	was	changing
we	were	changing
you	were	changing
they	were	changing

Present Perfect Continuous
I	have	been	changing
you	have	been	changing
he/she/it	has	been	changing
we	have	been	changing
you	have	been	changing
they	have	been	changing

Past Perfect Continuous
I	had	been	changing
you	had	been	changing
he/she/it	had	been	changing
we	had	been	changing
you	had	been	changing
they	had	been	changing

Future I
I	will	change
you	will	change
he/she/it	will	change
we	will	change
you	will	change
they	will	change

Future I Continuous
I	will be	changing
you	will be	changing
he/she/it	will be	changing
we	will be	changing
you	will be	changing
they	will be	changing

Future II
I	will have changed
you	will have changed
he/she/it	will have changed
we	will have changed
you	will have changed
they	will have changed

Future II Continuous
I	will have been changing
you	will have been changing
he/she/it	will have been changing
we	will have been changing
you	will have been changing
they	will have been changing

Conditional II
I	would change
you	would change
he/she/it	would change
we	would change
you	would change
they	would change

Conditional Past
I	would have changed
you	would have changed
he/she/it	would have changed
we	would have changed
you	would have changed
they	would have changed

Imperative
change

Gerund
changing

Past Participle
changed

+ *-ing* wird ∉(siehe S. 153)

choose | (aus)wählen

Simple

Present Simple

I	choose
you	choose
he/she/it	chooses
we	choose
you	choose
they	choose

Past Simple

I	chose
you	chose
he/she/it	chose
we	chose
you	chose
they	chose

Present Perfect

I	have	chosen
you	have	chosen
he/she/it	has	chosen
we	have	chosen
you	have	chosen
they	have	chosen

Past Perfect

I	had	chosen
you	had	chosen
he/she/it	had	chosen
we	had	chosen
you	had	chosen
they	had	chosen

Continuous

Present Continuous

I	am	choosing
you	are	choosing
he/she/it	is	choosing
we	are	choosing
you	are	choosing
they	are	choosing

Past Continuous

I	was	choosing
you	were	choosing
he/she/it	was	choosing
we	were	choosing
you	were	choosing
they	were	choosing

Present Perfect Continuous

I	have	been	choosing
you	have	been	choosing
he/she/it	has	been	choosing
we	have	been	choosing
you	have	been	choosing
they	have	been	choosing

Past Perfect Continuous

I	had	been	choosing
you	had	been	choosing
he/she/it	had	been	choosing
we	had	been	choosing
you	had	been	choosing
they	had	been	choosing

Future

Future I

I	will	choose
you	will	choose
he/she/it	will	choose
we	will	choose
you	will	choose
they	will	choose

Future I Continuous

I	will be	choosing
you	will be	choosing
he/she/it	will be	choosing
we	will be	choosing
you	will be	choosing
they	will be	choosing

Future II

I	will have	chosen
you	will have	chosen
he/she/it	will have	chosen
we	will have	chosen
you	will have	chosen
they	will have	chosen

Future II Continuous

I	will have been choosing
you	will have been choosing
he/she/it	will have been choosing
we	will have been choosing
you	will have been choosing
they	will have been choosing

Conditional

Conditional II

I	would	choose
you	would	choose
he/she/it	would	choose
we	would	choose
you	would	choose
they	would	choose

Conditional Past

I	would have	chosen
you	would have	chosen
he/she/it	would have	chosen
we	would have	chosen
you	would have	chosen
they	would have	chosen

Imperative

choose

Gerund

choosing

Past Participle

chosen

Regelmäßig

close | schließen

+ **-ing** wird ~~e~~ (siehe S. 153)/
+ **-d** nicht **-ed** (siehe S. 152)

Simple

Present Simple
I	close
you	close
he/she/it	closes
we	close
you	close
they	close

Past Simple
I	closed
you	closed
he/she/it	closed
we	closed
you	closed
they	closed

Present Perfect
I	have	closed
you	have	closed
he/she/it	has	closed
we	have	closed
you	have	closed
they	have	closed

Past Perfect
I	had	closed
you	had	closed
he/she/it	had	closed
we	had	closed
you	had	closed
they	had	closed

Continuous

Present Continuous
I	am	closing
you	are	closing
he/she/it	is	closing
we	are	closing
you	are	closing
they	are	closing

Past Continuous
I	was	closing
you	were	closing
he/she/it	was	closing
we	were	closing
you	were	closing
they	were	closing

Present Perfect Continuous
I	have	been	closing
you	have	been	closing
he/she/it	has	been	closing
we	have	been	closing
you	have	been	closing
they	have	been	closing

Past Perfect Continuous
I	had	been	closing
you	had	been	closing
he/she/it	had	been	closing
we	had	been	closing
you	had	been	closing
they	had	been	closing

Future

Future I
I	will	close
you	will	close
he/she/it	will	close
we	will	close
you	will	close
they	will	close

Future I Continuous
I	will be	closing
you	will be	closing
he/she/it	will be	closing
we	will be	closing
you	will be	closing
they	will be	closing

Future II
I	will have closed
you	will have closed
he/she/it	will have closed
we	will have closed
you	will have closed
they	will have closed

Future II Continuous
I	will have been closing
you	will have been closing
he/she/it	will have been closing
we	will have been closing
you	will have been closing
they	will have been closing

Conditional

Conditional II
I	would	close
you	would	close
he/she/it	would	close
we	would	close
you	would	close
they	would	close

Conditional Past
I	would have closed
you	would have closed
he/she/it	would have closed
we	would have closed
you	would have closed
they	would have closed

Imperative
close

Gerund
closing

Past Participle
closed

Unregelmäßig

+ *-ing* wird ∉(siehe S. 153)

come | kommen

Simple

Present Simple

I	come
you	come
he/she/it	comes
we	come
you	come
they	come

Past Simple

I	came
you	came
he/she/it	came
we	came
you	came
they	came

Present Perfect

I	have come
you	have come
he/she/it	has come
we	have come
you	have come
they	have come

Past Perfect

I	had come
you	had come
he/she/it	had come
we	had come
you	had come
they	had come

Continuous

Present Continuous

I	am	coming
you	are	coming
he/she/it	is	coming
we	are	coming
you	are	coming
they	are	coming

Past Continuous

I	was	coming
you	were	coming
he/she/it	was	coming
we	were	coming
you	were	coming
they	were	coming

Present Perfect Continuous

I	have been coming
you	have been coming
he/she/it	has been coming
we	have been coming
you	have been coming
they	have been coming

Past Perfect Continuous

I	had been coming
you	had been coming
he/she/it	had been coming
we	had been coming
you	had been coming
they	had been coming

Future

Future I

I	will come
you	will come
he/she/it	will come
we	will come
you	will come
they	will come

Future I Continuous

I	will be coming
you	will be coming
he/she/it	will be coming
we	will be coming
you	will be coming
they	will be coming

Future II

I	will have come
you	will have come
he/she/it	will have come
we	will have come
you	will have come
they	will have come

Future II Continuous

I	will have been coming
you	will have been coming
he/she/it	will have been coming
we	will have been coming
you	will have been coming
they	will have been coming

Conditional

Conditional II

I	would come
you	would come
he/she/it	would come
we	would come
you	would come
they	would come

Conditional Past

I	would have come
you	would have come
he/she/it	would have come
we	would have come
you	would have come
they	would have come

Imperative

come

Gerund

coming

Past Participle

come

Regelmäßig

cook | kochen

Simple

Present Simple

I	cook
you	cook
he/she/it	cooks
we	cook
you	cook
they	cook

Past Simple

I	cooked
you	cooked
he/she/it	cooked
we	cooked
you	cooked
they	cooked

Present Perfect

I	have	cooked
you	have	cooked
he/she/it	has	cooked
we	have	cooked
you	have	cooked
they	have	cooked

Past Perfect

I	had	cooked
you	had	cooked
he/she/it	had	cooked
we	had	cooked
you	had	cooked
they	had	cooked

Continuous

Present Continuous

I	am	cooking
you	are	cooking
he/she/it	is	cooking
we	are	cooking
you	are	cooking
they	are	cooking

Past Continuous

I	was	cooking
you	were	cooking
he/she/it	was	cooking
we	were	cooking
you	were	cooking
they	were	cooking

Present Perfect Continuous

I	have	been	cooking
you	have	been	cooking
he/she/it	has	been	cooking
we	have	been	cooking
you	have	been	cooking
they	have	been	cooking

Past Perfect Continuous

I	had	been	cooking
you	had	been	cooking
he/she/it	had	been	cooking
we	had	been	cooking
you	had	been	cooking
they	had	been	cooking

Future

Future I

I	will	cook
you	will	cook
he/she/it	will	cook
we	will	cook
you	will	cook
they	will	cook

Future I Continuous

I	will	becooking
you	will	becooking
he/she/it	will	becooking
we	will	becooking
you	will	becooking
they	will	becooking

Future II

I	will have	cooked
you	will have	cooked
he/she/it	will have	cooked
we	will have	cooked
you	will have	cooked
they	will have	cooked

Future II Continuous

I	will have been	cooking
you	will have been	cooking
he/she/it	will have been	cooking
we	will have been	cooking
you	will have been	cooking
they	will have been	cooking

Conditional

Conditional II

I	would	cook
you	would	cook
he/she/it	would	cook
we	would	cook
you	would	cook
they	would	cook

Conditional Past

I	would have	cooked
you	would have	cooked
he/she/it	would have	cooked
we	would have	cooked
you	would have	cooked
they	would have	cooked

Imperative

cook

Gerund

cooking

Past Participle

cooked

Unregelmäßig

cost | kosten

Simple

Present Simple

I	cost
you	cost
he/she/it	costs
we	cost
you	cost
they	cost

Past Simple

I	cost
you	cost
he/she/it	cost
we	cost
you	cost
they	cost

Present Perfect

I	have	cost
you	have	cost
he/she/it	has	cost
we	have	cost
you	have	cost
they	have	cost

Past Perfect

I	had	cost
you	had	cost
he/she/it	had	cost
we	had	cost
you	had	cost
they	had	cost

Continuous

Present Continuous

I	am	costing
you	are	costing
he/she/it	is	costing
we	are	costing
you	are	costing
they	are	costing

Past Continuous

I	was	costing
you	were	costing
he/she/it	was	costing
we	were	costing
you	were	costing
they	were	costing

Present Perfect Continuous

I	have	been	costing
you	have	been	costing
he/she/it	has	been	costing
we	have	been	costing
you	have	been	costing
they	have	been	costing

Past Perfect Continuous

I	had	been	costing
you	had	been	costing
he/she/it	had	been	costing
we	had	been	costing
you	had	been	costing
they	had	been	costing

Future

Future I

I	will	cost
you	will	cost
he/she/it	will	cost
we	will	cost
you	will	cost
they	will	cost

Future I Continuous

I	will be	costing
you	will be	costing
he/she/it	will be	costing
we	will be	costing
you	will be	costing
they	will be	costing

Future II

I	will have	cost
you	will have	cost
he/she/it	will have	cost
we	will have	cost
you	will have	cost
they	will have	cost

Future II Continuous

I	will have been costing
you	will have been costing
he/she/it	will have been costing
we	will have been costing
you	will have been costing
they	will have been costing

Conditional

Conditional II

I	would cost
you	would cost
he/she/it	would cost
we	would cost
you	would cost
they	would cost

Conditional Past

I	would have	cost
you	would have	cost
he/she/it	would have	cost
we	would have	cost
you	would have	cost
they	would have	cost

Imperative

cost

Gerund

costing

Past Participle

cost

Unregelmäßig

cut | schneiden

Konsonantenverdopplung
(siehe S. 152)

Simple

Present Simple
I	cut
you	cut
he/she/it	cuts
we	cut
you	cut
they	cut

Past Simple
I	cut
you	cut
he/she/it	cut
we	cut
you	cut
they	cut

Present Perfect
I	have	cut
you	have	cut
he/she/it	has	cut
we	have	cut
you	have	cut
they	have	cut

Past Perfect
I	had	cut
you	had	cut
he/she/it	had	cut
we	had	cut
you	had	cut
they	had	cut

Continuous

Present Continuous
I	am	cutting
you	are	cutting
he/she/it	is	cutting
we	are	cutting
you	are	cutting
they	are	cutting

Past Continuous
I	was	cutting
you	were	cutting
he/she/it	was	cutting
we	were	cutting
you	were	cutting
they	were	cutting

Present Perfect Continuous
I	have	been	cutting
you	have	been	cutting
he/she/it	has	been	cutting
we	have	been	cutting
you	have	been	cutting
they	have	been	cutting

Past Perfect Continuous
I	had	been	cutting
you	had	been	cutting
he/she/it	had	been	cutting
we	had	been	cutting
you	had	been	cutting
they	had	been	cutting

Future

Future I
I	will	cut
you	will	cut
he/she/it	will	cut
we	will	cut
you	will	cut
they	will	cut

Future I Continuous
I	will be	cutting
you	will be	cutting
he/she/it	will be	cutting
we	will be	cutting
you	will be	cutting
they	will be	cutting

Future II
I	will have	cut
you	will have	cut
he/she/it	will have	cut
we	will have	cut
you	will have	cut
they	will have	cut

Future II Continuous
I	will have been cutting
you	will have been cutting
he/she/it	will have been cutting
we	will have been cutting
you	will have been cutting
they	will have been cutting

Conditional

Conditional II
I	would cut
you	would cut
he/she/it	would cut
we	would cut
you	would cut
they	would cut

Conditional Past
I	would have	cut
you	would have	cut
he/she/it	would have	cut
we	would have	cut
you	would have	cut
they	would have	cut

Imperative
cut

Gerund
cutting

Past Participle
cut

Regelmäßig

decide | entscheiden

+ *-ing* wird ∅(siehe S. 153)/
+ *-d* nicht *-ed* (siehe S. 152)

Simple

Present Simple

I	decide
you	decide
he/she/it	decides
we	decide
you	decide
they	decide

Past Simple

I	decided
you	decided
he/she/it	decided
we	decided
you	decided
they	decided

Present Perfect

I	have	decided
you	have	decided
he/she/it	has	decided
we	have	decided
you	have	decided
they	have	decided

Past Perfect

I	had	decided
you	had	decided
he/she/it	had	decided
we	had	decided
you	had	decided
they	had	decided

Continuous

Present Continuous

I	am	deciding
you	are	deciding
he/she/it	is	deciding
we	are	deciding
you	are	deciding
they	are	deciding

Past Continuous

I	was	deciding
you	were	deciding
he/she/it	was	deciding
we	were	deciding
you	were	deciding
they	were	deciding

Present Perfect Continuous

I	have	been	deciding
you	have	been	deciding
he/she/it	has	been	deciding
we	have	been	deciding
you	have	been	deciding
they	have	been	deciding

Past Perfect Continuous

I	had	been	deciding
you	had	been	deciding
he/she/it	had	been	deciding
we	had	been	deciding
you	had	been	deciding
they	had	been	deciding

Future

Future I

I	will	decide
you	will	decide
he/she/it	will	decide
we	will	decide
you	will	decide
they	will	decide

Future I Continuous

I	will be	deciding
you	will be	deciding
he/she/it	will be	deciding
we	will be	deciding
you	will be	deciding
they	will be	deciding

Future II

I	will have decided
you	will have decided
he/she/it	will have decided
we	will have decided
you	will have decided
they	will have decided

Future II Continuous

I	will have been deciding
you	will have been deciding
he/she/it	will have been deciding
we	will have been deciding
you	will have been deciding
they	will have been deciding

Conditional

Conditional II

I	would	decide
you	would	decide
he/she/it	would	decide
we	would	decide
you	would	decide
they	would	decide

Conditional Past

I	would have	decided
you	would have	decided
he/she/it	would have	decided
we	would have	decided
you	would have	decided
they	would have	decided

Imperative

decide

Gerund

deciding

Past Participle

decided

Unregelmäßig

do | tun/machen

+ **-es** in 3. Person Singular
(siehe S. 152)

Simple

Present Simple
I	do
you	do
he/she/it	does
we	do
you	do
they	do

Past Simple
I	did
you	did
he/she/it	did
we	did
you	did
they	did

Present Perfect
I	have	done
you	have	done
he/she/it	has	done
we	have	done
you	have	done
they	have	done

Past Perfect
I	had	done
you	had	done
he/she/it	had	done
we	had	done
you	had	done
they	had	done

Continuous

Present Continuous
I	am	doing
you	are	doing
he/she/it	is	doing
we	are	doing
you	are	doing
they	are	doing

Past Continuous
I	was	doing
you	were	doing
he/she/it	was	doing
we	were	doing
you	were	doing
they	were	doing

Present Perfect Continuous
I	have	been	doing
you	have	been	doing
he/she/it	has	been	doing
we	have	been	doing
you	have	been	doing
they	have	been	doing

Past Perfect Continuous
I	had	been	doing
you	had	been	doing
he/she/it	had	been	doing
we	had	been	doing
you	had	been	doing
they	had	been	doing

Future

Future I
I	will	do
you	will	do
he/she/it	will	do
we	will	do
you	will	do
they	will	do

Future I Continuous
I	will be	doing
you	will be	doing
he/she/it	will be	doing
we	will be	doing
you	will be	doing
they	will be	doing

Future II
I	will have	done
you	will have	done
he/she/it	will have	done
we	will have	done
you	will have	done
they	will have	done

Future II Continuous
I	will have been	doing
you	will have been	doing
he/she/it	will have been	doing
we	will have been	doing
you	will have been	doing
they	will have been	doing

Conditional

Conditional II
I	would do
you	would do
he/she/it	would do
we	would do
you	would do
they	would do

Conditional Past
I	would have	done
you	would have	done
he/she/it	would have	done
we	would have	done
you	would have	done
they	would have	done

Imperative
do

Gerund
doing

Past Participle
done

Unregelmäßig

drink | trinken

Simple

Present Simple

I	drink
you	drink
he/she/it	drinks
we	drink
you	drink
they	drink

Past Simple

I	drank
you	drank
he/she/it	drank
we	drank
you	drank
they	drank

Present Perfect

I	have	drunk
you	have	drunk
he/she/it	has	drunk
we	have	drunk
you	have	drunk
they	have	drunk

Past Perfect

I	had	drunk
you	had	drunk
he/she/it	had	drunk
we	had	drunk
you	had	drunk
they	had	drunk

Continuous

Present Continuous

I	am	drinking
you	are	drinking
he/she/it	is	drinking
we	are	drinking
you	are	drinking
they	are	drinking

Past Continuous

I	was	drinking
you	were	drinking
he/she/it	was	drinking
we	were	drinking
you	were	drinking
they	were	drinking

Present Perfect Continuous

I	have	been	drinking
you	have	been	drinking
he/she/it	has	been	drinking
we	have	been	drinking
you	have	been	drinking
they	have	been	drinking

Past Perfect Continuous

I	had	been	drinking
you	had	been	drinking
he/she/it	had	been	drinking
we	had	been	drinking
you	had	been	drinking
they	had	been	drinking

Future

Future I

I	will	drink
you	will	drink
he/she/it	will	drink
we	will	drink
you	will	drink
they	will	drink

Future I Continuous

I	will be drinking
you	will be drinking
he/she/it	will be drinking
we	will be drinking
you	will be drinking
they	will be drinking

Future II

I	will have	drunk
you	will have	drunk
he/she/it	will have	drunk
we	will have	drunk
you	will have	drunk
they	will have	drunk

Future II Continuous

I	will have been	drinking
you	will have been	drinking
he/she/it	will have been	drinking
we	will have been	drinking
you	will have been	drinking
they	will have been	drinking

Conditional

Conditional II

I	would	drink
you	would	drink
he/she/it	would	drink
we	would	drink
you	would	drink
they	would	drink

Conditional Past

I	would have	drunk
you	would have	drunk
he/she/it	would have	drunk
we	would have	drunk
you	would have	drunk
they	would have	drunk

Imperative

drink

Gerund

drinking

Past Participle

drunk

Unregelmäßig

drive | fahren

+ *-ing* wird ∅ (siehe S. 153)

Simple

Present Simple

I	drive
you	drive
he/she/it	drives
we	drive
you	drive
they	drive

Past Simple

I	drove
you	drove
he/she/it	drove
we	drove
you	drove
they	drove

Present Perfect

I	have	driven
you	have	driven
he/she/it	has	driven
we	have	driven
you	have	driven
they	have	driven

Past Perfect

I	had	driven
you	had	driven
he/she/it	had	driven
we	had	driven
you	had	driven
they	had	driven

Continuous

Present Continuous

I	am	driving
you	are	driving
he/she/it	is	driving
we	are	driving
you	are	driving
they	are	driving

Past Continuous

I	was	driving
you	were	driving
he/she/it	was	driving
we	were	driving
you	were	driving
they	were	driving

Present Perfect Continuous

I	have	been	driving
you	have	been	driving
he/she/it	has	been	driving
we	have	been	driving
you	have	been	driving
they	have	been	driving

Past Perfect Continuous

I	had	been	driving
you	had	been	driving
he/she/it	had	been	driving
we	had	been	driving
you	had	been	driving
they	had	been	driving

Future

Future I

I	will	drive
you	will	drive
he/she/it	will	drive
we	will	drive
you	will	drive
they	will	drive

Future I Continuous

I	will be	driving
you	will be	driving
he/she/it	will be	driving
we	will be	driving
you	will be	driving
they	will be	driving

Future II

I	will have	driven
you	will have	driven
he/she/it	will have	driven
we	will have	driven
you	will have	driven
they	will have	driven

Future II Continuous

I	will have been driving
you	will have been driving
he/she/it	will have been driving
we	will have been driving
you	will have been driving
they	will have been driving

Conditional

Conditional II

I	would	drive
you	would	drive
he/she/it	would	drive
we	would	drive
you	would	drive
they	would	drive

Conditional Past

I	would have	driven
you	would have	driven
he/she/it	would have	driven
we	would have	driven
you	would have	driven
they	would have	driven

Imperative

drive

Gerund

driving

Past Participle

driven

Unregelmäßig

eat | essen

Simple	Continuous	Future	Conditional

Present Simple

I	eat
you	eat
he/she/it	eats
we	eat
you	eat
they	eat

Past Simple

I	ate
you	ate
he/she/it	ate
we	ate
you	ate
they	ate

Present Perfect

I	have	eaten
you	have	eaten
he/she/it	has	eaten
we	have	eaten
you	have	eaten
they	have	eaten

Past Perfect

I	had	eaten
you	had	eaten
he/she/it	had	eaten
we	had	eaten
you	had	eaten
they	had	eaten

Present Continuous

I	am	eating
you	are	eating
he/she/it	is	eating
we	are	eating
you	are	eating
they	are	eating

Past Continuous

I	was	eating
you	were	eating
he/she/it	was	eating
we	were	eating
you	were	eating
they	were	eating

Present Perfect Continuous

I	have	been	eating
you	have	been	eating
he/she/it	has	been	eating
we	have	been	eating
you	have	been	eating
they	have	been	eating

Past Perfect Continuous

I	had	been	eating
you	had	been	eating
he/she/it	had	been	eating
we	had	been	eating
you	had	been	eating
they	had	been	eating

Future I

I	will	eat
you	will	eat
he/she/it	will	eat
we	will	eat
you	will	eat
they	will	eat

Future I Continuous

I	will be	eating
you	will be	eating
he/she/it	will be	eating
we	will be	eating
you	will be	eating
they	will be	eating

Future II

I	will have	eaten
you	will have	eaten
he/she/it	will have	eaten
we	will have	eaten
you	will have	eaten
they	will have	eaten

Future II Continuous

I	will have been eating
you	will have been eating
he/she/it	will have been eating
we	will have been eating
you	will have been eating
they	will have been eating

Conditional II

I	would	eat
you	would	eat
he/she/it	would	eat
we	would	eat
you	would	eat
they	would	eat

Conditional Past

I	would have	eaten
you	would have	eaten
he/she/it	would have	eaten
we	would have	eaten
you	would have	eaten
they	would have	eaten

Imperative

eat

Gerund

eating

Past Participle

eaten

Regelmäßig

enjoy | genießen

Simple

Present Simple

	enjoy
	enjoy
you	enjoy
he/she/it	enjoys
we	enjoy
you	enjoy
they	enjoy

Past Simple

I	enjoyed
you	enjoyed
he/she/it	enjoyed
we	enjoyed
you	enjoyed
they	enjoyed

Present Perfect

I	have	enjoyed
you	have	enjoyed
he/she/it	has	enjoyed
we	have	enjoyed
you	have	enjoyed
they	have	enjoyed

Past Perfect

I	had	enjoyed
you	had	enjoyed
he/she/it	had	enjoyed
we	had	enjoyed
you	had	enjoyed
they	had	enjoyed

Continuous

Present Continuous

I	am	enjoying
you	are	enjoying
he/she/it	is	enjoying
we	are	enjoying
you	are	enjoying
they	are	enjoying

Past Continuous

I	was	enjoying
you	were	enjoying
he/she/it	was	enjoying
we	were	enjoying
you	were	enjoying
they	were	enjoying

Present Perfect Continuous

I	have	been	enjoying
you	have	been	enjoying
he/she/it	has	been	enjoying
we	have	been	enjoying
you	have	been	enjoying
they	have	been	enjoying

Past Perfect Continuous

I	had	been	enjoying
you	had	been	enjoying
he/she/it	had	been	enjoying
we	had	been	enjoying
you	had	been	enjoying
they	had	been	enjoying

Future

Future I

I	will	enjoy
you	will	enjoy
he/she/it	will	enjoy
we	will	enjoy
you	will	enjoy
they	will	enjoy

Future I Continuous

I	will be enjoying
you	will be enjoying
he/she/it	will be enjoying
we	will be enjoying
you	will be enjoying
they	will be enjoying

Future II

I	will have	enjoyed
you	will have	enjoyed
he/she/it	will have	enjoyed
we	will have	enjoyed
you	will have	enjoyed
they	will have	enjoyed

Future II Continuous

I	will have been	enjoying
you	will have been	enjoying
he/she/it	will have been	enjoying
we	will have been	enjoying
you	will have been	enjoying
they	will have been	enjoying

Conditional

Conditional II

I	would	enjoy
you	would	enjoy
he/she/it	would	enjoy
we	would	enjoy
you	would	enjoy
they	would	enjoy

Conditional Past

I	would have	enjoyed
you	would have	enjoyed
he/she/it	would have	enjoyed
we	would have	enjoyed
you	would have	enjoyed
they	would have	enjoyed

Imperative
enjoy

Gerund
enjoying

Past Participle
enjoyed

Unregelmäßig

fall | fallen/stürzen

Simple	Continuous	Future	Conditional

Present Simple

I	fall
you	fall
he/she/it	falls
we	fall
you	fall
they	fall

Present Continuous

I	am	falling
you	are	falling
he/she/it	is	falling
we	are	falling
you	are	falling
they	are	falling

Future I

I	will	fall
you	will	fall
he/she/it	will	fall
we	will	fall
you	will	fall
they	will	fall

Conditional II

I	would fall
you	would fall
he/she/it	would fall
we	would fall
you	would fall
they	would fall

Past Simple

I	fell
you	fell
he/she/it	fell
we	fell
you	fell
they	fell

Past Continuous

I	was	falling
you	were	falling
he/she/it	was	falling
we	were	falling
you	were	falling
they	were	falling

Future I Continuous

I	will be	falling
you	will be	falling
he/she/it	will be	falling
we	will be	falling
you	will be	falling
they	will be	falling

Conditional Past

I	would have	fallen
you	would have	fallen
he/she/it	would have	fallen
we	would have	fallen
you	would have	fallen
they	would have	fallen

Present Perfect

I	have	fallen
you	have	fallen
he/she/it	has	fallen
we	have	fallen
you	have	fallen
they	have	fallen

Present Perfect Continuous

I	have	been	falling
you	have	been	falling
he/she/it	has	been	falling
we	have	been	falling
you	have	been	falling
they	have	been	falling

Future II

I	will have	fallen
you	will have	fallen
he/she/it	will have	fallen
we	will have	fallen
you	will have	fallen
they	will have	fallen

Imperative

fall

Gerund

falling

Past Participle

fallen

Past Perfect

I	had	fallen
you	had	fallen
he/she/it	had	fallen
we	had	fallen
you	had	fallen
they	had	fallen

Past Perfect Continuous

I	had	been	falling
you	had	been	falling
he/she/it	had	been	falling
we	had	been	falling
you	had	been	falling
they	had	been	falling

Future II Continuous

I	will have been falling
you	will have been falling
he/she/it	will have been falling
we	will have been falling
you	will have been falling
they	will have been falling

Unregelmäßig

feel | fühlen

Simple

Present Simple

I	feel
you	feel
he/she/it	feels
we	feel
you	feel
they	feel

Past Simple

I	felt
you	felt
he/she/it	felt
we	felt
you	felt
they	felt

Present Perfect

I	have	felt
you	have	felt
he/she/it	has	felt
we	have	felt
you	have	felt
they	have	felt

Past Perfect

I	had	felt
you	had	felt
he/she/it	had	felt
we	had	felt
you	had	felt
they	had	felt

Continuous

Present Continuous

I	am	feeling
you	are	feeling
he/she/it	is	feeling
we	are	feeling
you	are	feeling
they	are	feeling

Past Continuous

I	was	feeling
you	were	feeling
he/she/it	was	feeling
we	were	feeling
you	were	feeling
they	were	feeling

Present Perfect Continuous

I	have	been	feeling
you	have	been	feeling
he/she/it	has	been	feeling
we	have	been	feeling
you	have	been	feeling
they	have	been	feeling

Past Perfect Continuous

I	had	been	feeling
you	had	been	feeling
he/she/it	had	been	feeling
we	had	been	feeling
you	had	been	feeling
they	had	been	feeling

Future

Future I

I	will	feel
you	will	feel
he/she/it	will	feel
we	will	feel
you	will	feel
they	will	feel

Future I Continuous

I	will be	feeling
you	will be	feeling
he/she/it	will be	feeling
we	will be	feeling
you	will be	feeling
they	will be	feeling

Future II

I	will have	felt
you	will have	felt
he/she/it	will have	felt
we	will have	felt
you	will have	felt
they	will have	felt

Future II Continuous

I	will have been feeling
you	will have been feeling
he/she/it	will have been feeling
we	will have been feeling
you	will have been feeling
they	will have been feeling

Conditional

Conditional II

I	would	feel
you	would	feel
he/she/it	would	feel
we	would	feel
you	would	feel
they	would	feel

Conditional Past

I	would have	felt
you	would have	felt
he/she/it	would have	felt
we	would have	felt
you	would have	felt
they	would have	felt

Imperative

feel

Gerund

feeling

Past Participle

felt

Unregelmäßig

find | finden

Simple

Present Simple
I	find
you	find
he/she/it	finds
we	find
you	find
they	find

Past Simple
I	found
you	found
he/she/it	found
we	found
you	found
they	found

Present Perfect
I	have found
you	have found
he/she/it	has found
we	have found
you	have found
they	have found

Past Perfect
I	had found
you	had found
he/she/it	had found
we	had found
you	had found
they	had found

Continuous

Present Continuous
I	am finding
you	are finding
he/she/it	is finding
we	are finding
you	are finding
they	are finding

Past Continuous
I	was finding
you	were finding
he/she/it	was finding
we	were finding
you	were finding
they	were finding

Present Perfect Continuous
I	have been finding
you	have been finding
he/she/it	has been finding
we	have been finding
you	have been finding
they	have been finding

Past Perfect Continuous
I	had been finding
you	had been finding
he/she/it	had been finding
we	had been finding
you	had been finding
they	had been finding

Future

Future I
I	will find
you	will find
he/she/it	will find
we	will find
you	will find
they	will find

Future I Continuous
I	will be finding
you	will be finding
he/she/it	will be finding
we	will be finding
you	will be finding
they	will be finding

Future II
I	will have found
you	will have found
he/she/it	will have found
we	will have found
you	will have found
they	will have found

Future II Continuous
I	will have been finding
you	will have been finding
he/she/it	will have been finding
we	will have been finding
you	will have been finding
they	will have been finding

Conditional

Conditional II
I	would find
you	would find
he/she/it	would find
we	would find
you	would find
they	would find

Conditional Past
I	would have found
you	would have found
he/she/it	would have found
we	would have found
you	would have found
they	would have found

Imperative
find

Gerund
finding

Past Participle
found

Unregelmäßig

fly | fliegen

-y wird *-ie* vor *-s* (siehe S. 152)

Simple

Present Simple

I	fly
you	fly
he/she/it	flies
we	fly
you	fly
they	fly

Past Simple

I	flew
you	flew
he/she/it	flew
we	flew
you	flew
they	flew

Present Perfect

I	have	flown
you	have	flown
he/she/it	has	flown
we	have	flown
you	have	flown
they	have	flown

Past Perfect

I	had	flown
you	had	flown
he/she/it	had	flown
we	had	flown
you	had	flown
they	had	flown

Continuous

Present Continuous

I	am	flying
you	are	flying
he/she/it	is	flying
we	are	flying
you	are	flying
they	are	flying

Past Continuous

I	was	flying
you	were	flying
he/she/it	was	flying
we	were	flying
you	were	flying
they	were	flying

Present Perfect Continuous

I	have	been	flying
you	have	been	flying
he/she/it	has	been	flying
we	have	been	flying
you	have	been	flying
they	have	been	flying

Past Perfect Continuous

I	had	been	flying
you	had	been	flying
he/she/it	had	been	flying
we	had	been	flying
you	had	been	flying
they	had	been	flying

Future

Future I

I	will	fly
you	will	fly
he/she/it	will	fly
we	will	fly
you	will	fly
they	will	fly

Future I Continuous

I	will be flying
you	will be flying
he/she/it	will be flying
we	will be flying
you	will be flying
they	will be flying

Future II

I	will have	flown
you	will have	flown
he/she/it	will have	flown
we	will have	flown
you	will have	flown
they	will have	flown

Future II Continuous

I	will have been flying
you	will have been flying
he/she/it	will have been flying
we	will have been flying
you	will have been flying
they	will have been flying

Conditional

Conditional II

I	would	fly
you	would	fly
he/she/it	would	fly
we	would	fly
you	would	fly
they	would	fly

Conditional Past

I	would have	flown
you	would have	flown
he/she/it	would have	flown
we	would have	flown
you	would have	flown
they	would have	flown

Imperative

fly

Gerund

flying

Past Participle

flown

Konsonantenverdopplung
(siehe S. 152)

Unregelmäßig

forget | vergessen

Simple

Present Simple

I	forget
you	forget
he/she/it	forgets
we	forget
you	forget
they	forget

Past Simple

I	forgot
you	forgot
he/she/it	forgot
we	forgot
you	forgot
they	forgot

Present Perfect

I	have	forgotten
you	have	forgotten
he/she/it	has	forgotten
we	have	forgotten
you	have	forgotten
they	have	forgotten

Past Perfect

I	had	forgotten
you	had	forgotten
he/she/it	had	forgotten
we	had	forgotten
you	had	forgotten
they	had	forgotten

Continuous

Present Continuous

I	am	forgetting
you	are	forgetting
he/she/it	is	forgetting
we	are	forgetting
you	are	forgetting
they	are	forgetting

Past Continuous

I	was	forgetting
you	were	forgetting
he/she/it	was	forgetting
we	were	forgetting
you	were	forgetting
they	were	forgetting

Present Perfect Continuous

I	have	been	forgetting
you	have	been	forgetting
he/she/it	has	been	forgetting
we	have	been	forgetting
you	have	been	forgetting
they	have	been	forgetting

Past Perfect Continuous

I	had	been	forgetting
you	had	been	forgetting
he/she/it	had	been	forgetting
we	had	been	forgetting
you	had	been	forgetting
they	had	been	forgetting

Future

Future I

I	will	forget
you	will	forget
he/she/it	will	forget
we	will	forget
you	will	forget
they	will	forget

Future I Continuous

I	will be	forgetting
you	will be	forgetting
he/she/it	will be	forgetting
we	will be	forgetting
you	will be	forgetting
they	will be	forgetting

Future II

I	will have	forgotten
you	will have	forgotten
he/she/it	will have	forgotten
we	will have	forgotten
you	will have	forgotten
they	will have	forgotten

Future II Continuous

I	will have been forgetting
you	will have been forgetting
he/she/it	will have been forgetting
we	will have been forgetting
you	will have been forgetting
they	will have been forgetting

Conditional

Conditional II

I	would forget
you	would forget
he/she/it	would forget
we	would forget
you	would forget
they	would forget

Conditional Past

I	would have	forgotten
you	would have	forgotten
he/she/it	would have	forgotten
we	would have	forgotten
you	would have	forgotten
they	would have	forgotten

Imperative
forget

Gerund
forgetting

Past Participle
forgotten

Unregelmäßig

get | bekommen

Im AE ist das Partizip Perfekt
gotten.

Simple

Present Simple

I	get
you	get
he/she/it	gets
we	get
you	get
they	get

Past Simple

I	got
you	got
he/she/it	got
we	got
you	got
they	got

Present Perfect

I	have	got
you	have	got
he/she/it	has	got
we	have	got
you	have	got
they	have	got

Past Perfect

I	had	got
you	had	got
he/she/it	had	got
we	had	got
you	had	got
they	had	got,

Continuous

Present Continuous

I	am	getting
you	are	getting
he/she/it	is	getting
we	are	getting
you	are	getting
they	are	getting

Past Continuous

I	was	getting
you	were	getting
he/she/it	was	getting
we	were	getting
you	were	getting
they	were	getting

Present Perfect Continuous

I	have	been	getting
you	have	been	getting
he/she/it	has	been	getting
we	have	been	getting
you	have	been	getting
they	have	been	getting

Past Perfect Continuous

I	had	been	getting
you	had	been	getting
he/she/it	had	been	getting
we	had	been	getting
you	had	been	getting
they	had	been	getting

Future

Future I

I	will	get
you	will	get
he/she/it	will	get
we	will	get
you	will	get
they	will	get

Future I Continuous

I	will be	getting
you	will be	getting
he/she/it	will be	getting
we	will be	getting
you	will be	getting
they	will be	getting

Future II

I	will have	got
you	will have	got
he/she/it	will have	got
we	will have	got
you	will have	got
they	will have	got

Future II Continuous

I	will have been getting
you	will have been getting
he/she/it	will have been getting
we	will have been getting
you	will have been getting
they	will have been getting

Conditional

Conditional II

I	would get
you	would get
he/she/it	would get
we	would get
you	would get
they	would get

Conditional Past

I	would have	got
you	would have	got
he/she/it	would have	got
we	would have	got
you	would have	got
they	would have	got

Imperative
get

Gerund
getting

Past Participle
got/gotten

Unregelmäßig

give | geben

+ *-ing* wird ~~e~~ (siehe S. 152)

Simple

Present Simple
I	give
you	give
he/she/it	gives
we	give
you	give
they	give

Past Simple
I	gave
you	gave
he/she/it	gave
we	gave
you	gave
they	gave

Present Perfect
I	have	given
you	have	given
he/she/it	has	given
we	have	given
you	have	given
they	have	given

Past Perfect
I	had	given
you	had	given
he/she/it	had	given
we	had	given
you	had	given
they	had	given

Continuous

Present Continuous
I	am	giving
you	are	giving
he/she/it	is	giving
we	are	giving
you	are	giving
they	are	giving

Past Continuous
I	was	giving
you	were	giving
he/she/it	was	giving
we	were	giving
you	were	giving
they	were	giving

Present Perfect Continuous
I	have	been	giving
you	have	been	giving
he/she/it	has	been	giving
we	have	been	giving
you	have	been	giving
they	have	been	giving

Past Perfect Continuous
I	had	been	giving
you	had	been	giving
he/she/it	had	been	giving
we	had	been	giving
you	had	been	giving
they	had	been	giving

Future

Future I
I	will	give
you	will	give
he/she/it	will	give
we	will	give
you	will	give
they	will	give

Future I Continuous
I	will be	giving
you	will be	giving
he/she/it	will be	giving
we	will be	giving
you	will be	giving
they	will be	giving

Future II
I	will have	given
you	will have	given
he/she/it	will have	given
we	will have	given
you	will have	given
they	will have	given

Future II Continuous
I	will have been giving
you	will have been giving
he/she/it	will have been giving
we	will have been giving
you	will have been giving
they	will have been giving

Conditional

Conditional II
I	would	give
you	would	give
he/she/it	would	give
we	would	give
you	would	give
they	would	give

Conditional Past
I	would have	given
you	would have	given
he/she/it	would have	given
we	would have	given
you	would have	given
they	would have	given

Imperative
give

Gerund
giving

Past Participle
given

Unregelmäßig

go | gehen

+ **-es** in 3. Person Singular
(siehe S. 152)

Simple

Present Simple

I	go
you	go
he/she/it	goes
we	go
you	go
they	go

Past Simple

I	went
you	went
he/she/it	went
we	went
you	went
they	went

Present Perfect

I	have	gone
you	have	gone
he/she/it	has	gone
we	have	gone
you	have	gone
they	have	gone

Past Perfect

I	had	gone
you	had	gone
he/she/it	had	gone
we	had	gone
you	had	gone
they	had	gone

Continuous

Present Continuous

I	am	going
you	are	going
he/she/it	is	going
we	are	going
you	are	going
they	are	going

Past Continuous

I	was	going
you	were	going
he/she/it	was	going
we	were	going
you	were	going
they	were	going

Present Perfect Continuous

I	have been	going
you	have been	going
he/she/it	has been	going
we	have been	going
you	have been	going
they	have been	going

Past Perfect Continuous

I	had been	going
you	had been	going
he/she/it	had been	going
we	had been	going
you	had been	going
they	had been	going

Future

Future I

I	will	go
you	will	go
he/she/it	will	go
we	will	go
you	will	go
they	will	go

Future I Continuous

I	will be	going
you	will be	going
he/she/it	will be	going
we	will be	going
you	will be	going
they	will be	going

Future II

I	will have	gone
you	will have	gone
he/she/it	will have	gone
we	will have	gone
you	will have	gone
they	will have	gone

Future II Continuous

I	will have been	going
you	will have been	going
he/she/it	will have been	going
we	will have been	going
you	will have been	going
they	will have been	going

Conditional

Conditional II

I	would go
you	would go
he/she/it	would go
we	would go
you	would go
they	would go

Conditional Past

I	would have	gone
you	would have	gone
he/she/it	would have	gone
we	would have	gone
you	would have	gone
they	would have	gone

Imperative

go

Gerund

going

Past Participle

gone

Unregelmäßig
Voll- und Hilfsverb

+ *-ing* wird ∉(siehe S. 152)

have | haben

Simple

Present Simple

I	have
you	have
he/she/it	has
we	have
you	have
they	have

Past Simple

I	had
you	had
he/she/it	had
we	had
you	had
they	had

Present Perfect

I	have had
you	have had
he/she/it	has had
we	have had
you	have had
they	have had

Past Perfect

I	had had
you	had had
he/she/it	had had
we	had had
you	had had
they	had had

Continuous

Present Continuous

I	am	having
you	are	having
he/she/it	is	having
we	are	having
you	are	having
they	are	having

Past Continuous

I	was	having
you	were	having
he/she/it	was	having
we	were	having
you	were	having
they	were	having

Present Perfect Continuous

I	have been having
you	have been having
he/she/it	has been having
we	have been having
you	have been having
they	have been having

Past Perfect Continuous

I	had been having
you	had been having
he/she/it	had been having
we	had been having
you	had been having
they	had been having

Future

Future I

I	will have
you	will have
he/she/it	will have
we	will have
you	will have
they	will have

Future I Continuous

I	will be having
you	will be having
he/she/it	will be having
we	will be having
you	will be having
they	will be having

Future II

I	will have had
you	will have had
he/she/it	will have had
we	will have had
you	will have had
they	will have had

Future II Continuous

I	will have been having
you	will have been having
he/she/it	will have been having
we	will have been having
you	will have been having
they	will have been having

Conditional

Conditional II

I	would have
you	would have
he/she/it	would have
we	would have
you	would have
they	would have

Conditional Past

I	would have had
you	would have had
he/she/it	would have had
we	would have had
you	would have had
they	would have had

Imperative

have

Gerund

having

Past Participle

had

Unregelmäßig

hear | hören

Simple

Present Simple

I	hear
you	hear
he/she/it	hears
we	hear
you	hear
they	hear

Past Simple

I	heard
you	heard
he/she/it	heard
we	heard
you	heard
they	heard

Present Perfect

I	have	heard
you	have	heard
he/she/it	has	heard
we	have	heard
you	have	heard
they	have	heard

Past Perfect

I	had	heard
you	had	heard
he/she/it	had	heard
we	had	heard
you	had	heard
they	had	heard

Continuous

Present Continuous

I	am	hearing
you	are	hearing
he/she/it	is	hearing
we	are	hearing
you	are	hearing
they	are	hearing

Past Continuous

I	was	hearing
you	were	hearing
he/she/it	was	hearing
we	were	hearing
you	were	hearing
they	were	hearing

Present Perfect Continuous

I	have	been	hearing
you	have	been	hearing
he/she/it	has	been	hearing
we	have	been	hearing
you	have	been	hearing
they	have	been	hearing

Past Perfect Continuous

I	had	been	hearing
you	had	been	hearing
he/she/it	had	been	hearing
we	had	been	hearing
you	had	been	hearing
they	had	been	hearing

Future

Future I

I	will	hear
you	will	hear
he/she/it	will	hear
we	will	hear
you	will	hear
they	will	hear

Future I Continuous

I	will be	hearing
you	will be	hearing
he/she/it	will be	hearing
we	will be	hearing
you	will be	hearing
they	will be	hearing

Future II

I	will have	heard
you	will have	heard
he/she/it	will have	heard
we	will have	heard
you	will have	heard
they	will have	heard

Future II Continuous

I	will have been	hearing
you	will have been	hearing
he/she/it	will have been	hearing
we	will have been	hearing
you	will have been	hearing
they	will have been	hearing

Conditional

Conditional II

I	would hear
you	would hear
he/she/it	would hear
we	would hear
you	would hear
they	would hear

Conditional Past

I	would have	heard
you	would have	heard
he/she/it	would have	heard
we	would have	heard
you	would have	heard
they	would have	heard

Imperative

hear

Gerund

hearing

Past Participle

heard

Regelmäßig

help | helfen

Simple

Present Simple
I	help
you	help
he/she/it	helps
we	help
you	help
they	help

Past Simple
I	helped
you	helped
he/she/it	helped
we	helped
you	helped
they	helped

Present Perfect
I	have	helped
you	have	helped
he/she/it	has	helped
we	have	helped
you	have	helped
they	have	helped

Past Perfect
I	had	helped
you	had	helped
he/she/it	had	helped
we	had	helped
you	had	helped
they	had	helped

Continuous

Present Continuous
I	am	helping
you	are	helping
he/she/it	is	helping
we	are	helping
you	are	helping
they	are	helping

Past Continuous
I	was	helping
you	were	helping
he/she/it	was	helping
we	were	helping
you	were	helping
they	were	helping

Present Perfect Continuous
I	have	been	helping
you	have	been	helping
he/she/it	has	been	helping
we	have	been	helping
you	have	been	helping
they	have	been	helping

Past Perfect Continuous
I	had	been	helping
you	had	been	helping
he/she/it	had	been	helping
we	had	been	helping
you	had	been	helping
they	had	been	helping

Future

Future I
I	will	help
you	will	help
he/she/it	will	help
we	will	help
you	will	help
they	will	help

Future I Continuous
I	will be helping
you	will be helping
he/she/it	will be helping
we	will be helping
you	will be helping
they	will be helping

Future II
I	will have helped
you	will have helped
he/she/it	will have helped
we	will have helped
you	will have helped
they	will have helped

Future II Continuous
I	will have been helping
you	will have been helping
he/she/it	will have been helping
we	will have been helping
you	will have been helping
they	will have been helping

Conditional

Conditional II
I	would help
you	would help
he/she/it	would help
we	would help
you	would help
they	would help

Conditional Past
I	would have	helped
you	would have	helped
he/she/it	would have	helped
we	would have	helped
you	would have	helped
they	would have	helped

Imperative
help

Gerund
helping

Past Participle
helped

Unregelmäßig

hit | schlagen

Konsonantenverdopplung
(siehe S. 152)

Simple	Continuous	Future	Conditional

Present Simple

I	hit
you	hit
he/she/it	hits
we	hit
you	hit
they	hit

Present Continuous

I	am	hitting
you	are	hitting
he/she/it	is	hitting
we	are	hitting
you	are	hitting
they	are	hitting

Future I

I	will	hit
you	will	hit
he/she/it	will	hit
we	will	hit
you	will	hit
they	will	hit

Conditional II

I	would hit
you	would hit
he/she/it	would hit
we	would hit
you	would hit
they	would hit

Past Simple

I	hit
you	hit
he/she/it	hit
we	hit
you	hit
they	hit

Past Continuous

I	was	hitting
you	were	hitting
he/she/it	was	hitting
we	were	hitting
you	were	hitting
they	were	hitting

Future I Continuous

I	will be	hitting
you	will be	hitting
he/she/it	will be	hitting
we	will be	hitting
you	will be	hitting
they	will be	hitting

Conditional Past

I	would have	hit
you	would have	hit
he/she/it	would have	hit
we	would have	hit
you	would have	hit
they	would have	hit

Present Perfect

I	have	hit
you	have	hit
he/she/it	has	hit
we	have	hit
you	have	hit
they	have	hit

Present Perfect Continuous

I	have been	hitting
you	have been	hitting
he/she/it	has been	hitting
we	have been	hitting
you	have been	hitting
they	have been	hitting

Future II

I	will have	hit
you	will have	hit
he/she/it	will have	hit
we	will have	hit
you	will have	hit
they	will have	hit

Imperative

hit

Gerund

hitting

Past Participle

hit

Past Perfect

I	had	hit
you	had	hit
he/she/it	had	hit
we	had	hit
you	had	hit
they	had	hit

Past Perfect Continuous

I	had	been	hitting
you	had	been	hitting
he/she/it	had	been	hitting
we	had	been	hitting
you	had	been	hitting
they	had	been	hitting

Future II Continuous

I	will have been hitting
you	will have been hitting
he/she/it	will have been hitting
we	will have been hitting
you	will have been hitting
they	will have been hitting

Unregelmäßig

hurt | wehtun

Simple

Present Simple

I	hurt
you	hurt
he/she/it	hurts
we	hurt
you	hurt
they	hurt

Past Simple

I	hurt
you	hurt
he/she/it	hurt
we	hurt
you	hurt
they	hurt

Present Perfect

I	have	hurt
you	have	hurt
he/she/it	has	hurt
we	have	hurt
you	have	hurt
they	have	hurt

Past Perfect

I	had	hurt
you	had	hurt
he/she/it	had	hurt
we	had	hurt
you	had	hurt
they	had	hurt

Continuous

Present Continuous

I	am	hurting
you	are	hurting
he/she/it	is	hurting
we	are	hurting
you	are	hurting
they	are	hurting

Past Continuous

I	was	hurting
you	were	hurting
he/she/it	was	hurting
we	were	hurting
you	were	hurting
they	were	hurting

Present Perfect Continuous

I	have	been	hurting
you	have	been	hurting
he/she/it	has	been	hurting
we	have	been	hurting
you	have	been	hurting
they	have	been	hurting

Past Perfect Continuous

I	had	been	hurting
you	had	been	hurting
he/she/it	had	been	hurting
we	had	been	hurting
you	had	been	hurting
they	had	been	hurting

Future

Future I

I	will	hurt
you	will	hurt
he/she/it	will	hurt
we	will	hurt
you	will	hurt
they	will	hurt

Future I Continuous

I	will be	hurting
you	will be	hurting
he/she/it	will be	hurting
we	will be	hurting
you	will be	hurting
they	will be	hurting

Future II

I	will have	hurt
you	will have	hurt
he/she/it	will have	hurt
we	will have	hurt
you	will have	hurt
they	will have	hurt

Future II Continuous

I	will have been hurting
you	will have been hurting
he/she/it	will have been hurting
we	will have been hurting
you	will have been hurting
they	will have been hurting

Conditional

Conditional II

I	would	hurt
you	would	hurt
he/she/it	would	hurt
we	would	hurt
you	would	hurt
they	would	hurt

Conditional Past

I	would have	hurt
you	would have	hurt
he/she/it	would have	hurt
we	would have	hurt
you	would have	hurt
they	would have	hurt

Imperative

hurt

Gerund

hurting

Past Participle

hurt

Regelmäßig

invite | einladen

+ **-ing** wird ø (siehe S. 153)/
+ **-d** nicht **-ed** (siehe S. 152)

Simple

Present Simple

I	invite
you	invite
he/she/it	invites
we	invite
you	invite
they	invite

Past Simple

I	invited
you	invited
he/she/it	invited
we	invited
you	invited
they	invited

Present Perfect

I	have	invited
you	have	invited
he/she/it	has	invited
we	have	invited
you	have	invited
they	have	invited

Past Perfect

I	had	invited
you	had	invited
he/she/it	had	invited
we	had	invited
you	had	invited
they	had	invited

Continuous

Present Continuous

I	am	inviting
you	are	inviting
he/she/it	is	inviting
we	are	inviting
you	are	inviting
they	are	inviting

Past Continuous

I	was	inviting
you	were	inviting
he/she/it	was	inviting
we	were	inviting
you	were	inviting
they	were	inviting

Present Perfect Continuous

I	have	been	inviting
you	have	been	inviting
he/she/it	has	been	inviting
we	have	been	inviting
you	have	been	inviting
they	have	been	inviting

Past Perfect Continuous

I	had	been	inviting
you	had	been	inviting
he/she/it	had	been	inviting
we	had	been	inviting
you	had	been	inviting
they	had	been	inviting

Future

Future I

I	will	invite
you	will	invite
he/she/it	will	invite
we	will	invite
you	will	invite
they	will	invite

Future I Continuous

I	will be	inviting
you	will be	inviting
he/she/it	will be	inviting
we	will be	inviting
you	will be	inviting
they	will be	inviting

Future II

I	will have invited
you	will have invited
he/she/it	will have invited
we	will have invited
you	will have invited
they	will have invited

Future II Continuous

I	will have been inviting
you	will have been inviting
he/she/it	will have been inviting
we	will have been inviting
you	will have been inviting
they	will have been inviting

Conditional

Conditional II

I	would invite
you	would invite
he/she/it	would invite
we	would invite
you	would invite
they	would invite

Conditional Past

I	would have	invited
you	would have	invited
he/she/it	would have	invited
we	would have	invited
you	would have	invited
they	would have	invited

Imperative

invite

Gerund

inviting

Past Participle

invited

Know hat keine Verlaufsform

know | wissen/kennen

Simple

Present Simple
I	know
you	know
he/she/it	knows
we	know
you	know
they	know

Past Simple
I	knew
you	knew
he/she/it	knew
we	knew
you	knew
they	knew

Present Perfect
I	have	known
you	have	known
he/she/it	has	known
we	have	known
you	have	known
they	have	known

Past Perfect
I	had	known
you	had	known
he/she/it	had	known
we	had	known
you	had	known
they	had	known

Continuous

Present Continuous
—

Past Continuous
—

Present Perfect Continuous
—

Past Perfect Continuous
—

Future

Future I
I	will	know
you	will	know
he/she/it	will	know
we	will	know
you	will	know
they	will	know

Future I Continuous
—

Future II
I	will have	known
you	will have	known
he/she/it	will have	known
we	will have	known
you	will have	known
they	will have	known

Future II Continuous
—

Conditional

Conditional II
I	would know
you	would know
he/she/it	would know
we	would know
you	would know
they	would know

Conditional Past
I	would have	known
you	would have	known
he/she/it	would have	known
we	would have	known
you	would have	known
they	would have	known

Imperative
know

Gerund
knowing

Past Participle
known

Unregelmäßig

learn | lernen

Im AE ist das Partizip Perfekt *learned*.

Simple

Present Simple
I	learn
you	learn
he/she/it	learns
we	learn
you	learn
they	learn

Past Simple
I	learnt
you	learnt
he/she/it	learnt
we	learnt
you	learnt
they	learnt

Present Perfect
I	have	learnt
you	have	learnt
he/she/it	has	learnt
we	have	learnt
you	have	learnt
they	have	learnt

Past Perfect
I	had	learnt
you	had	learnt
he/she/it	had	learnt
we	had	learnt
you	had	learnt
they	had	learnt

Continuous

Present Continuous
I	am	learning
you	are	learning
he/she/it	is	learning
we	are	learning
you	are	learning
they	are	learning

Past Continuous
I	was	learning
you	were	learning
he/she/it	was	learning
we	were	learning
you	were	learning
they	were	learning

Present Perfect Continuous
I	have	been	learning
you	have	been	learning
he/she/it	has	been	learning
we	have	been	learning
you	have	been	learning
they	have	been	learning

Past Perfect Continuous
I	had	been	learning
you	had	been	learning
he/she/it	had	been	learning
we	had	been	learning
you	had	been	learning
they	had	been	learning

Future

Future I
I	will	learn
you	will	learn
he/she/it	will	learn
we	will	learn
you	will	learn
they	will	learn

Future I Continuous
I	will be	learning
you	will be	learning
he/she/it	will be	learning
we	will be	learning
you	will be	learning
they	will be	learning

Future II
I	will have	learnt
you	will have	learnt
he/she/it	will have	learnt
we	will have	learnt
you	will have	learnt
they	will have	learnt

Future II Continuous
I	will have been	learning
you	will have been	learning
he/she/it	will have been	learning
we	will have been	learning
you	will have been	learning
they	will have been	learning

Conditional

Conditional II
I	would learn
you	would learn
he/she/it	would learn
we	would learn
you	would learn
they	would learn

Conditional Past
I	would have	learnt
you	would have	learnt
he/she/it	would have	learnt
we	would have	learnt
you	would have	learnt
they	would have	learnt

Imperative
learn

Gerund
learning

Past Participle
learnt/learned

Unregelmäßig

+ *-ing* wird ~~e~~ (siehe S. 153)

leave | verlassen

Simple

Present Simple
I	leave
you	leave
he/she/it	leaves
we	leave
you	leave
they	leave

Past Simple
I	left
you	left
he/she/it	left
we	left
you	left
they	left

Present Perfect
I	have	left
you	have	left
he/she/it	has	left
we	have	left
you	have	left
they	have	left

Past Perfect
I	had	left
you	had	left
he/she/it	had	left
we	had	left
you	had	left
they	had	left

Continuous

Present Continuous
I	am	leaving
you	are	leaving
he/she/it	is	leaving
we	are	leaving
you	are	leaving
they	are	leaving

Past Continuous
I	was	leaving
you	were	leaving
he/she/it	was	leaving
we	were	leaving
you	were	leaving
they	were	leaving

Present Perfect Continuous
I	have	been	leaving
you	have	been	leaving
he/she/it	has	been	leaving
we	have	been	leaving
you	have	been	leaving
they	have	been	leaving

Past Perfect Continuous
I	had	been	leaving
you	had	been	leaving
he/she/it	had	been	leaving
we	had	been	leaving
you	had	been	leaving
they	had	been	leaving

Future

Future I
I	will	leave
you	will	leave
he/she/it	will	leave
we	will	leave
you	will	leave
they	will	leave

Future I Continuous
I	will be	leaving
you	will be	leaving
he/she/it	will be	leaving
we	will be	leaving
you	will be	leaving
they	will be	leaving

Future II
I	will have	left
you	will have	left
he/she/it	will have	left
we	will have	left
you	will have	left
they	will have	left

Future II Continuous
I	will have been leaving
you	will have been leaving
he/she/it	will have been leaving
we	will have been leaving
you	will have been leaving
they	will have been leaving

Conditional

Conditional II
I	would leave
you	would leave
he/she/it	would leave
we	would leave
you	would leave
they	would leave

Conditional Past
I	would have	left
you	would have	left
he/she/it	would have	left
we	would have	left
you	would have	left
they	would have	left

Imperative
leave

Gerund
leaving

Past Participle
left

Unregelmäßig

lend | (aus)leihen

Simple

Present Simple

I	lend
you	lend
he/she/it	lends
we	lend
you	lend
they	lend

Past Simple

I	lent
you	lent
he/she/it	lent
we	lent
you	lent
they	lent

Present Perfect

I	have	lent
you	have	lent
he/she/it	has	lent
we	have	lent
you	have	lent
they	have	lent

Past Perfect

I	had	lent
you	had	lent
he/she/it	had	lent
we	had	lent
you	had	lent
they	had	lent

Continuous

Present Continuous

I	am	lending
you	are	lending
he/she/it	is	lending
we	are	lending
you	are	lending
they	are	lending

Past Continuous

I	was	lending
you	were	lending
he/she/it	was	lending
we	were	lending
you	were	lending
they	were	lending

Present Perfect Continuous

I	have	been	lending
you	have	been	lending
he/she/it	has	been	lending
we	have	been	lending
you	have	been	lending
they	have	been	lending

Past Perfect Continuous

I	had	been	lending
you	had	been	lending
he/she/it	had	been	lending
we	had	been	lending
you	had	been	lending
they	had	been	lending

Future

Future I

I	will	lend
you	will	lend
he/she/it	will	lend
we	will	lend
you	will	lend
they	will	lend

Future I Continuous

I	will be	lending
you	will be	lending
he/she/it	will be	lending
we	will be	lending
you	will be	lending
they	will be	lending

Future II

I	will have	lent
you	will have	lent
he/she/it	will have	lent
we	will have	lent
you	will have	lent
they	will have	lent

Future II Continuous

I	will have been lending
you	will have been lending
he/she/it	will have been lending
we	will have been lending
you	will have been lending
they	will have been lending

Conditional

Conditional II

I	would lend
you	would lend
he/she/it	would lend
we	would lend
you	would lend
they	would lend

Conditional Past

I	would have	lent
you	would have	lent
he/she/it	would have	lent
we	would have	lent
you	would have	lent
they	would have	lent

Imperative

lend

Gerund

lending

Past Participle

lent

Regelmäßig

Like hat keine Verlaufsform

like | mögen

Simple

Present Simple
I	like
you	like
he/she/it	likes
we	like
you	like
they	like

Past Simple
I	liked
you	liked
he/she/it	liked
we	liked
you	liked
they	liked

Present Perfect
I	have	liked
you	have	liked
he/she/it	has	liked
we	have	liked
you	have	liked
they	have	liked

Past Perfect
I	had	liked
you	had	liked
he/she/it	had	liked
we	had	liked
you	had	liked
they	had	liked

Continuous

Present Continuous
—

Past Continuous
—

Present Perfect Continuous
—

Past Perfect Continuous
—

Future

Future I
I	will	like
you	will	like
he/she/it	will	like
we	will	like
you	will	like
they	will	like

Future I Continuous
—

Future II
I	will have	liked
you	will have	liked
he/she/it	will have	liked
we	will have	liked
you	will have	liked
they	will have	liked

Future II Continuous
—

Conditional

Conditional II
I	would like
you	would like
he/she/it	would like
we	would like
you	would like
they	would like

Conditional Past
I	would have	liked
you	would have	liked
he/she/it	would have	liked
we	would have	liked
you	would have	liked
they	would have	liked

Imperative
like

Gerund
liking

Past Participle
liked

Regelmäßig

listen | zuhören

Simple

Present Simple

I	listen
you	listen
he/she/it	listens
we	listen
you	listen
they	listen

Past Simple

I	listened
you	listened
he/she/it	listened
we	listened
you	listened
they	listened

Present Perfect

I	have	listened
you	have	listened
he/she/it	has	listened
we	have	listened
you	have	listened
they	have	listened

Past Perfect

I	had	listened
you	had	listened
he/she/it	had	listened
we	had	listened
you	had	listened
they	had	listened

Continuous

Present Continuous

I	am	listening
you	are	listening
he/she/it	is	listening
we	are	listening
you	are	listening
they	are	listening

Past Continuous

I	was	listening
you	were	listening
he/she/it	was	listening
we	were	listening
you	were	listening
they	were	listening

Present Perfect Continuous

I	have	been	listening
you	have	been	listening
he/she/it	has	been	listening
we	have	been	listening
you	have	been	listening
they	have	been	listening

Past Perfect Continuous

I	had	been	listening
you	had	been	listening
he/she/it	had	been	listening
we	had	been	listening
you	had	been	listening
they	had	been	listening

Future

Future I

I	will listen
you	will listen
he/she/it	will listen
we	will listen
you	will listen
they	will listen

Future I Continuous

I	will be listening
you	will be listening
he/she/it	will be listening
we	will be listening
you	will be listening
they	will be listening

Future II

I	will have	listened
you	will have	listened
he/she/it	will have	listened
we	will have	listened
you	will have	listened
they	will have	listened

Future II Continuous

I	will have been	listening
you	will have been	listening
he/she/it	will have been	listening
we	will have been	listening
you	will have been	listening
they	will have been	listening

Conditional

Conditional II

I	would listen
you	would listen
he/she/it	would listen
we	would listen
you	would listen
they	would listen

Conditional Past

I	would have	listened
you	would have	listened
he/she/it	would have	listened
we	would have	listened
you	would have	listened
they	would have	listened

Imperative

listen

Gerund

listening

Past Participle

listened

Regelmäßig

live | leben/wohnen

+ -*ing* wird ∉(siehe S. 153)/
+ -*d* statt -*ed* (siehe S. 152)

Simple

Present Simple
I	live
you	live
he/she/it	lives
we	live
you	live
they	live

Past Simple
I	lived
you	lived
he/she/it	lived
we	lived
you	lived
they	lived

Present Perfect
I	have	lived
you	have	lived
he/she/it	has	lived
we	have	lived
you	have	lived
they	have	lived

Past Perfect
I	had	lived
you	had	lived
he/she/it	had	lived
we	had	lived
you	had	lived
they	had	lived

Continuous

Present Continuous
I	am	living
you	are	living
he/she/it	is	living
we	are	living
you	are	living
they	are	living

Past Continuous
I	was	living
you	were	living
he/she/it	was	living
we	were	living
you	were	living
they	were	living

Present Perfect Continuous
I	have	been	living
you	have	been	living
he/she/it	has	been	living
we	have	been	living
you	have	been	living
they	have	been	living

Past Perfect Continuous
I	had	been	living
you	had	been	living
he/she/it	had	been	living
we	had	been	living
you	had	been	living
they	had	been	living

Future

Future I
I	will	live
you	will	live
he/she/it	will	live
we	will	live
you	will	live
they	will	live

Future I Continuous
I	will be	living
you	will be	living
he/she/it	will be	living
we	will be	living
you	will be	living
they	will be	living

Future II
I	will have	lived
you	will have	lived
he/she/it	will have	lived
we	will have	lived
you	will have	lived
they	will have	lived

Future II Continuous
I	will have been living
you	will have been living
he/she/it	will have been living
we	will have been living
you	will have been living
they	will have been living

Conditional

Conditional II
I	would live
you	would live
he/she/it	would live
we	would live
you	would live
they	would live

Conditional Past
I	would have	lived
you	would have	lived
he/she/it	would have	lived
we	would have	lived
you	would have	lived
they	would have	lived

Imperative
live

Gerund
living

Past Participle
lived

Regelmäßig

look | sehen

Simple		Continuous		Future		Conditional	

Present Simple

I	look
you	look
he/she/it	looks
we	look
you	look
they	look

Past Simple

I	looked
you	looked
he/she/it	looked
we	looked
you	looked
they	looked

Present Perfect

I	have looked
you	have looked
he/she/it	has looked
we	have looked
you	have looked
they	have looked

Past Perfect

I	had looked
you	had looked
he/she/it	had looked
we	had looked
you	had looked
they	had looked

Present Continuous

I	am	looking
you	are	looking
he/she/it	is	looking
we	are	looking
you	are	looking
they	are	looking

Past Continuous

I	was	looking
you	were	looking
he/she/it	was	looking
we	were	looking
you	were	looking
they	were	looking

Present Perfect Continuous

I	have been	looking
you	have been	looking
he/she/it	has been	looking
we	have been	looking
you	have been	looking
they	have been	looking

Past Perfect Continuous

I	had been	looking
you	had been	looking
he/she/it	had been	looking
we	had been	looking
you	had been	looking
they	had been	looking

Future I

I	will	look
you	will	look
he/she/it	will	look
we	will	look
you	will	look
they	will	look

Future I Continuous

I	will be	looking
you	will be	looking
he/she/it	will be	looking
we	will be	looking
you	will be	looking
they	will be	looking

Future II

I	will have looked
you	will have looked
he/she/it	will have looked
we	will have looked
you	will have looked
they	will have looked

Future II Continuous

I	will have been looking
you	will have been looking
he/she/it	will have been looking
we	will have been looking
you	will have been looking
they	will have been looking

Conditional II

I	would look
you	would look
he/she/it	would look
we	would look
you	would look
they	would look

Conditional Past

I	would have looked
you	would have looked
he/she/it	would have looked
we	would have looked
you	would have looked
they	would have looked

Imperative

look

Gerund

looking

Past Participle

looked

Unregelmäßig

+ *-ing* wird ɇ (siehe S. 153)

lose | verlieren

Simple

Present Simple
I	lose
you	lose
he/she/it	loses
we	lose
you	lose
they	lose

Past Simple
I	lost
you	lost
he/she/it	lost
we	lost
you	lost
they	lost

Present Perfect
I	have	lost
you	have	lost
he/she/it	has	lost
we	have	lost
you	have	lost
they	have	lost

Past Perfect
I	had	lost
you	had	lost
he/she/it	had	lost
we	had	lost
you	had	lost
they	had	lost

Continuous

Present Continuous
I	am	losing
you	are	losing
he/she/it	is	losing
we	are	losing
you	are	losing
they	are	losing

Past Continuous
I	was	losing
you	were	losing
he/she/it	was	losing
we	were	losing
you	were	losing
they	were	losing

Present Perfect Continuous
I	have	been	losing
you	have	been	losing
he/she/it	has	been	losing
we	have	been	losing
you	have	been	losing
they	have	been	losing

Past Perfect Continuous
I	had	been	losing
you	had	been	losing
he/she/it	had	been	losing
we	had	been	losing
you	had	been	losing
they	had	been	losing

Future

Future I
I	will	lose
you	will	lose
he/she/it	will	lose
we	will	lose
you	will	lose
they	will	lose

Future I Continuous
I	will be	losing
you	will be	losing
he/she/it	will be	losing
we	will be	losing
you	will be	losing
they	will be	losing

Future II
I	will have	lost
you	will have	lost
he/she/it	will have	lost
we	will have	lost
you	will have	lost
they	will have	lost

Future II Continuous
I	will have been losing
you	will have been losing
he/she/it	will have been losing
we	will have been losing
you	will have been losing
they	will have been losing

Conditional

Conditional II
I	would lose
you	would lose
he/she/it	would lose
we	would lose
you	would lose
they	would lose

Conditional Past
I	would have	lost
you	would have	lost
he/she/it	would have	lost
we	would have	lost
you	would have	lost
they	would have	lost

Imperative
lose

Gerund
losing

Past Participle
lost

Unregelmäßig

make | machen

+ -*ing* wird ∅ (siehe S. 153)

Simple

Present Simple
I	make
you	make
he/she/it	makes
we	make
you	make
they	make

Past Simple
I	made
you	made
he/she/it	made
we	made
you	made
they	made

Present Perfect
I	have	made
you	have	made
he/she/it	has	made
we	have	made
you	have	made
they	have	made

Past Perfect
I	had	made
you	had	made
he/she/it	had	made
we	had	made
you	had	made
they	had	made

Continuous

Present Continuous
I	am	making
you	are	making
he/she/it	is	making
we	are	making
you	are	making
they	are	making

Past Continuous
I	was	making
you	were	making
he/she/it	was	making
we	were	making
you	were	making
they	were	making

Present Perfect Continuous
I	have	been	making
you	have	been	making
he/she/it	has	been	making
we	have	been	making
you	have	been	making
they	have	been	making

Past Perfect Continuous
I	had	been	making
you	had	been	making
he/she/it	had	been	making
we	had	been	making
you	had	been	making
they	had	been	making

Future

Future I
I	will	make
you	will	make
he/she/it	will	make
we	will	make
you	will	make
they	will	make

Future I Continuous
I	will be	making
you	will be	making
he/she/it	will be	making
we	will be	making
you	will be	making
they	will be	making

Future II
I	will have	made
you	will have	made
he/she/it	will have	made
we	will have	made
you	will have	made
they	will have	made

Future II Continuous
I	will have been making
you	will have been making
he/she/it	will have been making
we	will have been making
you	will have been making
they	will have been making

Conditional

Conditional II
I	would make
you	would make
he/she/it	would make
we	would make
you	would make
they	would make

Conditional Past
I	would have	made
you	would have	made
he/she/it	would have	made
we	would have	made
you	would have	made
they	would have	made

Imperative
make

Gerund
making

Past Participle
made

Unregelmäßig

meet | treffen

Simple

Present Simple

I	meet
you	meet
he/she/it	meets
we	meet
you	meet
they	meet

Past Simple

I	met
you	met
he/she/it	met
we	met
you	met
they	met

Present Perfect

I	have	met
you	have	met
he/she/it	has	met
we	have	met
you	have	met
they	have	met

Past Perfect

I	had	met
you	had	met
he/she/it	had	met
we	had	met
you	had	met
they	had	met

Continuous

Present Continuous

I	am	meeting
you	are	meeting
he/she/it	is	meeting
we	are	meeting
you	are	meeting
they	are	meeting

Past Continuous

I	was	meeting
you	were	meeting
he/she/it	was	meeting
we	were	meeting
you	were	meeting
they	were	meeting

Present Perfect Continuous

I	have	been	meeting
you	have	been	meeting
he/she/it	has	been	meeting
we	have	been	meeting
you	have	been	meeting
they	have	been	meeting

Past Perfect Continuous

I	had	been	meeting
you	had	been	meeting
he/she/it	had	been	meeting
we	had	been	meeting
you	had	been	meeting
they	had	been	meeting

Future

Future I

I	will	meet
you	will	meet
he/she/it	will	meet
we	will	meet
you	will	meet
they	will	meet

Future I Continuous

I	will be	meeting
you	will be	meeting
he/she/it	will be	meeting
we	will be	meeting
you	will be	meeting
they	will be	meeting

Future II

I	will have	met
you	will have	met
he/she/it	will have	met
we	will have	met
you	will have	met
they	will have	met

Future II Continuous

I	will have been	meeting
you	will have been	meeting
he/she/it	will have been	meeting
we	will have been	meeting
you	will have been	meeting
they	will have been	meeting

Conditional

Conditional II

I	would meet
you	would meet
he/she/it	would meet
we	would meet
you	would meet
they	would meet

Conditional Past

I	would have	met
you	would have	met
he/she/it	would have	met
we	would have	met
you	would have	met
they	would have	met

Imperative
meet

Gerund
meeting

Past Participle
met

Unregelmäßig
Modalverb

must/have to | müssen/sollen

Must kann nur in seiner Grundform gebraucht werden. Ansonsten wird *have to* benutzt. /*Have to* im *Present*- und *Past Continuous* wird meistens mit *always* verwendet und drückt ein negatives Empfinden aus.

Simple

Present Simple
I	must/have to
you	must/have to
he/she/it	must/has to
we	must/have to
you	must/have to
they	must/have to

Past Simple
I	had to
you	had to
he/she/it	had to
we	had to
you	had to
they	had to

Present Perfect
I	have	had to
you	have	had to
he/she/it	has	had to
we	have	had to
you	have	had to
they	have	had to

Past Perfect
I	had	had to
you	had	had to
he/she/it	had	had to
we	had	had to
you	had	had to
they	had	had to

Continuous

Present Continuous
I	am	having to
you	are	having to
he/she/it	is	having to
we	are	having to
you	are	having to
they	are	having to

Past Continuous
I	was	having to
you	were	having to
he/she/it	was	having to
we	were	having to
you	were	having to
they	were	having to

Present Perfect Continuous
I	have	been	having to
you	have	been	having to
he/she/it	has	been	having to
we	have	been	having to
you	have	been	having to
they	have	been	having to

Past Perfect Continuous
I	had	been	having to
you	had	been	having to
he/she/it	had	been	having to
we	had	been	having to
you	had	been	having to
they	had	been	having to

Future

Future I
I	will	have	to
you	will	have	to
he/she/it	will	have	to
we	will	have	to
you	will	have	to
they	will	have	to

Future I Continuous
I	will be	having to
you	will be	having to
he/she/it	will be	having to
we	will be	having to
you	will be	having to
they	will be	having to

Future II
I	will have	had to
you	will have	had to
he/she/it	will have	had to
we	will have	had to
you	will have	had to
they	will have	had to

Future II Continuous
I	will have been having to
you	will have been having to
he/she/it	will have been having to
we	will have been having to
you	will have been having to
they	will have been having to

Conditional

Conditional II
I	would have	to
you	would have	to
he/she/it	would have	to
we	would have	to
you	would have	to
they	would have	to

Conditional Past
I	would have	had to
you	would have	had to
he/she/it	would have	had to
we	would have	had to
you	would have	had to
they	would have	had to

Imperative
—

Gerund
having to

Past Participle
had to

Regelmäßig

need | brauchen

Simple

Present Simple

I	need
you	need
he/she/it	needs
we	need
you	need
they	need

Past Simple

I	needed
you	needed
he/she/it	needed
we	needed
you	needed
they	needed

Present Perfect

I	have needed
you	have needed
he/she/it	has needed
we	have needed
you	have needed
they	have needed

Past Perfect

I	had needed
you	had needed
he/she/it	had needed
we	had needed
you	had needed
they	had needed

Continuous

Present Continuous

I	am needing
you	are needing
he/she/it	is needing
we	are needing
you	are needing
they	are needing

Past Continuous

I	was needing
you	were needing
he/she/it	was needing
we	were needing
you	were needing
they	were needing

Present Perfect Continuous

I	have been needing
you	have been needing
he/she/it	has been needing
we	have been needing
you	have been needing
they	have been needing

Past Perfect Continuous

I	had been needing
you	had been needing
he/she/it	had been needing
we	had been needing
you	had been needing
they	had been needing

Future

Future I

I	will need
you	will need
he/she/it	will need
we	will need
you	will need
they	will need

Future I Continuous

I	will be needing
you	will be needing
he/she/it	will be needing
we	will be needing
you	will be needing
they	will be needing

Future II

I	will have needed
you	will have needed
he/she/it	will have needed
we	will have needed
you	will have needed
they	will have needed

Future II Contlimous

I	will have been needing
you	will have been needing
he/she/it	will have been needing
we	will have been needing
you	will have been needing
they	will have been needing

Conditional

Conditional II

I	would need
you	would need
he/she/it	would need
we	would need
you	would need
they	would need

Conditional Past

I	would have needed
you	would have needed
he/she/it	would have needed
we	would have needed
you	would have needed
they	would have needed

Imperative

—

Gerund

needing

Past Participle

needed

Regelmäßig

open | öffnen

Simple

Present Simple

I	open
you	open
he/she/it	opens
we	open
you	open
they	open

Past Simple

I	opened
you	opened
he/she/it	opened
we	opened
you	opened
they	opened

Present Perfect

I	have opened
you	have opened
he/she/it	has opened
we	have opened
you	have opened
they	have opened

Past Perfect

I	had opened
you	had opened
he/she/it	had opened
we	had opened
you	had opened
they	had opened

Continuous

Present Continuous

I	am	opening
you	are	opening
he/she/it	is	opening
we	are	opening
you	are	opening
they	are	opening

Past Continuous

I	was	opening
you	were	opening
he/she/it	was	opening
we	were	opening
you	were	opening
they	were	opening

Present Perfect Continuous

I	have been	opening
you	have been	opening
he/she/it	has been	opening
we	have been	opening
you	have been	opening
they	have been	opening

Past Perfect Continuous

I	had been	opening
you	had been	opening
he/she/it	had been	opening
we	had been	opening
you	had been	opening
they	had been	opening

Future

Future I

I	will	open
you	will	open
he/she/it	will	open
we	will	open
you	will	open
they	will	open

Future I Continuous

I	will be opening
you	will be opening
he/she/it	will be opening
we	will be opening
you	will be opening
they	will be opening

Future II

I	will have	opened
you	will have	opened
he/she/it	will have	opened
we	will have	opened
you	will have	opened
they	will have	opened

Future II Continuous

I	will have been	opening
you	will have been	opening
he/she/it	will have been	opening
we	will have been	opening
you	will have been	opening
they	will have been	opening

Conditional

Conditional II

I	would open
you	would open
he/she/it	would open
we	would open
you	would open
they	would open

Conditional Past

I	would have	opened
you	would have	opened
he/she/it	would have	opened
we	would have	opened
you	would have	opened
they	would have	opened

Imperative

open

Gerund

opening

Past Participle

opened

Unregelmäßig

pay | zahlen

Simple

Present Simple

I	pay
you	pay
he/she/it	pays
we	pay
you	pay
they	pay

Past Simple

I	paid
you	paid
he/she/it	paid
we	paid
you	paid
they	paid

Present Perfect

I	have	paid
you	have	paid
he/she/it	has	paid
we	have	paid
you	have	paid
they	have	paid

Past Perfect

I	had	paid
you	had	paid
he/she/it	had	paid
we	had	paid
you	had	paid
they	had	paid

Continuous

Present Continuous

I	am	paying
you	are	paying
he/she/it	is	paying
we	are	paying
you	are	paying
they	are	paying

Past Continuous

I	was	paying
you	were	paying
he/she/it	was	paying
we	were	paying
you	were	paying
they	were	paying

Present Perfect Continuous

I	have	been	paying
you	have	been	paying
he/she/it	has	been	paying
we	have	been	paying
you	have	been	paying
they	have	been	paying

Past Perfect Continuous

I	had	been	paying
you	had	been	paying
he/she/it	had	been	paying
we	had	been	paying
you	had	been	paying
they	had	been	paying

Future

Future I

I	will	pay
you	will	pay
he/she/it	will	pay
we	will	pay
you	will	pay
they	will	pay

Future I Continuous

I	will be	paying
you	will be	paying
he/she/it	will be	paying
we	will be	paying
you	will be	paying
they	will be	paying

Future II

I	will have	paid
you	will have	paid
he/she/it	will have	paid
we	will have	paid
you	will have	paid
they	will have	paid

Future II Continuous

I	will have been paying
you	will have been paying
he/she/it	will have been paying
we	will have been paying
you	will have been paying
they	will have been paying

Conditional

Conditional II

I	would pay
you	would pay
he/she/it	would pay
we	would pay
you	would pay
they	would pay

Conditional Past

I	would have	paid
you	would have	paid
he/she/it	would have	paid
we	would have	paid
you	would have	paid
they	would have	paid

Imperative

pay

Gerund

paying

Past Participle

paid

Regelmäßig

play | spielen

Simple		Continuous			Future			Conditional	
Present Simple		**Present Continuous**			**Future I**			**Conditional II**	
I	play	I	am	playing	I	will	play	I	would play
you	play	you	are	playing	you	will	play	you	would play
he/she/it	plays	he/she/it	is	playing	he/she/it	will	play	he/she/it	would play
we	play	we	are	playing	we	will	play	we	would play
you	play	you	are	playing	you	will	play	you	would play
they	play	they	are	playing	they	will	play	they	would play

Simple		Continuous			Future			Conditional		
Past Simple		**Past Continuous**			**Future I Continuous**			**Conditional Past**		
I	played	I	was	playing	I	will be	playing	I	would have	played
you	played	you	were	playing	you	will be	playing	you	would have	played
he/she/it	played	he/she/it	was	playing	he/she/it	will be	playing	he/she/it	would have	played
we	played	we	were	playing	we	will be	playing	we	would have	played
you	played	you	were	playing	you	will be	playing	you	would have	played
they	played	they	were	playing	they	will be	playing	they	would have	played

Simple			Continuous				Future		
Present Perfect			**Present Perfect Continuous**				**Future II**		
I	have	played	I	have	been	playing	I	will have	played
you	have	played	you	have	been	playing	you	will have	played
he/she/it	has	played	he/she/it	has	been	playing	he/she/it	will have	played
we	have	played	we	have	been	playing	we	will have	played
you	have	played	you	have	been	playing	you	will have	played
they	have	played	they	have	been	playing	they	will have	played

Imperative

play

Gerund

playing

Past Participle

played

Simple			Continuous				Future	
Past Perfect			**Past Perfect Continuous**				**Future II Continuous**	
I	had	played	I	had	been	playing	I	will have been playing
you	had	played	you	had	been	playing	you	will have been playing
he/she/it	had	played	he/she/it	had	been	playing	he/she/it	will have been playing
we	had	played	we	had	been	playing	we	will have been playing
you	had	played	you	had	been	playing	you	will have been playing
they	had	played	they	had	been	playing	they	will have been playing

Unregelmäßig

Konsonantenverdopplung
(siehe S. 152)

put | setzen/stellen/ legen

Simple

Present Simple
I	put
you	put
he/she/it	puts
we	put
you	put
they	put

Past Simple
I	put
you	put
he/she/it	put
we	put
you	put
they	put

Present Perfect
I	have	put
you	have	put
he/she/it	has	put
we	have	put
you	have	put
they	have	put

Past Perfect
I	had	put
you	had	put
he/she/it	had	put
we	had	put
you	had	put
they	had	put

Continuous

Present Continuous
I	am	putting
you	are	putting
he/she/it	is	putting
we	are	putting
you	are	putting
they	are	putting

Past Continuous
I	was	putting
you	were	putting
he/she/it	was	putting
we	were	putting
you	were	putting
they	were	putting

Present Perfect Continuous
I	have	been	putting
you	have	been	putting
he/she/it	has	been	putting
we	have	been	putting
you	have	been	putting
they	have	been	putting

Past Perfect Continuous
I	had	been	putting
you	had	been	putting
he/she/it	had	been	putting
we	had	been	putting
you	had	been	putting
they	had	been	putting

Future

Future I
I	will	put
you	will	put
he/she/it	will	put
we	will	put
you	will	put
they	will	put

Future I Continuous
I	will be	putting
you	will be	putting
he/she/it	will be	putting
we	will be	putting
you	will be	putting
they	will be	putting

Future II
I	will have	put
you	will have	put
he/she/it	will have	put
we	will have	put
you	will have	put
they	will have	put

Future II Continuous
I	will have been putting
you	will have been putting
he/she/it	will have been putting
we	will have been putting
you	will have been putting
they	will have been putting

Conditional

Conditional II
I	would put
you	would put
he/she/it	would put
we	would put
you	would put
they	would put

Conditional Past
I	would have	put
you	would have	put
he/she/it	would have	put
we	would have	put
you	would have	put
they	would have	put

Imperative
put

Gerund
putting

Past Participle
put

Unregelmäßig

read | lesen

Die *Past simple*-Form und das *Partizip Perfekt* werden wie die Farbe rot – *red* ausgesprochen [red].

Simple

Present Simple
I	read
you	read
he/she/it	reads
we	read
you	read
they	read

Past Simple
I	read
you	read
he/she/it	read
we	read
you	read
they	read

Present Perfect
I	have	read
you	have	read
he/she/it	has	read
we	have	read
you	have	read
they	have	read

Past Perfect
I	had	read
you	had	read
he/she/it	had	read
we	had	read
you	had	read
they	had	read

Continuous

Present Continuous
I	am	reading
you	are	reading
he/she/it	is	reading
we	are	reading
you	are	reading
they	are	reading

Past Continuous
I	was	reading
you	were	reading
he/she/it	was	reading
we	were	reading
you	were	reading
they	were	reading

Present Perfect Continuous
I	have	been	reading
you	have	been	reading
he/she/it	has	been	reading
we	have	been	reading
you	have	been	reading
they	have	been	reading

Past Perfect Continuous
I	had	been	reading
you	had	been	reading
he/she/it	had	been	reading
we	had	been	reading
you	had	been	reading
they	had	been	reading

Future

Future I
I	will	read
you	will	read
he/she/it	will	read
we	will	read
you	will	read
they	will	read

Future I Continuous
I	will be	reading
you	will be	reading
he/she/it	will be	reading
we	will be	reading
you	will be	reading
they	will be	reading

Future II
I	will have	read
you	will have	read
he/she/it	will have	read
we	will have	read
you	will have	read
they	will have	read

Future II Continuous
I	will have been reading
you	will have been reading
he/she/it	will have been reading
we	will have been reading
you	will have been reading
they	will have been reading

Conditional

Conditional II
I	would read
you	would read
he/she/it	would read
we	would read
you	would read
they	would read

Conditional Past
I	would have	read
you	would have	read
he/she/it	would have	read
we	would have	read
you	would have	read
they	would have	read

Imperative
read

Gerund
reading

Past Participle
read

Konsonantenverdopplung
(siehe S. 152)

Unregelmäßig

run | laufen/rennen

Simple

Present Simple

I	run
you	run
he/she/it	runs
we	run
you	run
they	run

Past Simple

I	ran
you	ran
he/she/it	ran
we	ran
you	ran
they	ran

Present Perfect

I	have	run
you	have	run
he/she/it	has	run
we	have	run
you	have	run
they	have	run

Past Perfect

I	had	run
you	had	run
he/she/it	had	run
we	had	run
you	had	run
they	had	run

Continuous

Present Continuous

I	am	running
you	are	running
he/she/it	is	running
we	are	running
you	are	running
they	are	running

Past Continuous

I	was	running
you	were	running
he/she/it	was	running
we	were	running
you	were	running
they	were	running

Present Perfect Continuous

I	have	been	running
you	have	been	running
he/she/it	has	been	running
we	have	been	running
you	have	been	running
they	have	been	running

Past Perfect Continuous

I	had	been	running
you	had	been	running
he/she/it	had	been	running
we	had	been	running
you	had	been	running
they	had	been	running

Future

Future I

I	will	run
you	will	run
he/she/it	will	run
we	will	run
you	will	run
they	will	run

Future I Continuous

I	will berunning
you	will berunning
he/she/it	will berunning
we	will berunning
you	will berunning
they	will berunning

Future II

I	will have run
you	will have run
he/she/it	will have run
we	will have run
you	will have run
they	will have run

Future II Contlimous

I	will have been running
you	will have been running
he/she/it	will have been running
we	will have been running
you	will have been running
they	will have been running

Conditional

Conditional II

I	would run
you	would run
he/she/it	would run
we	would run
you	would run
they	would run

Conditional Past

I	would have run
you	would have run
he/she/it	would have run
we	would have run
you	would have run
they	would have run

Imperative

run

Gerund

running

Past Participle

run

Unregelmäßig

say | sagen

Die Aussprache von *says* weicht von den restlichen Formen ab. Es wird [sez] ausgesprochen

Simple

Present Simple
I	say
you	say
he/she/it	says
we	say
you	say
they	say

Past Simple
I	said
you	said
he/she/it	said
we	said
you	said
they	said

Present Perfect
I	have said
you	have said
he/she/it	has said
we	have said
you	have said
they	have said

Past Perfect
I	had said
you	had said
he/she/it	had said
we	had said
you	had said
they	had said

Continuous

Present Continuous
I	am	saying
you	are	saying
he/she/it	is	saying
we	are	saying
you	are	saying
they	are	saying

Past Continuous
I	was	saying
you	were	saying
he/she/it	was	saying
we	were	saying
you	were	saying
they	were	saying

Present Perfect Continuous
I	have been	saying
you	have been	saying
he/she/it	has been	saying
we	have been	saying
you	have been	saying
they	have been	saying

Past Perfect Continuous
I	had been	saying
you	had been	saying
he/she/it	had been	saying
we	had been	saying
you	had been	saying
they	had been	saying

Future

Future I
I	will	say
you	will	say
he/she/it	will	say
we	will	say
you	will	say
they	will	say

Future I Continuous
I	will be	saying
you	will be	saying
he/she/it	will be	saying
we	will be	saying
you	will be	saying
they	will be	saying

Future II
I	will have said
you	will have said
he/she/it	will have said
we	will have said
you	will have said
they	will have said

Future II Continuous
I	will have been saying
you	will have been saying
he/she/it	will have been saying
we	will have been saying
you	will have been saying
they	will have been saying

Conditional

Conditional II
I	would say
you	would say
he/she/it	would say
we	would say
you	would say
they	would say

Conditional Past
I	would have said
you	would have said
he/she/it	would have said
we	would have said
you	would have said
they	would have said

Imperative
say

Gerund
saying

Past Participle
said

see | sehen

Simple

Present Simple

I	see
you	see
he/she/it	sees
we	see
you	see
they	see

Past Simple

I	saw
you	saw
he/she/it	saw
we	saw
you	saw
they	saw

Present Perfect

I	have seen
you	have seen
he/she/it	has seen
we	have seen
you	have seen
they	have seen

Past Perfect

I	had seen
you	had seen
he/she/it	had seen
we	had seen
you	had seen
they	had seen

Continuous

Present Continuous

I	am seeing
you	are seeing
he/she/it	is seeing
we	are seeing
you	are seeing
they	are seeing

Past Continuous

I	was seeing
you	were seeing
he/she/it	was seeing
we	were seeing
you	were seeing
they	were seeing

Present Perfect Continuous

I	have been seeing
you	have been seeing
he/she/it	has been seeing
we	have been seeing
you	have been seeing
they	have been seeing

Past Perfect Continuous

I	had been seeing
you	had been seeing
he/she/it	had been seeing
we	had been seeing
you	had been seeing
they	had been seeing

Future

Future I

I	will see
you	will see
he/she/it	will see
we	will see
you	will see
they	will see

Future I Continuous

I	will be seeing
you	will be seeing
he/she/it	will be seeing
we	will be seeing
you	will be seeing
they	will be seeing

Future II

I	will have seen
you	will have seen
he/she/it	will have seen
we	will have seen
you	will have seen
they	will have seen

Future II Continuous

I	will have been seeing
you	will have been seeing
he/she/it	will have been seeing
we	will have been seeing
you	will have been seeing
they	will have been seeing

Conditional

Conditional II

I	would see
you	would see
he/she/it	would see
we	would see
you	would see
they	would see

Conditional Past

I	would have seen
you	would have seen
he/she/it	would have seen
we	would have seen
you	would have seen
they	would have seen

Imperative

see

Gerund

seeing

Past Participle

seen

Unregelmäßig

sell | verkaufen

Simple	Continuous	Future	Conditional

Present Simple
I	sell
you	sell
he/she/it	sells
we	sell
you	sell
they	sell

Past Simple
I	sold
you	sold
he/she/it	sold
we	sold
you	sold
they	sold

Present Perfect
I	have	sold
you	have	sold
he/she/it	has	sold
we	have	sold
you	have	sold
they	have	sold

Past Perfect
I	had	sold
you	had	sold
he/she/it	had	sold
we	had	sold
you	had	sold
they	had	sold

Present Continuous
I	am	selling
you	are	selling
he/she/it	is	selling
we	are	selling
you	are	selling
they	are	selling

Past Continuous
I	was	selling
you	were	selling
he/she/it	was	selling
we	were	selling
you	were	selling
they	were	selling

Present Perfect Continuous
I	have	been	selling
you	have	been	selling
he/she/it	has	been	selling
we	have	been	selling
you	have	been	selling
they	have	been	selling

Past Perfect Continuous
I	had	been	selling
you	had	been	selling
he/she/it	had	been	selling
we	had	been	selling
you	had	been	selling
they	had	been	selling

Future I
I	will	sell
you	will	sell
he/she/it	will	sell
we	will	sell
you	will	sell
they	will	sell

Future I Continuous
I	will be	selling
you	will be	selling
he/she/it	will be	selling
we	will be	selling
you	will be	selling
they	will be	selling

Future II
I	will have	sold
you	will have	sold
he/she/it	will have	sold
we	will have	sold
you	will have	sold
they	will have	sold

Future II Continuous
I	will have been selling
you	will have been selling
he/she/it	will have been selling
we	will have been selling
you	will have been selling
they	will have been selling

Conditional II
I	would sell
you	would sell
he/she/it	would sell
we	would sell
you	would sell
they	would sell

Conditional Past
I	would have	sold
you	would have	sold
he/she/it	would have	sold
we	would have	sold
you	would have	sold
they	would have	sold

Imperative

sell

Gerund

selling

Past Participle

sold

Unregelmäßig

send | schicken

Simple

Present Simple
I	send
you	send
he/she/it	sends
we	send
you	send
they	send

Past Simple
I	sent
you	sent
he/she/it	sent
we	sent
you	sent
they	sent

Present Perfect
I	have	sent
you	have	sent
he/she/it	has	sent
we	have	sent
you	have	sent
they	have	sent

Past Perfect
I	had	sent
you	had	sent
he/she/it	had	sent
we	had	sent
you	had	sent
they	had	sent

Continuous

Present Continuous
I	am	sending
you	are	sending
he/she/it	is	sending
we	are	sending
you	are	sending
they	are	sending

Past Continuous
I	was	sending
you	were	sending
he/she/it	was	sending
we	were	sending
you	were	sending
they	were	sending

Present Perfect Continuous
I	have	been	sending
you	have	been	sending
he/she/it	has	been	sending
we	have	been	sending
you	have	been	sending
they	have	been	sending

Past Perfect Continuous
I	had	been	sending
you	had	been	sending
he/she/it	had	been	sending
we	had	been	sending
you	had	been	sending
they	had	been	sending

Future

Future I
I	will	send
you	will	send
he/she/it	will	send
we	will	send
you	will	send
they	will	send

Future I Continuous
I	will be sending
you	will be sending
he/she/it	will be sending
we	will be sending
you	will be sending
they	will be sending

Future II
I	will have	sent
you	will have	sent
he/she/it	will have	sent
we	will have	sent
you	will have	sent
they	will have	sent

Future II Continuous
I	will have been sending
you	will have been sending
he/she/it	will have been sending
we	will have been sending
you	will have been sending
they	will have been sending

Conditional

Conditional II
I	would send
you	would send
he/she/it	would send
we	would send
you	would send
they	would send

Conditional Past
I	would have	sent
you	would have	sent
he/she/it	would have	sent
we	would have	sent
you	would have	sent
they	would have	sent

Imperative
send

Gerund
sending

Past Participle
sent

Unregelmäßig

shut | schließen

Konsonantenverdopplung
(siehe S. 152)

Simple

Present Simple
I	shut
you	shut
he/she/it	shuts
we	shut
you	shut
they	shut

Past Simple
I	shut
you	shut
he/she/it	shut
we	shut
you	shut
they	shut

Present Perfect
I	have shut
you	have shut
he/she/it	has shut
we	have shut
you	have shut
they	have shut

Past Perfect
I	had shut
you	had shut
he/she/it	had shut
we	had shut
you	had shut
they	had shut

Continuous

Present Continuous
I	am	shutting
you	are	shutting
he/she/it	is	shutting
we	are	shutting
you	are	shutting
they	are	shutting

Past Continuous
I	was	shutting
you	were	shutting
he/she/it	was	shutting
we	were	shutting
you	were	shutting
they	were	shutting

Present Perfect Continuous
I	have been	shutting
you	have been	shutting
he/she/it	has been	shutting
we	have been	shutting
you	have been	shutting
they	have been	shutting

Past Perfect Continuous
I	had been	shutting
you	had been	shutting
he/she/it	had been	shutting
we	had been	shutting
you	had been	shutting
they	had been	shutting

Future

Future I
I	will	shut
you	will	shut
he/she/it	will	shut
we	will	shut
you	will	shut
they	will	shut

Future I Continuous
I	will be	shutting
you	will be	shutting
he/she/it	will be	shutting
we	will be	shutting
you	will be	shutting
they	will be	shutting

Future II
I	will have shut
you	will have shut
he/she/it	will have shut
we	will have shut
you	will have shut
they	will have shut

Future II Continuous
I	will have been shutting
you	will have been shutting
he/she/it	will have been shutting
we	will have been shutting
you	will have been shutting
they	will have been shutting

Conditional

Conditional II
I	would shut
you	would shut
he/she/it	would shut
we	would shut
you	would shut
they	would shut

Conditional Past
I	would have shut
you	would have shut
he/she/it	would have shut
we	would have shut
you	would have shut
they	would have shut

Imperative
shut

Gerund
shutting

Past Participle
shut

Unregelmäßig

sit | sitzen

Konsonantenverdopplung
(siehe S. 152)

Simple

Present Simple

I	sit
you	sit
he/she/it	sits
we	sit
you	sit
they	sit

Past Simple

I	sat
you	sat
he/she/it	sat
we	sat
you	sat
they	sat

Present Perfect

I	have	sat
you	have	sat
he/she/it	has	sat
we	have	sat
you	have	sat
they	have	sat

Past Perfect

I	had	sat
you	had	sat
he/she/it	had	sat
we	had	sat
you	had	sat
they	had	sat

Continuous

Present Continuous

I	am	sitting
you	are	sitting
he/she/it	is	sitting
we	are	sitting
you	are	sitting
they	are	sitting

Past Continuous

I	was	sitting
you	were	sitting
he/she/it	was	sitting
we	were	sitting
you	were	sitting
they	were	sitting

Present Perfect Continuous

I	have	been	sitting
you	have	been	sitting
he/she/it	has	been	sitting
we	have	been	sitting
you	have	been	sitting
they	have	been	sitting

Past Perfect Continuous

I	had	been	sitting
you	had	been	sitting
he/she/it	had	been	sitting
we	had	been	sitting
you	had	been	sitting
they	had	been	sitting

Future

Future I

I	will	sit
you	will	sit
he/she/it	will	sit
we	will	sit
you	will	sit
they	will	sit

Future I Continuous

I	will be	sitting
you	will be	sitting
he/she/it	will be	sitting
we	will be	sitting
you	will be	sitting
they	will be	sitting

Future II

I	will have	sat
you	will have	sat
he/she/it	will have	sat
we	will have	sat
you	will have	sat
they	will have	sat

Future II Continuous

I	will have been sitting
you	will have been sitting
he/she/it	will have been sitting
we	will have been sitting
you	will have been sitting
they	will have been sitting

Conditional

Conditional II

I	would sit
you	would sit
he/she/it	would sit
we	would sit
you	would sit
they	would sit

Conditional Past

I	would have	sat
you	would have	sat
he/she/it	would have	sat
we	would have	sat
you	would have	sat
they	would have	sat

Imperative
sit

Gerund
sitting

Past Participle
sat

Unregelmäßig

sleep | schlafen

Simple

Present Simple

I	sleep
you	sleep
he/she/it	sleeps
we	sleep
you	sleep
they	sleep

Past Simple

I	slept
you	slept
he/she/it	slept
we	slept
you	slept
they	slept

Present Perfect

I	have slept
you	have slept
he/she/it	has slept
we	have slept
you	have slept
they	have slept

Past Perfect

I	had slept
you	had slept
he/she/it	had slept
we	had slept
you	had slept
they	had slept

Continuous

Present Continuous

I	am	sleeping
you	are	sleeping
he/she/it	is	sleeping
we	are	sleeping
you	are	sleeping
they	are	sleeping

Past Continuous

I	was	sleeping
you	were	sleeping
he/she/it	was	sleeping
we	were	sleeping
you	were	sleeping
they	were	sleeping

Present Perfect Continuous

I	have been	sleeping
you	have been	sleeping
he/she/it	has been	sleeping
we	have been	sleeping
you	have been	sleeping
they	have been	sleeping

Past Perfect Continuous

I	had been	sleeping
you	had been	sleeping
he/she/it	had been	sleeping
we	had been	sleeping
you	had been	sleeping
they	had been	sleeping

Future

Future I

I	will	sleep
you	will	sleep
he/she/it	will	sleep
we	will	sleep
you	will	sleep
they	will	sleep

Future I Continuous

I	will be	sleeping
you	will be	sleeping
he/she/it	will be	sleeping
we	will be	sleeping
you	will be	sleeping
they	will be	sleeping

Future II

I	will have	slept
you	will have	slept
he/she/it	will have	slept
we	will have	slept
you	will have	slept
they	will have	slept

Future II Continuous

I	will have been	sleeping
you	will have been	sleeping
he/she/it	will have been	sleeping
we	will have been	sleeping
you	will have been	sleeping
they	will have been	sleeping

Conditional

Conditional II

I	would sleep
you	would sleep
he/she/it	would sleep
we	would sleep
you	would sleep
they	would sleep

Conditional Past

I	would have	slept
you	would have	slept
he/she/it	would have	slept
we	would have	slept
you	would have	slept
they	would have	slept

Imperative
sleep

Gerund
sleeping

Past Participle
slept

Unregelmäßig

speak | sprechen

Simple

Present Simple
I	speak
you	speak
he/she/it	speaks
we	speak
you	speak
they	speak

Past Simple
I	spoke
you	spoke
he/she/it	spoke
we	spoke
you	spoke
they	spoke

Present Perfect
I	have	spoken
you	have	spoken
he/she/it	has	spoken
we	have	spoken
you	have	spoken
they	have	spoken

Past Perfect
I	had	spoken
you	had	spoken
he/she/it	had	spoken
we	had	spoken
you	had	spoken
they	had	spoken

Continuous

Present Continuous
I	am	speaking
you	are	speaking
he/she/it	is	speaking
we	are	speaking
you	are	speaking
they	are	speaking

Past Continuous
I	was	speaking
you	were	speaking
he/she/it	was	speaking
we	were	speaking
you	were	speaking
they	were	speaking

Present Perfect Continuous
I	have	been	speaking
you	have	been	speaking
he/she/it	has	been	speaking
we	have	been	speaking
you	have	been	speaking
they	have	been	speaking

Past Perfect Continuous
I	had	been	speaking
you	had	been	speaking
he/she/it	had	been	speaking
we	had	been	speaking
you	had	been	speaking
they	had	been	speaking

Future

Future I
I	will	speak
you	will	speak
he/she/it	will	speak
we	will	speak
you	will	speak
they	will	speak

Future I Continuous
I	will be speaking
you	will be speaking
he/she/it	will be speaking
we	will be speaking
you	will be speaking
they	will be speaking

Future II
I	will have	spoken
you	will have	spoken
he/she/it	will have	spoken
we	will have	spoken
you	will have	spoken
they	will have	spoken

Future II Continuous
I	will have been speaking
you	will have been speaking
he/she/it	will have been speaking
we	will have been speaking
you	will have been speaking
they	will have been speaking

Conditional

Conditional II
I	would speak
you	would speak
he/she/it	would speak
we	would speak
you	would speak
they	would speak

Conditional Past
I	would have	spoken
you	would have	spoken
he/she/it	would have	spoken
we	would have	spoken
you	would have	spoken
they	would have	spoken

Imperative
speak

Gerund
speaking

Past Participle
spoken

Unregelmäßig

spend | ausgeben/verbringen

Simple

Present Simple
I	spend
you	spend
he/she/it	spends
we	spend
you	spend
they	spend

Past Simple
I	spent
you	spent
he/she/it	spent
we	spent
you	spent
they	spent

Present Perfect
I	have	spent
you	have	spent
he/she/it	has	spent
we	have	spent
you	have	spent
they	have	spent

Past Perfect
I	had	spent
you	had	spent
he/she/it	had	spent
we	had	spent
you	had	spent
they	had	spent

Continuous

Present Continuous
I	am	spending
you	are	spending
he/she/it	is	spending
we	are	spending
you	are	spending
they	are	spending

Past Continuous
I	was	spending
you	were	spending
he/she/it	was	spending
we	were	spending
you	were	spending
they	were	spending

Present Perfect Continuous
I	have	been	spending
you	have	been	spending
he/she/it	has	been	spending
we	have	been	spending
you	have	been	spending
they	have	been	spending

Past Perfect Continuous
I	had	been	spending
you	had	been	spending
he/she/it	had	been	spending
we	had	been	spending
you	had	been	spending
they	had	been	spending

Future

Future I
I	will	spend
you	will	spend
he/she/it	will	spend
we	will	spend
you	will	spend
they	will	spend

Future I Continuous
I	will be	spending
you	will be	spending
he/she/it	will be	spending
we	will be	spending
you	will be	spending
they	will be	spending

Future II
I	will have	spent
you	will have	spent
he/she/it	will have	spent
we	will have	spent
you	will have	spent
they	will have	spent

Future II Continuous
I	will have been spending
you	will have been spending
he/she/it	will have been spending
we	will have been spending
you	will have been spending
they	will have been spending

Conditional

Conditional II
I	would spend
you	would spend
he/she/it	would spend
we	would spend
you	would spend
they	would spend

Conditional Past
I	would have	spent
you	would have	spent
he/she/it	would have	spent
we	would have	spent
you	would have	spent
they	would have	spent

Imperative
spend

Gerund
spending

Past Participle
spent

Unregelmäßig

stand | stehen

Simple

Present Simple

I	stand
you	stand
he/she/it	stands
we	stand
you	stand
they	stand

Past Simple

I	stood
you	stood
he/she/it	stood
we	stood
you	stood
they	stood

Present Perfect

I	have	stood
you	have	stood
he/she/it	has	stood
we	have	stood
you	have	stood
they	have	stood

Past Perfect

I	had	stood
you	had	stood
he/she/it	had	stood
we	had	stood
you	had	stood
they	had	stood

Continuous

Present Continuous

I	am	standing
you	are	standing
he/she/it	is	standing
we	are	standing
you	are	standing
they	are	standing

Past Continuous

I	was	standing
you	were	standing
he/she/it	was	standing
we	were	standing
you	were	standing
they	were	standing

Present Perfect Continuous

I	have been	standing
you	have been	standing
he/she/it	has been	standing
we	have been	standing
you	have been	standing
they	have been	standing

Past Perfect Continuous

I	had been	standing
you	had been	standing
he/she/it	had been	standing
we	had been	standing
you	had been	standing
they	had been	standing

Future

Future I

I	will	stand
you	will	stand
he/she/it	will	stand
we	will	stand
you	will	stand
they	will	stand

Future I Continuous

I	will be standing
you	will be standing
he/she/it	will be standing
we	will be standing
you	will be standing
they	will be standing

Future II

I	will have	stood
you	will have	stood
he/she/it	will have	stood
we	will have	stood
you	will have	stood
they	will have	stood

Future II Continuous

I	will have been	standing
you	will have been	standing
he/she/it	will have been	standing
we	will have been	standing
you	will have been	standing
they	will have been	standing

Conditional

Conditional II

I	would stand
you	would stand
he/she/it	would stand
we	would stand
you	would stand
they	would stand

Conditional Past

I	would have	stood
you	would have	stood
he/she/it	would have	stood
we	would have	stood
you	would have	stood
they	would have	stood

Imperative
stand

Gerund
standing

Past Participle
stood

Regelmäßig

stay | bleiben/übernachten

Simple

Present Simple

I	stay
you	stay
he/she/it	stays
we	stay
you	stay
they	stay

Past Simple

I	stayed
you	stayed
he/she/it	stayed
we	stayed
you	stayed
they	stayed

Present Perfect

I	have	stayed
you	have	stayed
he/she/it	has	stayed
we	have	stayed
you	have	stayed
they	have	stayed

Past Perfect

I	had	stayed
you	had	stayed
he/she/it	had	stayed
we	had	stayed
you	had	stayed
they	had	stayed

Continuous

Present Continuous

I	am	staying
you	are	staying
he/she/it	is	staying
we	are	staying
you	are	staying
they	are	staying

Past Continuous

I	was	staying
you	were	staying
he/she/it	was	staying
we	were	staying
you	were	staying
they	were	staying

Present Perfect Continuous

I	have	been	staying
you	have	been	staying
he/she/it	has	been	staying
we	have	been	staying
you	have	been	staying
they	have	been	staying

Past Perfect Continuous

I	had	been	staying
you	had	been	staying
he/she/it	had	been	staying
we	had	been	staying
you	had	been	staying
they	had	been	staying

Future

Future I

I	will	stay
you	will	stay
he/she/it	will	stay
we	will	stay
you	will	stay
they	will	stay

Future I Continuous

I	will be	staying
you	will be	staying
he/she/it	will be	staying
we	will be	staying
you	will be	staying
they	will be	staying

Future II

I	will have stayed
you	will have stayed
he/she/it	will have stayed
we	will have stayed
you	will have stayed
they	will have stayed

Future II Continuous

I	will have been staying
you	will have been staying
he/she/it	will have been staying
we	will have been staying
you	will have been staying
they	will have been staying

Conditional

Conditional II

I	would stay
you	would stay
he/she/it	would stay
we	would stay
you	would stay
they	would stay

Conditional Past

I	would have	stayed
you	would have	stayed
he/she/it	would have	stayed
we	would have	stayed
you	would have	stayed
they	would have	stayed

Imperative

stay

Gerund

staying

Past Participle

stayed

Konsonantenverdopplung
(siehe S. 152)

Unregelmäßig

swim | schwimmen

Simple

Present Simple

I	swim
you	swim
he/she/it	swims
we	swim
you	swim
they	swim

Past Simple

I	swam
you	swam
he/she/it	swam
we	swam
you	swam
they	swam

Present Perfect

I	have	swum
you	have	swum
he/she/it	has	swum
we	have	swum
you	have	swum
they	have	swum

Past Perfect

I	had	swum
you	had	swum
he/she/it	had	swum
we	had	swum
you	had	swum
they	had	swum

Continuous

Present Continuous

I	am	swimming
you	are	swimming
he/she/it	is	swimming
we	are	swimming
you	are	swimming
they	are	swimming

Past Continuous

I	was	swimming
you	were	swimming
he/she/it	was	swimming
we	were	swimming
you	were	swimming
they	were	swimming

Present Perfect Continuous

I	have	been	swimming
you	have	been	swimming
he/she/it	has	been	swimming
we	have	been	swimming
you	have	been	swimming
they	have	been	swimming

Past Perfect Continuous

I	had	been	swimming
you	had	been	swimming
he/she/it	had	been	swimming
we	had	been	swimming
you	had	been	swimming
they	had	been	swimming

Future

Future I

I	will	swim
you	will	swim
he/she/it	will	swim
we	will	swim
you	will	swim
they	will	swim

Future I Continuous

I	will be	swimming
you	will be	swimming
he/she/it	will be	swimming
we	will be	swimming
you	will be	swimming
they	will be	swimming

Future II

I	will have	swum
you	will have	swum
he/she/it	will have	swum
we	will have	swum
you	will have	swum
they	will have	swum

Future II Continuous

I	will have been swimming
you	will have been swimming
he/she/it	will have been swimming
we	will have been swimming
you	will have been swimming
they	will have been swimming

Conditional

Conditional II

I	would swim
you	would swim
he/she/it	would swim
we	would swim
you	would swim
they	would swim

Conditional Past

I	would have	swum
you	would have	swum
he/she/it	would have	swum
we	would have	swum
you	would have	swum
they	would have	swum

Imperative

swim

Gerund

swimming

Past Participle

swum

Unregelmäßig

take | nehmen

+ *-ing* wird ∉ (siehe S. 153)

Simple

Present Simple

I	take
you	take
he/she/it	takes
we	take
you	take
they	take

Past Simple

I	took
you	took
he/she/it	took
we	took
you	took
they	took

Present Perfect

I	have taken
you	have taken
he/she/it	has taken
we	have taken
you	have taken
they	have taken

Past Perfect

I	had taken
you	had taken
he/she/it	had taken
we	had taken
you	had taken
they	had taken

Continuous

Present Continuous

I	am taking
you	are taking
he/she/it	is taking
we	are taking
you	are taking
they	are taking

Past Continuous

I	was taking
you	were taking
he/she/it	was taking
we	were taking
you	were taking
they	were taking

Present Perfect Continuous

I	have been taking
you	have been taking
he/she/it	has been taking
we	have been taking
you	have been taking
they	have been taking

Past Perfect Continuous

I	had been taking
you	had been taking
he/she/it	had been taking
we	had been taking
you	had been taking
they	had been taking

Future

Future I

I	will take
you	will take
he/she/it	will take
we	will take
you	will take
they	will take

Future I Continuous

I	will be taking
you	will be taking
he/she/it	will be taking
we	will be taking
you	will be taking
they	will be taking

Future II

I	will have taken
you	will have taken
he/she/it	will have taken
we	will have taken
you	will have taken
they	will have taken

Future II Continuous

I	will have been taking
you	will have been taking
he/she/it	will have been taking
we	will have been taking
you	will have been taking
they	will have been taking

Conditional

Conditional II

I	would take
you	would take
he/she/it	would take
we	would take
you	would take
they	would take

Conditional Past

I	would have taken
you	would have taken
he/she/it	would have taken
we	would have taken
you	would have taken
they	would have taken

Imperative

take

Gerund

taking

Past Participle

taken

Unregelmäßig

think | denken

Simple

Present Simple
I	think
you	think
he/she/it	thinks
we	think
you	think
they	think

Past Simple
I	thought
you	thought
he/she/it	thought
we	thought
you	thought
they	thought

Present Perfect
I	have	thought
you	have	thought
he/she/it	has	thought
we	have	thought
you	have	thought
they	have	thought

Past Perfect
I	had	thought
you	had	thought
he/she/it	had	thought
we	had	thought
you	had	thought
they	had	thought

Continuous

Present Continuous
I	am	thinking
you	are	thinking
he/she/it	is	thinking
we	are	thinking
you	are	thinking
they	are	thinking

Past Continuous
I	was	thinking
you	were	thinking
he/she/it	was	thinking
we	were	thinking
you	were	thinking
they	were	thinking

Present Perfect Continuous
I	have	been	thinking
you	have	been	thinking
he/she/it	has	been	thinking
we	have	been	thinking
you	have	been	thinking
they	have	been	thinking

Past Perfect Continuous
I	had	been	thinking
you	had	been	thinking
he/she/it	had	been	thinking
we	had	been	thinking
you	had	been	thinking
they	had	been	thinking

Future

Future I
I	will	think
you	will	think
he/she/it	will	think
we	will	think
you	will	think
they	will	think

Future I Continuous
I	will be	thinking
you	will be	thinking
he/she/it	will be	thinking
we	will be	thinking
you	will be	thinking
they	will be	thinking

Future II
I	will have	thought
you	will have	thought
he/she/it	will have	thought
we	will have	thought
you	will have	thought
they	will have	thought

Future II Continuous
I	will have been	thinking
you	will have been	thinking
he/she/it	will have been	thinking
we	will have been	thinking
you	will have been	thinking
they	will have been	thinking

Conditional

Conditional II
I	would think
you	would think
he/she/it	would think
we	would think
you	would think
they	would think

Conditional Past
I	would have	thought
you	would have	thought
he/she/it	would have	thought
we	would have	thought
you	would have	thought
they	would have	thought

Imperative
think

Gerund
thinking

Past Participle
thought

Regelmäßig

travel | reisen

Konsonantenverdopplung
im BE (siehe S. 152). Im AE keine
Verdopplung.

Simple		Continuous			Future			Conditional	
Present Simple		**Present Continuous**			**Future I**			**Conditional II**	
I	travel	I	am	travelling	I	will	travel	I	would travel
you	travel	you	are	travelling	you	will	travel	you	would travel
he/she/it	travels	he/she/it	is	travelling	he/she/it	will	travel	he/she/it	would travel
we	travel	we	are	travelling	we	will	travel	we	would travel
you	travel	you	are	travelling	you	will	travel	you	would travel
they	travel	they	are	travelling	they	will	travel	they	would travel
Past Simple		**Past Continuous**			**Future I Continuous**			**Conditional Past**	
I	travelled	I	was	travelling	I	will be	travelling	I	would have travelled
you	travelled	you	were	travelling	you	will be	travelling	you	would have travelled
he/she/it	travelled	he/she/it	was	travelling	he/she/it	will be	travelling	he/she/it	would have travelled
we	travelled	we	were	travelling	we	will be	travelling	we	would have travelled
you	travelled	you	were	travelling	you	will be	travelling	you	would have travelled
they	travelled	they	were	travelling	they	will be	travelling	they	would have travelled
Present Perfect		**Present Perfect Continuous**			**Future II**				
I	have travelled	I	have been	travelling	I	will have	travelled	**Imperative**	
you	have travelled	you	have been	travelling	you	will have	travelled	travel	
he/she/it	has travelled	he/she/it	has been	travelling	he/she/it	will have	travelled		
we	have travelled	we	have been	travelling	we	will have	travelled	**Gerund**	
you	have travelled	you	have been	travelling	you	will have	travelled	travelling	
they	have travelled	they	have been	travelling	they	will have	travelled		
Past Perfect		**Past Perfect Continuous**			**Future II Continuous**			**Past Participle**	
I	had travelled	I	had been	travelling	I	will have been travelling		travelled	
you	had travelled	you	had been	travelling	you	will have been travelling			
he/she/it	had travelled	he/she/it	had been	travelling	he/she/it	will have been travelling			
we	had travelled	we	had been	travelling	we	will have been travelling			
you	had travelled	you	had been	travelling	you	will have been travelling			
they	had travelled	they	had been	travelling	they	will have been travelling			

Regelmäßig

visit | besuchen/ besichtigen

Simple

Present Simple
I	visit
you	visit
he/she/it	visits
we	visit
you	visit
they	visit

Past Simple
I	visited
you	visited
he/she/it	visited
we	visited
you	visited
they	visited

Present Perfect
I	have	visited
you	have	visited
he/she/it	has	visited
we	have	visited
you	have	visited
they	have	visited

Past Perfect
I	had	visited
you	had	visited
he/she/it	had	visited
we	had	visited
you	had	visited
they	had	visited

Continuous

Present Continuous
I	am	visiting
you	are	visiting
he/she/it	is	visiting
we	are	visiting
you	are	visiting
they	are	visiting

Past Continuous
I	was	visiting
you	were	visiting
he/she/it	was	visiting
we	were	visiting
you	were	visiting
they	were	visiting

Present Perfect Continuous
I	have	been	visiting
you	have	been	visiting
he/she/it	has	been	visiting
we	have	been	visiting
you	have	been	visiting
they	have	been	visiting

Past Perfect Continuous
I	had	been	visiting
you	had	been	visiting
he/she/it	had	been	visiting
we	had	been	visiting
you	had	been	visiting
they	had	been	visiting

Future

Future I
I	will	visit
you	will	visit
he/she/it	will	visit
we	will	visit
you	will	visit
they	will	visit

Future I Continuous
I	will be	visiting
you	will be	visiting
he/she/it	will be	visiting
we	will be	visiting
you	will be	visiting
they	will be	visiting

Future II
I	will have visited
you	will have visited
he/she/it	will have visited
we	will have visited
you	will have visited
they	will have visited

Future II Contlimous
I	will have been visiting
you	will have been visiting
he/she/it	will have been visiting
we	will have been visiting
you	will have been visiting
they	will have been visiting

Conditional

Conditional II
I	would visit
you	would visit
he/she/it	would visit
we	would visit
you	would visit
they	would visit

Conditional Past
I	would have	visited
you	would have	visited
he/she/it	would have	visited
we	would have	visited
you	would have	visited
they	would have	visited

Imperative
visit

Gerund
visiting

Past Participle
visited

Regelmäßig

wait | warten

Simple

Present Simple
I	wait
you	wait
he/she/it	waits
we	wait
you	wait
they	wait

Past Simple
I	waited
you	waited
he/she/it	waited
we	waited
you	waited
they	waited

Present Perfect
I	have	waited
you	have	waited
he/she/it	has	waited
we	have	waited
you	have	waited
they	have	waited

Past Perfect
I	had	waited
you	had	waited
he/she/it	had	waited
we	had	waited
you	had	waited
they	had	waited

Continuous

Present Continuous
I	am	waiting
you	are	waiting
he/she/it	is	waiting
we	are	waiting
you	are	waiting
they	are	waiting

Past Continuous
I	was	waiting
you	were	waiting
he/she/it	was	waiting
we	were	waiting
you	were	waiting
they	were	waiting

Present Perfect Continuous
I	have	been	waiting
you	have	been	waiting
he/she/it	has	been	waiting
we	have	been	waiting
you	have	been	waiting
they	have	been	waiting

Past Perfect Continuous
I	had	been	waiting
you	had	been	waiting
he/she/it	had	been	waiting
we	had	been	waiting
you	had	been	waiting
they	had	been	waiting

Future

Future I
I	will	wait
you	will	wait
he/she/it	will	wait
we	will	wait
you	will	wait
they	will	wait

Future I Continuous
I	will be	waiting
you	will be	waiting
he/she/it	will be	waiting
we	will be	waiting
you	will be	waiting
they	will be	waiting

Future II
I	will have	waited
you	will have	waited
he/she/it	will have	waited
we	will have	waited
you	will have	waited
they	will have	waited

Future II Continuous
I	will have been waiting
you	will have been waiting
he/she/it	will have been waiting
we	will have been waiting
you	will have been waiting
they	will have been waiting

Conditional

Conditional II
I	would wait
you	would wait
he/she/it	would wait
we	would wait
you	would wait
they	would wait

Conditional Past
I	would have	waited
you	would have	waited
he/she/it	would have	waited
we	would have	waited
you	would have	waited
they	would have	waited

Imperative
wait

Gerund
waiting

Past Participle
waited

Regelmäßig
Modalverb

want | wollen/mögen

Keine *Present Continuous* Form
möglich.

Simple

Present Simple
I	want
you	want
he/she/it	wants
we	want
you	want
they	want

Past Simple
I	wanted
you	wanted
he/she/it	wanted
we	wanted
you	wanted
they	wanted

Present Perfect
I	have	wanted
you	have	wanted
he/she/it	has	wanted
we	have	wanted
you	have	wanted
they	have	wanted

Past Perfect
I	had	wanted
you	had	wanted
he/she/it	had	wanted
we	had	wanted
you	had	wanted
they	had	wanted

Continuous

Present Continuous
—

Past Continuous*
I	was	wanting
you	were	wanting
he/she/it	was	wanting
we	were	wanting
you	were	wanting
they	were	wanting

Present Perfect Continuous
I	have	been	wanting
you	have	been	wanting
he/she/it	has	been	wanting
we	have	been	wanting
you	have	been	wanting
they	have	been	wanting

Past Perfect Continuous
I	had	been	wanting
you	had	been	wanting
he/she/it	had	been	wanting
we	had	been	wanting
you	had	been	wanting
they	had	been	wanting

Future

Future I
I	will	want
you	will	want
he/she/it	will	want
we	will	want
you	will	want
they	will	want

Future I Continuous
I	will be	wanting
you	will be	wanting
he/she/it	will be	wanting
we	will be	wanting
you	will be	wanting
they	will be	wanting

Future II
I	will have	wanted
you	will have	wanted
he/she/it	will have	wanted
we	will have	wanted
you	will have	wanted
they	will have	wanted

Future II Continuous
I	will have been	wanting
you	will have been	wanting
he/she/it	will have been	wanting
we	will have been	wanting
you	will have been	wanting
they	will have been	wanting

Conditional

Conditional II
I	would want
you	would want
he/she/it	would want
we	would want
you	would want
they	would want

Conditional Past
I	would have	wanted
you	would have	wanted
he/she/it	would have	wanted
we	would have	wanted
you	would have	wanted
they	would have	wanted

Imperative
want*

Gerund
wanting

Past Participle
wanted

241

Regelmäßig

wash | waschen

+ **-es** in 3. Person Singular (siehe S. 152, Aussprache siehe S. 154)

Simple

Present Simple

I	wash
you	wash
he/she/it	washes
we	wash
you	wash
they	wash

Past Simple

I	washed
you	washed
he/she/it	washed
we	washed
you	washed
they	washed

Present Perfect

I	have washed
you	have washed
he/she/it	has washed
we	have washed
you	have washed
they	have washed

Past Perfect

I	had washed
you	had washed
he/she/it	had washed
we	had washed
you	had washed
they	had washed

Continuous

Present Continuous

I	am	washing
you	are	washing
he/she/it	is	washing
we	are	washing
you	are	washing
they	are	washing

Past Continuous

I	was	washing
you	were	washing
he/she/it	was	washing
we	were	washing
you	were	washing
they	were	washing

Present Perfect Continuous

I	have been washing
you	have been washing
he/she/it	has been washing
we	have been washing
you	have been washing
they	have been washing

Past Perfect Continuous

I	had been washing
you	had been washing
he/she/it	had been washing
we	had been washing
you	had been washing
they	had been washing

Future

Future I

I	will	wash
you	will	wash
he/she/it	will	wash
we	will	wash
you	will	wash
they	will	wash

Future I Continuous

I	will be washing
you	will be washing
he/she/it	will be washing
we	will be washing
you	will be washing
they	will be washing

Future II

I	will have washed
you	will have washed
he/she/it	will have washed
we	will have washed
you	will have washed
they	will have washed

Future II Continuous

I	will have been washing
you	will have been washing
he/she/it	will have been washing
we	will have been washing
you	will have been washing
they	will have been washing

Conditional

Conditional II

I	would wash
you	would wash
he/she/it	would wash
we	would wash
you	would wash
they	would wash

Conditional Past

I	would have washed
you	would have washed
he/she/it	would have washed
we	would have washed
you	would have washed
they	would have washed

Imperative

wash

Gerund

washing

Past Participle

washed

Unregelmäßig

wear | tragen

Simple

Present Simple

I	wear
you	wear
he/she/it	wears
we	wear
you	wear
they	wear

Past Simple

I	wore
you	wore
he/she/it	wore
we	wore
you	wore
they	wore

Present Perfect

I	have	worn
you	have	worn
he/she/it	has	worn
we	have	worn
you	have	worn
they	have	worn

Past Perfect

I	had	worn
you	had	worn
he/she/it	had	worn
we	had	worn
you	had	worn
they	had	worn

Continuous

Present Continuous

I	am	wearing
you	are	wearing
he/she/it	is	wearing
we	are	wearing
you	are	wearing
they	are	wearing

Past Continuous

I	was	wearing
you	were	wearing
he/she/it	was	wearing
we	were	wearing
you	were	wearing
they	were	wearing

Present Perfect Continuous

I	have	been	wearing
you	have	been	wearing
he/she/it	has	been	wearing
we	have	been	wearing
you	have	been	wearing
they	have	been	wearing

Past Perfect Continuous

I	had	been	wearing
you	had	been	wearing
he/she/it	had	been	wearing
we	had	been	wearing
you	had	been	wearing
they	had	been	wearing

Future

Future I

I	will	wear
you	will	wear
he/she/it	will	wear
we	will	wear
you	will	wear
they	will	wear

Future I Continuous

I	will be wearing
you	will be wearing
he/she/it	will be wearing
we	will be wearing
you	will be wearing
they	will be wearing

Future II

I	will have	worn
you	will have	worn
he/she/it	will have	worn
we	will have	worn
you	will have	worn
they	will have	worn

Future II Continuous

I	will have been wearing
you	will have been wearing
he/she/it	will have been wearing
we	will have been wearing
you	will have been wearing
they	will have been wearing

Conditional

Conditional II

I	would wear
you	would wear
he/she/it	would wear
we	would wear
you	would wear
they	would wear

Conditional Past

I	would have	worn
you	would have	worn
he/she/it	would have	worn
we	would have	worn
you	would have	worn
they	would have	worn

Imperative

wear

Gerund

wearing

Past Participle

worn

Regelmäßig

work | arbeiten

Simple		Continuous		Future		Conditional	

Present Simple

I	work
you	work
he/she/it	works
we	work
you	work
they	work

Present Continuous

I	am	working
you	are	working
he/she/it	is	working
we	are	working
you	are	working
they	are	working

Future I

I	will	work
you	will	work
he/she/it	will	work
we	will	work
you	will	work
they	will	work

Conditional II

I	would work
you	would work
he/she/it	would work
we	would work
you	would work
they	would work

Past Simple

I	worked
you	worked
he/she/it	worked
we	worked
you	worked
they	worked

Past Continuous

I	was	working
you	were	working
he/she/it	was	working
we	were	working
you	were	working
they	were	working

Future I Continuous

I	will be working
you	will be working
he/she/it	will be working
we	will be working
you	will be working
they	will be working

Conditional Past

I	would have worked
you	would have worked
he/she/it	would have worked
we	would have worked
you	would have worked
they	would have worked

Present Perfect

I	have worked
you	have worked
he/she/it	has worked
we	have worked
you	have worked
they	have worked

Present Perfect Continuous

I	have been working
you	have been working
he/she/it	has been working
we	have been working
you	have been working
they	have been working

Future II

I	will have worked
you	will have worked
he/she/it	will have worked
we	will have worked
you	will have worked
they	will have worked

Imperative

work

Gerund

working

Past Participle

worked

Past Perfect

I	had worked
you	had worked
he/she/it	had worked
we	had worked
you	had worked
they	had worked

Past Perfect Continuous

I	had been working
you	had been working
he/she/it	had been working
we	had been working
you	had been working
they	had been working

Future II Continuous

I	will have been working
you	will have been working
he/she/it	will have been working
we	will have been working
you	will have been working
they	will have been working

Unregelmäßig

write | schreiben

+ *-ing* wird ∉ (siehe S. 153)

Simple

Present Simple
I	write
you	write
he/she/it	writes
we	write
you	write
they	write

Past Simple
I	wrote
you	wrote
he/she/it	wrote
we	wrote
you	wrote
they	wrote

Present Perfect
I	have	written
you	have	written
he/she/it	has	written
we	have	written
you	have	written
they	have	written

Past Perfect
I	had	written
you	had	written
he/she/it	had	written
we	had	written
you	had	written
they	had	written

Continuous

Present Continuous
I	am	writing
you	are	writing
he/she/it	is	writing
we	are	writing
you	are	writing
they	are	writing

Past Continuous
I	was	writing
you	were	writing
he/she/it	was	writing
we	were	writing
you	were	writing
they	were	writing

Present Perfect Continuous
I	have	been	writing
you	have	been	writing
he/she/it	has	been	writing
we	have	been	writing
you	have	been	writing
they	have	been	writing

Past Perfect Continuous
I	had	been	writing
you	had	been	writing
he/she/it	had	been	writing
we	had	been	writing
you	had	been	writing
they	had	been	writing

Future

Future I
I	will	write
you	will	write
he/she/it	will	write
we	will	write
you	will	write
they	will	write

Future I Continuous
I	will be	writing
you	will be	writing
he/she/it	will be	writing
we	will be	writing
you	will be	writing
they	will be	writing

Future II
I	will have	written
you	will have	written
he/she/it	will have	written
we	will have	written
you	will have	written
they	will have	written

Future II Continuous
I	will have been writing
you	will have been writing
he/she/it	will have been writing
we	will have been writing
you	will have been writing
they	will have been writing

Conditional

Conditional II
I	would write
you	would write
he/she/it	would write
we	would write
you	would write
they	would write

Conditional Past
I	would have	written
you	would have	written
he/she/it	would have	written
we	would have	written
you	would have	written
they	would have	written

Imperative
write

Gerund
writing

Past Participle
written

Infinitive	Past Simple	Past Participle	German

Unregelmäßige englische Verben

Infinitiv	Vergangenheit	Partizip Perfekt	Deutsch
arise	arose	arisen	sich ergeben, entstehen
awake	awoke	awoken	erwachen
be	was/were	been	sein
bear	bore	borne	tragen, ertragen
beat	beat	beaten	schlagen
become	became	become	werden
begin	began	begun	beginnen
bend	bent	bent	beugen, verbiegen
bet	bet, betted	bet, betted	wetten
bind	bound	bound	binden
bleed	bled	bled	bluten
bite	bit	bitten	beißen
blow	blew	blown	blasen
break	broke	broken	(zer)brechen
breed	bred	bred	züchten, brüten
bring	brought	brought	(her)bringen
build	built	built	bauen
burn	burnt	burnt	verbrennen
burst	burst	burst	platzen, aufbrechen
buy	bought	bought	kaufen
can	could	(been able)	können
cast	cast	cast	werfen
catch	caught	caught	fangen
choose	chose	chosen	wählen
come	came	come	kommen
cost	cost	cost	kosten
creep	crept	crept	schleichen, kriechen
cut	cut	cut	schneiden
dig	dug	dug	graben

do	did	done	machen, tun
draw	drew	drawn	zeichnen
dream	dreamt	dreamt	träumen
drink	drank	drunk	trinken
drive	drove	driven	fahren
eat	ate	eaten	essen
fall	fell	fallen	fallen
feed	fed	fed	füttern
feel	felt	felt	(sich) fühlen
fight	fought	fought	kämpfen
find	found	found	finden
flee	fled	fled	fliehen, flüchten
fling	flung	flung	schleudern
fly	flew	flown	fliegen
forbid	forbad, forbade	forbidden	verbieten
forecast	forecast, forecasted	forecast, forecasted	vorhersagen
forget	forgot	forgotten	vergessen
forgive	forgave	forgiven	verzeihen
freeze	froze	frozen	(ge)frieren
get	got	got, AE: gotten	bekommen
give	gave	given	geben
go	went	gone	gehen
grind	ground	ground	(zer)mahlen
grow	grew	grown	wachsen
hang	hung	hung	hängen
have	had	had	haben
hear	heard	heard	hören
hide	hid	hidden	(sich) verstecken
hit	hit	hit	schlagen
hold	held	held	halten
hurt	hurt	hurt	wehtun
keep	kept	kept	behalten
kneel	knelt	knelt	knien
know	knew	known	wissen, kennen
lay	laid	laid	legen

lead	led	led	führen
lean	leant, leaned	leant, leaned	lehnen, sich neigen
leap	leapt, leaped	leapt, leaped	springen
learn	learnt, learned	learnt, learned	lernen
leave	left	left	(ver)lassen
lend	lent	lent	(aus)leihen
let	let	let	lassen
lie	lay	lain	liegen
light	lit	lit	anzünden
lose	lost	lost	verlieren
make	made	made	machen
may	might	—	dürfen
mean	meant	meant	bedeuten, meinen
meet	met	met	treffen
mistake	mistook	mistaken	falsch verstehen
must	(had to)	(had to)	müssen
pay	paid	paid	bezahlen
put	put	put	legen, stellen, setzen
quit	quit, quitted	quit, quitted	aufhören
read	read	read	lesen
ride	rode	ridden	reiten, fahren
ring	rang	rung	klingeln
rise	rose	risen	aufstehen, (an)steigen
run	ran	run	rennen
saw	sawed	sawn, sawed	sägen
say	said	said	sagen
see	saw	seen	sehen
seek	sought	sought	suchen, streben
sell	sold	sold	verkaufen
send	sent	sent	schicken
set	set	set	setzen, legen, festsetzen
sew	sewed	sewn	nähen
shake	shook	shaken	schütteln
shine	shone	shone	scheinen
shoot	shot	shot	(er)schießen

show	showed	shown	zeigen
shrink	shrank	shrunk	einlaufen, schrumpfen
shut	shut	shut	schließen
sing	sang	sung	singen
sink	sank	sunk	versenken, sinken
sit	sat	sat	sitzen
sleep	slept	slept	schlafen
slide	slid	slid	rutschen
smell	smelt	smelt	riechen
sow	sowed	sown, sowed	säen
speak	spoke	spoken	sprechen
spell	spelt, spelled	spelt, spelled	buchstabieren
spend	spent	spent	ausgeben, verbringen
spill	spilt, spilled	spilt, spilled	verschütten
spin	spun	spun	spinnen, drehen
spit	spat	spat	spucken
split	split	split	spalten
spoil	spoilt, spoiled	spoilt, spoiled	verderben
spread	spread	spread	ausbreiten, bestreichen
stand	stood	stood	stehen
steal	stole	stolen	stehlen
stick	stuck	stuck	kleben
sting	stung	stung	stechen
stink	stank	stunk	stinken
stride	strode	stridden	schreiten
strike	struck	struck	schlagen
strive	strove	striven	sich bemühen
swear	swore	sworn	schwören
sweep	swept	swept	kehren
swim	swam	swum	schwimmen
swing	swung	swung	schwingen
take	took	taken	nehmen
teach	taught	taught	lehren
tear	tore	torn	zerreißen
tell	told	told	erzählen
think	thought	thought	denken

throw	threw	thrown	werfen
understand	understood	understood	verstehen
upset	upset	upset	umstoßen, erschüttern
wake	woke	woken	(auf)wachen
wear	wore	worn	tragen
weave	wove	woven	weben
weep	wept	wept	weinen
win	won	won	gewinnen
wind	wound	wound	wickeln, spulen
wring	wrung	wrung	auswringen
write	wrote	written	schreiben

Alphabetische Verbliste Deutsch – Englisch

A

		Seite
absagen	cancel	175
ändern	change	178
anfangen	begin	168
ankommen	arrive	164
anrufen	call	173
antworten	answer	163
arbeiten	work	244
ausgeben	spend	232
ausleihen	lend	208
auswählen	choose	179

B

beginnen	begin	168
bekommen	get	196
besichtigen	visit	239
besuchen	visit	239
bleiben	stay	234
brauchen	need	217
brechen	break	170
bringen	bring	171
buchen	book	169

D

denken	think	237

E

einladen	invite	204
entscheiden	decide	185
erlauben	allow	162
essen	eat	189

F

fahren	drive	188
fallen	fall	191
fangen	catch	177
finden	find	193
fliegen	fly	194
fragen	ask	165
fühlen	feel	192

G

geben	give	197
gehen	go	198
genießen	enjoy	190

H

haben	have	199
helfen	help	201
hören	hear	200

K

kaufen	buy	172
kennen	know	205
kochen	cook	182
können	can/be able to	174
kommen	come	181
kosten	cost	183

L

laufen	run	223
leben	live	211
legen	put	221
leihen	lend	208
lernen	learn	206
lesen	read	222

M

machen	make	214
mitbringen	bring	171
mögen	like	209
mögen	want	241
müssen	must	216

3 | Übungsgrammatik

Inhalt

So ist die Übungsgrammatik aufgebaut

Die Übungsgrammatik besteht aus 12 Modulen und 12 Tests. Jedes Modul beginnt mit einer leichten Einführung zu den jeweiligen Themen. Im Anschluss erhalten Sie genaue Erklärungen und haben die Möglichkeit, in zahlreichen Übungen das Gelernte anzuwenden. Nach jedem Modul können Sie einen Test machen, um zu überprüfen, ob Sie die Inhalte auch sicher beherrschen.

Die Übungsgrammatik wird durch **Audio-Dateien** zum Download ergänzt. Viele der Übungen und Texte finden Sie auch hier, wodurch Sie zusätzlich ihr Hörverstehen und ihre Aussprache üben können.

Bildsymbole

 Dieses Bildsymbol zeigt Ihnen, dass Sie den Text der Übung auch anhören können, indem Sie die jeweilige Sounddatei unter www.pons.de/grammatik-komplett-englisch herunterladen.

 Für eine Übung mit diesem Symbol brauchen Sie einen Stift, um etwas zu schreiben oder einzutragen.

 Auch für diese Übungen brauchen Sie einen Stift, diesmal um etwas anzukreuzen oder zu verbinden.

 Bei diesem Symbol werden Sie aufgefordert ein zusätzliches Blatt zu verwenden, um die Übung zu machen.

 Mit diesem Symbol werden Sie darauf hingewiesen, dass Sie die Inhalte besonders aufmerksam lesen sollten.

Nice to know Im gesprochenen Englisch sagt man sehr oft **I guess** an Stelle von **I think**.	In der Box erhalten Sie nützliche und interessante Hinweise zur englischen Sprache und landesüblichen Besonderheiten.
book – *Buch* **kiss** – *Kuss* **knive** – *Messer* **half** – *Hälfte* ▸	Das Wortschatzfeld enthält Wörter und Wendungen, die für die jeweiligen Übungen hilfreich sind.
Lerntipp! Oft müssen Sie sich noch unbekannte Wörter selbst erschließen. Stellen Sie sich dabei z.B. folgende Frage: Kenne ich ein deutsches Wort, das ähnlich ist?	In dieser Box finden Sie Tipps, die Ihnen das Lernen erleichtern können.

Lösungen:
Wortverzeichnis:

In diesem Teil finden Sie die Lösungen zu allen Übungen. In diesem alphabetisch sortierten Wortverzeichnis finden Sie schnell alle verwendeten Wörter mit deren Übersetzungen.

Die Einkaufsliste / Englische Substantive

1

Die Familie Smith, Paul, seine Frau Kate und ihre beiden Kinder Ben und Jane leben in Manchester. Montags gehen Paul und Kate immer einkaufen. Kate ist gerade dabei, die Einkaufsliste zu schreiben.
Lesen Sie den Dialog und markieren Sie im Text die Pluralformen (Mehrzahl) der Substantive (Hauptwörter).
Sie können den Dialog auch hören.

Kate: What do we need?

Paul: Oranges, apples, pears and bananas.

Kate: There are apples in the fruit bowl.

Paul: Yes, I know, but I prefer green apples. Oh, and we definitely need a bottle of milk and a piece of butter.

Kate: Do we have salad?

Paul: No, we don't. Write it down, please. What about Ben's birthday present? Does he need new trousers?

Kate: Hmm ... We can buy him tickets for the Manchester United football match. There's a ticket-office near the supermarket.

Paul: That's a good idea. How about for dinner tonight?

Kate: We can buy a bottle of wine for us and an apple pie for dessert for the children.

Paul: Why only for the children? I love apple pie with vanilla ice cream.

> **need** – *brauchen*
> **apple** – *Apfel*
> **pear** – *Birne*
> **banana** – *Banane*
> **fruit bowl** – *Obstschale*
> **know** – *wissen*
> **prefer** – *bevorzugen*
> **definitely** – *unbedingt*
> **bottle** – *Flasche*
> **milk** – *Milch*
> **piece** – *Stück*
> **birthday present** – *Geburtstagsgeschenk*
> **trousers** – *Hose*
> **near** – *in der Nähe von*
> **office** – *Büro*
> **idea** – *Idee*
> **wine** – *Wein*
> **apple pie** – *Apfelkuchen*
> **dessert** – *Nachtisch*
> **children** – *Kinder*
> **vanilla ice cream** – *Vanilleeis*

2

Hier sehen Sie englische Substantive mit dem bestimmten Artikel **the**.
Sprechen Sie die Wörter laut aus. Wenn Sie möchten, können Sie sich die Begriffe anhören. Achten Sie dabei auf die unterschiedliche
Aussprache des Artikels.

> 1. the apple   2. the pear   3. the trousers
> 4. the office   5. the children

Groß- und Kleinschreibung

3 👓

Groß- und **Kleinschreibung**
Im Gegensatz zum Deutschen werden Substantive im Englischen meist kleingeschrieben: **bus, love, child, dog.**

Es gibt aber auch Substantive, die immer großgeschrieben werden.
Hierzu gehören
- die Wochentage: **Monday, Tuesday, Wednesday, Thursday, Friday,
        Saturday, Sunday**

- die Monate: **January, February, March, April, May, June, July, August,
        September, October, November, December**

- Länder, Sprachen und Nationalitäten:

England	**English**
France	**French**
the United States of America	**American**
Germany	**German**

- sowie Eigennamen: z.B. **Paul Smith**, **the Beatles** oder **Top Line Software Company.**

Nice to know

Das Wort für Sprache und Nationalität ist im Englischen oft gleich.
I'm English.
Ich bin Engländer.
She speaks English.
Sie spricht Englisch.

4 ✐

Schreiben Sie die englischen Übersetzungen der Wörter in die Lücken.
Achten Sie besonders auf die Groß- und Kleinschreibung.

1. *Nachtisch* _____
2. *Hose* _____
3. *französisch* _____
4. *Hund* _____
5. *März* _____
6. *Samstag* _____
7. *Kinder* _____
8. *Freitag* _____
9. *Abendessen* _____
10. *Spanien* _____

The und *a/an*

5

Die Artikel

Im Englischen gibt es nur einen bestimmten Artikel: **the**.

the computer	*der Computer*
the door	*die Tür*
the car	*das Auto*

Die Aussprache stellt dabei eine Besonderheit dar:
Beginnt das nachfolgende Substantiv mit einem Vokal (a, e, i, o, u), so wird der Artikel **the** mit **i** ausgesprochen. Folgt ein Substantiv, das mit einem Konsonanten (b, m, t, r, w, s, etc.) beginnt, so bleibt die Aussprache von **the** so wie Sie sie bereits kennen.
Wenn Sie möchten, finden Sie hierzu Hörbeispiele, die Sie nachsprechen können.

Der unbestimmte Artikel (*ein, eine*) heißt **a** oder **an**.
Beginnt das nachfolgende Wort mit einem Konsonanten, verwendet man **a**, wie in **a pear**.
Beginnt das nachfolgende Wort mit einem Vokal, verwendet man **an**, wie in **an apple**. Auch diese Beispiele können Sie sich anhören.

> **Nice to know**
>
> Bei Wörtern, die mit **h** beginnen, wird **a** zu **an**, wenn das **h** nicht gesprochen wird.
> Man sagt **a house**, aber **an hour**.

6 🖉

Welcher unbestimmte Artikel ist hier richtig? Schreiben Sie **a** oder **an** in die Lücken.

1. _____ office

2. _____ bottle

3. _____ dog

4. _____ ice cream

5. _____ hour

6. _____ minute

7. _____ orange

8. _____ computer

9. _____ idea

10. _____ banana

11. _____ office

12. _____ pear

> ◁ **dog** – *Hund*
> **hour** – *Stunde*
> **minute** – *Minute*
> **orange** – *Orange*

Pluralbildung

7

Die Bildung des Plural

Der Plural (Mehrzahl) von Substantiven wird gebildet, indem man einfach ein **-s** an die Singularform anhängt: **book – books.**

Bei Wörtern, die auf einen Zischlaut enden, **-s**, **-ss**, **-sh**, **-ch**, **-x** oder **-z**, wird im Plural ein **-es** als Endung angehängt: **kiss – kisses.**

Endet ein Wort auf einen **Konsonanten + -y**, fällt das **y** weg und es wird **-ies** angehängt: **family – families.**
Endet das Wort jedoch auf einen **Vokal + -y**, wird nur ein **-s** angehängt:
    day – days.

book – *Buch*
kiss – *Kuss*
knive – *Messer*
half – *Hälfte*
roof – *Dach*

Bei Substantiven, die auf **-f** oder **-fe** enden, ändert sich das **f** zu **v** und es wird **-ves** angehängt.
    knife – knives
    half – halves
Es gibt allerdings einige Ausnahmen, die den Plural regelmäßig bilden wie zum Beispiel **roof – roofs.**

Die häufigsten unregelmäßigen Pluralformen lauten:

child	**children**	*Kinder*
man	**men**	*Männer*
woman	**women**	*Frauen*
foot	**feet**	*Füße*
tooth	**teeth**	*Zähne*
mouse	**mice**	*Mäuse*
tomato	**tomatoes**	*Tomaten*
fish	**fish**	*Fische*

Nice to know

Es gibt auch Substantive, die nur im Plural gebraucht werden.
glasses *Brille*
trousers *Hose*
news *Nachrichten*

8

Verbinden Sie die Wörter links jeweils mit der richtigen Pluralform rechts.
Die Aussprache der Vokabeln können Sie sich auch anhören.

1. knife
2. woman
3. orange
4. house
5. child

a. houses
b. children
c. knives
d. oranges
e. women

house – *Haus*

Plural / Zählbare und nicht zählbare Substantive

9 ✏

Schreiben Sie die Pluralformen der folgenden Wörter in die Lücken.

1. **book** _____   6. **knife** _____

2. **city** _____   7. **ticket** _____

3. **tomato** _____   8. **kiss** _____

4. **fish** _____   9. **mouse** _____

5. **present** _____   10. **roof** _____

10 👓

Zählbar oder **nicht zählbar**?
Im Englischen wird zwischen zählbaren (**apple**, **car** etc.) und nicht zählbaren
(**love**, **milk** etc.) Substantiven unterschieden.

Zählbare Substantive haben sowohl eine Plural- als auch eine Singularform und
können mit **a/an** oder einer Zahl verwendet werden:
That's a good idea. We need four bananas.

Nicht zählbare Substantive haben nur eine Form. **A** oder **an** können nie direkt vor
dem betreffenden Wort stehen.
> **Too much coffee isn't good for you.**
> *Zu viel Kaffee ist nicht gut für dich.*
> **Music helps me to relax.** *Musik hilft mir zu entspannen.*

Durch a ... of ... können nicht zählbare Dinge eine zählbare Form bekommen.

a cup of coffee	*eine Tasse Kaffee*
a slice of toast	*eine Scheibe Toast*
a packet of rice	*eine Packung Reis*
a piece of cake	*ein Stück Kuchen*
a bottle of coke	*eine Flasche Cola*

Zählbar oder nicht zählbar?

11 ✏️

Kreuzen Sie jeweils das Wort an, das **nicht** zählbar ist.

1. ☐ a. office
   ☐ b. child
   ☐ c. coffee
   ☐ d. supermarket

2. ☐ a. music
   ☐ b. house
   ☐ c. woman
   ☐ d. banana

3. ☐ a. bottle
   ☐ b. butter
   ☐ c. ticket
   ☐ d. knife

4. ☐ a. present
   ☐ b. party
   ☐ c. football
   ☐ d. love

12 ✏️

Schauen Sie sich die Bilder an und schreiben Sie das fehlende Wort in die Lücken.

cheese – *Käse* ▸
wine – *Wein*
hot chocolate
– *heiße Schokolade*
bread – *Brot*
sugar – *Zucker*

1. a _____ of cheese

2. a _____ of wine

3. a _____ of hot chocolate

4. a _____ of bread

5. a _____ of sugar

*There is und **there are***

13 👓

There is und **there are**

There is und there are entsprechen etwa den deutschen Konstruktionen *es gibt* und *es ist/sind*.

Steht das Substantiv, auf das Bezug genommen wird, im Singular (Einzahl), verwendet man there is oder abgekürzt there's.

> There's **a ticket-office near the supermarket.**
> *Es gibt ein Kartenbüro in der Nähe des Supermarktes.*

Auch mit nicht zählbaren Substantiven wird **there is** gebraucht.

> There's **live music at the party.**
> *Es gibt Live-Musik auf dem Fest.*

Steht das Substantiv, auf das Bezug genommen wird, im Plural (Mehrzahl), verwendet man there are.

> There are **apples in the fruit bowl.**
> *Es sind Äpfel in der Obstschale.*

14 ✏️

Nach dem Besuch im Supermarkt ist der Kühlschrank von Kate und Paul wieder gut gefüllt. Was ist im Kühlschrank?
Schreiben Sie **There is** oder **There are** in die Lücken.

1. _____ an apple pie.

2. _____ a bottle of wine.

3. _____ oranges.

4. _____ a piece of butter.

5. _____ two bottles of milk.

6. _____ green apples.

Plural / Länder und Sprachen

15

A	C	T	O	M	A	T	O	E	S
K	C	P	W	F	I	S	H	T	B
I	N	E	B	G	E	P	U	W	O
C	H	I	L	D	R	E	N	O	T
A	M	N	V	G	L	A	T	M	T
K	M	I	C	E	P	R	Z	E	L
E	B	O	O	K	S	S	T	N	E
S	K	T	R	O	U	S	E	R	S

Finden Sie die Pluralformen, die diese Bilder darstellen, im Buchstaben-gitter. Die Wörter können senkrecht, waagerecht und diagonal im Gitter versteckt sein.

16

Ordnen Sie jedem Land die Landessprache zu, indem Sie den richtigen Buchstaben in das jeweilige Kästchen eintragen.

1. ☐ England   a. Swedish

2. ☐ Germany   b. French

3. ☐ France   c. German

4. ☐ Norway   d. English

5. ☐ Sweden   e. Norwegian

6. ☐ Portugal   f. Portuguese

Groß oder klein? / Nicht zählbare

1

Ergänzen Sie die fehlenden Anfangsbuchstaben der Wörter. Achten Sie dabei auf die Groß- und Kleinschreibung.

1. ___erman

5. ___uesday

2. ___ootball

6. ___inner

3. ___anchester ___nited

7. ___nglish

4. ___arch

8. ___anana

2

Kreuzen Sie jeweils das passende Wort an.

1. a cup of
   - ◼ a. sugar
   - ◼ b. wine
   - ◼ c. tea

2. a packet of
   - ◼ a. milk
   - ◼ b. rice
   - ◼ c. apple

3. a slice of
   - ◼ a. bread
   - ◼ b. coke
   - ◼ c. coffee

4. a bottle of
   - ◼ a. chocolate
   - ◼ b. butter
   - ◼ c. water

*Substantive **A** oder **an**? / Substantive im Plural*

3 ✏

Schreiben Sie **a** oder **an** in die Lücke vor dem Substantiv.

1. _____ kiss   4. _____ house

2. _____ idea   5. _____ match

3. _____ hour   6. _____ apple pie

4 ✏

Schreiben Sie die Pluralformen der abgebildeten Gegenstände in die Lücken.

1. _____

2. _____

3. _____

4. _____

5. _____

6. _____

Ein ganz normaler Tag / Fragen und Antworten

1 ✏

Diese Sätze schildern einen typischen Tag im Leben von Paul und Kate aus Manchester. Ordnen Sie den Sätzen die dazugehörenden Bilder zu.
Wenn Sie möchten, können Sie sich den Text auch anhören.

a b c d
e f g h

> ◀ **get up** – *aufstehen*
> **at** – *um*
> **o'clock** – *Uhr*
> **breakfast** – *Frühstück*
> **leave** – *verlassen*
> **take** – *nehmen*
> **half past nine** – *halb neun*
> **work** – *Arbeit*
> **finish** – *beenden/ fertig sein mit*
> **come** – *kommen*
> **home** – *nach Hause*
> **together** – *zusammen*
> **evening** – *Abend*
> **watch TV** – *fernsehen*
> **go to bed** – *ins Bett gehen*

1. Paul and Kate get up at seven o'clock. ☐

2. They have breakfast together with their children, Ben and Jane. ☐

3. Paul leaves the house at eight o'clock. ☐

4. Ben and Jane take the bus to school. ☐

5. Kate goes to work at half past nine. ☐

6. The children come home from school at half past four. ☐

7. At six o'clock, they have dinner together. ☐

8. They all go to bed at eleven o'clock. ☐

2

Verbinden Sie die Fragen auf der linken Seite mit den jeweils korrekten Antworten auf der rechten Seite.

> ◀ **live** – *wohnen, leben*
> **be called** – *heißen*

1. Does Paul live in London?
2. Do Paul and Kate have two children?
3. Are the Beatles from Manchester?
4. Is Edinburgh in England?

a. No, they aren't. They are from Liverpool.
b. Yes, they do. The children are called Ben and Jane.
c. No, it isn't. It's in Scotland.
d. No, he doesn't. He lives in Manchester.

*Das **present simple** / Unregelmäßige Verben*

3

Bildung des present simple

Die Bildung des englischen present simple (einfache Gegenwart) ist sehr einfach, da es bei **regelmäßigen** Verben nur zwei Formen aufweist. Man benutzt für alle Personen die Grundform des Verbs, ausgenommen die 3. Person Singular (**he**, **she**, **it**), bei der ein -s an das Verb angehängt wird.

> **Nice to know**
>
> Merken Sie sich als Faustregel für das **present simple** einfach den folgenden Reim: „Bei **he**, **she**, **it** - das **s** muss mit!"

They get up at seven o'clock.   **Jane gets up at seven o'clock.**
Sie stehen um sieben Uhr auf.   *Jane steht um sieben Uhr auf.*
The children leave the house at a quarter past eight.
Die Kinder verlassen um Viertel nach acht das Haus.
Paul leaves the house at eight o'clock.
Paul verlässt um acht Uhr das Haus.

4 ✏

Schreiben Sie die fehlenden Verben in die Lücken.

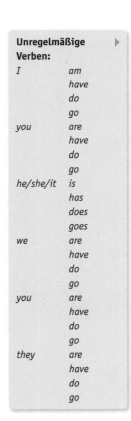

Unregelmäßige Verben:	
I	am
	have
	do
	go
you	are
	have
	do
	go
he/she/it	is
	has
	does
	goes
we	are
	have
	do
	go
you	are
	have
	do
	go
they	are
	have
	do
	go

> gets up   live   works
>   loves   take

1. We _____ in Manchester.

2. Ben and Jane _____ the bus to school.

3. Paul _____ at seven o'clock.

4. Kate _____ in a shop.

5. She _____ shopping.

5

Unregelmäßige Verben

Einige Verben haben eine **unregelmäßige** Form im present simple. Dies sind vor allem die Hilfsverben **do** (*tun*), **be** (*sein*), **have** (*haben*) sowie das Verb **go** (*gehen*). Sehen Sie sich dazu die Tabelle links an.

Ben and Jane go to school.   **Paul goes to work.**
Ben und Jane gehen in die Schule. *Paul geht zur Arbeit.*
Paul and Kate have two children. **Ben has a little sister.**
Paul und Kate haben zwei Kinder.   *Ben hat eine kleine Schwester.*

*Verwendung des **present simple***

6

Diese Bilder zeigen einen typischen Montag im Leben von Jane.
Sehen Sie sich die Bilder an und schreiben Sie dann in der dritten Person
(z.B. **She gets up.**) in die Lücken, was Jane auf den Bildern macht.
Was Jane Ihnen über ihren Montag erzählt, können Sie sich auch anhören.

> I have breakfast at home.

> Then I go to school by bus.

> In the morning, I have maths.

> In the break, I go to the library.

> After lunch, I have sports.

1. Jane _____

2. Then she _____

3. _____

4. _____

5. _____

◄ **maths** – *Mathe*
break – *Pause*
library – *Bibliothek/ Bücherei*
lunch – *Mittagessen*

7

Verwendung des present simple
Das present simple wird für allgemein gültige Aussagen oder Feststellungen
in der Gegenwart benutzt. Man kann damit generelle Informationen über Personen
oder Dinge geben, die sich normalerweise nicht ständig verändern.

> **Kate works in a shop.**   *Kate arbeitet in einem Laden.*
> **Paul drives to work every day.** *Paul fährt jeden Tag zur Arbeit.*

Man kann das present simple auch benutzen, um Gewohnheiten oder sich regelmäßig wiederholende Handlungen zu beschreiben, wobei oftmals Signalwörter wie **usually** (*normalerweise*), **always** (*immer*), **every day** (*jeden Tag*) oder **never** (*nie*) vorkommen. Achtung! Hierbei steht das Signalwort immer vor dem Verb, nicht danach!

> **She always drinks coffee on Sundays.**
> *Sie trinkt sonntags immer Kaffee.*
> **Kate usually goes shopping on Mondays.**
> *Normalerweise geht Kate montags einkaufen.*

Present simple / *Kate trifft eine Freundin*

8

Sehen Sie sich die Bilder an. Schreiben Sie dann ein passendes Verb aus der Box im **present simple** in der richtigen Form in die Lücken.

watch – *ansehen, schauen*
drive – *fahren*
clean – *saubermachen, putzen*
dishes – *Geschirr*
cycle – *Fahrrad fahren*

1. We _____ TV every evening.
2. He _____ to work every day.
3. She _____ the dishes every day.
4. They _____ home every evening.

9

Beim Einkaufen trifft Kate eine alte Schulfreundin. Lesen Sie den Dialog und versuchen Sie, so viel wie möglich zu verstehen. Sie können sich das Gespräch auch anhören.

believe – *glauben*
fine – *gut/prima*
still – *noch/immer noch*
remember – *sich erinnern*
really – *wirklich*
married – *verheiratet*
primary school – *Grundschule*
visit – *Besuch*
as – *als*
sister – *Schwester*
wedding – *Hochzeit*
listen – *zuhören*
a lot of – *viel*
meet – *treffen*
sure – *sicher*
maybe – *vielleicht*
station – *Bahnhof*
by – *an/bei*
there – *dorthin*
often – *oft*
nice – *nett/schön*
see you – *bis bald*

Kate: Louise? Is that you?
Louise: Kate? Oh, I don't believe it! It's you! How are you?
Kate: I'm fine. How are you?
Louise: Fine, fine. Do you still live here in Manchester?
Kate: Yes, I still live here. Do you remember Paul?
Louise: Yes, I do. Does he still live here?
Kate: Yes, he does. We're married now. Paul works in a bank. But what about you? Are you here on a visit?
Louise: Yes, I am. It's my sister's wedding on Saturday, so I'm here for that. I now live in Edinburgh.
Kate: Oh, really? And what do you do there?
Louise: I work as a teacher in a primary school. And you? What do you do?
Kate: I work in a shop.
Louise: Listen, I don't have a lot of time now. Can we meet for a coffee tomorrow?
Kate: Yes, sure. What time?
Louise: Two o'clock, maybe?
Kate: That's OK. Two o'clock at the coffee bar by the station? I often go there. It's a nice place.
Louise: Fine. See you tomorrow!
Kate: Bye!

Verneinung / Fragen

10 ✏

Verneinung

Man kann Sätze im present simple verneinen, indem man dem Hauptverb **do not/ don't** bzw. **does not/doesn't** voranstellt. Hierbei wechselt in der 3. Person Singular das **-s** vom Hauptverb zum Hilfsverb (**does**). Das Hauptverb bleibt für alle Personen immer unverändert.

Kate lives in Manchester.	*Kate wohnt in Manchester.*
Kate doesn't live in London.	*Kate wohnt nicht in London.*
I remember Paul.	*Ich erinnere mich an Paul.*
I don't remember John.	*Ich erinnere mich nicht an John.*

11 ✏

Als Paul noch keine Familie hatte, hatte er viel mehr Zeit für seine Hobbys.
Lesen Sie, was Paul jetzt alles nicht mehr (**not any more**) macht, und unterstreichen Sie die korrekte Form der Verneinung.
Die Lösungen können Sie sich auch anhören.

1. Well, I have a family, so I *don't have / haven't / not have* so much time for myself any more.
2. I *go not / don't go / isn't go* to the pub with my mates any more. Well, not so often, anyway.
3. And I *go not / 'm not go / don't go* swimming so often, either.
4. I *never / isn't / always* go out during the week. I'm always at home.
5. But the good thing is, I *isn't / don't / not* work so much overtime either!

◀ **well** – *nun/na ja*
any more – *nicht mehr*
much – *viel*
myself – *mich/ mich selbst*
pub – *Kneipe*
mate – *Kumpel/ Freund*
anyway – *jedenfalls*
either – *auch nicht*
during – *während*
week – *Woche*
overtime – *Überstunden*

12 👓

Fragen

Zur Bildung von **Fragen** benötigt man, wie bei der Verneinung, ebenfalls das Hilfsverb **do** bzw. **does**. Dieses stellt man einfach an den Anfang des Fragesatzes.

Do you still **live** here?	*Wohnst du immer noch hier?*
Does Louise **work** in a school?	*Arbeitet Louise in einer Schule?*

Auch bei Fragen steht das Hauptverb immer in der Grundform,
d.h. ohne **s**-Endung in der dritten Person Singular.

*Das Verb **be** / Fragen*

13

Das Verb be

Wir haben bereits gesehen, dass das Verb **be** (*sein*) im present simple unregelmäßig ist. Die Formen von **be** sind:

I	**am** (*bin*)	we	**are** (*sind*)
you	**are** (*bist*)	you	**are** (*seid/sind*)
he/she/it	**is** (*ist*)	they	**are** (*sind*)

Aus den Personalpronomen (**I**, **you**, **he**, etc.) und dem Verb **be** im present simple
wird sehr häufig eine verkürzte Form gebildet. Der erste Buchstabe des Verbs wird
weggelassen und durch einen Apostroph ersetzt.

I'm	**we're**
you're	**you're**
he's/she's/it's	**they're**

Wenn man **be** verneinen oder Fragen damit bilden möchte, braucht man das Hilfsverb **do** nicht.

Bei **Verneinungen** wird einfach nur not hinter das Verb gestellt.

I'm not **stupid.**	**He's** not **the best.**
Ich bin nicht blöd.	*Er ist nicht der Beste.*

In **Fragen** werden Subjekt und Objekt vertauscht.

Are you **not cold?**	Is he **still in Manchester?**
Ist dir nicht kalt?	*Ist er immer noch in Manchester?*

Nice to know

In verneinten Sätzen
gibt es zwei Formen der
Verkürzung:
He's not German.
oder
He isn't German.
You're not Italian.
oder
You aren't Italian.
They're not late.
oder
They aren't late.
We're not angry.
oder
We aren't angry.

14

Bringen Sie diese Fragen und Sätze in die richtige Reihenfolge und schreiben Sie sie
in die Lücken.

1. John / you / Do / know / ?   _____

2. he / Is / Japanese / ?   _____

3. at / Jane / school / isn't / .   _____

4. not / happy / We're / very / .   _____

5. read / she / a / book / Does / ?   _____

6. tired / you / Are / ?   _____

15 👓

Kurzantworten

Auf Fragen, die mit **Ja** oder **Nein** beantwortet werden können, reagiert man im Englischen häufig mit einer so genannten Kurzantwort. Hierzu wird das Hilfsverb aus der Frage wieder aufgenommen und in der entsprechenden Form in der Antwort wiederholt. Wird die Frage verneint, hängt man einfach **not** an das Verb an.

Do you like Manchester? *Mögen sie Manchester?*

Yes, I do.   **No, I don't.**
Ja, (das tu ich).   *Nein, (das tu ich nicht).*

Does Ben like chocolate? *Mag Ben Schokolade?*

Yes, he does.   **No, he doesn't.**
Ja, (das tut er).   *Nein, (das tut er nicht).*

Is London beautiful? *Ist London schön?*

Yes, it is.   **No, it isn't.**
Ja, (das ist es).   *Nein, (das ist es nicht).*

Are you tired? *Bist du müde?*

Yes, I am.   **No, I'm not.**
Ja, (das bin ich).   *Nein, (das bin ich nicht).*

> **Nice to know**
>
> Im Englischen klingt es oft sehr direkt und unhöflich, wenn man Fragen nur mit **Yes** oder **No** beantwortet. Benutzen Sie immer die entsprechende Kurzantwort und Sie werden gleich viel freundlicher klingen!

16 ✏️

Sehen Sie sich die Bilder an und beantworten Sie dann die Fragen, indem Sie die passende Kurzantwort in die Lücke schreiben
(z.B. **Is he tired? Yes, he is. / No, he isn't.**).

Is he fat?

Are they thin?

Does he cycle?

_____   _____   _____

> ◀ **fat** – *dick, fett*
> **thin** – *dünn*
> **cycle** – *Fahrrad fahren*
> **angry** – *wütend, verärgert*

Do they play football?

Is she angry?

_____   _____

Present simple

17 🖉

Sehen Sie sich die Sätze an und schreiben Sie das jeweils fehlende Wort in das Gitter. Achtung! Auch Apostrophe (') benötigen ein eigenes Kästchen!

1. Kate ... from London.
2. Does Paul work in a bank?
Yes, he ... .
3. Ben's ... a football player.
4. Louise ... in a school.
5. Are you tired? Yes, I ... .
6. Are Kate and Paul married?
Yes, they ... .

7. Does Louise work in a bank?
No, she ... .
8. Jane ... a book.
9. Ben ... Jane's brother.
10. Do you remember John?
Yes, I ... .

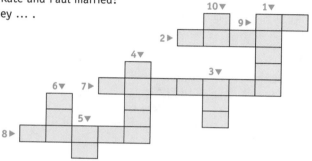

18 🖉

Großtante Hermione ist zu Besuch und fragt Jane über ihren Schulalltag aus. Die Zeiten haben sich geändert, seit sie selbst einmal zur Schule ging. Ergänzen Sie das Gespräch, indem Sie die fehlenden Wörter in die Lücken schreiben.

| does   do   wear   don't   wear   don't   does |

1. **Great Aunt:** So, Jane, _____ you _____ a tie to school?

2. **Jane:** No, we _____. We _____ a uniform, but it's a jumper and skirt.

3. **Great Aunt:** I see. What about your brother, _____ he wear a tie?

4. **Jane:** Yes, he _____. Boys wear ties in our school, and girls _____.

5. **Great Aunt:** No ties for girls ... I see ... Very modern.

---

great aunt – *Groß-tante*
wear – *tragen*
tie – *Krawatte*
jumper – *Pullover*
skirt – *Rock*
brother – *Bruder*

Nice to know

Im Englischen sagt man oft **I see.** um auszudrücken, dass man etwas zwar versteht, es darum aber noch lange nicht gutheißt!

*3. Person **present simple** / Verneinung*

1

Wandeln Sie diese Sätze in die dritte Person Singular (**he**) um
(z.B. **I walk home. - He walks home.**).

1. I drive to work. _____

2. I like swimming. _____

3. I don't go
to work by bus. _____

4. I don't read
many books. _____

5. I'm very thin. _____

6. I'm not angry. _____

2

Verneinen Sie diese Sätze, indem Sie die Verben in der entsprechenden Form
in die Lücken schreiben (z.B. Hermione **lives** in Manchester. - Hermione **doesn't**
live in Manchester.)

1. Paul is Japanese.   Paul _____ Japanese.

2. Kate reads books.   Kate _____ books.

3. Ben and Jane like bananas.   Ben and Jane _____ bananas.

4. We watch TV every evening.   We _____ TV every evening.

5. I'm very angry.   I _____ very angry.

6. They play football.   They _____ football.

7. The apples are green.   The apples _____ green.

Kurzantworten

3 ✎

Lesen Sie die Fragen und wählen Sie durch Ankreuzen die korrekte
Antwort aus.

1. Do you like chocolate?
▢ a. No, I'm not.
▢ b. Yes, I do.
▢ c. Yes, I doesn't.

2. Does Ben like swimming?
▢ a. No, he doesn't.
▢ b. Yes, he is.
▢ c. No, he don't.

3. Do you go to work by bus?
▢ a. No, I do.
▢ b. Yes, I do.
▢ c. Yes, I does.

4. Is Kate a teacher?
▢ a. No, she aren't.
▢ b. No, she isn't.
▢ c. No, she doesn't.

5. Are you a teacher?
▢ a. Yes, I'm not.
▢ b. Yes, I do.
▢ c. Yes, I am.

4 ✎

Bilden Sie Fragen, indem Sie die korrekte Wortgruppe unterstreichen und wählen
Sie dann die passende Antwort aus.
Die Lösungen können Sie sich auch anhören.

1. *Know you / Do you know / You know* Kate? _____

smoke – *rauchen* ▶

2. *Does Kate / Kate does / Is Kate* smoke?_____

3. *Jane is / Is Jane / Does Jane* from Birmingham?_____

4. *You are / Do you / Are you* cold? _____

Yes, I do.   No, she isn't.   Yes, I am.   No, she doesn't.

Paul und seine Familie / Nur halbe Sätze

1

Auf diesem Bild sehen Sie Pauls Familie. Lesen Sie, was Paul über seine Familienmitglieder zu sagen hat, oder hören Sie es sich an. Ordnen Sie dann die Sätze den
richtigen Personen zu, indem Sie die entsprechende Ziffer in die Kästchen schreiben.

> **mother** – *Mutter*
> **father** – *Vater*
> **homework** – *Haus-*
> *aufgaben*
> **visit** – *besuchen*

a. These are my kids. I help them with their homework.

b. This is my sister. She often visits us.

c. This is my mother. I like her very much.

d. This is my father. He comes to see me every day.

e. That is my brother. I often play tennis with him.

2

Können Sie die Satzanfänge auf der linken Seite mit den passenden Enden auf
der rechten Seite verbinden? Die Lösungen können Sie sich auch anhören.

1. Ben's got
2. He has to
3. My daughter's always
4. She's
5. Do you want to

a. out. I never see her.
b. see them?
c. his exams this year.
d. fifteen years old.
e. study a lot.

> **have got** – *haben*
> **have to** – *müssen*
> **daughter** – *Tochter*
> **want** – *wollen*
> **out** – *aus/weg*
> **her** – *sie/ihr*
> **them** – *sie/ihnen*
> **his** – *sein/seine*
> **exam** – *Prüfung*
> **year** – *Jahr*
> **study** – *studieren/*
> *lernen*
> **a lot** – *viel*

Personalpronomen

3 🕶

Personalpronomen

Wenn man die handelnde Person (das Subjekt) in einem Satz nicht immer wiederholen möchte, kann man sie durch ein **Personalpronomen** (**he**, **she**, **it**, ...)
ersetzen.

Paul arrives at the bank.	**He arrives at the bank.**
Paul kommt in der Bank an.	*Er kommt in der Bank an.*
Ben and Jane go to school.	**They go to school.**
Ben und Jane gehen in die Schule.	*Sie gehen in die Schule.*

Die Form des **Personalpronomens** kann sich ändern, wenn es nicht die handelnde
Person (das Subjekt), sondern das Objekt im Satz ersetzt.

Paul speaks to Kate.	**Paul speaks to her.**
Paul spricht mit Kate.	*Paul spricht mit ihr.*
Kate speaks to Paul.	**Kate speaks to him.**
Kate spricht mit Paul.	*Kate spricht mit ihm.*

Subjektpronomen

I (*ich*)	I go home.
you (*du/Sie*)	You are very nice.
he (*er*)	He plays tennis.
she (*sie*)	She reads.
it (*es*)	It is very nice.
we (*wir*)	We are a family.
you (*ihr/Sie*)	You are wonderful.
they (*sie*)	They go home.

Objektpronomen

me (*mir/mich*)	He likes me.
you (*dir/dich*)	He likes you.
him (*ihm/ihn*)	I like him.
her (*ihr/sie*)	I like her.
it (*ihm/es*)	I like it.
us (*uns*)	He likes us.
you (*euch/Sie*)	He likes you.
them (*ihnen/sie*)	He likes them.

4

Kate und Louise sitzen zusammen im Café. Sie haben sich wirklich lange nicht mehr gesehen und tauschen nun Neuigkeiten aus.
Lesen Sie den Dialog oder hören Sie sich ihn an.
Markieren Sie dann alle **Personalpronomen** im Text.

Louise: Kate, it's so good to see you! And you're married to Paul, that's wonderful!

Kate: Yes, I'm married to him. And we've got two teenage kids.

Louise: Really? Oh, tell me all about them!

Kate: Well, Ben's sixteen now and Jane's fourteen. They're both at school, and they're out a lot. We don't see them much.

Louise: Yeah, I know all about that. I've got a daughter, you know. She's fifteen. She's always out, too. I never see her at all.

Kate: Well, at that age they really have their own life ...

Louise: That's true.

Kate: Well, what can we do? Anyway, Ben's got his exams this year, so he has to be at home more to study.

Louise: Oh, yes, school exams ... Do you remember when we ...?

Kate: Yes, of course. Wait, I've got some pictures here from last year, with some people you know. Do you want to see them?

Louise: Oh yes, please.

5

Entziffern Sie diese Sätze und schreiben Sie sie auf ein Blatt Papier
(z.B. **I s e e t h e m .** – **I see them**.).

1. S h e o f t e n s e e s h e r .
2. I n e v e r p l a y t e n n i s w i t h h i m .
3. T h e y a l w a y s v i s i t u s .
4. S h e v i s i t s h e r i n t h e e v e n i n g .
5. S h e n e v e r t a l k s a b o u t t h e m .
6. W e p l a y f o o t b a l l o n S a t u r d a y s .
7. D o y o u r e m e m b e r h e r ?

tell – *sagen/erzählen*
both – *beide*
too – *auch*
at all – *überhaupt*
age – *Alter*
own – *eigener/eigen/ eigenes*
life – *Leben*
true – *wahr*
when – *wenn/als*
wait – *warten*
some – *einige, ein paar*
picture – *Bild, Foto*
last – *letzter/letzte/ letztes*
people – *Leute*

Lerntipp!

Oft müssen Sie sich noch unbekannte Wörter selbst erschließen. Stellen Sie sich dabei z.B. folgende Frage: Kenne ich ein deutsches Wort, das ähnlich ist?
Manchmal kennt man auch schon eine Vokabel, die denselben Wortstamm hat. Wenn Sie z.B. wissen, was **know** heißt, können Sie sicher auch erraten was **knowledge** bedeutet. Und zu guter Letzt lassen sich viele Wörter auch aus dem Zusammenhang erschließen.

Personalpronomen

6 ✎

Lesen Sie die Sätze und schreiben Sie dann die Sätze mit den korrekten Personalpronomen in die Lücken.

> He meets him.   They talk about him.
> We see them.   She meets her.
> He talks about them.   She sees her.

1. Jane and I see Ben and Paul. _____

2. Kate sees Jane. _____

3. Paul meets Ben. _____

4. Kate meets Louise. _____

5. Ben and Jane talk about Paul. _____

6. Paul talks about his children. _____

7 ✎

Zur Familie gehört auch Hermione, Kates Tante.
Lesen Sie den Text über Hermione und schreiben Sie jeweils das passende **Personalpronomen** in die Lücken.

nearly – *fast* ▶
visit – *besuchen*
enjoy – *genießen*
talk – *sich unterhalten/sprechen*
however – *jedoch/wie auch immer*
say – *sagen*
think – *denken/glauben*
question – *Frage*
ask – *fragen*
should – *sollten*

Hermione is Kate's aunt. 1. _____ is nearly 80 years old and lives near Kate and Paul. 2. _____ often visits 3. _____. Kate really likes 4. _____ and enjoys 5. _____ visits. 6. _____ drink tea and talk. Ben and Jane, however, are not so happy. Ben says: "7. _____ don't think my great aunt likes 8. _____. 9. _____ always asks 10. _____ stupid questions about school. 11. _____ should listen to 12. _____!" And Aunt Hermione says: "Kate's children are wonderful. Ben really likes 13. _____. He enjoys talking about his school so much. And Paul, I really like 14. _____, too."

Have und *have got*

8

Have und **have got**
Im britischen Englisch wird anstatt **have** oft die Form **have got** benutzt. In der gesprochenen Sprache wird **have** dann meist zu **'ve** und **has** zu **'s** verkürzt.

Sehen Sie sich noch einmal diese Beispiele aus dem Dialog an bzw. hören Sie sie sich an:

We've got two kids.	*Wir haben zwei Kinder.*
I've got some pictures.	*Ich habe ein paar Fotos.*

Wenn man **have got** verneint, braucht man das Hilfsverb **do** nicht. Nach **have** wird einfach **not** eingefügt, wobei dann oft zu **haven't** bzw. **hasn't** verkürzt wird.

Kate hasn't got three children.
Kate hat keine drei Kinder.
Paul and Kate haven't got a big house.
Paul und Kate haben kein großes Haus.

Bei Fragen wird **have/has** an den Anfang der Frage gestellt und **got** steht direkt nach dem Subjekt (der handelnden Person).

Has Kate got three children? *Hat Kate drei Kinder?*
Have we got apples? *Haben wir Äpfel?*

9 ✏

Sehen Sie sich die Bilder an. Schreiben Sie dann die jeweils korrekte Form von **have got** in die Lücke.

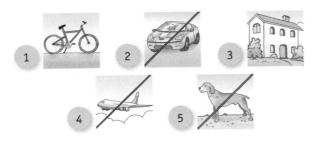

1. Ben _____ a bicycle.
2. I _____ a car.
3. We _____ a house.
4. They _____ an airplane.
5. He _____ a dog.

> **Nice to know**
>
> Im amerikanischen Englisch wird **have got** nicht benutzt. Man sagt dort nur **have**:
> **He has a lot of money.**
> **I don't have a lot of time.**

> **Lerntipp!**
>
> Sicherlich haben Sie schon bemerkt, dass das britische und das amerikanische Englisch sich nicht nur in der Aussprache unterscheiden, sondern dass manche Vokabeln auch ganz verschieden sind oder unterschiedlich geschrieben werden. In diesem Kurs lernen Sie britisches Englisch, im Wortverzeichnis finden Sie jedoch auch amerikanische Varianten.

◀ **bicycle** – *Fahrrad*
airplane – *Flugzeug*

Im Café / Demonstrativpronomen

10

recognize – *erkennen* ▶

recognize – *erkennen* ▶
let – *lassen*
where – *wo*
look – *schauen/ aussehen*
different – *anders*
my goodness – *meine Güte*
same – *gleich*
who – *wer*
next to – *neben*
those – *jene*
hope – *hoffen*

Lerntipp!

Das Markieren von Textstellen oder Wörtern kann sehr hilfreich sein. Nehmen Sie sich ab und an die Zeit, einen Text aus einer englischen Zeitung oder eine Passage aus einem Buch nach Ihren eigenen Vorgaben zu bearbeiten. So können Sie zum Beispiel eine Zeitform, die Sie gerade gelernt haben, im Text markieren und in den unterschiedlichen Zusammenhängen lernen. Oder Sie können Wörter, die Ihnen nicht geläufig sind, hervorheben und gezielt üben. Ihren eigenen Ideen sind da keine Grenzen gesetzt.

Hier sehen Sie den zweiten Teil des Gesprächs zwischen Kate und Louise im Café. Lesen Sie den Dialog oder hören Sie sich ihn an.
Der Text enthält viele der englischen Demonstrativpronomen **this**, **that**, **these** und **those**. Markieren Sie alle Demonstrativpronomen, die Sie finden können.

Kate: Let me see, where have I got them? Ah, here they are. Look, do you recognize these people?
Louise: No, I don't. Oh, wait, is that Julia?
Kate: Yes, that's right. That is Julia. She looks very different now!
Louise: Yes, totally. And this? Is this Paul?
Kate: Yes, it is.
Louise: My goodness, he still looks just the same. And here, next to him? Who's that?
Kate: That's Keith. Do you remember him? The best in our class at school? He now works at the airport. And those two are his children.
Louise: We really are old now. Everyone's got teenage children.
Kate: I know. Listen, have you got some time on Sunday? We could have a barbecue in the garden.
Louise: Sounds good. Can I bring my daughter?
Kate: Yes, sure. Let's hope for good weather!

11

Demonstrativpronomen

Wenn man etwas besonders herausheben möchte, benutzt man die **Demonstrativpronomen this** und **that** für einzelne Personen oder Objekte, oder **these** und **those** für mehrere. Dabei stehen **this** und **these** immer für Personen oder Sachen, die dem Betrachter näher sind, und **that** und **those** für Personen oder Sachen, die weiter entfernt sind.

Demonstrativpronomen

12

Sehen Sie sich die Bildpaare an. Lesen Sie den Satz bzw. hören Sie ihn sich an und entscheiden Sie, zu welchem Bild er besser passt, indem Sie den entsprechenden Buchstaben in das Kästchen eintragen.

This is a banana and that's an orange. ☐

This is Kate and that's Paul. ☐

These are apples and those are lemons. ☐

◀ **lemon** – *Zitrone*

These are Ben and Jane,
and those are Paul and Kate. ☐

13

Unterstreichen Sie das Wort, das den Satz korrekt ergänzt.

1. *These / That / This* are bananas.
2. *These / This / Those* is an apple.
3. *That / Those / These* is Paul.
4. *Those / These / This* is a dog.

Have got / *Pronomen raten*

14 🖉

Schreiben Sie das passende Wort aus dem Kasten in die Lücken.
Aber Vorsicht! Wenn sie alle Wörter richtig in die Lücken eingetragen und dann im Kasten durchgestrichen haben, bleiben zwei Wörter übrig.
Welcher Satz lässt sich daraus bilden?

they	Have	got	This	fun	him
her	them	Has	Those		

1. Ben's _____ a bicycle.

2. _____ are tomatoes.

3. Louise? Oh, yes, Kate knows _____.

4. The family? Yes, _____'ve got a garden.

5. _____ here is my car.

6. _____ Jane got a bicycle?

7. Ben and Jane? Yes, we know _____.

8. Paul? Do you know _____?

15 ✎

Unterstreichen Sie jeweils das Pronomen, das nicht zu den anderen passt.

1. this	that	those	him
2. he	me	she	it
3. those	that	these	her
4. that	him	her	you
5. we	they	us	it
6. he	she	it	him
7. them	she	it	he
8. us	we	you	those
9. him	her	it	I
10. this	that	you	those
11. them	us	me	he
12. him	she	I	we
13. she	her	I	they
14. them	we	he	she
15. it	she	he	that

1 ✏️

Ersetzen Sie die in Klammern angegebenen Personen durch das passende Personalpronomen.

1. Jane likes _____ (Ben and I).

2. _____ (Paul and Ben) often play football.

3. _____ (Louise and I) like shopping.

4. Kate goes to visit _____ (Louise).

5. Paul speaks to _____ (Ben).

6. We all like _____ (Paul and Kate).

2 ✏️

Welcher Satz passt zum Bild? Markieren Sie die passende Aussage durch Ankreuzen. Wenn Sie möchten, können Sie sich die Sätze auch anhören.

▨ a. Ben's got two bicycles.
▨ b. Ben's got a bicycle.
▨ c. Ben's got a car.

▨ a. Jane's got a book.
▨ b. Jane's not got a book.
▨ c. Jane's got two books.

▨ a. Paul and Kate have got a house.
▨ b. Paul and Kate haven't got a house.
▨ c. Jane's got a house.

▨ a. Ben hasn't got a car.
▨ b. Ben's got two cars.
▨ c. Ben hasn't got a dog.

▨ a. Jane hasn't got two dogs.
▨ b. Jane's got two dogs.
▨ c. Jane hasn't got a dog.

Pronomen

3

Unterstreichen Sie das richtige Demonstrativpronomen.

1. *Those / This / These* is my sister Kate.
2. *That / These / Those* is a dog.
3. *This / These / That* are Ben and Jane.
4. *This / That / These* are bananas.
5. *Those / That / This* are apples.

4

Schreiben Sie ein passendes Demonstrativpronomen (**this that**, **these** oder **those**) in die Lücken.

_____ are apples.

_____ are apples.

_____ is a car.

_____ is a car.

5

Bringen Sie die Wörter in diesen kurzen Sätzen wieder in die richtige Reihenfolge und schreiben Sie sie auf ein Blatt Papier.

1. Sunday / her / He / every / visits / .
2. bring / They / us / cakes / often / .
3. many / We / together / do / things / .
4. much / very / like / you / I / .
5. café / You / go / the / me / to / with / .
6. We / play / with / never / him / football / .

*Die **ing-Form** / Zu Hause*

1

Verbinden Sie die Beispielsätze auf der linken Seite mit einem passenden Verb auf der rechten Seite. Sie können sich die Sätze auch anhören.

1. Ben's riding a bicycle.	a. watch
2. Jane's playing the piano.	b. go
3. We're watching TV.	c. drive
4. Paul's driving home.	d. ride
5. Are they going to the theatre?	e. play

Nice to know

Im Englischen gibt es zwei Möglichkeiten *Fahrrad fahren* auszudrücken: Man kann sagen **cycle** oder **ride a bike** – man fährt also nicht Fahrrad, sondern man reitet es!

2

Es ist Samstagnachmittag bei Kate und Paul. Sehen Sie sich an, was die Familienmitglieder gerade tun. Lesen Sie dann die Sätze und schreiben Sie die entsprechenden Verben in die Lücken.
Die Lösungen können Sie sich auch anhören.

sleeping	listening	playing
eating	watering	washing

1. Jane is _____ a cake.

2. Ben is _____ to music.

3. Kate is _____ the garden.

4. Jane is _____ the piano.

5. Paul is _____ the car.

6. The cat is _____ .

◀ **eat** – *essen*
water – *gießen*
cat – *Katze*
sleep – *schlafen*

We're having a barbecue! / Present continuous

was – *war*
on earth – *auf Erden*
roast dinner – *Bratengericht*
everything – *alles*
ourselves – *selbst*
by the way – *übrigens*
early – *früh*
afternoon – *Nachmittag*
no problem – *kein Problem*
famous – *berühmt*
egg salad – *Eiersalat*
perhaps – *vielleicht*

Nice to know

Ein typisch englisches **roast dinner** besteht aus **meat** (*Fleisch*), **roast potatoes** (*Röstkartoffeln*), **vegetables** (*Gemüse*) und **gravy** (*Bratensoße*). Manchmal gibt es auch **Yorkshire puddings** (ähnlich wie herzhafte Windbeutel) dazu.

3

Lesen Sie den Text bzw. hören Sie sich den Dialog an.
Markieren Sie alle **ing-Formen** (**present continuous**) im Text.

Kate: Hi everyone. I'm back!
Paul: Hi, how was the coffee with Louise?
Kate: Really nice. What on earth are you doing?
Paul: We're cooking dinner!
Ben: We're making a roast dinner for tonight …
Paul: … and you're not helping us! We're doing everything ourselves!
Kate: OK, fantastic! By the way, Louise and her daughter are coming here on Saturday.
Paul: Really? Good, we can have a barbecue then. But you know I'm playing tennis with Michael in the early afternoon.
Kate: Yes, sure, I know. Louise is coming at six. I hope that's not too early for you?
Paul: Oh, that's no problem. We usually finish at four o'clock. Are you making your famous egg salad?
Ben: Yes, please, Mum!
Kate: Well, perhaps …

4

Formen des present continuous
Eine weitere englische Form der Gegenwart ist das so genannte present continuous. Es wird gebildet, indem man an die Grundform des Verbs **-ing** anhängt.
Diese Verbform wird immer in Kombination mit einer passenden Form des Hilfsverbs **be** benutzt.

Einige Verben haben bei der Bildung der **ing-Form** Besonderheiten.
Endet ein Verb auf **–e**, so fällt dieser Buchstabe weg:

mak**e**	mak**ing**	**We're making a cake.**
		Wir machen einen Kuchen.
tak**e**	tak**ing**	**I'm taking an aspirin.**
		Ich nehme ein Aspirin.

Endet ein Verb auf einen Vokal + einen Konsonant, so wird der letzte Konsonant verdoppelt:

sit	si**tt**ing	**They're sitting in the garden.**
		Sie sitzen im Garten.
shop	sho**pp**ing	**Kate's shopping in the supermarket.**
		Kate kauft im Supermarkt ein.

Present continuous

5

Gebrauch des present continuous

Das **present continuous** wird verwendet, wenn:

- etwas genau im Moment des Sprechens geschieht,

    It's four o'clock. Ben and Paul are making dinner.

    Es ist vier Uhr. Ben und Paul machen gerade das Abendessen.

- etwas im Moment gültig ist, aber nicht notwendigerweise genau zum Zeitpunkt des Sprechens geschieht,

    Paul is very tired. He's working too much at the moment.

    Paul ist sehr müde. Er arbeitet im Moment zu viel.

- etwas in naher Zukunft geschehen wird und schon so fest geplant ist, dass es sich aller Voraussicht nach nicht mehr ändern wird.

    Louise is coming to visit.   *Louise kommt zu Besuch.*

Für routinemäßige Abläufe und sich regelmäßig wiederholende Handlungen verwendet man dagegen das **present simple**.

Man benutzt das **present continuous** daher auch oft, um etwas, das im Moment geschieht, mit etwas zu vergleichen, das normalerweise geschieht.

    Kate usually cooks on Saturdays.

    Normalerweise kocht Kate samstags.

    This Saturday, Paul and Ben are cooking.

    Diesen Samstag kochen Paul und Ben.

> **Nice to know**
>
> Wenn Sie im Deutschen *momentan*, *im Moment*, oder *gerade* sagen würden, dann können Sie im Englischen das **present continuous** benutzen!

> **Nice to know**
>
> **Study** kann im Englischen sowohl *lernen* als auch *studieren* bedeuten. Sehr junge Schüler bezeichnet man als **pupils**, ab 16 Jahren ist aber jeder Schüler ein **student**.

6 🖊

Lesen Sie, worüber Ben sich beschwert, und ergänzen Sie die fehlenden Verben im **present continuous**.

> do   work   do   learn   give   study   write   be

Well, this year is really horrible. We 1. _____ so hard,

I don't believe it. The teachers 2. _____ us so much

homework that we 3. _____ until late in the evening.

Today I 4. _____ two essays for English, one for history,

and then I 5. _____ my maths homework as well!

Jane's lucky, she 6. _____ nothing at all! She plays

with the cat all afternoon and then she comes and asks me: "7. _____

you _____ again?"

> ◄ **horrible** – *fürchterlich/ schrecklich*
> **homework** – *Hausaufgaben*
> **late** – *spät*
> **until** – *bis*
> **essay** – *Aufsatz*
> **as well** – *auch noch*
> **nothing** – *nichts*
> **history** – *Geschichte*
> **be lucky** – *Glück haben*
> **again** – *wieder*

*Verneinung und Fragen im **present continuous***

7

Verneinung

Sätze im **present continuous** verneint man, indem man dem Hilfsverb **be** ein **not** nachstellt. Dabei wird die Form von **be** oft verkürzt und entweder mit dem Subjekt oder mit **not** zusammengezogen:

You're not **helping us!**   **You** aren't **helping us!**
Du hilfst uns nicht!   *Du hilfst uns nicht!*
Jane's not **riding a bicycle.**   **Jane** isn't **riding a bicycle.**
Jane fährt nicht Fahrrad.   *Jane fährt nicht Fahrrad.*

8

Schreiben Sie die fehlenden Wörter in die Lücken.

isn't	'm not	not	aren't

1. We _____ playing golf.

2. She's _____ a good swimmer.

3. He _____ a fast driver.

tired – *müde*   ▶

4. I _____ tired.

9

Fragen

Zur Bildung von Fragen wird einfach das Subjekt mit der Form von **be** vertauscht.

You are making egg salad.   **Are you making egg salad?**
Du machst Eiersalat.   *Machst du Eiersalat?*
Louise is staying for dinner.   **Is Louise staying for dinner?**
Louise bleibt zum Abendessen.   *Bleibt Louise zum Abendessen?*

10

Unterstreichen Sie die korrekte Form der Fragebildung.

1. *Is you / you are / Are you* staying for dinner?
2. *Paul is / Is Paul / Paul has* playing tennis with Michael?
3. *Are they / they are / Is they* riding a bicycle?
4. *She is / Are she / Is she* a good cook?

11

Kurzantworten

Auf Fragen im **present continuous**, die mit **ja** oder **nein** beantwortet werden können, kann man oft kurz antworten, indem man ein **Personalpronomen** und das Verb **be** in der passenden Form wiederholt.

Is Kate cooking dinner?	**Are you learning English?**
Yes, she is.	**Yes, I am.**
No, she isn't./No, she's not.	**No, I'm not.**

> **Lerntipp!**
> Kurzantworten können mit allen englischen Zeitformen gebildet werden. Schauen Sie sich daher ruhig noch einmal die Bildung der Kurzantworten im **present simple** im Modul 2 an. Je öfter Sie ein Thema wiederholen oder es mit einem neuen Thema vergleichen, umso besser können Sie es sich merken und das Gelernte auch anwenden.

12

Kreuzen Sie die korrekte Antwort auf die Frage an.

1. Are you watching TV?
   - a. No, I'm not.
   - b. No, I don't.
   - c. No, I isn't.

2. Is Paul drinking a beer?
   - a. Yes, he are.
   - b. Yes, he does.
   - c. Yes, he is.

3. Are the children sleeping?
   - a. Yes, they aren't.
   - b. No, they don't.
   - c. No, they aren't.

4. Are you tired?
   - a. No, I not.
   - b. Yes, I am.
   - c. Yes, I do.

13

Sehen Sie sich die Bilder an und beantworten Sie dann die Fragen mit einer passenden Kurzantwort (z. B. **Yes, he is.** / **No, they aren't.**).
Wenn Sie möchten, können Sie sich die Fragen auch anhören.

 1 2  3 4

1. Is he playing football? _____

2. Are they dancing? _____

3. Are they cleaning their room? _____

4. Is he doing his homework? _____

> **Nice to know**
> Vorsicht Falle! Im Englischen heißt es **I'm doing my homework** (nicht **making**!).

Present simple oder **continuous**?

14 👓

Present simple oder **continuous**?
Im Englischen gibt es zwei Zeitformen, um die Gegenwart auszudrücken:
das present continuous und das present simple.

Sie haben gelernt, dass das present continuous dann benutzt wird, wenn etwas
im Moment des Sprechens geschieht oder gültig ist oder wenn etwas für die Zukunft
fest geplant ist.

Im Gegensatz dazu wird das present simple nur dann benutzt, wenn man eine
allgemein gültige Aussage oder Feststellung macht oder um eine Gewohnheit oder
regelmäßig wiederkehrende Handlung auszudrücken.

Je nachdem, welche Zeitform man benutzt, kann ein Satz also eine andere Bedeutung bekommen.

> **I don't** drink **coffee**.
> bedeutet, dass ich nie Kaffee trinke.
> **I'm not** drinking **coffee**.
> bedeutet, dass ich im Moment keinen Kaffee trinke,
> sondern etwas anderes.

> **Nice to know**
>
> Im Deutschen werden
> **present simple** und
> **present continuous**
> genau gleich übersetzt:
> **Kate cooks every day.**
> *Kate kocht jeden Tag.*
> **Kate is cooking today.**
> *Kate kocht heute.*

15 ✏

Schreiben Sie die Verben in die passende Lücke. Achten Sie dabei darauf, ob Sie
das **present continuous** oder das **present simple** benötigen.

> is reading   reads   Are ... going   go
> works   isn't working   plays   is playing

1. Paul _____ tennis this Saturday. He always

   _____ tennis on Saturdays.

2. It's nine o'clock and Kate _____ a book.

   She often _____ in the evening.

3. It's Sunday and Louise _____. She never

   _____ on Sundays.

4. _____ you _____

   home now? Yes, I usually _____ home at

   five o'clock.

Present continuous

16

Entscheiden Sie bei jedem Satz, ob er etwas beschreibt, das die Person normalerweise (**usually**) macht, oder ob er etwas beschreibt, dass die Person nur im Moment
(**at the moment**) tut. Schreiben Sie dann **A** für **usually** bzw. **B** für **at the moment**
in das Kästchen daneben. Die Lösung können Sie sich auch anhören. Erst werden
alle Sätze im **present simple**, dann die im **present continuous** gesprochen.

1. I go swimming once a week. ☐

   I'm going swimming a lot. ☐

2. Paul is taking the train. ☐

   Paul drives to work. ☐

3. Ben plays football on Mondays. ☐

   Ben's playing in a big match! ☐

4. She's not working late today. ☐

   Kate works late. ☐

Nice to know

Im Englischen sagt man
oft **go + -ing**:
I go swimming.
Ich gehe schwimmen.
I go jogging.
Ich gehen joggen.

Im **present continuous**
sagt man dann **going +
-ing**:
I'm going swimming.
I'm going jogging.

◀ **once** – *einmal*
  complain – *sich
beschweren*

Nice to know

Anstatt *Ich freue mich
wahnsinnig!* sagt man
mit typisch britischer
Untertreibung oft **I'm
not complaining.** (*Ich
beschwere mich nicht.*),
wenn man über etwas
glücklich ist.

17

Im folgenden Text spricht Kate über die Sommerferien der Familie.
Ergänzen Sie die Verben in der korrekten Form - manchmal benötigen Sie das
present continuous, manchmal das **present simple**. Als Hilfestellung sind
die Grundformen der benötigten Verben in Klammern angegeben!

Well, normally we 1. _____ (spend) our holidays in the

South of England. We 2. _____ (rent) a small cottage

by the sea and 3. _____ (relax) on the beach. We

4. _____ (cook) in the evenings and we

5. _____ (play) games together. But this year,

we 6. _____ (go) to France. We 7. _____

(drive) there and we 8. _____ (stay) on a camping

site in Southern France. It'll be a wonderful holiday, so I

9. _____ (not complain)!

◀ **normally**
  – *normalerweise*
  spend – *verbringen*
  holiday – *Ferien/
Urlaub*
  South of England –
Südengland
  rent – *mieten*
  small – *klein*
  cottage – *Hütte/
kleines Haus*
  sea – *Meer*
  beach – *Strand*
  game – *Spiel*
  camping site
  – *Campingplatz*
  Southern France –
Südfrankreich

Ing-Formen

18

Die **ing-Formen** folgender Verben sind im Gitter versteckt (waagerecht, senkrecht oder diagonal). Können Sie alle Verben finden?

1. look	7. listen	13. take
2. dance	8. drive	14. make
3. feed	9. drink	15. need
4. be	10. speak	16. work
5. have	11. live	17. leave
6. learn	12. write	

J	Z	O	P	L	O	O	K	I	N	G	B	O	O	S
U	U	E	J	I	D	U	K	Y	E	A	E	P	K	J
L	Q	K	O	L	J	X	F	E	E	D	I	N	G	P
J	I	L	U	E	A	L	G	D	P	N	W	S	K	
W	P	V	L	A	W	O	R	K	I	N	G	P	U	U
R	U	J	I	R	E	A	D	I	N	G	H	A	Y	T
I	P	U	S	N	D	P	R	R	G	U	G	J	J	T
T	D	Q	T	I	G	U	I	J	I	O	I	J	N	W
I	A	J	E	N	B	H	N	P	D	V	V	L	M	A
N	N	K	N	G	M	A	K	I	N	G	I	D	E	U
G	C	J	I	J	N	V	I	L	Z	A	N	N	P	J
U	I	U	N	N	M	I	N	J	J	E	G	Q	G	Q
J	N	O	G	L	G	N	G	Z	Q	F	O	J	L	K
Z	G	L	X	U	Z	G	S	P	E	A	K	I	N	G
L	E	A	V	I	N	G	H	N	O	E	J	C	H	E

19

Nun sind Sie fast fertig mit dem Modul. **Very good!**
Schreiben Sie nun noch diese Sätze in ihrer richtigen Reihenfolge auf.

1. garden / watering / We / the / 're / .
2. He / book / a / reading / 's / .
3. driving / 's / a / car / He / .
4. 's / She / armchair / in / sitting / an / .
5. We / dinner / 're / making / .

*Verben im **present continuous***

1

Finden Sie zu jedem Bild einen passenden Satz und schreiben Sie die entsprechende
Ziffer in das Kästchen.

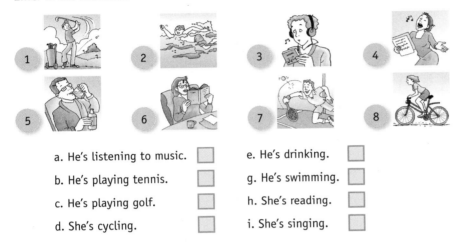

a. He's listening to music. ☐   e. He's drinking. ☐

b. He's playing tennis. ☐   g. He's swimming. ☐

c. He's playing golf. ☐   h. She's reading. ☐

d. She's cycling. ☐   i. She's singing. ☐

2

Was tun die Leute auf den Bildern? Ergänzen Sie die Sätze mit einem passenden
Verb im present continuous.

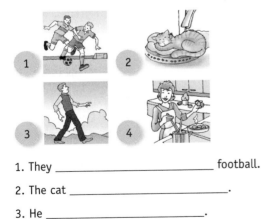

1. They _____ football.

2. The cat _____.

3. He _____.

4. She _____ dinner.

*Verneinung / Fragen und Antworten / **Present simple** oder **continuous**?*

3

Ergänzen Sie jeden Satz mit der korrekten Form, indem Sie diese unterstreichen.

1. She *not going / isn't going / isn't go* there.
2. I *not being / be not / 'm not* leaving.
3. *Is you / Are you / You're* working?
4. *She are / Are she / Is she* coming?

4

Lesen Sie die Frage und wählen Sie dann die korrekte Antwort aus.

1. Is he sleeping?	Yes, he is. / No, he is. / No, he doesn't.
2. Does she drive?	No, she don't. / No, she isn't. / No, she doesn't.
3. Are you going jogging?	No, I am. / Yes, I am. / Yes, I'm.
4. Are they leaving?	No, they're not. / Yes, they aren't. / No, they don't.

5 ✏

Schreiben Sie die fehlenden Verben in der korrekten Form (**present simple** oder **present continuous**) in die Lücken!
Die Grundform der Verben, die Sie benötigen, ist jeweils in Klammern angegeben.

1. I usually _____ (read) a book in the evening.
2. Today, I _____ (drive) to work. I need the car there.
3. She often _____ (prepare) dinner for the family.
4. Today, she _____ (prepare) a roast dinner.
5. They never _____ (leave) the house before seven in the morning.
6. I always _____ (eat) breakfast.

So viele Pläne! / Die Zukunft

1

Ben und Jane haben große Pläne, was sie in der Zukunft alles machen möchten –
und sie sind sehr überzeugt davon, dass sie das alles auch schaffen werden!
Diese Sätze, die Sie sich auch anhören können, beschreiben die Pläne von Ben und
Jane. Verbinden Sie sie mit dem jeweils passenden Bild.

1

2

3

4

5

a. I'll drive a big car!
b. I'll become a doctor!
c. I'll go to university and study law!
d. I'll earn a lot of money!
e. I won't drive a big car!

◀ **law** – *Jura/Recht*
earn – *verdienen*
will – *werden*
won't – *nicht werden*
waiter – *Kellner*

2

Auch Kate hat Pläne für Ben und Jane - diese befassen sich aber mehr mit
der direkten Zukunft ihrer Kinder.
Lesen Sie die Sätze laut bzw. hören Sie sich an, was Kates Pläne
für ihre Kinder sind. Sprechen Sie
dann die Sätze laut nach.

◀ **driving test** – *Führer-
scheinprüfung*

1. Ben will go to college next year.
2. Jane will learn to dance.
3. Ben will take his driving test next year.
4. Jane won't learn French any more.
5. Ben won't have time to play football.

*Das **will future** / Vorbereitungen fürs Grillfest*

3

Bildung des will future

Das **will future** wird aus dem Hilfsverb **will** und der Grundform des Vollverbs gebildet. Hierbei steht **will** immer vor dem Verb und wird oft zu **'ll** verkürzt. Verneinte Sätze bildet man, indem man nach dem **will** ein **not** einfügt. Dies wird dann meist verkürzt zu **won't**.

> **I'll** prepare the steaks.
> **I won't** put garlic in the salad.

Bei der Bildung des **will future** muss man nicht auf das **-s** in der 3. Person Singular achten. Die Form ist für alle Personen gleich.

4 ✎

Es ist Samstagnachmittag und heute kommen Louise und ihre Tochter zum Grillen. Paul und Kate sind in der Küche und bereiten das Essen vor.
Lesen Sie den Dialog oder hören Sie ihn sich an.

need – *müssen, brauchen*
set up – *aufstellen*
barbecue – *Grill*
kitchen – *Küche*
manage – *schaffen*
fridge – *Kühlschrank*
garlic – *Knoblauch*
use – *benutzen*
enough – *genug*
break – *zerbrechen /kaputtmachen*
if – *wenn/falls*
careful – *vorsichtig*
already – *schon*
soon – *bald*

Paul: OK then, what do we need to do?
Kate: Well, I'm making the salad now, and then I think, I'll prepare the steaks.
Paul: I'll set up the barbecue, then. Will you need me in the kitchen later?
Kate: Let me think ... No, I won't. I'll manage.
Paul: All right. I'll look after the drinks. I'll put some white wine in the fridge.
Kate: Fine. Now, the salad. I won't put garlic in it, is that all right?
Paul: Yes, sure. Oh, and we won't use the good glasses, I think.
Kate: Why not? The children are old enough, they won't break them if they are careful.
Paul: OK, we'll use them, then. Oh, it's five o'clock already! They'll be here soon.

Entscheiden Sie nun, ob die Sätze falsch (Kreuz) oder richtig (Häkchen) sind.

1. Kate will prepare the steaks. ▪
2. Paul will put some beer in the fridge. ▪
3. Kate won't put garlic in the salad. ▪
4. They will use the good glasses. ▪

*Das **will future** / Urlaubspläne*

5

Gebrauch des will future

Das will future wird benutzt, um über zukünftige Ereignisse zu sprechen.
Man kann damit:

- Vorhersagen machen,

> **I think it**'ll rain **tomorrow.** *Ich denke, es wird morgen regnen.*

- spontane Entscheidungen ausdrücken,

> **I** won't put **garlic in the salad.** *Ich werde keinen Knoblauch in den Salat tun.*

- über die Zukunft nachdenken

> **Maybe I**'ll go **to the cinema tomorrow.** *Vielleicht werde ich morgen ins Kino gehen.*

- und Dinge zusagen oder absagen.

> **I**'ll set up **the barbecue.** *Ich werde den Grill aufstellen.*
> **I** won't need **you in the kitchen later.** *Ich werde dich später nicht in der Küche brauchen.*

> **Nice to know**
>
> Das **will future** können Sie auch im Restaurant benutzen, wenn Sie Ihr Essen bestellen. Sagen Sie einfach **I'll have** + das Gericht, welches Sie bestellen möchten.
> **Waiter: What can I get you?**
> **Customer: I'll have a steak, please.**

6 ✏

Paul und Kate besprechen den geplanten Urlaub in Südfrankreich.
Schreiben Sie die fehlenden Verben im **will future** in die Lücken. Die Verben,
die Sie benötigen, stehen in ihrer Grundform in Klammern neben der Lücke. Manchmal brauchen Sie die **positive**, manchmal die **negative** Form.

Kate: We 1. _____ (leave) the house at

8 in the morning, so we 2. _____

(arrive) in Dover at about 4 in the afternoon.

Paul: Oh, no, it 3. _____ (take) us that

long. I think the drive 4. _____

(take) 5 hours at most.

Kate: OK, so we 5. _____ (have) extra

time in Dover.

Paul: Yes, we 6. _____ (need) that

because I 7. _____ (want) to go

duty-free shopping!

◀ **leave** – *verlassen*
arrive – *ankommen*
about – *ungefähr*
drive – *Fahrt*
it takes us – *wir brauchen (Zeit)*
hour – *Stunde*
at most – *höchstens*
that long – *so lange*
because – *weil*
duty-free – *zollfrei*

Fragen und Kurzantworten

7

Fragen und Kurzantworten

Fragen im **will future** bildet man, indem man das Subjekt und **will** vertauscht.

Auf Fragen im **will future**, die mit *ja* oder *nein* beantwortet werden können, kann man eine Kurzantwort geben, indem man nach **yes** oder **no** das Personalpronomen und die passende Form von **will** anhängt.

Negative Fragen bildet man, indem man **will** durch **won't** ersetzt oder indem man nach dem Subjekt ein **not** einfügt:

> Won't **you come tomorrow?** *Wirst du morgen nicht kommen?*
> Will **you** not **come tomorrow?** *Wirst du morgen nicht kommen?*

Nice to know

Negative Fragen werden oft benutzt, um Überraschung auszudrücken. Wenn jemand Sie fragt: **Won't you be here tomorrow?**, dann erwartet er/sie eigentlich, dass Sie da sein werden.

8

Die folgenden Fragen im **will future** sind durcheinander gepurzelt! Schreiben Sie sie in ihrer richtigen Reihenfolge auf.

1. come / Will / tomorrow / they / here / ?
2. his / Ben / take / driving test / Won't / ?
3. you / Will / him / later / phone / ?
4. Won't / the / cake / he / bring / ?
5. you / way / find / the / Will / ?
6. go / Jane / university / Will / to / ?

9

Lesen Sie die Fragen oder hören Sie sie sich an.
Kreuzen Sie dann die grammatikalisch richtigen Antworten an.
Es können auch mehrere Antworten richtig sein!

Nice to know

Pommes heißen nur in Großbritannien **chips**. In Nordamerika heißen sie **French fries**.

1. Will you go home early today?
   - a. Yes, I will.
   - b. No, I won't.
   - c. Yes, I'll.
   - d. Yes, I do.

2. Will they buy the apples?
   - a. No, they will.
   - b. No, they won't.
   - c. No, they don't.
   - d. No, they aren't.

3. Will Kate make chips?
   - a. Yes, she will.
   - b. No, she willn't.
   - c. No, she want.
   - d. No, she woesn't.

4. Will he drive to work?
   - a. Yes, he will.
   - b. No, he won't.
   - c. He'll.
   - d. No, she won't.

*Das **will future** mit **if***

10

Das will future mit if

Wenn man Bedingungen in der Zukunft ausdrücken will, benutzt man im Hauptsatz
das will future und im Nebensatz mit if (*wenn/falls*) das
present simple.

> **I'll make a salad if you help me.**
> *Ich mache einen Salat, wenn Du mir hilfst.*

Die Stellung von Haupt- und Nebensatz kann dabei ohne Bedeutungsunterschied
vertauscht werden. Man muss aber beachten, dass im Englischen nur dann ein
Komma gesetzt wird, wenn der if-Satz zuerst kommt.

> **I won't go swimming if it rains tomorrow.**
> *Ich werde nicht schwimmen gehen, wenn es morgen regnet.*
> **If it rains tomorrow, I won't go swimming.**
> *Wenn es morgen regnet, werde ich nicht schwimmen gehen.*

11

Entziffern Sie diese Sätze! Schreiben Sie sie richtig auf.

1. I'llbebackearlyifthereisn'tsomuchtraffic.
2. PaulwillsetupthebarbecueifKatepreparesthesteaks.
3. Theywillphoneusiftheycan'tfindtheway.

traffic – *Verkehr*
phone – *anrufen/
telefonieren*

12

Unterstreichen Sie zu den Satzanfängen das jeweils richtige Ende. Denken Sie dabei
daran, dass man das **will future** nur in den Nebensätzen mit **if** benutzt.

1. I won't go to the park tomorrow if *it rains. / it will rain. / it is
   raining*.
2. She'll go to university if *she will work hard. / she works hard. /
   she is working hard*.
3. If I finish my work, *I'll go home early. / I go home early. / I going
   home early*.
4. If he gets the job, *he is very happy. / he be very happy. / he will
   be very happy*.

Will future oder *present continuous?*

13

Will future oder nicht?

Wenn man über feste Pläne und Vereinbarungen spricht, die sich aller Voraussicht nach nicht mehr ändern werden, benutzt man nicht das will future, sondern das present continuous.

Nice to know

Wenn man über das englische Lieblingsthema Wetter diskutieren will, nimmt man immer das **will future** – denn das kann man ja nie 100%ig vorhersagen!

Paul and Kate are going on holiday to Southern France.

> heißt, dass sie diese Entscheidung bereits in der Vergangenheit getroffen haben, dass die Reise gebucht und geplant ist und aller Voraussicht nach nicht mehr abgesagt wird.

Paul and Kate will go on holiday to Southern France.

> heißt, dass sie diese Entscheidung jetzt gerade treffen oder dass es sich bis jetzt nur um eine Idee handelt, die sich noch ändern kann.

Wenn man über die Zukunft spricht, benutzt man oft Ausdrücke wie **I think** (*ich denke*), **I hope** (*ich hoffe*), **I fear** (*ich fürchte*), **I suppose** (*ich nehme an*). Nach diesen Ausdrücken benutzt man immer das will future.

14

Lesen Sie die Sätze oder hören Sie sie sich an. Entscheiden Sie jeweils, ob das **present continuous** oder das **will-future** vorliegt, und geben Sie dann die Zeitform in der Lücke an (**pc = present continuous**, **wf = will-future**).

1. Will you come back later? _____

2. Are you leaving? _____

3. Paul isn't preparing the barbecue. _____

4. He won't come. _____

5. We're going on holiday. _____

6. I think it'll rain soon. _____

Will future oder present continuous?

15

Unterstreichen Sie die korrekten Formen.

1. Kate and Paul *are having / will have / have* a barbecue tonight.
2. I *'m going / 'll go / go* on holiday tomorrow.
3. I think I *'ll phone / phone / 'm phoning* you later.
4. Jane hopes she *studies / is studying / will study* law when she is older.

16

Ergänzen Sie die Sätze mit dem angegebenen Verb im **present continuous** oder **will future**.

1. I think it _____ (rain) soon. There are many

   clouds in the sky.

2. I _____ (go) to the cinema tonight. I have

   the tickets.

3. Maybe I _____ (phone) him later.

4. We _____ (have) a barbecue tomorrow.

   We already have the food.

5. Paul _____ (come). He is ill.

6. I hope he _____ (be) back soon.

7. I think I _____ (do) my homework now.

8. Paul _____ (drive) us back. He knows he has

   to do that.

Nice to know

Wenn man über feste Pläne und Vereinbarungen spricht, die sich aller Voraussicht nach nicht mehr ändern werden, benutzt man das present continuous.

Das will future benutzt man hingegen, wenn man eine spontane Entscheidung trifft oder wenn man von Ideen oder Ereignissen spricht, die sich noch ändern können.

Nach Ausdrücken wie **I think, I hope, I fear** oder **I suppose** benutzt man immer das will future.

◀ **cloud** – *Wolke*
sky – *Himmel*
ill – *krank*

*Rätselspaß mit dem **will future***

17

Bringen Sie diese Sätze in die richtige Reihenfolge.

1. year / Ben / next / go / will / to / college / .
2. French / will / learn / not / any / more / Jane / .
3. up / I'll / barbecue / the / set / .
4. put / I / the / garlic / won't / in / salad / .

18

Lösen Sie das Kreuzworträtsel, indem Sie die Sätze mit einem jeweils passenden Verb ergänzen.

1. Louise won't ... the flowers.
2. Jane will ... the piano.
3. Kate will ... the steaks.
4. Jane will ... to university.
5. Paul will ... a book.
6. Paul will ... the car home.
7. We'll ... at the table and eat.
8. I'm very tired. I'll ... very well.
9. I'll ... him later. I want to speak to him.
10. Ben will ... a doctor.
11. Louise and Kate will ... in a café.
12. I'll ... the bus.
13. They're having a baby, and they'll ... her Emma.
14. I'll ... a lot of English if I practise.

practise – *üben* ▶

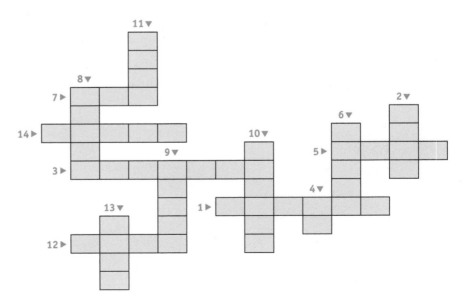

*Verben im **will future***

1

Unterstreichen Sie die für den Satz passende Verbform.

1. Paul and Jane *will goes / will go / is going* on holiday next year.
2. Jane *will go / will going / are go* to university.
3. Ben *not will become / won't become/ will becoming* a doctor.
4. Next year, Kate *will learning/ will learns / will learn* Spanish.
5. Paul *won't works / won't work / won't working* more next year.
6. Kate*'ll come / 'll comes / does coming* home early today.
7. Ben *will finishes / is finishing / will finish* the work tomorrow.
8. Jane *will studies / 'll study / not will study* law.

2

Setzen Sie in den folgenden Text die fehlenden Verben im **will future** ein! Die deutsche Übersetzung der gesuchten Verben steht in Klammern hinter der Lücke.

They 1. _____ (*verlassen*) the house at 8 in the

morning, and they 2. _____ (*ankommen*) in Dover

at about 1 in the afternoon. The drive 3. _____ (*sein*)

about 5 hours, so they 4. _____ (*haben*) extra time

in Dover. They 5. _____ (*brauchen*) that because Paul

6. _____ (*wollen*) to go duty-free shopping.

*Kurzantworten / Sätze mit **if***

3

Lesen Sie die Fragen oder hören Sie sie sich an. Unterstreichen
Sie dann jeweils die passende Antwort.

1. Will they be here soon?   Yes, they will. / Yes, they are. /
Yes, they do.

2. Will it rain tomorrow?   No, it doesn't. / No, it won't. /
No, it isn't.

3. Will you phone me?   Yes, I will. / Yes, I won't. /
No, I want.

4. Will she bring the cake?   No, she isn't. / No, she doesn't. /
No, she won't.

5. Will you drive?   Yes, I will. / Yes, I. / No, I will.

4

Lesen Sie die Satzanfänge und kreuzen Sie jeweils das korrekte Ende an.

1. I'll go home early if
☐ a. I'll finish my work.
☐ b. I am finishing my work.
☐ c. I finish my work.

2. She won't go out if
☐ a. it rains.
☐ b. it is raining.
☐ c. it'll rain.

3. If you buy the bananas,
☐ a. I'll buy the apples.
☐ b. I buy the apples.
☐ c. I'm buying the apples.

4. If they arrive early,
☐ a. we'll have more time.
☐ b. we're having more time.
☐ c. we have more time.

5

Schreiben Sie diese Sätze in ihrer richtigen Reihenfolge auf.

1. to / Kate / isn't / cinema / coming / the / .
2. now / I / I / 'll / my / think / homework / finish / .
3. I / it / hope / won't / tonight / rain / .
4. phone / Maybe / will / us / Paul / later / .
5. Ben / Next / test / year, / will / his / driving / take / .

*Was war am Nachmittag? / Das **past simple***

1

Erinnern Sie sich, was die Familie Smith diesen Samstagnachmittag gemacht hat?
Ordnen Sie den Sätzen die richtigen Bilder zu.
Die Sätze können Sie sich auch anhören.

1. Kate prepared dinner. ☐
2. Jane ate a piece of cake. ☐
3. Paul drank a beer. ☐

4. Jane cleaned her room. ☐
5. Jane played the piano. ☐

◀ **ate** – *aß/aßt/aßen*
drank – *trank/*
trankst/tranken/trankt

2

Können Sie die Fragen auf der linken Seite mit den passenden Antworten
auf der rechten Seite verbinden?
Die Lösungen können Sie sich auch anhören.

1. Did she go swimming?
2. Did he take his test?
3. Did they buy the apples?
4. Did you find the way?
5. Did it rain yesterday?
6. Did Paul and you know that?

a. Yes, he did.
b. No, it didn't.
c. No, we didn't.
d. No, she didn't.
e. Yes, I did.
f. Yes, they did.

◀ **find** – *finden*
yesterday – *gestern*

*Erinnerungen / Das **past simple***

3

Es ist Samstagabend und Louise und ihre Tochter sind zum Grillen gekommen.
Jetzt werden Erinnerungen ausgetauscht.
Lesen Sie den Dialog bzw. hören Sie sich ihn an und versuchen Sie,
so viel wie möglich zu verstehen.

Louise: Mmh, this salad is delicious! Did you make it?
Kate: Yes, I did. I got the recipe from Suzanne.
Do you remember her?
Louise: Yes, I do. Didn't she go to the USA to study?
Kate: Yes, she did, but she wasn't there for very long.
She now lives just outside Manchester.
Louise: Oh, really? I must contact her.
Have you got her number?
Kate: Yes, remind me later and I'll give it to you. But what about you?
What did you do after you left Manchester?
Louise: Well, I went to university in Exeter and studied teaching. When I finished
I got a job in Edinburgh so I decided to move up there.
Kate: Didn't you apply for jobs around Manchester?
Louise: Well – no, I didn't. You see, I fell in love with a fellow student. James
was from Edinburgh and he really wanted to go back there. He didn't like
the South at all, so I followed him to Scotland.
Kate: And do you like it there?
Louise: Yes, it's great. There is so much to do ...

4

Bildung des past simple
Zur Bildung des past simple - der einfachen Vergangenheit - hängt man bei regelmäßigen Verben an die Grundform des Verbs (**work**, **listen**, **play**) die Endung **-ed**
an.

> **Jane** played **the piano.**
> **Louise** decided **to move up to Edinburgh.**

Endet die Grundform des Verbs auf **-e**, so hängt man nur **-d** an.

> **Louise** moved **to Edinburgh.**
> **Kate** arrived **home late from work.**

Endet die Grundform des Verbs auf einen Konsonanten **+ y**, so wird das **-y** weggelassen und **-ied** angehängt:

> **Suzanne** studied **in the USA.**

Die **past simple** Form der Verben ist für alle Personen gleich.

delicious – *lecker*
recipe – *Kochrezept*
remind – *jemanden
erinnern*
decide – *sich ent-
scheiden*
apply – *sich bewerben*
fellow student –
*Kommilitone/Studien-
kollege*

Nice to know

Ein **recipe** gibt es nur
im Kochbuch! Der Zet-
tel, den Sie beim Arzt
bekommen, heißt im
Englischen **prescripti-
on**. Beim Einkaufen
oder im Restaurant be-
kommen Sie auch oft
ein **receipt** – eine Quit-
tung.

*Unregelmäßige Verben im **past simple***

5

Unregelmäßige Verben
Viele der häufig gebrauchten englischen Verben haben eine unregelmäßige **past simple**-Form.

> **Kate had no time yesterday.**　von　have
> **Kate got the recipe from Suzanne.**　von　get
> **Kate made the salad.**　von　make
> **Louise went to university in Exeter.**　von　go

Eine Liste aller unregelmäßigen Verben, die bis Modul 6 in diesem Kurs vorgekommen sind, finden Sie rechts am Rand.

Infinitiv	past simple
write	wrote
have	had
go	went
speak	spoke
do	did
be	was, were
make	made
read	read
drive	drove
know	knew
buy	bought
drink	drank
see	saw
tell	told
leave	left
say	said
think	thought
swim	swam
ride	rode
sleep	slept
sit	sat
feed	fed
sing	sang
meet	met
take	took
eat	ate
fall	fell
wear	wore
drink	drank
get	got

6

Diese **past simple**-Formen sind durcheinander geraten!
Schreiben Sie die Verben in die Lücken.

1. wtoer _____
2. ovred _____
3. ubogth _____
4. gttuhho _____

5. akdrn _____
6. pesok _____
7. nwek _____
8. tem _____

7 ✏

Finden Sie heraus, was Tante Hermione zu erzählen hat. Schreiben Sie die angegebenen Verben im **past simple** in die Lücken.

> Well, when I 1. _____ (be) young, life 2. _____ (be) very different. I 3. _____ (have) four sisters, and we all 4. _____ (go) to the same school. We 5. _____ (walk) there, and it 6. _____ (take) us an hour. Nobody 7. _____ (drive) cars then. Sometimes we 8. _____ (buy) sweets in a little shop. At school, I 9. _____ (learn) a lot. Our teachers 10. _____ (ask) us so many questions! We 11. _____ (read) Shakespeare and we 12. _____ (sit) still all day. We 13. _____ (think) our teachers 14. _____ (know) everything!

◀ **young** – *jung*
nobody – *niemand*
sweets – *Süßigkeiten*
little – *klein*
all day – *den ganzen Tag*

*Zeitangaben und das **past simple***

8

Verwendung des past simple
Man benutzt das past simple, um über abgeschlossene Handlungen oder Ereignisse in der Vergangenheit zu sprechen.

> **Kate went to school with Louise.**
> *Kate ging mit Louise zur Schule.*
> **Paul and Kate got married.**
> *Paul und Kate haben geheiratet.*

Zusammen mit dem **past simple** werden oft Zeitangaben benutzt, die sich auf die Vergangenheit beziehen, wie z.B. **yesterday** (*gestern*), **last week** (*letzte Woche*), **a year ago** (*vor einem Jahr*) oder **in 1989** (*1989*).

Diese Zeitangaben können entweder am Anfang eines Satzes stehen oder an dessen Ende. Stehen Sie am Anfang, dann steht nach der Zeitangabe ein Komma.

> **Paul and Kate got married in 1987.**
> **In 1987, Paul and Kate got married.**

9

Unterstreichen Sie das passende Verb.

1. Kate *drank / made / wrote* the salad.
2. Paul *spoke / left / was* to Louise.
3. Kate *said / thought / bought* a dress.
4. Jane *met / learned / saw* French.

10

Schreiben Sie das passende Verb im **past simple** in die Lücken.
Die Lösung können Sie sich auch anhören.

> sit   leave   meet   buy

1. Kate _____ Louise in a café last Thursday.

2. Aunt Hermione _____ on a chair all evening.

3. Kate _____ a new dress.

4. Paul _____ the office late.

Nice to know

Im Deutschen können Sie das **past simple** auf zwei Arten übersetzen:
Kate went to school with Louise.
Kate ging mit Louise in die Schule.
Kate ist mit Louise in die Schule gegangen.

Nice to know

Meet ist im Englischen nicht reflexiv. Man sagt immer **We met** und niemals **We met us**.
We met in a café.
Wir trafen uns in einem Café.

11 👓

Fragen

Bei Fragen im past simple benutzt man **did** (**past simple** von **do**) und die Grundform des Vollverbs.

> **What did you do after you left Manchester?**
> *Was hast du gemacht, nachdem du aus Manchester weggegangen bist?*

Man kann auch negative Fragen bilden, indem man **didn't** (**did not**) und das Vollverb benutzt.

> **Didn't she go to the USA to study?**
> *Ist sie nicht in die USA gegangen, um zu studieren?*

Auf Fragen, die mit *ja* oder *nein* beantwortet werden können, gibt man oft Kurzantworten, indem man **did/didn't** mit einem passenden Personalpronomen verwendet.

> **Nice to know**
>
> **Did you?** Wird im Eng-
> lischen sehr oft ge-
> braucht, um auf eine
> Aussage zu reagieren:
> **I went to Australia
> last year.**
> **Oh, did you? What did
> you do there?**

12 ✎

Jane interessiert sich immer sehr für alles, was Tante Hermione zu erzählen hat,
und sie stellt ihr viele Fragen. Lesen Sie Janes Fragen und kreuzen Sie die richtigen
Antworten an.

1. Did you have a bicycle?
   - ▦ a. No, I didn't.
   - ▦ b. No, I hadn't.
   - ▦ c. No, I do not.

2. Did you always wear dresses?
   - ▦ a. Yes, I wore.
   - ▦ b. Yes, I did.
   - ▦ c. Yes, I do.

3. Did you go to school
   all day?
   - ▦ a. Yes, we do.
   - ▦ b. No, we don'tid.
   - ▦ c. Yes, we did.

4. Did you go dancing on
   Saturdays?
   - ▦ a. Yes, we danced.
   - ▦ b. Yes, we did.
   - ▦ c. Yes, we dance.

13 👓

Verneinung

Möchte man Sätze verneinen, benutzt man **didn't/did not** und die Grundform
des Vollverbs.

> **James didn't like the South at all.**
> **Kate didn't study teaching.**

Das Verb be im past simple

14 👓

Das Verb be im past simple

Das Verb **be** funktioniert im past simple nicht wie andere Vollverben.

Zunächst hat es zwei Vergangenheitsformen: **was** und **were**. Schauen Sie sich die Tabelle rechts an.

Bei Verneinungen, Fragen und Kurzantworten mit **be** benutzt man nicht **did**, sondern nur **was** oder **were**.

I was
you were
he/she/it was

we were
you were
they were

Paul was **at work yesterday**.	*Paul war gestern bei der Arbeit.*
Louise wasn't **in London**.	*Louise war nicht in London.*
Were **you at home last night?**	**Yes, I** was. **No, I** wasn't.
Warst du gestern Abend zu Hause?	*Ja.* *Nein.*

15 ✎

Unterstreichen Sie die korrekte Form.

1. Louise *wasn't / were / weren't* at university in Manchester.
2. *Were / Was / Did* you at the theatre last Saturday?
3. Were you at home yesterday? Yes, I *did / was / were*.
4. Paul and Kate *was / were / did* at the pub yesterday.

16 ✎

Schreiben Sie die folgenden Sätze im **past simple** in die Lücken.

1. I don't go to school. _____
2. I buy cakes. _____
3. I am happy. _____
4. I'm not fat. _____
5. You're ready. _____
6. You're not angry. _____
7. Paul is at work. _____
8. Louise is tired. _____

*Be oder **do**? / Tante Hermione erzählt*

17

Wählen Sie die richtige Verbform aus. Sie können dann die entsprechende Audio-Datei anhören und auch so kontrollieren, ob Sie alles richtig gemacht haben.

1. We *listened not / didn't listened / didn't listen* to the radio.
2. They *did be / were / was* on holiday.
3. Louise *was / didn't / were* at university.
4. *Did you made / You made / Did you make* the salad?
5. Paul *did work / worked / was work* a lot.
6. He *didn't drove / didn't drive / didn't drived* home.
7. We *wasn't / didn't be / weren't* angry.
8. I *wasn't / weren't / didn't* tired.

18

Tante Hermione hat noch mehr zu erzählen.
Ergänzen Sie ihre Erzählung, indem Sie die Verben in der richtigen Form des **past simple** (positiv oder negativ) in die Lücken schreiben.

walk	think	stay	be	be	be
	not be	live	not work		
work	not go	eat	work	not have	

Well, we 1. _____ a car, and in the summer we

2. _____ on holiday, we 3. _____

at home. The summers in England 4. _____ beautiful then,

and we 5. _____ unhappy at all. We

6. _____ ice cream in the evenings and 7. _____

in the fields. We 8. _____ in the country, and we

9. _____ it 10. _____ wonderful.

We 11. _____ very hard, oh no! We only

12. _____ hard at school, and our teachers

13. _____ very strict!

summer – *Sommer*
unhappy – *unglück-lich*
field – *Feld*
country – *Land*
hard – *hart*
strict – *streng*

*Verbformen im **past simple***

19 🖉

Schreiben Sie das passende Verb im **past simple** unter das Bild! Sie werden sehen, wie viele Verbformen Sie bereits kennen.

*Verben im **past simple***

1 🖊

Diese unregelmäßigen **past simple**-Formen sind durcheinander gepurzelt!
Schreiben Sie sie in die Lücken.
Die Bilder helfen Ihnen herauszufinden, welche Verben gesucht sind.

1. ewotr

_____

2. roved

_____

3. dkrna

_____

4. amsw

_____

5. epslt

_____

6. nags

_____

2 🖊

Ergänzen Sie die Sätze mit der richtigen Verbform im **past simple**, indem Sie diese unterstreichen.

1. I *am not going / didn't went / didn't* go to school.
2. She *didn't study / didn't studied / study* law.
3. Did you *know / knew / knows* him?
4. She *plays / was playing / played* the piano.
5. She *didn't go / isn't going / goes* home early.

*Was haben sie gestern getan? / **Be** im **past simple** / Kurzantworten*

3 🖉

Beschreiben Sie mit einem Verb im **past simple**, was die Person im Bild gestern gemacht hat.

They _____ home.   She _____ a piece of cake.

The cat _____.   They _____ TV.

4 🖉

Schreiben Sie die passende Form von **be** im **past simple** (positiv oder verneint) in die Lücken.

1. He _____ a good student, really good!

2. Where _____ you yesterday?

   I thought you wanted to come!

3. I _____ very good at school. I didn't like it.

4. We _____ at the café yesterday because we had no time.

5 🖉

Beantworten Sie die Fragen mit einer passenden Kurzantwort im **past simple**! Sie können dabei positiv oder negativ antworten, wie Sie möchten.

1. Did he go swimming?   _____

2. Did you see me?   _____

3. Were you at home?   _____

4. Was he there?   _____

Bens Zimmer / Landeskunde

1

In Bens Zimmer herrscht Chaos. Betrachen Sie das Bild und ordnen Sie den darunter stehenden Sätzen jeweils den entsprechenden Bildausschnitt zu, indem Sie den korrekten Buchstaben notieren.

> ◀ **bag** – *Tasche*
> **nice** – *schön*
> **trousers** – *Hosen*
> **black** – *schwarz*
> **white** – *weiß*
> **wardrobe** – *Kleider-schrank*
> **desk** – *Schreibtisch*
> **untidy** – *unordentlich*

1. This is a big poster. ☐

2. This is a nice bag. ☐

3. These are black trousers. ☐

4. This is an open wardrobe. ☐

5. This is an untidy desk. ☐

> **Nice to know**
>
> *Hosen* (**trousers**) sind im Englischen immer Plural. Man sagt auch oft *ein Paar Hosen* (**a pair of trousers**).

2

Testen Sie Ihre Kenntnisse der britischen Landeskunde und verbinden Sie die Satzanfänge auf der linken Seite mit einem passenden Ende auf der rechten Seite.

1. London is
2. Ben Nevis is
3. Scotland is
4. Ireland is as large as
5. Oxford has got
6. Big Ben is
7. The London Underground has got
8. The Thames is

a. larger than Wales.
b. the Serengeti in East Africa.
c. the UK's most famous bell.
d. the biggest city in the UK.
e. the world's longest escalators.
f. the UK's oldest university.
g. much smaller than the Rhine.
h. the highest mountain in the UK.

> ◀ **city** – *Großstadt*
> **mountain** – *Berg*
> **bell** – *Glocke*
> **escalator** – *Rolltreppe*

Shopping for the summer holiday / *Adjektive*

3

Kate und Jane sind im Kaufhaus, um einige Sachen für den Urlaub einzukaufen. Lesen bzw. hören Sie den Dialog und sehen Sie sich die Bilder an. Können Sie alles verstehen?

> **Nice to know**
>
> Es gibt im Englischen keinen Unterscheid zwischen *rosa* und *pink*. **Pink** bedeutet beides. Oft sagt man **light pink**, wenn man *rosa* meint, und **bright pink**, wenn man *pink* meint.

more – *mehr*
most – *am meisten*
go with – *passen zu*
than – *als*
as ... as – *so ... wie*
try on – *anprobieren*
go ahead! – *tu das!*
changing room – *Umkleidekabine*

Kate: Jane, what about this T-shirt? Do you like it?
Jane: Mum, you know I don't like blue. This red one here is much nicer!
Kate: Yes, you're right, but it's more expensive. How about this one? It's red, too, but it's a bit cheaper.
Jane: Hmm, that one's OK. Ooooh, look at this pink one! It's nicer than all the others!
Kate: That's the most expensive T-shirt in the shop!
Jane: Yes, but it's also the nicest. I love pink, and it'll go nicely with my new trousers!
Kate: Well, if you want that one, you can only have one T-shirt. That one's

as expensive as two others!
Jane: Thanks! Can I try it on?
Kate: Go ahead, the changing room's over there.
Jane: It's too big! I need a smaller size.

Kate: What size have you got there?
Jane: A ten.
Kate: I'll get you a size eight, then ...

4

Ein **Adjektiv** beschreibt, wie jemand oder etwas ist.
Adjektive sind im Englischen unveränderlich und stehen normalerweise direkt vor dem Wort, das sie beschreiben.

> **two brown bags**   *zwei braune Taschen*
> **an untidy desk**   *ein unordentlicher Schreibtisch*

In manchen Fällen steht das Adjektiv aber auch nicht direkt vor dem Substantiv, sondern wird dem Verb **be** im Satz nachgestellt.

> **The bags we bought are brown.**
> *Die Taschen, die wir gekauft haben, sind braun.*

Steigerung von Adjektiven

5

Steigerung von Adjektiven

Adjektive können gesteigert werden.
Von einsilbigen Adjektiven bildet man den Komparativ – die erste Steigerungsform
– indem man einfach **-er** an das Adjektiv anhängt.
Um den Superlativ – die zweite Steigerungsform – zu bilden, wird **-est** an das
Adjektiv angehängt.

cheap	**cheap**er	**cheap**est
billig	*billiger*	*am billigsten*
high	**high**er	**high**est
hoch	*höher*	*am höchsten*

Auch einige zweisilbige Adjektive bilden so den Komparativ und den Superlativ.

clever	**clever**er	**clever**est
klug	*klüger*	*am klügsten*

Es gibt aber auch einige Besonderheiten:
Bei Adjektiven, die auf **-e** enden, wird nur **-r** oder **-st** angehängt:

nice	**nice**r	**nice**st

Bei zweisilbigen Adjektiven, die auf **-y** enden, fällt das **-y** weg, und es wird **-ier**
oder **-iest** angehängt:

happy	**happ**ier	**happ**iest

Besteht ein Adjektiv aus der Kombination Konsonant – Vokal – Konsonant, so wird
der letzte Konsonant verdoppelt:

big	**bi**gger	**bi**ggest

6 ✏

Schreiben Sie die passenden Adjektive in die Lücken.

> highest   cheaper   oldest   bigger

1. Russia is _____ than the UK.

2. A T-shirt is _____ than a winter coat.

3. Mount Kilimanjaro is the _____ mountain in Africa.

4. Ben is Paul and Kate's _____ child.

More und *most* / *Unregelmäßige Adjektive*

7

More und **most**

Sehen und hören Sie sich, wenn möglich, die folgenden Sätze an.

> **A winter coat is more expensive than a T-shirt.**
> *Ein Wintermantel ist teurer als ein T-Shirt.*
> **Jane buys the most expensive T-shirt in the shop.**
> *Jane kauft das teuerste T-Shirt im Laden.*
> **This book is more interesting than the author's other books.**
> *Dieses Buch ist interessanter als die anderen Bücher dieses Autors.*
> **This book is the most interesting one by this author.**
> *Dieses Buch ist das Interessanteste von diesem Autor.*

Können Sie jetzt die folgenden Regeln vervollständigen?

1. Mehrsilbige Adjektive bilden den **Komparativ** mit
- ☐ a. **more** + Grundform.
- ☐ b. **over** + Grundform.
- ☐ c. Grundform + **-er**.

2. Den **Superlativ** bilden mehrsilbige Adjektive mit
- ☐ a. **over** + Grundform.
- ☐ b. Grundform + **-er**.
- ☐ c. **most** + Grundform.

8

Bilden diese Adjektive den Komparativ und Superlativ mit **-er/-est** oder mit **more/ most**? Bilden Sie zwei Gruppen.

> big   expensive   boring   quiet   clever   hot   tired
> slow   frustrating   interesting   exciting   heavy

-er / -est	more / most

9

Folgende Adjektive haben eine unregelmäßige Steigerung:

good (*gut*)	**better** (*besser*)	**best** (*am besten*)
bad (*schlecht*)	**worse** (*schlechter*)	**worst** (*am schlechtesten*)
much/many (*viel*)	**more** (*mehr*)	**most** (*am meisten*)
little (*wenig*)	**less** (*weniger*)	**least** (*am wenigsten*)
far (*weit*)	**further** (*weiter*)	**furthest** (*am weitesten*)

boring – *langweilig* ▶
exciting – *spannend, aufregend*
frustrating – *frustrierend*

Früher und heute / Dinge vergleichen

10 ✎

Paul hat es manchmal nicht leicht mit Tante Hermione, die so gern von früher erzählt. Lesen Sie, was er zu sagen hat, und ergänzen Sie die fehlenden Adjektive in der richtigen Form (**Grundform** oder **Komparativ**). Die Grundform ist jeweils in Klammern angegeben.

Well, Aunt Hermione is very 1. _____ (old). She thinks every-thing was 2. _____ (good) when she was 3. _____ (young). For her, everything is 4. _____ (bad) now. Life was 5. _____ (slow), she says, and that is probably 6. _____ (true). People walked 7. _____ (much) and used cars 8. _____ (little). She also thinks people were 9. _____ (nice) and 10. _____ (happy). And, of course, she thinks that everything is 11. _____ (expensive) today than it was. Well, she's right! But I think life is much 12. _____ (exciting) now than when she was young, and, of course, many things are much 13. _____ (easy)!

Nice to know

Im Englischen hat man nicht Recht, man ist es:
Du hast Recht!
You're right!
Sie hat Recht.
She's right.

11 👓

Um Personen oder Dinge miteinander zu vergleichen, verwendet man den **Komparativ + than** (*als*), oder man benutzt eine Konstruktion mit **not as + Adjektiv + as** (*nicht so ... wie*).

> **Scotland is** larger than **Wales.**
> *Schottland ist größer als Wales.*
> **Wales is** not as large as **Scotland.**
> *Wales ist nicht so groß wie Schottland.*

Um auszudrücken, dass zwei Dinge gleich sind, benutzt man **as + Adjektiv + as** (*so ... wie*).

> **Paul is** as old as **Kate.**   *Paul ist so alt wie Kate.*

Möchte man sagen, dass etwas am besten, schnellsten etc. ist, benutzt man den **Superlativ.** Vor dem Superlativ steht oft **the.**

> **Big Ben is** the most famous **bell in the UK.**
> *Big Ben ist die berühmteste Glocke in Großbritannien.*

Nice to know

Der eigentliche **Big Ben** ist nicht der Uhrturm am Londoner Parlamentsgebäude, sondern nur die Glocke!

Vergleiche / Adverbien der Art und Weise

12 ✐

Sehen Sie sich die Bilder an und schreiben Sie die fehlenden Wörter in die Lücken
(**as ... as**, **not as ... as**, **than**).

1. A car is more expensive _____ a bicycle.

2. Jane is _____ tall _____ Ben.

3. The white T-shirt is _____ big _____ the black one.

4. Apples are healthier _____ cake.

healthy – *gesund* ▷

13 👓

Adjektive beschreiben Dinge oder Personen. **Adverbien der Art und Weise**
beschreiben Verben. Sie werden dazu benutzt, näher zu schildern, wie man etwas
macht oder wie etwas geschieht.

It's raining heavily.	**He drives** slowly.
Es regnet stark.	*Er fährt langsam.*

Viele **Adverbien der Art und Weise** werden gebildet, indem man einfach **-ly** an
das entsprechende Adjektiv anhängt.

slow	**My car is very** slow.	*Mein Auto ist sehr langsam.*
slowly	**He walks** slowly.	*Er geht langsam.*

Endet das Adjektiv in **-y**, so fällt das **-y** weg und es wird **-ily** angehängt.

heavy	heavily
happy	happily

Unregelmäßige Adjektive und Adverbien

14

Leider gibt es auch hier viele Ausnahmen und nicht aus jedem Adjektiv kann ein Adverb gebildet werden. So ist das Adverb zu **good** beispielsweise **well** und manchmal sind Adverb und Adjektiv auch gleich.

She's a good student.
Sie ist eine gute Schülerin.
It's a hard job.
Es ist eine harte Arbeit.

She plays the piano well.
Sie spielt gut Klavier.
He works hard.
Er arbeitet hart.

> **Nice to know**
>
> Vorsicht! **Hardly** gibt es im Englischen zwar auch, aber es bedeutet *kaum*! Vergleichen Sie:
> **I work hard.**
> *Ich arbeite hart.*
> **I hardly work.**
> *Ich arbeite kaum.*

15

Lesen Sie die Sätze und schauen Sie sich die darin enthaltenen Adjektive an. Suchen Sie dann das passende Adverb in der Buchstabenschlange und unterstreichen Sie es!

1. He is a bad singer.   fdgebadlyfggsingzuasjnvx
2. She is a happy woman.   saddffrguhappilyvcghappy
3. He is a fast driver.   drivefhfastghfhfastlyfgh
4. He is a good football player. dfghikfflwelljkfgstzhzb
5. This is a hard job.   dfgjdkgvbharddfgbjhardlydfj

> **Nice to know**
>
> **Heavy** bedeutet im Englischen wirklich nur *schwer* im Sinne von *„es wiegt viel"*.
> Eine schwere Zeit ist **a hard time** oder **a difficult time**!

16

In diesen Sätzen, die Sie sich auch anhören können, fehlt entweder das Adverb oder das Adjektiv. Schreiben Sie das fehlende Wort in die Lücke.

 1 2 3 4

| gut | schwer | glücklich | schlecht |

1. He drives _____.

2. She sings very _____.

3. The desk is _____.

4. The child is _____.

Rätselspaß mit Adjektiven

17

Finden Sie die **Grundform** von Adjektiven im Buchstabengitter. Das Adjektiv kann senkrecht, waagerecht oder diagonal versteckt sein.

C	L	E	A	N	B	K	L	S	S
E	X	P	E	N	S	I	V	E	H
K	Y	A	Y	O	U	N	G	T	O
J	P	F	L	I	T	T	L	E	R
W	M	A	N	I	C	E	S	R	T
L	A	R	G	E	K	R	B	L	P
O	S	M	O	C	H	E	A	P	E
N	L	M	U	C	H	S	D	P	H
G	O	Q	U	I	E	T	P	S	D
U	W	L	E	Q	U	I	C	K	O
P	K	W	M	E	D	N	R	L	L
T	I	D	Y	U	W	G	O	O	D

18

Unterstreichen Sie jeweils das Wort, das nicht zu den anderen passt.

1. red / brown / black / longer
2. quickly / slow / nice / hot
3. more expensive / more interesting / more careful / slower
4. cleanest / tidiest / short / nicest
5. slow / fast / quickly / well
6. easier / happy / heavier / sunnier
7. nicest / longer / hottest / tidiest
8. bigger / hotter / young / older
9. quietly / cheaply / expensively / good
10. large / small / big / well
11. largest / brown / smallest / reddest
12. black / well / quickly / shortly
13. worse / better / less / worst
14. least / most / more / furthest
15. less / least / most

Vergleiche

1

Sehen Sie sich das Bild an, und entscheiden Sie, welche Sätze falsch (Kreuz) und welche richtig (Häkchen) sind.

1. Paul's mother is smaller than his father. ■
2. Jane is taller than Ben. ■
3. Paul's sister is younger than Paul. ■
4. Ben is taller than Jane. ■
5. Paul is smaller than his mother. ■

2

Bringen Sie die folgenden Sätze in die richtige Reihenfolge.

1. is / This / very / big / house / .
2. the / The / than / garden / larger / is / house / .
3. The / is / happy / woman / .
4. book / heavy / The / is / not / as / the / bag / as / .
5. shirt / is / The / T- / as / trousers / as / the / bright / .

3

Sehen Sie sich die Bilder an und schreiben Sie die richtige Form des Adjektivs in Klammern in die Lücke.

1. A house is _____ (expensive) than a car.

2. The cat is not as _____ (big) as the dog.

3. Bananas are _____ (healthy) than chocolate.

4. The glass is not as _____ (tall) as the fruit bowl.

Welches Bild passt? / Adverbien / Superlativea

4

Sehen Sie sich die Bilder an und lesen bzw. hören Sie die Sätze. Tragen Sie die Zahl des Bildes ein, zu dem der Satz am besten passt.

This is the biggest house. ☐

This is the smallest bag. ☐

These are the cheapest trousers. ☐

This is the most expensive T-shirt. ☐

5

Unterstreichen Sie die korrekte Form des Adverbs.

1. He speaks French *good / well / goodly*.
2. He drives *fast / slow / fastly*.
3. They sing *beautiful / beautifully / beautifly*.
4. He works very *hard / hardly / harder*.

6 🖉

Schreiben Sie den dazugehörigen Superlativ in die Lücke.

1. bad	worse	_____
2. big	bigger	_____
3. good	better	_____
4. little	less	_____

Hausarbeit / Was können wir im Urlaub tun?

1 ✏

Paul und Kate haben sich die Hausarbeit aufgeteilt. Paul erzählt hier, was seine
Aufgaben sind und was nicht.
Betrachen Sie die Bilder und lesen bzw. hören Sie sich die Sätze an.
Was muss er tun (**has to do**), was muss er nicht tun (**doesn't have to do**) und
 was darf er nicht vergessen (**mustn't forget to do**)?
Ordnen Sie den Sätzen die richtigen Bilder zu.

◄ **do not have to/
don't have to** – *nicht
müssen*
must – *müssen*
must not/mustn't –
nicht dürfen

 a  b c d

1. I sometimes have to cook. ☐

2. I have to wash the car. ☐

3. I don't have to clean the windows. ☐

4. I mustn't forget to hoover the house. ☐

Nice to know

Im Englischen benutzt
man manchmal bekann-
te Produktnamen für
alltägliche Aktivitäten.
Staubsaugen kann so-
wohl **vacuum clean** als
auch **hoover** heißen.

2 ✏

Paul und Kate sind dabei, sich zu überlegen, was sie im Urlaub in Südfrankreich
alles tun könnten oder tun sollten.
Verbinden Sie die Sätze mit dem passenden Bild.

a   b   c

d   e

1. We might buy some wine. ☐

2. We may go sailing for a day. ☐

3. We'll be able to relax on the beach. ☐

4. We should take a lot of suntan lotion. ☐

5. We could visit some old churches. ☐

◄ **suntan lotion**
– *Sonnencreme*
be able to – *können*
might – *könnten*
may – *könnten*

Don't forget the suntan lotion! / Have to

3

Lesen bzw. hören Sie jetzt Paul und Kate zu, wie sie ihren Urlaub planen.

Kate: We may have the time to visit some vineyards. I would love to see how they make wine!
Paul: Yes, good idea, and we might buy some wine there, too.
Kate: Sure, and we could also go sailing for a day. What do you think?
Paul: That would be fantastic! I'm really beginning to look forward to this holiday! The sunshine, the beach …
Kate: That reminds me … we really must buy some more suntan lotion! I think we should take a lot with us.
Paul: Yes, but we don't have to buy it here. Everything is cheaper in France.
Kate: True. Oh, and we have to ask the neighbours if they can look after the cat.
Paul: Yes, we mustn't forget that. I'll do it tonight, don't let me forget!
Kate: I won't. Let's look at the map and plan our route!

Nice to know

Im Englischen gibt es zwei Worte für *erinnern*:
remember = *sich erinnern*
I can't remember the name of the hotel.
remind = *jemanden erinnern*
Remind me to buy some suntan lotion.

---

vineyard – *Weingut/ Weinberg*
would – *wäre*
look forward to – *sich freuen auf*
neighbour – *Nachbar*
if – *ob*
map – *Karte*
towel – *Handtuch*
sleeping bag – *Schlafsack*
ferry – *Fähre*

4

Unterstreichen Sie jeweils das Wort, das den Satz richtig ergänzt.

1. They may visit some *churches. / vineyards. / boutiques.*
2. They might buy some *wine. / souvenirs. / postcards.*
3. They must buy some more *suntan lotion. / towels. / sleeping bags.*
4. They mustn't forget to ask *their parents. / Louise. / the neighbours.*

5

Have to
Um ganz allgemein auszudrücken, dass man etwas *tun muss*, benutzt man im Englischen **have to**.

I have to wash the car.
Ich muss das Auto waschen.

Verneint wird **have to** mit **don't** bzw. **doesn't**.

We don't have to buy the suntan lotion here.
Wir müssen die Sonnencreme nicht hier kaufen.
He doesn't have to work on Sundays.
Er muss Sonntags nicht arbeiten.

Nice to know

Die Bedeutung von **look** verändert sich mit der Präposition, die darauf folgt:
look at – *anschauen*
look after – *sich kümmern um*
look forward to – *sich freuen auf*

6

Must

Um zu betonen, dass etwas unbedingt notwendig ist, benutzt man statt **have to** oft auch must. Must kann allerdings nur in der Gegenwart verwendet werden. Im **will-future** und im **past simple** bleibt es bei **have to**.

> **I really must go to bed early tonight. I am so tired!**
> *Ich muss heute wirklich früh ins Bett gehen. Ich bin so müde!*
> **I really had to go to bed early. I was so tired!**
> *Ich musste wirklich früh ins Bett gehen. Ich war so müde!*

Vorsicht! **Must not/mustn't** bedeutet nicht, wie man vermuten könnte, *nicht müssen*, sondern *nicht dürfen*.

> **You mustn't smoke in the kitchen.**
> *Man darf in der Küche nicht rauchen.*

7 ✎

Kate und Paul denken weiter über das nach, was sie noch tun bzw. nicht tun müssen. Lesen Sie den Dialog und schreiben Sie die Wörter im Kasten in die passende Lücke.

> has to   have to   didn't have to   'll have to
> do we have to   don't have to   have to

Kate: Well, we 1. _____ give the neighbours a key to the house.

Paul: No, we 2. _____. I think they've still got one.

Kate: Really? I'll ask them later. We also 3. _____ cancel the newspaper.

Paul: Do we? We 4. _____ do that last year.

Kate: Well, I think we just forgot ... What else 5. _____ do?

Paul: I'm not sure. Oh, Jane 6. _____ take her French books, so she can translate for us.

Kate: Yes, but we 7. _____ speak a little French, too!

◀ **cancel** – *abbestellen*
translate – *übersetzen*
else – *sonst noch*

*Die modalen Hilfsverben **should** und **can***

8

Should

Das Hilfsverb should wird benutzt, um auszudrücken, dass man etwas tun sollte oder dass es ratsam ist, etwas zu tun.

You shouldn't eat so much chocolate.

In Fragen wird es benutzt, um jemanden um Rat zu bitten.

What do you think he should do?

Man kann **should** auch verwenden, um Vermutungen zu äußern:

Louise should be here soon. *Louise sollte bald hier sein.*

Should bleibt im Präsens für alle Personen gleich, das heißt, bei **he/she/it** wird kein **-s** angehängt.

9 ✏

Ergänzen Sie die Sätze mit **should** oder **shouldn't**.
Die Lösung können Sie sich auch anhören.

dentist – *Zahnarzt*
stay up – *aufbleiben*

1. He _____ go to the dentist.

2. She _____ stay up so late.

3. He _____ go home.

10

Can

Can drückt aus, dass man fähig oder bereit ist, etwas zu tun.

Jane can play the piano. *Jane kann Klavier spielen.*

Can bleibt für alle Personen gleich. In der Verneinung wird **can** zu **can't** oder **cannot**.

Man kann can auch benutzen, um eine Erlaubnis zu erteilen oder jemanden um etwas zu bitten.

Mum, can I go to the cinema? Yes, sure, you can.
Mama, kann ich ins Kino gehen? Ja, sicher kannst du das.

*Can oder **be able to?***

11 👓

Could

Can existiert nur im **present simple** und im **past simple**.
Die **past simple** Form von **can** ist could.

In anderen Zeitformen als dem **present simple** und dem **past simple** (z.B. im **will-future**) existiert **can/could** nicht. Hier benutzt man be able to, um eine Fähigkeit oder Bereitschaft auszudrücken:

> **Jane will** be able to **play the piano very well if she practises a lot.**
> *Jane wird sehr gut Klavier spielen können, wenn sie viel übt.*

Um sehr höflich um etwas zu bitten, benutzt man statt **can** oft auch **could**.

> Can **I have an apple, please?**
> *Kann ich bitte einen Apfel haben?*
> Could **I have an apple, please?**
> *Könnte ich bitte einen Apfel haben?*

Nice to know

Merken Sie sich, dass **could** sowohl *konnte* als auch *könnte* bedeuten kann!

12 ✏️

Manchmal sinniert Paul darüber nach, was er als Student alles tun konnte und was er tun können wird, wenn er in Rente geht.
Ergänzen Sie den Text mit einer passenden Form – positiv oder negativ und in der richtigen Zeitform – von **can** oder **be able to**.

When I was a student, I (1.) _____ sleep late during the week, but I (2.) _____ go on holiday, because I didn't have any money. Well, I (3.) _____ go on holiday now, but I (4.) _____ sleep late in the mornings. Oh, and I (5.) _____ stay out as long as I wanted to, it was great! At the moment, I (6.) _____ read many books, because I haven't got the time. I (7.) _____ do that when I retire, I guess. Oh, and then I (8.) _____ go on holiday for as long as I want.

Nice to know

Im gesprochenen Englisch sagt man sehr oft **I guess** an Stelle von **I think**.

◀ **retire** – *in Rente gehen*
guess – *raten/denken*
not any – *kein/keine*

Would, may und *might*

13

Would, may und **might**

Mit would kann man Angebote machen, Ratschläge erteilen oder hypothetische Situationen ausdrücken.

> Would **you like an apple?** *Möchtest du einen Apfel?*
> I wouldn't **talk to him**. *Ich würde nicht mit ihm sprechen.*
> **That** would **be great.** *Das wäre großartig.*
> I'd **like to go home now.** *Ich würde jetzt gerne nach Hause gehen.*

May und might benutzt man, um die Zukunft betreffende Vermutungen auszu-drücken, wobei may eine etwas höhere Wahrscheinlichkeit ausdrückt als might.

> **We** may **have the time to visit some vineyards.**
> *Wir werden vielleicht die Zeit haben, um ein paar Weingüter zu besuchen.*
> **We** might **buy some wine.**
> *Wir könnten vielleicht etwas Wein kaufen.*

Wenn man um Erlaubnis bitten oder eine Erlaubnis erteilen möchte, kann man ebenfalls may benutzen.

> May **I leave now?** *Darf ich jetzt gehen?*
> **You** may **leave now.** *Du darfst jetzt gehen.*

Nice to know

Für *vielleicht* können Sie im Englischen auch **perhaps** sagen. Aber **We might buy some wine.** klingt eleganter als **Perhaps we'll buy some wine.**

14 ✎

Von den folgenden Sätzen passt jeweils einer nicht zu den anderen, weil er entweder eine andere Situation beschreibt oder in einer anderen Zeitform steht. Können Sie ihn finden? Dann unterstreichen Sie ihn!

1. I may go. / I might go. / Perhaps I'll go. / I can't go.
2. He really should go. / He must go. / He has to go. / He doesn't have to go.
3. She may see us. / She can't see us. / Perhaps she'll see us. / She might see us.
4. I could work. / I mustn't work. / I can work. / I may work.
5. They played. / They had to play. / They were able to play. / They might play.
6. I must buy food. / I have to buy food. / She must buy food. / She could buy food.

15 👓 📀

Let's und Imperativ
Der **Imperativ** (Befehlsform) entspricht im Englischen immer der Grundform
eines Verbs, und man verneint ihn mit **don't**. Man kann ihn benutzen, um direkte
Aufforderungen auszusprechen.

> **Go home!**   *Geh nach Hause!*
> **Don't let me forget that!**   *Lass mich das nicht vergessen!*

Der Imperativ kann oft direkt und unhöflich klingen. Wenn Sie möchten, dass Ihre
Aufforderung mehr wie eine Bitte als wie ein Befehl klingt, benutzen Sie stattdessen
lieber **Could you ...?**

> **Tell him I called!**
> *Sagen Sie ihm, dass ich angerufen habe!*
> **Could you tell him I called?**
> *Könnten Sie ihm sagen, dass ich angerufen habe?*

Möchte man jemanden auffordern, etwas gemeinsam zu tun, benutzt man im
Englischen **let's** (die Kurzform von **let us**) + den **Imperativ**. Diese Form wird
verneint durch das Einfügen von **not** nach **let's**.

> **Let's look at the map and plan our route!**
> *Lass uns auf die Karte schauen und unsere Route planen!*
> **Let's not forget that!**
> *Lass uns das nicht vergessen!*

> **Nice to know**
>
> Man kann den Imperativ auch benutzen, um gute Wünsche oder Aufforderungen auszudrücken:
> **Take care!**
> *Pass auf dich auf!*
> **Get better soon!**
> *Gute Besserung!*
> **Have a nice day!**
> *Einen schönen Tag!*

16 ✏️

Wenn man jemanden auffordert, etwas zu tun, dann hat man meist einen Grund
dafür.
Ordnen Sie jedem Grund eine passende Aufforderung zu.

1. I'm cold.
2. I'm hungry.
3. I'm tired.
4. I've got too much work.
5. I like tennis.
6. I like music.

a. Go and speak to your boss!
b. Close the window!
c. Don't stay up so late!
d. Let's go to a concert.
e. Let's have lunch!
f. Let's go and play!

> ◂ **cold** – *kalt*
> **close** – *schließen*
> **window** – *Fenster*
> **hungry** – *hungrig*
> **boss** – *Chef*
> **concert** – *Konzert*

Hilfsverben gesucht! / Endlich Urlaub!

17 ✎

Schreiben Sie das fehlende Wort in das Kreuzworträtsel.

1. Jane ... study law. She is not sure, but she wants to.
2. Ben ... go to university. He is really not sure.
3. I don't ... to go to work on Sundays. I can stay at home.
4. ... you like a cup of tea?
5. I was not ... to come earlier.
6. Louise ... be here soon.
7. You ... forget to clean the house!
8. I ... help you, I have no time.
9. ... you help me, please?

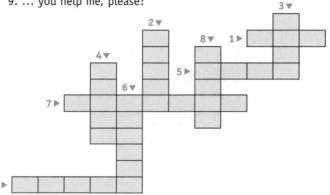

18 📃

Erinnern Sie sich noch an die Urlaubspläne von Paul und Kate? Hier sind Sätze gesucht, die ihren Urlaub betreffen. Schreiben Sie sie in der richtigen Reihenfolge auf.

1. beach / able / be / They / to / relax / the / on / 'll / .
2. They / buy / may / wine / some / .
3. could / They / sailing / go / .
4. would / fantastic / be / Sailing / .
5. should / They / take / lotion / suntan / .
6. take / should / books / They / .
7. Jane / French / have / to / will / speak / .
8. the / forget / They / cat / mustn't / .
9. many / England / don't / have / They / to / buy / in / things / .
10. 'll / They / able / to / buy / be / a / in / France / lot / .

Must oder *have to?*

1

Sehen Sie sich diese Schilder (**signs**) an, und ergänzen Sie die Sätze mit **have to** oder **mustn't**!

1 2 3 4

◀ **mph** – *Meilen in der Stunde*

1. You _____ smoke here!

2. You _____ drive faster than 30 mph here!

3. You _____ be very quiet here!

4. You _____ take this road!

Nice to know

In England werden Distanzen und Geschwindigkeiten in Meilen angegeben. 1 Meile entspricht ca. 1,6 km und 30 mph entsprechen ca. 50km/h.

2

Sehen Sie sich die Bilder an, und ergänzen Sie die Sätze mit **must** oder **have to** in der richtigen Zeitform.

1 2 3 4

1. Yesterday I _____ work very late.

2. I really _____ go to the dentist!

3. Ben will _____ tidy up his room soon or Kate will

   get very angry!

4. The Smith family _____ feed their cat every day.

3

Unterstreichen Sie die passende Form.

1. You *don't have to / didn't have to / mustn't* smoke here!
   Can't you see the sign?
2. Paul *doesn't have to / mustn't / have to* work on Sundays.
3. I *don't have to / mustn't / have to* forget to feed the cat.
4. You *mustn't / must / don't have to* finish today.
   Tomorrow will be early enough.

Can oder *be able to?* / *Should, would, could* und *might* / *Imperative*

4

Schreiben Sie die vorgegeben Sätze im **present simple** in die Lücken.
Benutzen Sie entweder **can** oder **be able to**.

    1. I'll be able to swim. _____

    2. I couldn't dance. _____

    3. I won't be able to drive. _____

    4. I was able to read. _____

5

Sehen Sie sich die Bilder an, und ergänzen Sie die Sätze mit **should**, **would**,
could oder **might**.
Benutzen Sie jedes dieser Hilfsverben genau einmal.

1   2    3   4

    1. I _____ like a cup of tea, please.

    2. It _____ rain soon.

    3. You _____ go home!

    4. _____ you help me, please?

6

Die folgenden Sätze sind durcheinander gepurzelt! Bringen Sie sie auf einem Blatt
Papier wieder in die richtige Reihenfolge.

    1. let / to / cat / me / the / forget / Don't / feed / !
    2. stay / too / Don't / late / out / !
    3. him / Tell / called / I / !
    4. some / and / milk / Go / buy / !
    5. have / Let's / a / next / Saturday / party / !
    6. Let's / tomorrow / tennis / play / together / !

Der Zeitschriftenladen / Was nehmen wir mit?

1 🖋

Der Zeitschriftenladen (**corner shop**) in der Straße der Smiths verkauft viele verschiedene Dinge, die Sie sich auch anhören können. Betrachen Sie das Bild und ordnen Sie den darunter stehenden Sätzen jeweils den entsprechenden Bildausschnitt zu, indem Sie den korrekten Buchstaben notieren.

> **Nice to know**
>
> Neben den vielen **corner shops** gibt es in England auch so genannte **off-licences**. Diese haben ein ähnliches Sortiment wie **corner shops**, dürfen aber auch alkoholische Getränke verkaufen.

1. They sell many magazines. ☐

2. They sell a lot of chocolate. ☐

3. They don't sell much milk. ☐

4. They sell some newspapers. ☐

5. They sell little mineral water. ☐

6. They sell a lot of cigarettes. ☐

7. They don't sell many birthday cards. ☐

8. They sell a few stamps. ☐

◀ **sell** – *verkaufen*
stamp – *Briefmarke*
a few – *ein paar*
off–licence – *Wein- und Spirituosen- geschäft*

2 🖋

Der Sommerurlaub der Familie Smith steht kurz bevor. Da sie zelten wollen, müssen Sie sich sehr genau überlegen, was sie mitnehmen und was nicht. Ordnen Sie den Sätzen, die Sie sich auch anhören können, die richtigen Bilder zu.

> **Nice to know**
>
> Handys gibt es im Englischen nicht. Mobiltelefone heißen in Großbritannien **mobile (phone)** und in Nordamerika **cellphone**.

 a   b   c   d

◀ **tent** – *Zelt*
travel guide – *Reise- führer*

1. They're taking a tent. ☐

2. Paul's not taking his mobile phone. ☐

3. They're taking some travel guides. ☐

4. They're not taking any wine.

Die Packliste / Arten von Substantiven

3

Paul und Kate sind dabei, eine detaillierte Packliste für ihren Urlaub zusammen-zustellen. Lesen Sie den Dialog. Wenn Sie möchten, können Sie diesen auch hören.

large – *groß*
raincoat – *Regenjacke*
get in – *hineinbe-kommen*
few – *wenige*
medicine – *Medika-mente*

Paul: How many bags will we need?
Kate: Oh, one large bag per person, I think – and we'll need some plastic bags for shoes.
Paul: Are we taking raincoats for everybody?
Kate: Well, I think we should. We should also take some food. It's easier to organise that here, and I don't want to do too much shopping in France – nobody will speak English!
Paul: I think we should take very little food. We'll be able to buy a lot of things there.
Kate: But we should take a few things – just for the first few days.
Paul: All right, but don't forget we're already taking so many other things.
Kate: Well, I just hope we'll be able to get everything in the car!
Paul: Oh, and we must pack a bag with some medicine.
Kate: Yes, we mustn't forget. Let's just hope nobody will need it!

4

Die meisten Substantive im Englischen sind zählbar und besitzen eine
Pluralform: **house – houses   mouse – mice**
Es gibt aber auch Substantive, die nicht zählbar sind. Diese bilden keine Pluralform und werden ohne unbestimmten Artikel gebraucht.
Einige der wichtigsten nicht zählbaren Substantive, denen Sie immer wieder begeg-nen werden und die sie sich deshalb gut einprägen sollten, sind:

work (*Arbeit*)	**I have a lot of work.**
information (*Information*)	**I've got no information.**
advice (*Rat*)	**He gave me some advice.**
time (*Zeit*)	**I haven't got a lot of time.**

5

Sind die folgenden Wörter
zählbar oder nicht?
Bilden Sie zwei Gruppen.

zählbar	nicht zählbar

water   cheese   apple   money   glass   dog   advice
euro   information   wine   child   towel

Much, many und *a lot of*

6

Much, **many** und **a lot of**
Zählbare Substantive werden im Englischen oft mit many (*viele*) oder a lot of (*viele*) benutzt.

> **We are taking so many other things.**
> *Wir nehmen so viele andere Dinge mit.*
> **Are we taking a lot of towels?**
> *Nehmen wir viele Handtücher mit?*

Nicht zählbare Substantive benutzt man mit much (*viel*), normalerweise aber nur in Fragen und negativen Sätzen. In positiven Sätzen bleibt es bei a lot of (*viel*).

> **I don't want to do much shopping in France.**
> *Ich will in Frankreich nicht viel einkaufen gehen.*
> **We'll need a lot of time to drive to France.**
> *Wir werden viel Zeit brauchen, um nach Frankreich zu fahren.*

Wenn Sie sich unsicher sind, können Sie immer a lot of benutzen. Diese Form ist nie falsch.

7

Benutzt man diese Wörter mit **much** oder mit **many**?
Bilden Sie zwei Gruppen.

much	many

bottle	wine	advice	computer	flower	house
butter	time	car	money	information	apple

8

Lesen Sie die Sätze und unterstreichen Sie dann das Wort, das den Satz richtig ergänzt.

1. I don't have *many / a / much* time.
2. We're taking *much / many / a* bags.
3. They're not taking *much / many / a* food.
4. He's got *much / a / many* friends.

Little und *few*

9

Little und **few**

Wenn man ausdrücken will, dass man von einer Sache wenig oder wenige hat, so tut man dies bei zählbaren Substantiven mit **few** und bei nicht zählbaren Substantiven mit **little**.

> **There's little milk in the bottle.**
> *Es ist wenig Milch in der Flasche.*
> **There are very few flowers in the garden.**
> *Es sind wenige Äpfel in der Schale.*

10

Lesen Sie die Sätze bzw. hören Sie sie sich an und entscheiden Sie, welches der Bilder am besten zu dem Satz passt.

1a 1b 2a 2b

3a 3b 4a 4b

1. There's a lot of water in the glass. ☐
2. There's little milk in the bottle. ☐
3. There are many apples in the bowl. ☐
4. There are very few flowers in the garden. ☐

11

Verwandeln Sie die vorgegeben Sätze jeweils in ihr Gegenteil, indem Sie diese mit **few** oder **little** schreiben (z.B. **There are many people.** / **There are few people.**).

1. There are many apples. _____
2. There is a lot of milk. _____
3. I have a lot of time. _____
4. He has many friends. _____

Some und *any*

12 👓

Some und **any**
Das Wort some (*einige, etwas*) benutzt man sowohl mit zählbaren als auch mit nicht zählbaren Substantiven. Es wird meist in positiven Aussagesätzen verwendet und in Fragen, auf die man eine positive Antwort erwartet.

> **We should take** some **food.**
> **Did you meet** some **friends?**
> **Would you like** some **tea?**

Any, welches man ebenfalls sowohl mit zählbaren als auch mit nicht zählbaren Substantiven benutzen kann, hat in negativen Sätzen die Bedeutung *kein/keine*.

> **I don't have** any **time!**   *Ich habe keine Zeit!*

In positiven Sätzen und Fragen bedeutet any *irgendein/e* oder *irgendwelche*.

> **I can come at** any **time.**   *Ich kann jederzeit kommen.*
> **Are there** any **questions?**   *Gibt es irgendwelche Fragen?*

Some bezeichnet immer einen Teil aus der Gesamtheit dessen, was möglich wäre.

> **I like** some **cheese.** heißt, dass *ich manchen Käse mag.*

Any bezeichnet hingegen immer alle oder alles.

> **I like** any **cheese.** heißt, dass *ich allen/jeden Käse mag.*

> **Nice to know**
>
> Das Wörtchen **some** wird im Deutschen oft gar nicht übersetzt.
> **He took some pictures.**
> *Er hat Fotos gemacht.*

13 ✏

Ergänzen Sie die Sätze mit **some** oder **any**.

1. Would you like _____ tea?

2. I would like _____ milk, please.

3. I don't have _____ time now. I'm sorry.

4. Can you help Kate? She's got _____ problems with the computer.

5. I need new furniture for my house! I haven't got _____ at the moment.

6. Paul and Kate haven't got _____ vegetables in the house.

◀ **furniture** – *Möbel*
left – *übrig*

Someone, no one und *anyone*

14 👓

Someone, no one und **anyone**
Die folgenden Wörter können im Englischen in beliebiger Kombination zusammengesetzt werden.

every *(jede/r/s)*	**thing** *(Ding, Sache)*
any *(irgendein/e/er/es)*	**body** *(Körper, Person)*
some *(einige)*	**one** *(eine/r/s)*
no *(keine/r/s)*	**where** *(wo)*

Entsprechend erhält man:

everything	**Do we have everything?**
alle	*Haben wir alles?*
everybody/everyone	**Everyone knows that!**
jeder	*Das weiß doch jeder!*
everywhere	**He walks everywhere.**
überall	*Er geht überall zu Fuß hin.*

Folgende Sätze verdeutlichen Kombinationen im Englischen mit **any**, **some** und **no**:

Would you like anything **to drink?**	*irgendetwas*
I don't know anybody **here.**	*niemanden*
We can go anywhere **we like.**	*überall*
I would like something **to drink, please.**	*etwas*
Somebody **told me that.**	*jemand*
I left my bag somewhere.	*irgendwo*
I know nothing **about that!**	*nichts*
Let's hope nobody**'ll need the medicine.**	*niemand*
I can find him nowhere**!**	*nirgendwo*

Vorsicht! Everybody bedeutet *jeder* im Sinne von *alle zusammen*, und anybody bedeutet *jeder* im Sinne von *irgendein beliebiger*.

Everybody **knows that.**	*Jeder weiß das.*
	(Wir alle wissen das.)
Anybody **could do that.**	*Jeder könnte das tun.*
	(Jeder Beliebige könnte das tun.)

In Fragen hat anything die Bedeutung von *irgendetwas*, in der Verneinung bedeutet es *nichts*.

Do you know anything**?**	*Weißt du irgendetwas?*
I don't know anything**.**	*Ich weiß nichts.*

Ebenso verhält es sich mit anybody, anyone und anywhere.

Die kennt doch jeder! / Wir hatten so wenig ...

15 ✎

Lesen Sie die Sätze und schreiben Sie die Wörter im Kasten in die passenden Lücken.

> everywhere   somewhere
> anybody   everybody   something

1. Margaret Thatcher? Well, _____ knows her!

   She was the prime minister of the UK!

2. Where are my keys? They must be _____

   in the house!

3. Does _____ know where I can buy chocolate here?

4. We are going to Louise's tomorrow, and we need _____

   _____ to take!

5. Kate likes walking. She walks _____.

◀ **prime minister** –
Premierminister/
Premierministerin

16 ✎

Lesen Sie, was Tante Hermione erzählt, und ergänzen Sie den Text mit **few**, **little**, **much**, **many**, **a lot of**, **some** oder **any**.

Well, when I was young, I had very (1.) _____

_____ nice dresses to wear. My family had

(2.) _____ money, so we never spent

(3.) _____. We never had

(4.) _____ expensive things, but we

had (5.) _____ toys. My sisters and me

knew (6.) _____ nice games that we could play, and for these

we did not need (7.) _____ things. We had (8.) _____

work for school, so we did not have (9.) _____ time to play in

the evenings. On (10.) _____ evenings we had to work at home

to help our parents, too.

◀ **spend** – *ausgeben*
toy – *Spielzeug*

Gegensätze / Wörter suchen

17

Schreiben Sie jeweils das Gegenteil in die Lücken.

1. everybody _____

2. everywhere _____

3. everything _____

4. few people _____

5. only some families _____

6. little time _____

7. no teacher _____

8. a lot of dishes _____

9. only here _____

10. only now _____

18

In diesem Buchstabengitter sind zehn Wörter versteckt, die Sie in dieser Lektion gelernt haben.
Welche sind es?

K	M	U	C	H	Z	K	X	H	G	L	P
P	X	A	P	A	K	P	Z	X	P	I	X
F	P	P	N	N	N	N	K	H	P	T	K
E	V	E	R	Y	B	O	D	Y	E	T	W
W	P	U	P	W	S	B	T	A	X	L	T
P	U	X	C	H	P	O	P	H	Q	E	P
Q	K	X	M	E	X	D	M	B	I	W	K
Q	A	Z	E	R	K	Y	X	E	K	N	K
Z	A	K	L	E	S	S	O	P	P	T	G

Much, many oder a lot of? / Few oder little? / Gegenteile

1 🖋

Ergänzen Sie die Sätze mit **much**, **many** oder **a lot of**.

1. There is _____ cheese in the fridge.

2. There are _____ towels in the bag.

3. There isn't _____ milk in the bottle.

4. Are there _____ apples?

2 🖋

Ergänzen Sie die folgenden Sätze mit **few** oder **little**.

1. There are _____ children at school today.

2. They have _____ milk left in the fridge.

3. I have _____ books at home.

4. She has _____ time to play.

3 🖋

Schreiben Sie die Wörter aus dem Kasten neben den Begriff, der ihr Gegenteil ausdrückt.

not anybody	few things	nowhere
no one	nowhere	

1. everywhere   _____

2. somebody   _____

3. everyone   _____

4. many things   _____

5. somewhere   _____

Welches Bild passt? / Sätze ordnen

4

Welches Bild passt am besten zu dem Satz?
Die Sätze können Sie sich auch anhören.

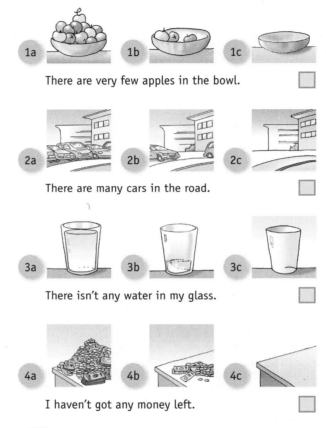

There are very few apples in the bowl. ☐

There are many cars in the road. ☐

There isn't any water in my glass. ☐

I haven't got any money left. ☐

5

Bringen Sie die folgenden Sätze wieder in die richtige Reihenfolge.

1. do / I / time / not / any / have / .
2. him / knows / Nobody / well / very / .
3. much / did / money / not / They / have / .
4. problems / few / had / They / .
5. did / problems / They / not / many / have / .

Wann war das? / Wo schläft Oscar?

1

Verbinden Sie die Satzanfänge auf der linken Seite mit einem passenden Ende
auf der rechten Seite.

1. Paul went to university
2. On Mondays, Paul and
3. The family usually watch TV
4. Ben and Jane come home from school
5. Kate went to school
6. The family go for long walks

a. for 12 years. She didn't go to university.
b. Kate go shopping.
c. at 4:30. They take the school bus.
d. 20 years ago, when he was 19 years old.
e. at the weekend. They enjoy walking very much.
f. in the evening.

from – *von*
between – *zwischen*
flat – *Wohnung*
ago – *vor*
in the evening –
abends

2

Oscar, die Katze der Familie Smith, legt sich gerne an den verschiedensten Orten
im Haus zum Schlafen hin. Wo befindet sich Oscar gerade?
Ordnen Sie den Sätzen das jeweils passende Bild zu, indem Sie den korrekten
Buchstaben notieren.

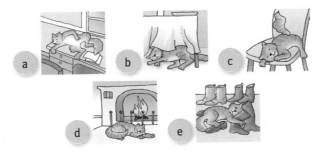

dining table – *Es-
stisch*
under – *unter*
in front of – *vor*

Nice to know

Die meisten englischen
Häuser haben zwar Zen-
tralheizung, besitzen
aber zusätzlich auch
noch einen offenen
Kamin (**fireplace**).
Allerdings wird dieser
heute oft elektrisch
betrieben.

1. Oscar is sleeping under the dining table. ☐

2. Oscar is sleeping between the shoes. ☐

3. Oscar is sleeping on the desk. ☐

4. Oscar is sleeping in front of the fireplace. ☐

5. Oscar is sleeping on a chair. ☐

Breakfast on the way / *Präpositionen der Zeit*

3

by – *um* ▶
in the afternoon – *nachmittags*
in the morning – *morgens*
mean – *meinen/heißen/bedeuten*
before – *vorher*
out of – *heraus/hinaus*
into – *hinein/herein*
on the way – *unterwegs*
stuff – *Zeug/Sachen*
be used to – *an etwas gewöhnt sein*
down – *herunter/hinunter*
around – *um ... herum*
along – *entlang*
straight – *geradeaus/direkt*
towards – *in Richtung*

Lesen Sie den Dialog bzw. hören Sie ihn sich an. Achten Sie dabei besonders auf die Präpositionen **on**, **at** und **in**.

Paul: Let's see ... The ferry leaves Dover at six o'clock, so we'll have to be there by five.
Kate: Earlier, I'd say. Let's plan to be there early in the afternoon.
Paul: OK. That means we'll have to leave here early in the morning.
Kate: Yes, but that's no problem. I'll pack us a picnic basket the night before and then we can be out of bed and into the car at seven. We'll have breakfast on the way.
Paul: Good idea. We'll have to take all the picnic stuff anyway, because we'll need it in France.
Kate: Yes, and during the drive, the basket can sit on the back seat between the children. They are used to that.
Paul: Good. Let's plan our route now. We'll take the M6 down to Birmingham and then go along the M1 and around London, then straight towards Dover.
Kate: I'm not looking forward to going around London. Let's hope the traffic isn't too bad.
Paul: True. But we're going on a Sunday, and we're also going in the middle of the school holidays. So I don't think we'll have too many problems.

4

Präpositionen der Zeit
Bei **Zeitangaben** werden am häufigsten die Präpositionen **on**, **at** und **in** verwendet.
On verwendet man, wenn man über einen Wochentag oder ein Datum spricht.

We're going on a Sunday.	*an einem Sonntag*
We're going on the 14th of July.	*am 14. Juli*

At wird mit Uhrzeiten oder auch Mahlzeiten verwendet.

The ferry leaves Dover at six o'clock.	*um sechs Uhr*
I'll see you at lunch.	*beim Mittagessen*

In wird mit Jahreszeiten, Jahren, Monaten und Tageszeiten verwendet.

Let's plan to be there in the afternoon.	*nachmittags*
They go on holiday in the summer.	*im Sommer*
Their holiday is in June.	*im Juni*

At und *by* / *Paul im Stress*

5

Es gibt einige Zeitangaben, die mit **at** benutzt werden, ohne dass es sich dabei um Uhrzeiten handelt.

at the weekend	*am Wochenende*
at the moment	*im Moment, jetzt gerade*
at night	*in der Nacht, nachts*
at Christmas	*an Weihnachten*
at the end	*am Ende*

6

Um auszudrücken, dass etwas bis zu einem bestimmten Zeitpunkt geschehen sein muss, benutzt man die Präposition **by**.

We'll have to be in Dover by **five o'clock.** *bis/um fünf Uhr*

Zeitangaben wie **tonight** (*heute Abend*), **tomorrow** (*morgen*) oder **this afternoon** (*heute Nachmittag*) benötigen keine Präposition.

7

Lesen Sie, was Paul vor dem Urlaub noch alles erledigen und bis wann er damit fertig sein muss. Schreiben Sie dann passende Präpositionen in die Lücken. Wenn Sie meinen, dass die Lücke leer bleiben muss, schreiben sie einen Bindestrich (-) in die Lücke.

We're leaving (1.) _____ tomorrow morning (2.) _____ seven o'clock. We have to finish all our packing (3.) _____ this evening, so that we'll be able to leave as early as we can (4.) _____ the morning. (5.) _____ five o'clock (6.) _____ this afternoon, I have to pick Kate up from work. Later (7.) _____ the evening, I have to pick Jane up from her friend. (8.) _____ seven, we're seeing the neighbours. Oh, and I also have to phone my brother (9.) _____ tonight, because it's his birthday. I'm just glad that we're going (10.) _____ a Sunday. There won't be so much traffic!

Tipp zur Lösung!

On verwendet man, wenn man über einen Wochentag oder ein Datum spricht.
At wird mit Uhrzeiten oder auch Mahlzeiten verwendet.
In wird mit Jahreszeiten, Jahren, Monaten und Tageszeiten verwendet.
Zeitangaben wie **tonight, tomorrow** oder **this afternoon** benötigen keine Präposition.

Zeiträume

8

Zeiträume

Um auszudrücken, wie lange ein Ereignis dauert, gedauert hat oder dauern wird, benutzt man die Präposition **for**.

> **Louise is in Manchester for two weeks.**
> *Louise ist zwei Wochen lang in Manchester.*
> **Paul went to university for three years.**
> *Paul ging drei Jahre lang zur Universität.*

Wenn man von einem zukünftigen Ereignis spricht und sagen möchte, wie lange es noch dauert, bis es passiert, benutzt man die Präposition **in**.

> **The ferry leaves in ten minutes.**
> *Die Fähre fährt in 10 Minuten ab.*
> **Ben will finish school in two years.**
> *Ben wird in zwei Jahren mit der Schule fertig sein.*

Die Präposition **ago** wird mit der Vergangenheit benutzt, um auszudrücken, wie lange etwas her ist. Vorsicht! **Ago** steht immer nach der Zeitangabe.

> **Kate finished school 19 years ago.**
> *Kate beendete vor 19 Jahren die Schule.*
> **I saw him 10 minutes ago.**
> *Ich habe ihn vor 10 Minuten gesehen.*

9

Lesen Sie die Sätze und unterstreichen Sie die passende Präposition.

> 1. Don't worry. He'll be here *in / for / ago* ten minutes.
> 2. I moved to London six years *for / in / ago*.
> 3. Ben usually studies *in / for / ago* three hours every day.
> 4. He went to school 19 years *for / ago / in*.
> 5. They will be here *in / ago / for* ten minutes.
> 6. Louise is staying in Manchester *ago / for / in* two weeks.
> 7. They went on holiday three years *in / for / ago*.
> 8. I'll be there *for / in / ago* half an hour. I'll stay all evening if you like.

Präpositionen des Ortes / Wo ist der Ball?

10

Präpositionen des Ortes
Im Englischen benutzt man verschiedene Präpositionen, um die Position von Dingen und Personen relativ zueinander zu beschreiben.
Die folgenden Sätze, die Sie sich auch anhören können, illustrieren einige dieser Präpositionen.
Können Sie die beschriebenen Objekte und deren Position auf den Illustrationen identifizieren?

Paul is sitting at the desk.
Paul sitzt am Schreibtisch.
The bin is under the desk.
Der Papierkorb ist unter dem Schreibtisch.
The lamp is on the desk.
Die Lampe ist auf dem Schreibtisch.
There is some paper in the drawer.
Da ist etwas Papier in der Schublade.

Ben is standing next to Jane.
Ben steht neben Jane.
Kate is standing behind Jane.
Kate steht hinter Jane.
Ben is standing in front of Paul.
Ben steht vor Paul.
Oscar is sitting between Ben and Jane.
Oscar sitzt zwischen Ben und Jane.

11 ✎

Sehen Sie sich die Zeichnungen an und schreiben Sie dann die Präposition aus
Übung 10 in die Lücke, die am besten beschreibt, wo sich der Ball gerade befindet.

◀ **above** – *über*

_____   _____   _____   _____

Tante Hermiones Wohnung / Ort und Richtung

12

Bei Tante Hermione ist immer alles an seinem angestammten Platz. Sehen Sie sich die Bilder an und vervollständigen Sie die Sätze mit einer passenden Präposition.

 1  2 3 4

1. The picture is _____ the fireplace.

2. The sofa is _____ the TV.

3. The phone book is _____ the phone.

4. The newspaper is _____ the coffee table.

13

Lesen Sie die Sätze bzw. hören Sie sie sich an.
Zwei der verwendeten Präpositionen drücken eine Bewegungsrichtung aus. Können Sie diese durch Ankreuzen identifizieren?

1. The post office is **opposite** the bank.
2. The hairdresser's is **above** the post office.
3. The post office is **below** the hairdresser's.
4. The children are playing **in the middle** of the road.
5. The car is parked **near** the corner.
6. The cat is sitting **among** the flowers.
7. The man is walking **through** the post office door.
8. The woman is walking **back** to her car.

Nice to know

Between heißt zwischen zwei genau definierten Objekten, und **among** heißt *irgendwo mittendrin*:
between the sofa and the table
zwischen dem Sofa und dem Tisch
among the people
zwischen/unter den Leuten

opposite – *gegenüber* ▶
hairdresser's
– *Friseurgeschäft*
below – *unter*
among – *zwischen/ inmitten/unter*
through – *durch*

14

Präpositionen der Richtung
Sehen Sie sich die Bilder an und schreiben Sie die korrekte Präposition in die Lücke.
Als Hilfe können Sie sich die Sätze auch anhören.

1. He is walking _____ the hill.
2. He is walking _____ the house.
3. He is walking _____ the corner.
4. He is walking _____ the street.
5. Oh no! He's falling _____ the cliff!

round
off
up
across
past

◀ **across** – *über*
up – *hinauf*
past – *an ... vorbei*
round – *um ... herum*
off – *herab/herunter*

15

Paul und Kate gehen noch einmal zusammen ihre Reiseroute durch. Lesen Sie den
Text und schreiben Sie die fehlenden Präpositionen in die Lücken.

We'll take the M6 (1.) _____ (*hinunter*) to Birmingham
and then go (2.) _____ (*entlang*) the M1 and
(3.) _____ (*um ... herum*) London, then straight
(4.) _____ (*in Richtung*) Dover. We're taking the ferry,
so we're not going (5.) _____ (*durch*) the Channel
Tunnel. Then we'll drive (6.) _____ (*heraus*) Calais and
follow the motorway (7.) _____ (*bis*) Paris. We'll go
(8.) _____ (*an ... vorbei*) Paris and follow the motorway
(9.) _____ (*in ... hinein*) the Provence. We'll get
(10.) _____ (*herunter*) the motorway (11.) _____
_____ (*in der Nähe von*) Avignon.

Nice to know

Merken Sie sich das Wort **past** am besten als *vorbei*. Das **past simple** ist vorbei (schon geschehen), **past the shop** heißt *am Laden vorbei*, und **half past four** heißt, dass vier Uhr seit einer halben Stunde vorbei ist.

Over, under, in front of

16 ✎

Schreiben Sie die richtige Präposition in die Lücken. Ihre Lösung können Sie auch überprüfen, indem Sie sich die Sätze anhören.

> across   for   through   along   at   ago   on
> over   in   in front of   to   among

1. I'm staying here _____ two weeks.

2. The cat usually comes in _____ the window.

3. Paul often plays tennis _____ the weekend.

4. I met him three years _____.

5. _____ Mondays, they often go shopping.

6. They watch TV _____ the evening.

7. The cat is sleeping _____ the fireplace.

8. They walk _____ school.

9. He is going _____ the street.

10. He is driving _____ the street.

11. There is a plane flying _____ the house.

12. The cat is sitting _____ the flowers.

17 ✎

Wohin fährt das Auto? Sehen Sie sich die Bilder genau an und ergänzen Sie die Sätze mit einer passenden Präposition.

1. The car is going _____ the road.

2. The car is going _____ a bridge.

3. The car is going _____ a tunnel.

4. The car is going _____ the hill.

*Wann war das? / **For**, **in** oder **ago**? / Wo ist die Katze?*

1 🖉

Schreiben Sie die passenden Präpositionen in die Lücken.

1. _____ Monday   5. _____ Christmas

2. _____ June   6. _____ night

3. _____ the evening   7. _____ the morning

4. _____ six o'clock   8. _____ the 14th of December

2 🖉

Ergänzen Sie die Sätze mit **for**, **in** oder **ago**.

1. She will be here _____ ten minutes.

2. They are staying _____ one week.

3. He finished school two years _____.

4. He'll be back _____ two hours.

5. They're staying _____ two days.

3 🖉

Wo ist die Katze?
Schreiben Sie eine passende Präposition in die Lücke.

_____ the shoes

_____ the desk

_____ the table

_____ the fireplace

Präpositionen des Ortes / Welche Präposition ist richtig?

4

Sehen Sie sich die Bilder an und lesen bzw. hören Sie die Sätze. Kreuzen Sie dann den Satz an, der am besten zum Bild passt.

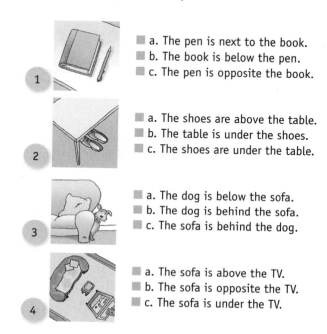

1.
- ◼ a. The pen is next to the book.
- ◼ b. The book is below the pen.
- ◼ c. The pen is opposite the book.

2.
- ◼ a. The shoes are above the table.
- ◼ b. The table is under the shoes.
- ◼ c. The shoes are under the table.

3.
- ◼ a. The dog is below the sofa.
- ◼ b. The dog is behind the sofa.
- ◼ c. The sofa is behind the dog.

4.
- ◼ a. The sofa is above the TV.
- ◼ b. The sofa is opposite the TV.
- ◼ c. The sofa is under the TV.

5 🖉

Ordnen Sie den Bildern die richtigen Präpositionen zu, indem Sie sie in die Lücken schreiben.

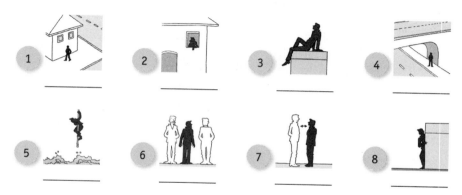

Es ist meins – es gehört mir! / Ich kann das selbst!

1

Verbinden Sie die Sätze auf der linken Seite jeweils mit einem Satz auf der rechten
Seite, der genau das Gleiche ausdrückt.

1. This is my book.
2. This is your camera.
3. This is his bag.
4. This is her pen.
5. This is our computer.
6. This is their living room.

◀ **mine** – *meiner/
meine/meins*
yours – *deiner/
deine/deins*
his – *seiner/
seine/seins*
hers – *ihrer/
ihre/ihres*
ours – *unserer/
unsere/unseres*
theirs – *ihrer/
ihre/ihres*

a. This living room is theirs.
b. This book is mine.
c. This bag is his.
d. This pen is hers.
e. This camera is yours.
f. This computer is ours.

2

Lesen Sie die Fragen und ordnen Sie ihnen dann die richtigen Antworten zu. Sie
können sich die Antworten auch anhören. Achten Sie dabei besonders auf die Betonung des letzten Wortes.

1. Can I help you with your bag?
2. Should I help Jane with
   her homework?
3. Do you and Kate need help
   with the tent?
4. Should we help Ben and Jane
   with dinner?
5. Do you need the pump for the
   air mattress?

◀ **put up** – *aufstellen*
air mattress – *Luft-
matratze*
inflate – *aufpumpen/
aufblasen*
myself – *selbst*
herself – *selbst*
ourselves – *selbst*
themselves – *selbst*
itself – *selbst*

a. No, thanks. I can carry it myself!
b. No, I think it inflates itself.
c. No, I think they can do that
   themselves.
d. No, she should really do it herself!
e. No, thanks. We can put it up
   ourselves.

Oh dear, where's our mattress? / *Possessivbegleiter*

3

Die Familie Smith ist in Südfrankreich angekommen, sie haben ihre Zelte aufgestellt und richten sich ein. Dabei geht es etwas chaotisch zu.
Lesen Sie den Dialog. Wenn Sie möchten, können Sie diesen auch hören.

Paul: Whose trousers are these?
Jane: I don't know. They're not mine. I think they're Ben's.
Paul: Ben? Are these your trousers? Could you put them away, please?
Ben: All right.
Jane: Does anybody know where my air mattress is?
Paul: Oh, I think it's in our tent. I'll get it for you.
Jane: No, it's all right, Dad. I'll get it myself.
Paul: Right. Now where's ours? I know we've got it. Kate packed it herself. Ben? Do you know where our air mattress is?
Ben: No idea.
Jane: I've got mine!
Paul: Let's see ... It's not in the car, it's not out here ... Oh dear, I hope we packed it. Kate? Kate?
Ben & Jane: Typical!
Jane: They always tell us not to forget anything and then they forget everything themselves!

> **whose** – *wessen* ►
> **put away** – *wegtun/ wegpacken*
> **right** – *also*
> **no idea** – *keine Ahnung*
> **typical** – *typisch*

4

Diese Sätze sind durcheinander gepurzelt.
Bringen Sie sie wieder in die richtige Reihenfolge.

1. These / trousers / Ben's / are / .
2. her / air mattress / is / This / .
3. is / air mattress / our / Where / ?
4. Paul / forget / and / themselves / everything / Kate / .
5. mine / I / got / 've / !
6. it / herself / packed / Kate / .

Possessivbegleiter / Mein Buch – dein Buch

5

Possessivbegleiter

Um Besitz oder Zugehörigkeit auszudrücken, benutzt man im Englischen die folgenden **Possessivbegleiter**:

my (*mein / meine*)	Where's **my** air mattress?
your (*dein / deine / ihr / ihre*)	Ben? Are these **your** trousers?
his (*sein / seine*)	These are **his** trousers.
her (*ihr / ihre*)	This is **her** air mattress.
its (*sein / seine*)	The dog ate **its** food.
our (*unser / unsere*)	I can't find **our** tent!
their (*ihr / ihre*)	This is **their** problem.
your (*euer / eure*)	Ben and Jane? Is this **your** cat?

> **Nice to know**
>
> Vorsicht! Der Possessivbegleiter **its** (*sein / seine*) wird oft mit **it's** (*es ist*) verwechselt.

Die englischen **Possessivbegleiter** stehen immer vor einem Substantiv und bleiben unveränderlich, egal ob dieses im Plural oder im Singular steht.

6

Unterstreichen Sie für jeden Satz den Possessivbegleiter, der sich auf die Person oder Personen bezieht, die vorher im Satz genannt worden sind.

1. Paul forgot to pack *his / her / its* air mattress.
2. Ben and Jane have got *its / our / their* mattresses.
3. Kate has got *our / her / his* sleeping bag.
4. We can't find *your / our / my* bag!

7

Ergänzen Sie die Sätze mit einem passenden Possessivbegleiter (**my**, **your**, **his**, etc.).

1. This book belongs to me. It's _____ book.

2. This car belongs to Paul. It's _____ car.

3. This pen belongs to you. It's _____ pen.

4. This house belongs to Paul and Kate. It's _____ house.

5. This basket belongs to the cat. It's _____ basket.

Possessivpronomen / Das ist meins

8

Possessivpronomen

Ist bereits klar, von welcher Person oder Sache die Rede ist, wird diese ausgespart und statt einem Possessivbegleiter ein Possessivpronomen verwendet.

Whose trousers are these?
Wessen Hose ist das?
Is this their house?
Ist das ihr Haus?
What's your phone number?
Wie ist deine Telefonnummer?

They're mine.
Das ist meine.
No, theirs **is over there.**
Nein, ihres ist dort drüben.
576345. What's yours**?**
576345. Wie ist deine?

Schauen Sie sich in der Abbildung noch einmal alle Possessivbegleiter und die entsprechenden Possessivpronomen an und prägen sie sich ein.

9

Schreiben Sie neben die Possessivbegleiter das entsprechende Possessivpronomen in die Lücke (zum Beispiel: **my - mine**)

1. our

_____

2. his

_____

3. their

_____

4. your

_____

10

Formen Sie die Sätze so um, dass sie anstatt des Possessivbegleiters ein Possessivpronomen enthalten (zum Beispiel: **This is my book. – This book is mine.**).

1. This is our house.

_____

2. These are my shoes.

_____

3. This is your umbrella.

_____

4. These are their photos.

_____

5. This is his car.

_____

6. These are her trousers.

_____

Der 's-Genitiv / Kates Katze

11

Der 's-Genitiv
Der 's-Genitiv wird verwendet, um aufzuzeigen, wem etwas gehört. Hierzu wird bei Personen, Tieren oder Ländern im Singular ein 's an das Substantiv angehängt. Werden zwei Personen zusammen genannt, so wird das 's nur an die letztgenannte Person angehängt.

Paul's car	*Pauls Auto*
Paul and Kate's house	*Paul und Kates Haus*

Endet ein Wort **im Plural** auf **-s**, bekommt es nur ein Apostroph.
  the parents' bedroom   *das Schlafzimmer der Eltern*

Bei Substantiven, deren Pluralformen nicht auf **-s** enden, wird 's angehängt.
  the children's bikes   *die Fahrräder der Kinder*

Statt 's wird oft auch eine Konstruktion mit of benutzt:
  Paul and Kate's house   **the house of Paul and Kate**

12 ✏

Lesen Sie, wem die abgebildeten Dinge gehören (**belong to**). Formen Sie dann den Satz so um, dass sie den 's-Genitiv benutzen können (zum Beispiel **This cat belongs to Kate. - This is Kate's cat.**).
Die Lösung können Sie auch überprüfen, indem Sie sich die Sätze anhören.

①   ②   ③   ④

1. This car belongs to Paul.

_____

2. This bike belongs to Kate

_____

3. This tent belongs to the children.

_____

4. This bedroom belongs to the parents.

_____

Wo sind meine Sandalen? / Reflexivpronomen

13 🖉

hang on – *warte mal* ▶
have a look – *nach-sehen*
tidy away – *weg-räumen*

Im Urlaub der Familie Smith geht es manchmal etwas drunter und drüber. Lesen Sie den Dialog und ergänzen Sie die fehlenden **Possessivbegleiter**, **Genitiv-'s** oder **Possessivpronomen**.

Kate: Does anyone know where 1. _____ sandals are?

Paul: No idea. 2. _____ are here. Hang on, are these 3. _____

_____?

Kate: No, I think they're Jane 4. _____. Jane? Are these sandals

5. _____?

Jane: No, they're Ben 6. _____.

Kate: Hmm, I'll have another look in 7. _____ tent ...

What's this? Jane, what's 8. _____ swimming costume doing

in 9. _____ tent?

Jane: Thanks, Mum! Oh, and 10. _____ sandals are here!

Paul: I wish these kids would tidy 11. _____ things away

a bit better!

Nice to know

I wish ... + would ... wird häufig benutzt, um unrealistische Wünsche zu äußern.
I wish I would win the first prize.
Ich wünschte ich würde den ersten Preis gewinnen.

Nice to know

Vorsicht!
I can do it myself. heißt *Ich kann das selbst machen.*
I can do it by myself. heißt *Ich kann das allein machen.*

---

14 👓

Reflexivpronomen
Im Englischen gibt es die folgenden Reflexivpronomen:

myself	*mich / mir*	**itself**	*sich*
yourself	*dich / dir*	**yourselves**	*euch*
himself	*sich*	**themselves**	*sich*
herself	*sich*	**ourselves**	*uns*

Diese werden verwendet, wenn sich das Verb im Satz auf die Person bezieht, welche die Handlung auch ausführt. Das heißt, wenn **Subjekt** und **Objekt** identisch sind.

I bought myself a new car.
Ich habe mir ein neues Auto gekauft.
They wash themselves every morning.
Sie waschen sich jeden Morgen.

Sie werden aber auch benutzt, um zu betonen, von wem etwas getan wird. Im Deutschen verwendet man dann das Wort *selbst*.

They forget everything themselves!
Sie vergessen selbst alles!

Welches Pronomen ist es? / Selbst gemachte Kuchen

15 ✏

Die Buchstaben dieser Reflexivpronomen sind durcheinander gepurzelt.
Können Sie sie wieder in die richtige Reihenfolge bringen?

1. ymfels _____

2. soyurlfe _____

3. mhfiels _____

4. hfeselr _____

5. ilseft _____

16 ✏

Schreiben Sie ein passendes Reflexivpronomen in die Lücke.

1. Did you make that cake _____?

2. We did everything _____.

3. They did all the work _____.

17 ✏

Wenn Menschen etwas ohne fremde Hilfe geleistet haben, sind sie oft stolz darauf
und möchten diese Tatsache besonders betonen.
Lesen Sie die Fragen. Schreiben Sie dann eine positive Antwort, die ein Reflexivpronomen enthält, in die Lücken. Es soll betont werden, dass die genannte Person
die Sache *selbst* gemacht hat (z.B. **Did you make the cake yourself? – Yes,
I made it myself.**).

1. Did you make the dress yourself?

   _____

2. Did Jane do her homework herself?

   _____

3. Did Paul and Kate do the garden themselves?

   _____

4. Did you and Louise make the cake yourselves?

   _____

Ordnen Sie die Sätze! / Finden Sie die Pronomen?

18

In diesen Sätzen sind die Wörter durcheinander geraten.
Schreiben Sie sie in der richtigen Reihenfolge auf.

1. bought / five / They / ago / their / years / house / .
2. can / that / I / myself / do / !
3. prepared / He / himself / everything / .
4. The / car / is / red / theirs / .
5. family / much / likes / He / his / very / .
6. opened / himself / the / door / He / .
7. That / Ben's / is / bicycle / .
8. Kate's / is / Paul / and / house / That / .

19

In diesem Buchstabengitter sind zehn Wörter versteckt, die Sie in dieser Lektion
gelernt haben.
Welche sind es?

K	Z	D	P	M	W	H	M	W	K	I	O
G	P	B	H	I	S	E	Y	J	K	T	U
J	C	D	A	N	B	R	S	D	A	S	R
D	A	T	H	E	M	S	E	L	V	E	S
A	Z	H	I	M	S	E	L	F	Z	L	B
Y	O	U	R	S	E	L	F	C	A	F	G
P	B	Y	O	U	R	S	E	L	V	E	S

1. _____   6. _____

2. _____   7. _____

3. _____   8. _____

4. _____   9. _____

5. _____   10. _____

Possessivbegleiter / Meins und deins / Welches Wort passt nicht?

1

Unterstreichen Sie jeweils den korrekten Possessivbegleiter.

1. This car belongs to you and me. It is *our / their / ours* car.
2. This bike belongs to Ben. It is *her / hers / his* bike.
3. This bag belongs to you. It is *his / yours / your* bag.
4. This house belongs to Paul and Kate. It is *their / theirs / her* house.
5. This book belongs to me. This is *its / my / mine* book.

2

Schreiben Sie die passenden Possessivpronomen neben die entsprechenden Possessivbegleiter.

1. my   _____
2. your   _____
3. his   _____
4. her   _____
5. its   _____
6. our   _____
7. their   _____

3

Unterstreichen Sie jeweils das Wort, das nicht zu den anderen in der Gruppe passt. Achten Sie darauf, ob es sich bei den Wörtern um Possessivpronomen, Possessivbegleiter oder Reflexivpronomen handelt.

1. mine / your / yours / his
2. myself / yourselves / our / ourselves
3. our / his / her / yours
4. theirs / their / yours / his
5. ours / ourselves / myself / himself

Wem gehört das? / Reflexivpronomen

4

Wem gehören diese Dinge? Schreiben Sie beispielsweise Jane's T-shirt in die Lücke, wenn Jane mit einem T-Shirt abgebildet ist.

5 ✐

Ergänzen Sie die Sätze mit dem jeweils passenden Reflexivpronomen.

1. I can do that _____.

2. You can do that _____.

3. You and Paul, you can do that _____.

4. They can do that _____.

5. We can do that _____.

*Im Urlaub / Das **past participle***

1

Die Familie Smith ist jetzt mitten in ihrem Sommerurlaub in Südfrankreich. Schauen Sie sich an, was sie zu diesem Zeitpunkt schon unternommen haben und was sie noch vorhaben. Wenn Sie möchten, können Sie sich die Sätze anhören.
Ordnen Sie dann den Sätzen das passende Bild zu.

1. They've visited a church. ☐

2. They haven't gone sailing yet. ☐

3. They haven't bought any wine yet. ☐

4. They've tried out the local cuisine. ☐

5. They've spent a lot of time on the beach. ☐

> **Nice to know**
>
> Für das deutsche Wort *Küche* gibt es im Englischen zwei Entsprechungen: **kitchen** ist der Ort, an dem gekocht wird, und **cuisine** sind die typischen Gerichte einer Region.

◄ **not … yet** – *noch nicht*
gone – *gegangen*
try out – *ausprobieren*

2

Die unregelmäßigen Verben unten kennen Sie bereits. Hier sind deren Infinitiv und **past simple**-Form angegeben. Verbinden Sie diese nun mit der passenden dritten Form im Kasten.

a. given	d. done	g. been	i. driven
b. had	e. written	h. eaten	j. made
c. gone	f. seen		

1. be, was / were ☐   6. have, had ☐

2. go, went ☐   7. drive, drove ☐

3. make, made ☐   8. give, gave ☐

4. do, did ☐   9. write, wrote ☐

5. see, saw ☐   10. eat, ate ☐

◄ **done** – *getan*
written – *geschrieben*
seen – *gesehen*
been – *gewesen*
eaten – *gegessen*
driven – *gefahren*
made – *gemacht*

Have you written to Louise? / *Das* **present perfect**

3

Der Urlaub von Kate und Paul neigt sich dem Ende zu. Bevor Sie zurückfahren, schreiben Sie noch einen ganzen Stapel Postkarten. Lesen Sie den Dialog oder hören Sie ihn sich an.

just – *gerade*
send – *schicken*
either – *auch nicht*
sign – *unterschreiben*

Paul: Hang on, here's the list. We've written to my parents ...
Kate: Yes, and I've just written to mine, too. Here's the postcard.
Paul: Great. Have we written the card to Louise?
Kate: No, we haven't. I'll do that next.
Paul: OK. What about Stephen and Sue? We should write them a card, too.
Kate: We've never written them postcards, I think. They never send us postcards, either.
Paul: They wrote to us last year, I think. Do you remember they went to Bali?
Kate: You're right. Let's write them a card, too.
Paul: OK. Have you written to Elizabeth?
Kate: Yes, and I've already written to James, too. Here's the card, if you want to sign it.
Paul: Sure. Oooh, hang on, have we written to Aunt Hermione?
Kate: Erm... no, we haven't. Let's do that now, we really mustn't forget!

4

Bildung des **present perfect**
Das present perfect wird aus **have/has** und der dritten Form (dem **past participle**) des Hauptverbs gebildet. **Have/has** wird dabei oft abgekürzt zu **'ve/'s**.

Bei regelmäßigen Verben wird das past participle gebildet, indem man **-ed** an die Grundform des Verbs anhängt. Endet das Hauptverb auf **-y**, so wird dieses zu **-ied**.
>   **They**'ve visited **a church.**
>   *Sie haben eine Kirche besichtigt.*
>   **They**'ve tried **out the local cuisine.**
>   *Sie haben die lokale Küche ausprobiert.*

Verneinung, Fragen, Kurzantworten / Unregelmäßige Verben I

5

In der Verneinung wird **not** zwischen **have/has** und dem **past participle** eingefügt. Hierbei wird besonders in der gesprochenen Sprache auf zwei Weisen verkürzt.

> **They** haven't visited **Marseille.**
> **They**'ve not watched **a lot of TV.**

Zur Bildung von Fragen vertauscht man die Position von **have** und dem Subjekt.

> Have **they watched a lot of TV?**

Kurzantworten werden mit **have/has** gebildet.

> Has **he watched a lot of TV?**   **No, he** hasn't.
> *Hat er viel ferngesehen?*   *Nein, hat er nicht.*
> Have **they visited Marseille?**   **Yes, they** have.
> *Haben sie Marseille besucht?*   *Ja, haben sie.*

6

Sie sehen hier Verben, deren **past participle** unregelmäßig ist. Lesen Sie die Beispielsätze laut bzw. hören Sie sie sich an und sprechen Sie diese laut nach. Versuchen Sie, sich die unregelmäßigen Verben samt **past participle** einzuprägen.

be, was/were, **been**	He's been to France.
go, went, **gone**	He's gone home.
make, made, **made**	They've made a mistake.
do, did, **done**	I've done my homework.
see, saw, **seen**	I've seen her!
have, had, **had**	We haven't had enough time.
drive, drove, **driven**	Have you driven him home?
give, gave, **given**	Have you given her the present?
write, wrote, **written**	Have you written to Louise?
eat, ate, **eaten**	You've eaten all the cake!
speak, spoke, **spoken**	She's spoken to me.
tell, told, **told**	Have you told him about the problem?
buy, bought, **bought**	Have you bought everything we need?
think, thought, **thought**	He hasn't thought of that.
sleep, slept, **slept**	I've slept really well.

Unregelmäßige Verben II / Welche Verbform passt?

7

Viele der häufig gebrauchten Verben im Englischen sind unregelmäßig. Es führt kein Weg daran vorbei, sich diese Verben einzeln einzuprägen. In Übung 6 sowie in diesem Kasten finden Sie alle wichtigen unregelmäßigen Verben dieses Kurses.

> **Nice to know**
>
> Vorsicht!
> **He's drunk the wine.**
> heißt *Er hat den Wein getrunken.*
> **He's drunk.** heißt aber *Er ist betrunken.*

begin	began	begun
build	built	built
drink	drank	drunk
fall	fell	fallen
feed	fed	fed
find	found	found
forget	forgot	forgotten
get	got	got/gotten
know	knew	known
leave	left	left
meant	meant	meant
meet	met	met
put	put	put
read	read	read
ride	rode	ridden
say	said	said
sell	sold	sold
send	sent	sent
sing	sang	sung
sit	sat	sat
spend	spent	spent
stand	stood	stood
swim	swam	swum
take	took	taken
wear	wore	worn

8

Lesen Sie die Fragen oder hören Sie sie, wenn Sie möchten, und unterstreichen Sie die Form, welche die Antwort korrekt ergänzt.

1. Have you spoken to Kate? Yes, I've just *speak / spoken / spoke* to her.
2. Has Jane been to France before? No, she's never *been / was / is* there.
3. Do we have any food left? No, the children've *eat / eaten / eating* it all.
4. Does Paul know the way? Yes, he's *drives / drove / driven* there many times.

*Gebrauch des **present perfect** / Los geht's an den Strand!*

9

Das **present perfect** wird verwendet, wenn man von etwas spricht, das in der Vergangenheit begonnen hat und bis in die Gegenwart reicht. Das heißt, wenn man von Handlungen spricht, die noch nicht abgeschlossen sind.

> **Paul and Kate** have gone **on holiday.**
> bedeutet, dass sie immer noch im Urlaub sind.

Man benutzt das **present perfect** auch dann, wenn eine Handlung zwar abgeschlossen ist, aber nur deren Ergebnis wichtig ist.

> Have **we** written **the card to Louise?**
> Hier ist es wichtig, ob die Karte geschrieben wurde, nicht wann.

Man findet im **present perfect** auch oft **not … yet** (*noch nicht*) oder **never** (*noch nie*).

> **They** haven't **bought any wine** yet.
> **They've** never **been to France.**

Fragen werden oft mit **ever** (*jemals*) oder **yet** (*schon*) gestellt.

> **Have we written to Aunt Hermione** yet**?**
> **Have you** ever **been to France?**

10 ✎

Die Familie Smith bereitet einen Strandtag vor. Lesen Sie den Dialog und ergänzen Sie die fehlenden **past participle** Formen.

Kate: Has anyone (1.) _____ (see) the big towels?

Paul: Yes, I've (2.) _____ (put) them in the car.
Do we have suntan lotion?

Kate: Yes, I've (3.) _____ (buy) some. I've (4.) _____
_____ (leave) it in the car.

Paul: Good. Oh, and have we (5.) _____ (pack) some
books?

Kate: I've (6.) _____ (read) all the ones we brought.

Paul: Have you really? I haven't even (7.) _____ (finish)
the first one. Oh my goodness!

*Zeitpunkt oder Zeitraum? / **For** oder **since**?*

11

Das **present perfect** wird oft in Verbindung mit **since** (*seit*), **for** (*seit*) oder **how long** verwendet. Es entspricht dann der deutschen Gegenwartsform mit *schon*.

Kate has worked in a shop for ten years.
Kate arbeitet seit zehn Jahren in einem Laden.
Kate has worked in a shop since 1993.
Kate arbeitet seit 1993 in einem Laden.

For steht immer für eine **Zeitdauer**. Es zeigt an, **wie lange** etwas geschieht oder geschehen ist. **Since** bezieht sich auf einen **Zeitpunkt**. Es zeigt an, **seit wann** etwas geschieht oder geschehen ist. Im **present perfect** werden beide Präpositionen mit *seit* übersetzt. Deshalb ist es hier besonders wichtig, darauf zu achten, ob es sich um einen **Zeitpunkt** (**since**) oder um eine **Zeitdauer** (**for**) handelt.

Hier einige Beispiele:
For wird mit Zeitbestimmungen verwendet, die einen **Zeitraum** beschreiben:

two hours	*zwei Stunden*	**a week**	*eine Woche*
20 minutes	*20 Minuten*	**40 years**	*40 Jahre*
six months	*sechs Monate*		

Since wird mit Zeitbestimmungen verwendet, die einen **Zeitpunkt** angeben:

9 o'clock	*9 Uhr*	**Monday**	*Montag*
yesterday	*gestern*	**December**	*Dezember*
Christmas	*(seit) Weihnachten*		

12

Ergänzen Sie die Sätze mit **for** oder **since**.

1. He's lived in this house _____ 10 years.

2. He's lived in this house _____ 1994.

3. She's been out _____ two o'clock.

4. She's been out _____ two hours.

5. Paul has worked at the bank _____ 15 years.

6. Paul has worked at the bank _____ last summer.

Present perfect – past simple / *Eine Postkarte an Louise*

13 👓

Present perfect – past simple

Das past simple wird dann verwendet, wenn man über eine abgeschlossene Handlung oder ein Ereignis in der Vergangenheit redet. Oft findet man Zeitbestimmungen wie **yesterday**, **a year ago**, **last August** oder in **1977**, die eindeutig auf einen Zeitpunkt in der Vergangenheit hinweisen.

> **They** wrote **to us last year.**

Das present perfect wird hingegen verwendet, wenn ein Bezug zur Gegenwart besteht. Zeitbestimmungen, die häufig im present perfect verwendet werden, sind **ever** (*jemals*), **never** (*nie*), **yet** (*schon*), **not ... yet** (*noch nicht*), **just** (*gerade*), **since** (*seit*), **so far** (*bis jetzt*) oder **this week/year** (*diese Woche/dieses Jahr*).

> **I**'ve **just** written **to my parents.**
> *Ich habe gerade meinen Eltern geschrieben.*

Im Deutschen werden beide Vergangenheitsformen meist ohne Bedeutungsunterschied benutzt. Im Englischen aber kann sich mit der Vergangenheitsform auch die Bedeutung des Satzes ändern.

> **They**'ve gone **on holiday.** heißt, dass sie noch im Urlaub sind.
> **They** went **on holiday.** heißt, dass sie bereits zurück sind.

14 ✏️

Kate schreibt Louise gerade eine Karte. Ergänzen Sie die Verben in Klammern im **present perfect** oder **past simple**.

Dear Louise,

We're having a fantastic time in France, and we (1.) _____

(be) very active. We (2.) _____ (not go) sailing yet,

but we're planning to do that soon. Yesterday we (3.) _____

(go) to a local market and (4.) _____ (buy) some fish. Then

we (5.) _____ (grill) the fish on the barbecue – it

(6.) _____ (be) delicious! (7.) _____ you ever

_____ (try) barbecued fish? The weather (8.) _____

_____ (be) fantastic so far, and we (9.) _____ (spend)

a lot of time on the beach. See you soon, Kate and family

Welches Verb ist das? / Unregelmäßige Verben gesucht!

15 ✏

Bei den folgenden unregelmäßigen **past participle**-Formen sind die Buchstaben durcheinander geraten. Bringen Sie sie wieder in die richtige Reihenfolge. Die Bilder helfen Ihnen herauszufinden, welches Verb gemeint ist.

1   tewnitr

2   rnkud

3   tanee

4   dera

_____   _____   _____   _____

16 ✏

Schreiben Sie das fehlende Verb in der korrekten Zeitform in das Kreuzworträtsel.

1. We know the place. We've ... there before.
2. Have you ... all the postcards yet?
3. I'm sorry, there is no more coffee. I've ... it all.
4. I've never ... those trousers before.
5. Yes, he knows that. I ... him.
6. John's never ... here before. He always sits over there.
7. I've ... to her. She's coming at 7 o'clock.
8. Have you ... that book? It's very good.
9. Where's all the cake? I'm sorry, I've ... it.
10. Yes, I know the way. I've ... there many times.

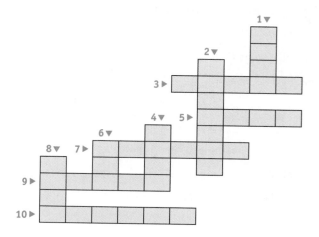

*Past participle – Formen / Das **present perfect***

1 ✏

Sehen Sie sich das Bild an und ergänzen Sie die Sätze mit der **past participle** Form eines passenden Verbs.

1. She's _____ a letter.

2. Somebody's _____ all the cake!

3. I've _____ the book.

4. You've _____ the dishes.

5. Have you _____ well?

2 ✏

Wandeln Sie die folgenden Sätze ins **present perfect** um und schreiben Sie diese in die Lücken.

1. We go shopping.

_____

2. She is speaking to her friend.

_____

3. He drives home.

_____

4. She buys apples.

_____

5. They take pictures.

_____

For oder *since?* / *Zeitangaben* / *Verbformen*

3

Werden diese Zeitangaben im **present perfect** mit **for** oder mit **since** verwendet?
Schreiben Sie die passende Präposition in die Lücken.

1. _____ two years

2. _____ last year

3. _____ one hour

4. _____ 2001

5. _____ one week

4

Unter den folgenden Gruppen von Wörtern ist jeweils ein Wort, das nicht mit dem
present perfect benutzt werden kann. Können Sie es identifizieren?
Kreuzen Sie es an.

1. ☐ a. ever
   ☐ b. yet
   ☐ c. last year
   ☐ d. already

2. ☐ a. never
   ☐ b. two hours ago
   ☐ c. for
   ☐ d. so far

3. ☐ a. yet
   ☐ b. already
   ☐ c. in 1999
   ☐ d. since

4. ☐ a. for
   ☐ b. ago
   ☐ c. since
   ☐ d. just

5

Unterstreichen Sie die Verbform, die den Satz korrekt ergänzt.

1. Yesterday, I *am walking / walked / have walked* home from work.
2. This morning, I *have worked / worked / work* a lot.
3. He *has lived / lives / lived* in this house for ten years, and he
   likes it very much.
4. Paul *knows / has known / knew* Kate since they went to school
   together.
5. They *have bought / bought / buy* a new kitchen last year.

Modul 1

1

Übung 1
oranges, apples, pears, bananas, trousers, tickets, children

Übung 4
1. dessert; 2. trousers; 3. French; 4. dog; 5. March; 6. Saturday; 7. children / kids;
8. Friday; 9. dinner; 10. Spain

Übung 6
1.an; 2. a; 3. a; 4. an; 5. an; 6. a; 7. an; 8. a; 9. an; 10. a; 11. an; 12. a

Übung 8
1. c; 2. e; 3. d; 4. a; 5. b

Übung 9
1. books; 2.cities; 3. tomatoes; 4. fish; 5. presents; 6. knives; 7. tickets; 8. kisses;
9. mice; 10. roofs

Übung 11
1. c; 2. a; 3. b; 4. d

Übung 12
1. piece; 2. bottle; 3. cup; 4. slice; 5. packet

Übung 14
1. There is / There's ; 2. There is / There's; 3. There are; 4. There is / There's;
5. There are; 6. There are

Übung 15

A	C	T	O	M	A	T	O	E	S
K	C	P	W	F	I	S	H	T	B
I	N	E	B	G	E	P	U	W	O
C	H	I	L	D	R	E	N	O	T
A	M	N	V	G	L	A	T	M	T
K	M	I	C	E	P	R	Z	E	L
E	B	O	O	K	S	S	T	N	E
S	K	T	R	O	U	S	E	R	S

Übung 16
1. d; 2. c; 3. b; 4. e; 5. a; 6. f

Test 1

Übung 1
1. G; 2. f; 3. M,U; 4. M; 5. T; 6. d; 7. E; 8. b

Module 1 bis 2

Übung 2
1. c; 2. b; 3. a; 4. c

Übung 3
1. a; 2. an; 3. an; 4. a; 5. a; 6. an

Übung 4
1. women; 2. mice; 3. books; 4. feet; 5. bottles; 6. knives

2

Übung 1
1. b; 2. f; 3. g; 4. c; 5. h; 6. e; 7. d; 8. a

Übung 2
1. d; 2. b; 3. a; 4. c

Übung 4
1. live; 2. take; 3. gets up; 4. works; 5. loves

Übung 6
1. Jane has breakfast at home. / Jane has breakfast. / She has breakfast.;
2. She goes to school by bus. / Jane goes to school by bus. / She goes to school. /
Jane goes to school.; 3. In the morning, she has maths. / In the morning, Jane has
maths. / Jane has maths. / She has maths. / Jane has maths in the morning. /
She has maths in the morning.; 4. In the break, she goes to the library. / In the
break, Jane goes to the library. / Jane goes to the library in the break. / She goes
to the library in the break. / She goes to the library. / Jane goes to the library.;
5. After lunch, she has sports. / After lunch, Jane has sports. / Jane has sports
after lunch. / She has sports after lunch. / Jane has sports. / She has sports.

Übung 8
1. watch; 2. drives; 3. cleans / washes; 4. cycle

Übung 11
1. don't have; 2. don't go; 3. don't go; 4. never; 5. don't

Übung 14
1. Do you know John?; 2. Is he Japanese?; 3. Jane isn't at school today. ; 4. We're
not very happy. 5. Does she read a book?; 6. Are you tired?

Übung 16
1. Yes, he is. 2. Yes, they are.; 3. No, he doesn't. / No, he does not.; 4. Yes, they do.;
5. Yes, she is.

Module 2 bis 3

Übung 17

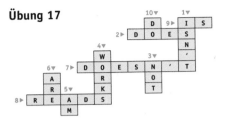

Übung 18

1. do, wear; 2. don't, wear; 3. does; 4. does, don't

Test **2**

Übung 1

1. He drives to work. 2. He likes swimming. 3. He doesn't go to work by bus. /
He does not go to work by bus. 4. He doesn't read many books. / He does not read
many books. 5. He's very thin. / He is very thin. 6. He's not angry. / He isn't angry.
/ He is not angry.

Übung 2

1. isn't / is not; 2. doesn't read / does not read; 3. don't like / do not like; 4. don't
watch / do not watch; 5. 'm not / am not; 6. don't play / do not play; 7. aren't /
are not

Übung 3

1. b; 2. a; 3. b; 4. b; 5. c

Übung 4

1. Do you know Kate? Yes, I do. 2. Does Kate smoke? No, she doesn't.
3. Is Jane from Birmingham? No, she isn't. 4. Are you cold? Yes, I am.

3

Übung 1

a. 3; b. 4; c. 1; d. 2; e. 5

Übung 2

1. c; 2. e; 3. a; 4. d

Übung 4

It, you, you, I, him, we, me, them, they, they, we, them, I, I, you, she, she, I, her,
they, we, he, you, we, I, you, you, them

Modul 3

Übung 5
1. She often sees her.
2. I never play tennis with him.
3. They always visit us.
4. She visits her in the evening.
5. She never talks about them.
6. We play football on Saturdays.
7. Do you remember her?

Übung 6
1. We see them.
2. She sees her.
3. He meets him.
4. She meets her.
5. They talk about him.
6. He talks about them.

Übung 7
1. She; 2. She; 3. them; 4. her; 5. her; 6. They; 7. I; 8. us / me; 9. She; 10. us / me; 11. You; 12. her; 13. me; 14. him

Übung 9
1. 's got / has got; 2. haven't got / 've not got / have not got; 3. 've got / have got; 4. haven't got / 've not got / have not got; 5. hasn't got / 's not got / has not got

Übung 10
these, that, that, that, this, this, that, that, those,

Übung 12
1. b; 2. b; 3. a; 4. a

Übung 13
1. These are bananas.
2. This is an apple.
3. That's Paul.
4. This is a dog.

Übung 14
1. got; 2. Those; 3. her; 4. they; 5. This; 6. Has; 7. them; 8. him; Satz: Have fun!

Übung 15
1. him; 2. me; 3. her; 4. that; 5. us; 6. him; 7. them; 8. those; 9. I; 10. you; 11. he; 12. him; 13. her; 14. them; 15. that

Module 3 bis 4

Test 3

Übung 1
1. us; 2. They / they; 3. We / we; 4. her; 5. him; 6. them

Übung 2
1. b; 2. a; 3. a; 4. a; 5. c

Übung 3
1. This; 2. That; 3. These; 4. These; 5. Those

Übung 4
1. Those / those; 2. These / these; 3. This / this; 4. That / that

Übung 5
1. He visits her every Sunday.
2. They often bring us cakes.
3. We do many things together.
4. I like you very much.
5. You go to the café with me.
6. We never play football with him.

4

Übung 1
1. d; 2. e; 3. a; 4. c; 5. b

Übung 2
1. Jane is eating a cake.
2. Ben is listening to music.
3. Kate is watering the garden.
4. Jane is playing the piano.
5. Paul is washing the car.
6. The cat is sleeping.

Übung 3
doing, cooking, making, doing, coming, playing, coming, making

Übung 6
1. 're working / are working; 2. are giving / 're giving; 3. 're studying / are studying;
4. 'm writing / am writing; 5. 'm doing / am doing; 6. 's doing / is doing;
7. Are ... learning / studying

Übung 8
1. aren't; 2. not; 3. isn't; 4. 'm not

Modul 4

Übung 10
1. Are you; 2. Is Paul; 3. Are they; 4. Is she

Übung 12
1. a; 2. c; 3. c; 4. b

Übung 13
1. No, he isn't. / No, he's not. / No, he is not. 2. Yes, they are. 3. No, they aren't. / No, they're not. / No, they are not. 4. Yes, he is.

Übung 15
1. is playing, plays; 2. is reading, reads; 3. isn't working, works; 4. Are, going, go

Übung 16
1. a, b; 2. b, a; 3. a, b; 4. b, a

Übung 17
1. spend; 2. rent; 3. relax; 4. cook; 5. play; 6. 're going / are going; 7. 're driving / are driving; 8. 're staying / are staying; 9. 'm not complaining / am not complaining

Übung 18

J	Z	O	P	L	O	O	K	I	N	G	B	O	O	S
U	U	E	J	I	D	U	K	Y	E	A	E	P	K	J
L	Q	K	O	L	J	X	F	E	E	D	I	N	G	P
J	I	L	U	E	A	L	G		D	P	N	W	S	K
W	P	V	L	A	W	O	R	K	I	N	G	P	U	U
R	U	J	I	R	E	A	D	I	N	G	H	A	Y	T
I	P	U	S	N	D	P	R	R	G	U	G	J	J	T
T	D	Q	T	I	G	U	I	J	I	O	I	J	N	W
I	A	J	E	N	B	H	N	P	D	V	V	L	M	A
N	N	K	N	G	M	A	K	I	N	G	I	D	E	U
G	C	J	I	J	N	V	I	L	Z	A	N	N	P	J
U	I	U	N	N	M	I	N	J	J	E	G	Q	G	Q
J	N	O	G	L	G	N	G	Z	Q	F	O	J	L	K
Z	G	L	X	U	Z	G	S	P	E	A	K	I	N	G
L	E	A	V	I	N	G	H	N	O	E	J	C	H	E

Übung 19
1. We're watering the garden.
2. He's reading a book.
3. He's driving a car.
4. She's sitting in an armchair.
5. We're making dinner.

Test 4

Übung 1
a. 3; b. 7; c. 1; d. 8; e. 5; f. 2; g. 6; h. 4

Übung 2
1. 're playing / are playing; 2. 's sleeping / is sleeping; 3. 's walking / is walking;
4. 's making / is making / 's preparing / is preparing

Übung 3
1. She isn't going there. 2. I'm not leaving. 3. Are you working? 4. Is she coming?

Übung 4
1. Yes, he is. 2. No, she doesn't. 3. Yes, I am. 4. No, they're not.

Übung 5
1. read; 2. 'm driving / am driving; 3. prepares; 4. 's preparing / is preparing;
5. leave; 6. eat

5

Übung 1
1. c; 2. d; 3. a; 4. e; 5. b

Übung 4
1. richtig; 2. falsch; 3. richtig; 4. richtig

Übung 6
1. 'll leave / will leave; 2. 'll arrive / will arrive; 3. won't take / will not take;
4. 'll be / will be / 'll take / will take; 5. 'll have / will have; 6. 'll need / will need;
7. 'll want / will want

Übung 8
1. Will they come here tomorrow?
2. Won't Ben take his driving test?
3. Will you phone him later?
4. Won't he bring the cake?
5. Will you find the way?
6. Will Jane go to university?

Übung 9
1. a, b; 2. b; 3. a; 4. a; b

Modul 5

Übung 11
1. I'll be back early if there isn't so much traffic.
2. Paul will set up the barbecue if Kate prepares the steaks.
3. They will phone us if they can't find the way.

Übung 12
1. it rains; 2. she works hard; 3. I'll go home early; 4. he will be very happy

Übung 14
1. wf; 2. pc; 3. pc; 4. wf; 5. pc; 6. wf

Übung 15
1. are having; 2. 'm going; 3. 'll phone; 4. will study

Übung 16
1. will rain / 'll rain; 2. 'm going / am going; 3. 'll phone / will phone; 4. 're having / are having; 5. isn't coming. / is not coming; 6. 'll be / will be; 7. 'll do / will do; 8. 's driving / is driving

Übung 17
1. Ben will go to college next year.
2. Jane will not learn French any more.
3. I'll set up the barbecue.
4. I won't put garlic in the salad.

Übung 18

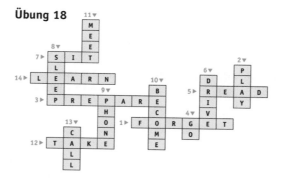

Test 5

Übung 1
1. will go; 2. will go; 3. won't become; 4. will learn; 5. won't work; 6. 'll come; 7. will finish; 8. 'll study

Übung 2
1. 'll leave / will leave; 2. 'll arrive / will arrive; 3. 'll be / will be; 4. 'll have / will have; 5. 'll need / will need; 6. 'll want / will want

Module 5 bis 6

Übung 3
1. Yes, they will. 2. No, it won't. 3. Yes, I will. 4. No, she won't. 5. Yes, I will

Übung 4
1. c; 2. a; 3. a; 4. a

Übung 5
1. Kate isn't coming to the cinema.
2. I think I 'll finish my homework now.
3. I hope it won't rain tonight.
4. Maybe Paul will phone us later.
5. Next year, Ben will take his driving test.

6

Übung 1
1. a; 2. e; 3. b; 4. d; 5. c

Übung 2
1. d; 2. a; 3. f; 4. e; 5. b; 6. c

Übung 6
1. wrote
2. drove
3. bought
4. thought
5. drank
6. spoke
7. knew
8. met

Übung 7
1. was; 2. was; 3. had; 4. went; 5. walked; 6. took; 7. drove; 8. bought; 9. learned; 10. asked; 11. read; 12. sat; 13. thought; 14. knew

Übung 9
1. made; 2. spoke; 3. bought; 4. learned

Übung 10
1. met; 2. sat; 3. bought; 4. left

Übung 12
1. a; 2. b; 3. c; 4. b

Übung 15
1. wasn't; 2. Were; 3. was; 4. were

Modul 6

Übung 16
1. I didn't go to school. / I did not go to school.
2. I bought cakes.
3. I was happy.
4. I wasn't fat. / I was not fat.
5. You were ready.
6. You weren't angry. / You were not angry.
7. Paul was at work.
8. Louise was tired.

Übung 17
1. didn't listen; 2. were; 3. was; 4. Did you make; 5. worked; 6. didn't drive; weren't;
8. wasn't

Übung 18
1. didn't have / did not have; 2. didn't go / did not go; 3. stayed / were; 4. were;
5. weren't / were not; 6. ate; 7. walked; 8. lived; 9. thought; 10. was;
11. didn't work / did not work; 12. worked; 13. were

Übung 19
1. drove; 2. watched (TV); 3. cycled; 4. walked; 5. played (football); 6. read; 7. ate;
8. drank; 9. listened (to music); 10. cooked; 11. played (the piano); 12. washed
(the car); 13. slept; 14. sat; 15. cleaned (the room); 16. studied; 17. played
(tennis); 18. played (chess); 19. swam; 20. took (the bus); 21. wrote; 22. shopped;
23. sang; 24. played (golf)

Test 6

Übung 1
1. wrote; 2. drove; 3. drank; 4. swam; 5. slept; 6. sang

Übung 2
1. didn't go; 2. didn't study; 3. know; 4. played; 5. didn't go

Übung 3
1. cycled; 2. ate; 3. slept; 4. watched

Übung 4
1. was; 2. were; 3. wasn't / was not; 4. weren't / were not

Übung 5
1. Yes, he did. / No, he didn't. / No, he did not.
2. Yes, I did. / No, I didn't. / No, I did not.
3. Yes, I was. / No, I wasn't. / No, I was not.
4. Yes, he was. / No, he wasn't. / No, he was not.

7

Übung 1
1. c; 2. d; 3. a; 4. e; 5. b

Übung 2
1. d; 2. h; 3. a; 4. b; 5. f; 6. c; 7. e; 8. g

Übung 6
1. bigger; 2. cheaper; 3. highest; 4. oldest

Übung 7
1. a. Mehrsilbige Adjektive bilden den Komparativ mit **more** + Grundform.
2. c. Den Superlativ bilden mehrsilbige Adjektive mit **most** + Grundform.

Übung 8
Gruppe 1: -er / -est
big, heavy, clever, quiet, hot, slow

Gruppe 2: more / most
expensive, interesting, boring, exciting, tired, frustrating

Übung 10
1. old; 2. better; 3. young; 4. worse; 5. slower; 6. true; 7. more; 8. less; 9. nicer;
10. happier; 11. more expensive; 12. more exciting; 13. easier

Übung 12
1. than; 2. not as … as; 3. as … as; 4. than

Übung 15
1. badly; 2. happily; 3. fast; 4. well; 5. hard

Übung 16
1. badly; 2. well; 3. heavy; 4. happy

Übung 17

C	L	E	A	N	B	K	L	S	S
E	X	P	E	N	S	I	V	E	H
K	Y	A	Y	O	U	N	G	T	O
J	P	F	L	I	T	T	L	E	R
W	M	A	N	I	C	E	S	R	T
L	A	R	G	E	K	R	B	L	P
O	S	M	O	C	H	E	A	P	E
N	L	M	U	C	H	S	D	P	H
G	O	Q	U	I	E	T	P	S	D
U	W	L	E	Q	U	I	C	K	O
P	K	W	M	E	D	N	R	L	L
T	I	D	Y	U	W	G	O	O	D

Modul 7 bis 8

Übung 18

1. longer; 2. quickly; 3. slower; 4. short; 5. slow; 6. happy; 7. longer; 8. young;
9. good; 10. well; 11. brown; 12. black; 13. worst; 14. more; 15. less

Test 7

Übung 1

1. richtig; 2. falsch; 3. richtig; 4. richtig; 5. falsch

Übung 2

1. This house is very big.
2. The garden is larger than the house. / The house is larger than the garden.
3. The woman is happy.
4. The book is not as heavy as the bag. / The bag is not as heavy as the book.
5. The T-shirt is as bright as the trousers.

Übung 3

1. more expensive; 2. big; 3. healthier; 4. tall

Übung 4

1. b; 2. a; 3. c; 4. a

Übung 5

1. well; 2. fast; 3. beautifully; 4. hard

Übung 6

1. worst; 2. biggest; 3. best; 4. least

8

Übung 1
1. d; 2. b; 3. c; 4. a

Übung 2
1. d; 2. e; 3. b; 4. a; 5. c

Übung 4
1. vineyards; 2. wine; 3. suntan lotion; 4. the neighbours

Übung 7
1. have to; 2. don't have to; 3. have to; 4. didn't have to; 5. do we have to;
6. has to; 7. 'll have to

Übung 9
1. should; 2. shouldn't; 3. should

Übung 12
1. could / was able to; 2. couldn't / could not / wasn't able to / was not able to;
3. can / am able to / 'm able to; 4. can't / cannot / 'm not able to / am not able to;
5. could / was able to; 6. can't / cannot / 'm not able to / am not able to;
7. 'll be able to / will be able to; 8. 'll be able to / will be able to

Übung 14
1. I can't go. 2. He doesn't have to go. 3. She can't see us. 4. I mustn't work.
5. They might play. 6. They might play.

Übung 16
1. b; 2. e; 3. c; 4. a; 5. f; 6. d

Übung 17

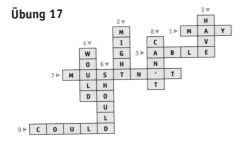

Übung 18
1. They'll be able to relax on the beach.
2. They may buy some wine.
3. They could go sailing.
4. Sailing would be fantastic.
5. They should take suntan lotion.
6. They should take books.
7. Jane will have to speak French.
8. They mustn't forget the cat.
9. They don't have to buy many things in England.
10. They'll be able to buy a lot in France.

Test 8

Übung 1
1. mustn't / must not; 2. mustn't / must not; 3. have to; 4. mustn't / mustn't

Übung 2
1. had to; 2. must / have to; 3. have to; 4. have to / must

Module 8 bis 9

Übung 3

1. mustn't; 2. doesn't have to; 3. mustn't; 4. don't have to

Übung 4

1. I can swim. / I'm able to swim. 2. I can't dance. / I cannot dance. / I'm not able to dance. 3. I can't drive. / I cannot drive. / I'm not able to drive. 4. I can read. / I am able to read.

Übung 5

1. would; 2. might; 3. should; 4. could

Übung 6

1. Don't let me forget to feed the cat!
2. Don't stay out too late!
3. Tell him I called!
4. Go and buy some milk!
5. Let's have a party next Saturday!
6. Let's play tennis together tomorrow!

9

Übung 1

1. e; 2. h; 3. a; 4. g; 5. c; 6. b; 7. f; 8. d

Übung 2

1. b; 2. d; 3. a; 4. c

Übung 5

Gruppe 1: nicht zählbar
water, cheese, money, advice, information, wine

Gruppe 2: zählbar
apple, glass, dog, euro, child, towel

Übung 7

Gruppe 1: much
wine, advice, butter, time, money, information

Gruppe 2: many
bottle, computer, flower, house, car, apple

Übung 8

1. much; 2. many; 3. much; 4. many

Modul 9

Übung 10
1. a; 2. b; 3. b; 4. b

Übung 11
1. There are few apples.
2. There is little milk. / There's little milk.
3. I have little time.
4. He has few friends.

Übung 13
1. some; 2. some; 3. any; 4. some; 5. any; 6. any

Übung 15
1. everybody; 2. somewhere; 3. anybody; 4. something; 5. everywhere

Übung 16
1. few; 2. little; 3. much / a lot / any; 4. any / many; 5. some / a few / many;
6. many / a lot of / some / a few; 7. many / a lot of / any; 8. a lot of / much;
9. much / a lot of / any; 10. some / many / a lot of / few

Übung 17
1. nobody; 2. nowhere; 3. nothing; 4. many people / a lot of people; 5. every family;
6. a lot of time / much time; 7. every teacher; 8. not any dishes; 9. anywhere;
10. any time

Übung 18

K	M	U	C	H	Z	K	X	H	G	L	P
P	X	A	P	A	K	P	Z	X	P	I	X
F	P	P	N	N	N	K	H	P	T	K
E	V	E	R	Y	B	O	D	Y	E	T	W
W	P	U	P	W	S	B	T	A	X	L	T
P	U	X	C	H	P	O	P	H	Q	E	P
Q	K	X	M	E	X	D	M	B	I	W	K
Q	A	Z	E	R	K	Y	X	E	K	N	K
Z	A	K	L	E	S	S	O	P	P	T	G

Test 9

Übung 1
1. much / a lot of; 2. many / a lot of; 3. much / a lot of; 4. many / a lot of

Übung 2
1. few; 2. little; 3. few; 4. little

Module 9 bis 10

Übung 3
1. nowhere; 2. not anybody; 3. no one; 4. few things; 5. nowhere

Übung 4
1. b; 2. a; 3. c; 4. c

Übung 5
1. I do not have any time.
2. Nobody knows him very well.
3. They did not have much money.
4. They had few problems.
5. They did not have many problems.

10

Übung 1
1. d; 2. b; 3. f; 4. c; 5. a; 6. e

Übung 2
1. b; 2. e; 3. a; 4. d; 5. c

Übung 7
1. -; 2. at; 3. by / -; 4. in; 5. At; 6. -; 7. in; 8. At; 9. -; 10. on

Übung 9
1. in; 2. ago; 3. for; 4. ago; 5. in; 6. for; 7. ago; 8. in

Übung 11
1. on; 2. above; 3. under; 4. next to; 5. between

Übung 12
1. above / over; 2. opposite / in front of; 3. next to / by; 4. on

Übung 13
Through und **back to** beschreiben eine Bewegungsrichtung.

Übung 14
1. up; 2. past; 3. round; 4. across; 5. off

Übung 15
1. down; 2. along; 3. around / round; 4. towards / to; 5. through; 6. out of; 7. to;
8. past; 9. into; 10. off; 11. near

Module 10 bis 11

Übung 16
1. for; 2. through; 3. at; 4. ago; 5. on; 6. in; 7. in front of; 8. to; 9. across;
10. along; 11. over; 12. among

Übung 17
1. along; 2. across; 3. through; 4. up

Test 10

Übung 1
1. on; 2. in; 3. in; 4. at; 5. at; 6. at; 7. in; 8. on

Übung 2
1. in / for; 2. for; 3. ago; 4. in; 5. for

Übung 3
1. between; 2. on; 3. under; 4. in front of

Übung 4
1. a; 2. c; 3. b; 4. b

Übung 5
1. next to; 2. in; 3. on; 4. under; 5. above; 6. between; 7. opposite; 8. behind

11

Übung 1
1. b; 2. e; 3. c; 4. d; 5. f; 6. a

Übung 2
1. a; 2. d; 3. e; 4. c; 5. b

Übung 4
1. These are Ben's trousers.
2. This is her air mattress.
3. Where is our air mattress?
4. Paul and Kate forget everything themselves.
5. I've got mine!
6. Kate packed it herself.

Übung 6
1. his; 2. their; 3. her; 4. our

Modul 11

Übung 7
1. my; 2. his; 3. your; 4. their; 5. its

Übung 9
1. our; 2. his; 3. theirs; 4. yours

Übung 10
1. This house is ours. / This is ours.
2. These shoes are mine. / These are mine.
3. This umbrella is yours. / This is yours. / This umbrella's yours.
4. These photos are theirs. / These are theirs.
5. This car is his. / This car's his. / This is his.
6. These trousers are hers. / These are hers.

Übung 12
1. This is Paul's car.
2. This is Kate's bike.
3. This is the children's tent.
4. This is the parents' bedroom.

Übung 13
1. my; 2. Mine; 3. yours; 4. 's; 5. yours; 6. 's; 7. our / my; 8. your; 9. our / my; 10. your; 11. their

Übung 15
1. myself; 2. yourself; 3. himself; 4. herself; 5. itself

Übung 16
1. yourself; 2. ourselves; 3. themselves

Übung 17
1. Yes, I made the dress myself. / Yes, I made it myself.
2. Yes, Jane did the homework herself. / Yes, she did it herself.
3. Yes, Paul and Kate did the garden themselves. / Yes, they did it themselves.
4. Yes, Louise and I made the cake ourselves. / Yes, we made it ourselves.

Übung 18
1. They bought their house five years ago.
2. I can do that myself!
3. He prepared everything himself.
4. The red car is theirs.
5. He likes his family very much.
6. He opened the door himself.
7. That bicycle is Ben's. / That is Ben's bicycle.
8. That is Paul and Kate's house. / That house is Paul and Kate's.

Module 11 bis 12

Übung 19

K	Z	D	P	M	W	H	M	W	K	I	O
G	P	B	H	I	S	E	Y	J	K	T	U
J	C	D	A	N	B	R	S	D	A	S	R
D	A	T	H	E	M	S	E	L	V	E	S
A	Z	H	I	M	S	E	L	F	Z	L	B
Y	O	U	R	S	E	L	F	C	A	F	G
P	B	Y	O	U	R	S	E	L	V	E	S

Test 11

Übung 1
1. our; 2. his; 3. your; 4. their; 5. my

Übung 2
1. mine; 2. yours; 3. his; 4. hers; 5. its; 6. ours; 7. theirs

Übung 3
1. your; 2. our; 3. yours; 4. ours

Übung 4
1. Ben's bike / Ben's bicycle; 2. Louise's bag; 3. Paul's car; 4. Kate's cat; 5. Jane's book

Übung 5
1. myself; 2. yourself; 3. yourselves; 4. themselves; 5. ourselves

12

Übung 1
1. c; 2. d; 3. a; 4. e; 5. b

Übung 2
1. g; 2. c; 3. j; 4. d; 5. f; 6. b; 7. i; 8. a; 9. e; 10. h

Übung 8
1. spoken; 2. been; 3. eaten; 4. driven; 5. told; 6. taken

Übung 10
1. seen; 2. put; 3. bought; 4. left; 5. packed; 6. read; 7. finished

Übung 12
1. for; 2. since; 3. since; 4. for; 5. for; 6. since

Modul 12

Übung 14

1. 've been / have been; 2. 've / have not gone / been; 3. went; 4. bought; 5. grilled; 6. was; 7. Have / have ... tried; 8. 's / has been; 9. 've spent / have spent

Übung 15

1. written; 2. drunk; 3. eaten; 4. read

Übung 16

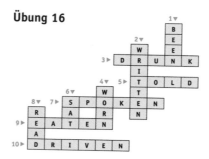

Test 12

Übung 1

1. written; 2. eaten; 3. read; 4. washed / cleaned; 5. slept

Übung 2

1. We've gone shopping. / We have gone shopping.
2. She 's spoken to her friend. / She has spoken to her friend.
3. He 's driven home. / He has driven home.
4. She 's bought apples. / She has bought apples.
5. They've taken pictures. / They have taken pictures.

Übung 3

1. for; 2. since; 3. for; 4. since; 5. for

Übung 4

1. c; 2. b; 3. c; 4. b

Übung 5

1. walked; 2. have worked; 3. has lived; 4. has known; 5. bought

Zielsprache/ Target language	Ausgangssprache/ Source language
A	
14th	14./vierzehnter
a	ein/eine
a few	ein paar
a little	ein bisschen
a lot	viel
a lot of	viel
about	über, ungefähr
above	über
across	über
active	aktiv
advice	Rat/Ratschlag
Africa	Afrika
after	nach/nachdem
afternoon	Nachmittag
again	wieder
age	Alter
ago	vor
air	Luft
air mattress	Luftmatratze
airport	Flughafen
all	alle
all day	den ganzen Tag
all evening	den ganzen Abend
all right	in Ordnung
along	entlang
already	schon
also	auch
always	immer
am	bin
American	amerikanisch Amerikaner/Amerikanerin
among	zwischen/inmitten/unter
an	ein/eine
and	und
angry	verärgert
another	noch ein/eine/einen
any	irgendein/irgendeine/ irgendeiner/irgendwelche
any more	nicht mehr
anybody	irgendjemand
anyone	irgendjemand
anything	irgendetwas
anyway	jedenfalls/sowieso
anywhere	irgendwo
apartment	Wohnung
apple	Apfel
apple pie	Apfelkuchen
apply	sich bewerben
April	April
are	bist/sind/seid
argue	streiten
armchair	Sessel
around	um/in der Gegend von um ... herum
arrive	ankommen
as	als
as ... as	so ... wie
as well	auch noch
ask	fragen
aspirin	Aspirin
at	auf, um, in/an
at all	überhaupt
at home	zu Hause
at most	höchstens
at night	nachts
at the moment	im Moment/momentan
ate	aß/aßt/aßen
August	August
aunt	Tante
Australia	Australien
author	Autor
Avignon	Avignon
B	
baby	Baby
back	zurück
back seat	Rücksitz
bad	schlecht
badminton	Badminton

banana	*Banane*	blue	*blau*
bank	*Bank*	book	*Buch*
barbecue	*Grillfest, Grill*	bored	*gelangweilt*
basket	*Korb*	boring	*langweilig*
bathroom	*Badezimmer*	boss	*Chef*
be	*sein*	both	*beide*
be able to	*können*	bottle	*Flasche*
be called	*heißen*	bought	*kaufte/kauftest/kauften/ kauftet/gekauft*
be lucky	*Glück haben*		
be used to	*an etwas gewöhnt sein*	boutique	*Boutique*
beach	*Strand*	bowl	*Schale*
Beatles	*Beatles*	boy	*Junge*
beautiful	*schön*	bread	*Brot*
because	*weil*	break	*Pause, zerbrechen/ kaputtmachen*
become	*werden*		
bed	*Bett*	breakfast	*Frühstück*
bedroom	*Schlafzimmer*	bright	*grell/leuchtend*
been	*gewesen*	bring	*bringen/mitbringen*
beer	*Bier*	brother	*Bruder*
before	*vor, vorher*	brought	*brachte/brachtest/ brachen/brachtet/ gebracht*
began	*begann/begannst/ begannen/begannt*		
		brown	*braun*
begin	*beginnen/anfangen*	build	*bauen*
begun	*begonnen*	built	*baute/bautest/bauten/ bautet/gebaut*
behind	*hinter*		
believe	*glauben*	bus	*Bus*
bell	*Glocke*	bush	*Busch*
belong to	*gehören*	but	*aber*
below	*unter*	butter	*Butter*
Ben Nevis	*Ben Nevis*	buy	*kaufen*
best	*bester/beste/bestes/ am besten*	by	*an/bei, von, um*
		by the way	*übrigens*
better	*besser*	bye	*Tschüss*
between	*zwischen*		
big	*groß*	**C**	
Big Ben	*Big Ben*		
bird	*Vogel*	cake	*Kuchen*
Birmingham	*Birmingham*	Calais	*Calais*
birthday	*Geburtstag*	call	*nennen*
birthday card	*Geburtstagskarte*	camera	*Fotoapparat/Kamera*
birthday present	*Geburtstags-geschenk*	camping site	*Campingplatz*
bit	*bisschen*	can	*können*

cancel	*abbestellen*
cannot	*nicht können*
car	*Auto*
card	*Karte*
careful	*vorsichtig*
carry	*tragen*
cat	*Katze*
cellphone	*Handy*
chair	*Stuhl*
changing room	*Umkleidekabine*
channel	*Kanal*
Channel Tunnel	*Kanaltunnel*
chat	*chatten/sich unterhalten*
cheap	*billig*
cheese	*Käse*
child	*Kind*
children	*Kinder*
China	*China*
Chinese	*chinesisch*
chips	*Pommes frites*
Christmas	*Weihnachten*
church	*Kirche*
cigarette	*Zigaretten*
cinema	*Kino*
city	*Stadt*
clean	*sauber machen/putzen sauber*
clever	*klug*
cliff	*Felsen*
close	*schließen/zumachen*
cloud	*Wolke*
coat	*Mantel*
coffee	*Kaffee*
coffee bar	*Café*
coffee table	*Beistelltisch*
coke	*Cola*
cold	*kalt*
college	*College*
come	*kommen*
complain	*sich beschweren*
computer	*Computer*
concert	*Konzert*

contact	*kontaktieren/anrufen*
corner	*Ecke*
corner shop	*Laden an der Ecke*
cottage	*Hütte/kleines Haus*
could	*könnte/könntest/könnten/ könntet*
	konnte
country	*Land*
course	*Kurs*
cuisine	*Küche*
cup	*Tasse*
cycle	*Fahrrad fahren*

D

Dad	*Papa/Vati*
dance	*tanzen*
daughter	*Tochter*
day	*Tag*
dear	*Lieber/Liebe*
December	*Dezember*
decide	*entscheiden/sich entschei- den*
definitely	*unbedingt*
delicious	*lecker*
dentist	*Zahnarzt*
desk	*Schreibtisch*
dessert	*Nachtisch/Dessert*
did	*tat/tatest/taten/tatet*
different	*anders/unterschiedlich*
difficult	*schwierig/schwer*
dining table	*Esstisch*
dinner	*Abendessen*
dishes	*Geschirr*
do	*tun*
doctor	*Arzt/Ärztin*
doesn't	*tut nicht*
dog	*Hund*
don't	*nicht tun*
done	*getan*
door	*Tür*
Dover	*Dover*
down	*herunter/hinunter*

drank	*trank/trankst/tranken/ trankt*
drawer	*Schublade*
dress	*Kleid*
drink	*trinken, Getränk*
drive	*Fahrt, fahren*
driven	*gefahren*
driver	*Fahrer/Fahrerin*
driving test	*Führerschein-prüfung*
drove	*fuhr/fuhrst/fuhren/fuhrt*
drunk	*getrunken betrunken*
during	*während*
duty-free	*zollfrei*

E

early	*früh*
earn	*verdienen*
earth	*Erde*
East Africa	*Ostafrika*
easy	*einfach*
eat	*essen*
eaten	*gegessen*
Edinburgh	*Edinburgh*
egg	*Ei*
egg salad	*Eiersalat*
eight	*acht*
either	*auch nicht*
eleven	*elf*
else	*sonst noch*
end	*Ende*
England	*England*
English	*englisch Engländer/Engländerin*
English course	*Englischkurs*
enjoy	*genießen*
enough	*genug*
escalator	*Rolltreppe*
essay	*Aufsatz*
euro	*Euro*
evening	*Abend*

every	*jede/jeder/jedes*
everybody	*jeder/alle*
everyone	*jeder/alle*
everything	*alles*
everywhere	*überall*
exam	*Prüfung*
exciting	*spannend/aufregend*
expensive	*teuer*
extra	*extra/zusätzlich*

F

fall	*fallen*
fall in love	*sich verlieben*
fallen	*gefallen*
family	*Familie*
famous	*berühmt*
fantastic	*fantastisch*
far	*weit*
fast	*schnell*
fat	*dick/fett*
father	*Vater*
fear	*fürchten*
February	*Februar*
fed	*fütterte/füttertest/ fütterten/füttertet/ gefüttert*
feed	*füttern*
feet	*Füße*
fell	*fiel/fielst/fielen/fielt/ gefallen*
fellow student	*Kommilitone/Studien-kollege*
ferry	*Fähre*
few	*wenige*
field	*Feld*
fifteen	*fünfzehn*
find	*finden*
find out	*herausfinden*
fine	*gut/prima*
finish	*beenden/fertig sein mit*
fireplace	*offener Kamin*
first	*erster/erste/erstes*

fish	Fisch
five	fünf
flat	Wohnung
flower	Blume
follow	folgen
food	Essen
foot	Fuß
football	Fußball
football match	Fußballspiel
for	für
forget	vergessen
forgot	vergaß/vergaßt/vergaßen
forgotten	vergessen
found	fand/fandest/fanden/ fandet/gefunden
four	vier
fourteen	vierzehn
France	Frankreich
French	französisch Franzose/Französin
French fries	Pommes frites
Friday	Freitag
fridge	Kühlschrank
friend	Freund
from	von
fruit	Obst/Früchte
fruit bowl	Obstschale
frustrating	frustrierend
fun	Spaß
furniture	Möbel
further	weiter
furthest	weitester/weiteste/ weitestes/am weitesten

G

game	Spiel
garage	Garage
garden	Garten
garlic	Knoblauch
German	deutsch Deutscher/Deutsche
Germany	Deutschland

get	holen/bringen
Get better soon!	Gute Besserung!
get in	hinein bekommen
get into	einsteigen
get married	heiraten
get out of	aussteigen
get stuck	stecken bleiben
get up	aufstehen
girl	Mädchen
glad	froh
glass	Glas
glasses	Brille
go	gehen
go ahead	tu das
go for a walk	spazieren gehen
go out	ausgehen
go to bed	ins Bett gehen
go with	passen zu
golf	Golf
gone	gegangen
good	gut
goodness	Güte
got	bekam/bekamst/bekamen/ bekamt/bekommen
gotten	bekommen
gravy	Bratensoße
great	toll/großartig
great aunt	Großtante
green	grün
grill	grillen
guess	raten/denken

H

had	hatte/hattest/hatten/ hattet/gehabt
hairdresser's	Friseurgeschäft
half	Hälfte, halb
hang on	warte mal
happen	geschehen/passieren
happily	glücklich
happy	glücklich
hard	hart

has	*hat*
have	*haben*
have a look	*nachsehen*
have breakfast	*frühstücken*
have got	*haben*
have to	*müssen*
he	*er*
healthy	*gesund*
heavily	*stark*
heavy	*schwer*
help	*helfen*
her	*sie/ihr*
here	*hier*
hers	*ihrer/ihre/ihres*
herself	*selbst, sich*
high	*hoch*
hill	*Hügel*
him	*ihm*
himself	*selbst, sich*
his	*sein/seine*
	seiner/seine/seins
history	*Geschichte*
holiday	*Ferien/Urlaub*
home	*nach Hause*
homework	*Hausaufgaben*
hoover	*staubsaugen*
hope	*hoffen*
horrible	*fürchterlich/schrecklich*
hot	*warm/heiß*
hot chocolate	*heiße Schokolade/Kakao*
hotel	*Hotel*
hour	*Stunde*
house	*Haus*
how	*wie*
how about	*wie ist es mit*
how many	*wie viele*
however	*wie auch immer*
hungry	*hungrig*

I

I	*ich*
I'm	*ich bin*
ice cream	*Eis*
idea	*Idee*
if	*wenn/falls, ob*
ill	*krank*
important	*wichtig*
in	*in*
in front of	*vor*
in the afternoon	*nachmittags*
in the evening	*abends*
in the middle of	*in der Mitte von*
in the morning	*morgens*
inflate	*aufpumpen/aufblasen*
information	*Information*
intelligent	*intelligent*
interesting	*interessant*
internet	*Internet*
into	*hinein/herein*
Ireland	*Irland*
is	*ist*
isn't	*ist nicht*
it	*es*
Italian	*italienisch*
	Italiener/Italienerin
Italy	*Italien*
its	*sein/seine*
itself	*selbst*
	sich

J

January	*Januar*
Japan	*Japan*
Japanese	*japanisch*
job	*Arbeit/Stelle*
jog	*joggen*
juice	*Saft*
July	*Juli*
jumper	*Pullover*
June	*Juni*

just	genau	living room	Wohnzimmer
	gerade	local	lokal/ortstypisch
		London	London
K		long	lang/lange
key	Schlüssel	look	schauen, aussehen
kid	Kind	look after	sich kümmern um
kiss	Kuss	look forward to	sich freuen auf
kitchen	Küche	lotion	Lotion/Creme
knew	wusste/wusstest/wussten/	love	lieben, Liebe
	wusstet	lunch	Mittagessen
knife	Messer		
know	wissen, kennen	**M**	
known	gekannt	made	machte/machtest/
			machten/machtet/
L			gemacht
lake	See	magazine	Zeitschrift
large	groß	make	machen
last	letzter/letzte/letztes	man	Mann
late	spät	manage	schaffen
later	später	Manchester	Manchester
law	Jura/Recht	Manchester United	Manchester United
learn	lernen	many	viele
least	am wenigsten	map	Karte
leave	verlassen	March	März
left	verließ/verließt/verließen/	Margaret Thatcher	Margaret Thatcher
	verlassen	market	Markt
	übrig	married	verheiratet
lemon	Zitrone	Marseille	Marseille
less	weniger	match	Spiel
let	lassen	mate	Kumpel/Freund
let's	lass uns	maths	Mathe
letter	Brief	mattress	Matratze
library	Bibliothek/Bücherei	May	Mai
life	Leben	may	könnten
light	hell	maybe	vielleicht
like	mögen	me	mir/mich
list	Liste	mean	meinen/heißen/bedeuten
listen	zuhören	meant	meinte/meintest/meinten/
little	klein, wenig		meintet/gemeint
live	wohnen/leben	meat	Fleisch
Liverpool	Liverpool	medicine	Medikamente
		meet	treffen

men	*Männer*
met	*traf/trafst/trafen/traft/ getroffen*
mice	*Mäuse*
middle	*Mitte*
might	*könnten*
milk	*Milch*
mine	*meiner/meine/meins*
mineral water	*Mineralwasser*
minister	*Minister/Ministerin*
minute	*Minute*
mistake	*Fehler*
mobile phone	*Handy*
modern	*modern*
Mom	*Mama*
moment	*Moment*
Monday	*Montag*
money	*Geld*
month	*Monat*
more	*mehr*
morning	*Morgen*
most	*am meisten*
mother	*Mutter*
motorway	*Autobahn*
mountain	*Berg*
mouse	*Maus*
move	*umziehen*
movie theater	*Kino*
mph	*Meilen in der Stunde*
much	*viel*
Mum	*Mama*
music	*Musik*
must	*müssen*
must not	*nicht dürfen*
mustn't	*nicht dürfen*
my	*mein/meine/meiner/ meines*
my goodness	*meine Güte*
myself	*mich/mich selbst selbst mich/mir*

N

name	*Name*
near	*in der Nähe von*
nearly	*fast*
need	*brauchen, müssen*
neighbor	*Nachbar*
neighbour	*Nachbar*
never	*nie*
new	*neu*
news	*Nachrichten*
newspaper	*Zeitung*
next	*nächster/nächste/nächstes*
next to	*neben*
nice	*nett/schön*
nicely	*gut/schön*
night	*Nacht/Abend*
nine	*neun*
nineteen	*neunzehn*
no	*nein, kein*
no idea	*keine Ahnung*
no one	*niemand*
nobody	*niemand*
normally	*normalerweise*
Norway	*Norwegen*
Norwegian	*norwegisch*
not	*nicht*
not ... yet	*noch nicht*
not any	*kein/keine*
not at all	*überhaupt nicht*
nothing	*nichts*
November	*November*
now	*jetzt*
nowhere	*nirgendwo*
number	*Nummer*

O

o'clock	*Uhr*
October	*Oktober*
of	*von*
of course	*natürlich*
off	*herab/herunter*

office	*Büro*	party	*Fest*
off-licence	*Wein- und Spirituosen-* *geschäft*	past	*nach, an … vorbei*
		pear	*Birne*
often	*oft*	pen	*Stift*
oh dear	*oh je*	people	*Leute*
OK	*in Ordnung*	per	*pro*
old	*alt*	perhaps	*vielleicht*
on	*auf, am, an/am*	person	*Person*
on earth	*auf Erden*	phone	*anrufen/telefonieren*
on Mondays	*montags*	phone book	*Telefonbuch*
on Sundays	*sonntags*	piano	*Klavier*
on the way	*unterwegs*	picnic	*Picknick*
once	*einmal*	picnic basket	*Picknickkorb*
only	*nur, erst*	picture	*Bild/Foto*
open	*offen*	pie	*Kuchen*
opposite	*gegenüber*	piece	*Stück*
orange	*Orange*	pink	*rosa/pink*
orange juice	*Orangensaft*	place	*Ort/Stelle/Platz*
organise	*organisieren*	plan	*Plan, planen*
other	*anderer/andere/anderes*	plastic bag	*Plastiktüte*
our	*unser/unsere*	play	*spielen*
ours	*unserer/unsere/unseres*	please	*bitte*
ourselves	*selbst, uns*	Portugal	*Portugal*
out	*aus/weg*	Portuguese	*portugiesisch*
out here	*hier draußen*	post office	*Postamt*
out of	*heraus/hinaus*	postcard	*Postkarte*
outside	*draußen/außerhalb von*	poster	*Poster*
over there	*da drüben*	potato	*Kartoffel*
overtime	*Überstunden*	pound	*Pfund*
own	*eigener/eigen/eigenes*	practice	*üben*
Oxford	*Oxford*	practise	*üben*
		prefer	*lieber mögen/bevorzugen*
P		prepare	*vorbereiten*
		present	*Geschenk*
pack	*packen*	primary school	*Grundschule*
packet	*Packung*	prime minister	*Premierminister/Premier-* *ministerin*
pants	*Hose*		
paper	*Papier*	probably	*wahrscheinlich*
parents	*Eltern*	problem	*Problem*
Paris	*Paris*	Provence	*Provence*
park	*Park, parken*	pub	*Kneipe*
parked	*geparkt*	pump	*Pumpe*

put	*stellen*
put away	*wegtun/wegpacken*
put in	*hineintun*
put up	*aufstellen*

Q

quarter	*viertel*
question	*Frage*
quiet	*ruhig*

R

radio	*Radio*
rain	*regnen*
raincoat	*Regenjacke*
read	*lesen, las/last/lasen/last/ gelesen*
ready	*fertig*
really	*wirklich*
recipe	*Kochrezept*
recognize	*erkennen*
red	*rot*
relax	*entspannen*
remember	*sich erinnern*
remind	*jemanden erinnern*
rent	*mieten*
retire	*in Rente gehen*
Rhine	*Rhein*
rice	*Reis*
ridden	*geritten/gefahren*
ride	*reiten*
right	*richtig, also*
road	*Straße*
roast	*rösten*
roast dinner	*Bratengericht*
roast potatoes	*Röstkartoffeln*
rode	*ritt/rittest/ritten/rittet*
roof	*Dach*
room	*Zimmer*
round	*um ... herum*
route	*Route/Strecke*
Russia	*Russland*

S

said	*sagte/sagtest/sagten/ sagtet/gesagt*
sailing	*Segeln*
salad	*Salat*
same	*gleich*
sandal	*Sandale*
sang	*sang/sangst/sangen/sangt*
sat	*saß/saßt/saßen/saßt/ gesessen*
Saturday	*Samstag*
saw	*sah/sahst/sahen/saht*
say	*sagen*
school	*Schule*
school bus	*Schulbus*
school holidays	*Schulferien*
Scotland	*Schottland*
sea	*Meer*
see	*sehen*
see you	*bis bald*
seen	*gesehen*
sell	*verkaufen*
send	*schicken*
sent	*schickte/schicktest/ schickte/geschickt*
September	*September*
Serengeti	*Serengeti*
set up	*aufstellen*
seven	*sieben*
Shakespeare	*Shakespeare*
she	*sie*
shoe	*Schuh*
shop	*Geschäft/Laden einkaufen*
shopping	*Einkaufen*
should	*sollen*
sign	*Schild, unterschreiben*
sing	*singen*
sir	*Herr*
sister	*Schwester*
sit	*sitzen*
six	*sechs*

sixteen	sechzehn	station	Bahnhof
size	Größe	stay	bleiben
skirt	Rock	stay up	aufbleiben
sky	Himmel	steak	Steak
sleep	schlafen	still	noch/immer noch
sleeping bag	Schlafsack	still	still
slept	schlief/schlieft/schliefen/ schlieft/geschlafen	stood	stand/standest/standen/ standet/gestanden
slice	Scheibe	straight	geradeaus/direkt
slow	langsam	street	Straße
slowly	langsam	strict	streng
small	klein	study	studieren/lernen
smoke	rauchen	stuff	Zeug/Sachen
so	so	stupid	dumm/blöd
so far	bis jetzt	sugar	Zucker
soccer	Fußball	summer	Sommer
soccer match	Fußballspiel	Sunday	Sonntag
sofa	Sofa	sung	gesungen
some	einige/ein paar	sunny	sonnig
somebody	jemand	sunshine	Sonnenschein
someone	jemand	suntan	Sonnenbräune
something	etwas	suntan lotion	Sonnencreme
sometimes	manchmal	supermarket	Supermarkt
somewhere	irgendwo	suppose	annehmen
soon	bald	sure	sicher
south	Süden	swam	schwamm/schwammst/ schwammen/schwammt
South of England	Südengland	sweater	Pullover
Southern France	Südfrankreich	Sweden	Schweden
souvenir	Souvenir/Andenken	Swedish	schwedisch
Spain	Spanien	sweets	Süßigkeiten
Spanish	spanisch	swimmer	Schwimmer/Schwimmerin
speak	sprechen	swimming	Schwimmen
spend	verbringen, ausgeben	swimming costume	Badeanzug
spent	gab aus/gabst aus/gaben aus/gabt aus/ausge- geben	swum	geschwommen
spoke	sprach/sprachst/sprachen/ spracht	**T**	
spoken	gesprochen	table	Tisch
sports	Sport	take	nehmen, dauern/brauchen, mitnehmen
stamp	Briefmarke	Take care!	Pass auf dich auf!
stand	stehen	taken	genommen

407

talk	sich unterhalten/sprechen	ticket-office	Kartenbüro
tea	Tee	tidy	ordentlich
teacher	Lehrer/Lehrerin	tidy away	wegräumen
teaching	Lehramt	tie	Krawatte
teenage	im Teenageralter	time	Zeit
teeth	Zähne	tired	müde
television	Fernseher	to	zu, zur
tell	sagen/erzählen	toast	Toast
ten	zehn	today	heute
tennis	Tennis	together	zusammen
tent	Zelt	told	erzälte/erzähltest/
Thames	Themse		erzählten/erzähltet/
than	als		erzählt
thanks	danke	tomato	Tomate
that	das, dieser/diese/dieses	tomorrow	morgen
that long	so lange	tonight	heute Abend/Nacht
that's	das ist	too	zu, auch
the	der/die/das	took	nahm/nahmst/nahmen/
theater	Theater		nahmt
theatre	Theater	tooth	Zahn
their	ihr/ihre/ihren	totally	total
theirs	ihrer/ihre/ihres	tourist	Tourist
them	sie/ihnen	towards	in Richtung
themselves	selbst	towel	Handtuch
	sich	toy	Spielzeug
then	dann	traffic	Verkehr
there	dort, dorthin	traffic jam	Stau
there are	es gibt/da sind	traffic lights	Ampel
there's	es gibt/da ist	translate	übersetzen
these	das/diese	travel guide	Reiseführer
they	sie	tree	Baum
thin	dünn	trousers	Hose
thing	Ding/Sache	true	wahr/richtig
think	denken/glauben	try	probieren
thirteen	dreizehn	try on	anprobieren
this	das	try out	ausprobieren
those	jene	T-shirt	T-Shirt
thought	dachte/dachtest/dachten/	Tuesday	Dienstag
	dachtet/gedacht	tunnel	Tunnel
through	durch	TV	Fernseher
Thursday	Donnerstag	two	zwei
ticket	Karte	typical	typisch

U

UK	Großbritannien
under	unter
underground	U-Bahn
unhappy	unglücklich
uniform	Uniform
United Kingdom	Vereinigtes Königreich
United States of America	Vereinigte Staaten von Amerika
university	Universität
untidy	unordentlich
until	bis
up	hinauf/nach oben
us	uns
USA	USA
use	benutzen
usually	normalerweise

V

vacation	Ferien/Urlaub
vacuum clean	staubsaugen
vanilla ice cream	Vanilleeis
vegetables	Gemüse
very	sehr
vineyard	Weingut/Weinberg
visit	Besuch
	besuchen

W

wait	warten
waiter	Kellner
Wales	Wales
walk	zu Fuß gehen
	Spaziergang
want	wollen
wardrobe	Kleiderschrank
was	war
wasn't	war nicht
watch	ansehen/schauen
watch TV	fernsehen
water	Wasser, gießen

way	Weg
we	wir
wear	tragen
weather	Wetter
wedding	Hochzeit
Wednesday	Mittwoch
week	Woche
weekend	Wochenende
well	nun/naja, gut
went	ging/gingst/gingen/gingt
were	warst/waren/wart
what	was
what about	was ist mit
when	wenn/als
where	wo
white	weiß
white wine	Weißwein
who	wer
whose	wessen
why	warum
will	werden
window	Fenster
windsurfing	Windsurfen
wine	Wein
winter	Winter
winter coat	Wintermantel
wish	Wunsch, wünschen
with	mit
woman	Frau
women	Frauen
won't	nicht werden
wonderful	wundervoll
wore	trug/trugst/trugen/trugt
work	Arbeit, arbeiten
world	Welt
worn	getragen
worry	sich sorgen
worse	schlimmer
worst	schlimmster/schlimmste/ schlimmstes/am schlimmsten
would	wäre

write	*schreiben*	yes	*ja*
write down	*aufschreiben*	yesterday	*gestern*
written	*geschrieben*	Yorkshire puddings	*Yorkshire Puddings*
wrote	*schrieb/schriebst/*	you	*du/dich/Sie/ihr/dir/euch*
	schrieben/schriebt	you're right	*du hast Recht*
		young	*jung*
		your	*dein/ihr/euer*
		yours	*deiner/deine/deins*
		yourself	*dich/dir, selbst*
		yourselves	*euch, selbst*

Y

yard	*Garten*
yeah	*ja*
year	*Jahr*

Lerntipps

Vokabeln lernen

Sie lernen in ihrem Englischkurs viele neue Wörter. Erwarten Sie nicht, dass Sie sich alles auf ein Mal merken können. Lernen Sie zunächst nur 4 oder 5 Wörter, die Ihnen wichtig oder schön erscheinen und wenn Sie diese beherrschen, lernen Sie die nächsten 4 oder 5 Wörter. Vieles wiederholt sich, so dass Sie Neues mit der Zeit ganz automatisch lernen.

Englisch und Deutsch

Englische Wörter sind ihrer deutschen Entsprechung oft sehr ähnlich: entweder in der Schreibweise, z. B. **diplomat** - *Diplomat*, oder in der Aussprache, z. B. **beer** – *Bier*, oder auch in beidem, z. B. **computer** – *Computer*.

Manche Wörter werden im Deutschen genauso wie im Englischen benutzt. Z. B. **shopping** (Einkaufen) oder **Park and Ride** (*Parken und Fahren*). Versuchen Sie also ruhig, Bedeutungen zu erraten. Das kann für Sie beim Erlernen der neuen Sprache sehr hilfreich sein.

Wortlisten

Es führt kein Weg daran vorbei, Wörter auswendig zu lernen. Daher ist es sinnvoll die Vokabeln für sich festzuhalten, z.B. in einer Liste oder auf Karteikarten. So haben Sie nicht nur die Möglichkeit, einzelne Wörter nachzuschlagen, sondern Sie können solche Listen zum Lernen überall hin mitnehmen.

Neue Wörter erkennen

Wenn Sie auf unbekannte Vokabeln stoßen, versuchen Sie zunächst einmal, deren Bedeutung aus dem Kontext zu erschließen. Viele Wörter können Sie bestimmt auf diese Weise erraten! Mut zum Raten ist beim Erlernen einer Fremdsprache sehr wichtig. Nur selten versteht man jedes Wort, aber man kann dennoch Zusammenhänge erkennen. Wenn Sie ein neues Wort überhaupt nicht verstehen, können Sie es im thematischen Wörterbuch nachschlagen.

Vokabeln lernen in Zusammenhang

Wenn Sie Wort für Wort übersetzen, können Sie manchmal in Schwierigkeiten geraten. **Here you are** heißt beispielsweise eben nicht *Hier du bist*, sondern *Bitte schön*. Deshalb ist es vernünftig, sich Wörter im Zusammenhang, d.h. innerhalb eines Satzes, und nicht nur alleine, zu merken.

Wenn Sie **I´m going to the beach** lernen, anstatt **go**, **to**, und **beach**, können Sie diese Vokabeln auch in einem anderen Satz richtig verwenden. Sie haben die Satzstruktur gleich mitgelernt.

Also murmeln Sie beim Vokabellernen nicht nur einzelne Wörter vor sich hin, sondern lernen Sie auch ganze Sätze und Satzteile. So lernen Sie gleichzeitig die Bedeutung von einzelnen Wörtern und wie man Sie anwendet.

Ausdrücke bildlich vorstellen

Viele Leute prägen sich neue Wörter schneller und besser ein, wenn sie diese mit einem Bild verknüpfen. Vor allem metaphorische Wendungen merkt man sich viel leichter, wenn man sich diese bildlich vorstellt. Denken Sie zum Beispiel an den Ausdruck **you´re breathing down my neck**. Im wörtlichen Sinne bezeichnet dieser Ausdruck *zu nahe stehen,* so dass es aufdringlich wird. Mit diesem Bild vor Augen können Sie sich die Bedeutung dieses Ausdrucks bestimmt besser merken; darüber hinaus erinnert dieses Bild an die deutsche Wendung *jemanden im Nacken haben*.

Bezeichnungen für Kleidungsstücke

Für viele Kleidungsstücke ist die Bezeichnung im Englischen und im Deutschen ähnlich. Auch bei den Größen trifft man oft auf englische Bezeichnungen – **S** für **Small** (*klein*); **M** für **Medium** (*mittel*); **L** für **Large** (*groß*) usw. Achten Sie beim nächsten Kleiderkauf auf die englischen Wörter und versuchen Sie, sie sich zu merken. Schreiben Sie sich eine Liste Ihrer Lieblingskleidungsstücke und deren Farbe auf Englisch!

413

Zahlen

Zahlen begegnen Ihnen in vielen Alltagssituationen. Um ein bisschen zu üben, können Sie versuchen, diese jedes Mal ins Englische zu übersetzen.

Den Wortschatz festigen

Wortschatzübungen sind zum Wiederholen da! Nehmen Sie sich zehn Minuten Zeit, und suchen Sie sich ein paar dieser Übungen aus früheren Lektionen aus. Natürlich haben Sie vieles vergessen, aber einige Wörter sind bestimmt hängen geblieben.

Gezielt Vokabeln lernen

Denken Sie nicht, dass Sie all diese Wörter sofort lernen müssen. Vieles ist zum Nachschlagen. Wählen Sie die Wörter aus, die für Sie persönlich nützlich sind.

Sprechen üben

Obwohl Sie sich vielleicht etwas komisch vorkommen, ist es wichtig, dass Sie immer wieder laut üben. Sie wollen doch Englisch nicht nur lesen und schreiben, sondern auch sprechen können – oder nicht? Schreiben Sie kleine Sätze aus der Lektion auf eine Karte oder einen Zettel, den Sie mitnehmen können und üben Sie unterwegs.

Lautes Sprechen

Wenn Sie englische Wörter oder Sätze lesen, sprechen Sie sie laut vor sich hin – ein leises Murmeln genügt. So gewöhnen Sie sich daran, sich selbst Englisch reden zu hören und wenn es wirklich darauf ankommt, fällt es Ihnen leichter.

Richtig betonen

Beim Lernen von Wörtern sollten Sie darauf achten, die Betonung immer gleich mitzulernen. Es gibt viele Methoden, sich diese zu merken. Sie könnten die betonte Silbe einfach unterstreichen. Oder Sie markieren die betonte Silbe mit einem großen O und die unbetonten Silben mit einem kleinem o.

z.B.   o   **O**   o
        ex   pen   sive

Sie können die betonte Silbe auch **fett** schreiben: **qual**ity. Sprechen Sie die Wörter laut nach, und klopfen Sie den Tisch bei der betonten Silbe ganz fest.

Hörverstehen

Wenn Sie einen neuen Text hören, konzentrieren Sie sich auf die Ihnen schon bekannten Wendungen und Ausdrücke und lassen Sie sich nicht von unbekannten Wörtern verunsichern. Hören Sie sich den Text mehrmals an, und Sie werden merken, dass Sie nach jedem Hören immer mehr verstehen.

Hör- und Leseverstehen

Bevor Sie einen Text mit Bildern lesen oder hören, ist es hilfreich, sich die begleitenden Bilder anzuschauen und sich die Situation vorzustellen. Filtern Sie die Informationen und notieren Sie sie. Dann wird es Ihnen beim Hören oder Lesen leichter fallen, den Text zu verstehen!

Grammatik nachschlagen

Wenn in Ihrem Englischkurs etwas erwähnt wird, was Sie nicht mehr im Kopf haben, oder einfach so wieder nachschauen möchten, können Sie jederzeit in die Grammatik gehen und noch einmal nachlesen.
Auch grammatikalische Begriffe können Sie dort immer nachschlagen.

Lernen in Reimen

Ein Reim oder Vers hilft Ihnen, gewisse Regeln leichter im Gedächtnis zu behalten, wie z. B.: Bei **he/she/it** das **s** muss mit. Wiederholen Sie diese Reime so oft wie möglich.

Unregelmäßige Verben

Eine Liste der häufigsten unregelmäßigen Verben mit ihren Vergangenheitsformen finden Sie im Grammatikteil. Sie können die Liste komplett kopieren und irgendwo zum Lernen hinlegen, oder Sie kopieren die Liste in eine Computerdatei und drucken zunächst nur paar wichtige Wörter aus.

Grammatik auffrischen

Frischen Sie, was Sie z.B. über das **will future** gelernt haben, noch einmal auf. Entweder mit der Grammatik oder indem Sie sich mit Hilfe der Suchmaschine im Internet ein paar Übungen dazu heraussuchen und diese wiederholen. Auf diese Weise können Sie jederzeit ein beliebiges Grammatikthema noch einmal anschauen und wiederholen.

Englisch üben im Alltag

Sie können Ihr Englisch in vielen Bereichen des täglichen Lebens üben. Versuchen Sie doch, wenn Sie das nächste Mal Einkaufen gehen, Ihren Einkaufszettel auf Englisch zu schreiben. Sie werden sehen, wie viele Wörter Sie schon kennen.

Telefonate auf Englisch

Wenn Sie sich hierzu eine Zusammenfassung ausdrucken und als Spickzettel auf Ihren Schreibtisch oder ins Telefonbuch legen, sind Sie für einen Telefonanruf auf Englisch immer gerüstet.

Buchstabieren von Namen und Adresse

Am wahrscheinlichsten werden Sie bei einem Auslandsaufenthalt Ihren Namen oder Ihre Adresse buchstabieren müssen. Sie können das laut vor sich hin üben. Dann kommen Sie nicht in Verlegenheit, wenn es von Ihnen verlangt wird.